STRENGTH TO STRENGTH

STRENGTH TO STRENGTH

DONNA L. HUISJEN

DEVOTIONAL
STEPPINGSTONES
FOR THE

Godly Woman

credo
house publishers

Strength to Strength

Published by Credo House Publishers, a division of
Credo Communications, LLC, Grand Rapids, Michigan;
www.credohousepublishers.com.

ISBN-10: 1-935391-58-5
ISBN-13: 978-1-935391-58-6

Cover and interior design: Sharon VanLoozenoord

First edition

Contents

"*B*lessed are those whose strength is in you,

whose hearts are set on pilgrimage. . . .

They go from strength to strength,

till each appears before God in Zion"

(Psalm 84:5, 7).

"You have no strength but what God gives

and you can have all the strength that God can give"

(ANDREW MURRAY).

$\mathcal{N}$ew every morning

Verses: "Because of the Lord's great love we are not consumed; for his compassions never fail. They are new every morning; great is your faithfulness" (Lamentations 3:22–23).

"Today's process is God's faithfulness to his promise"
(DAVID PARSONS).

Reflection: If you're reading this on the first morning of the year, "new every morning" suggests a layer of meaning that might not otherwise be apparent. The passing of the old year leaves in our minds a flavor, almost an aftertaste, most readily apparent on this first, still slow-paced, morning of the new year. Maybe afterglow sounds more positive.

Yet, although we're quick to assess the year that's gone, referring to it as good or bad or a host of other adjectives, we don't want to bask in it. We're ready to move on to new frontiers, possibilities, and surprises. We've been slowed by the holidays, despite their busyness, and want to delve into business as usual.

Before we jump in feet first, though, it's a good idea to review the year at our backs from a spiritual standpoint. God's faithfulness is the one constant in an ever-changing world. The two short clauses of verse 23, above, suggest a contrast: God's compassions are new every morning precisely because his "old" faithfulness (no pun intended) is steady and changeless. And it's wholly on the basis of this immovable backdrop that we face the new year with anticipation.

Prayer Prompt: In what ways was God's faithfulness in the past year most evident to you?

odly woman,

HIS FAITHFULNESS IS THE CONSTANT.

Our faithful God

Verses: "God is our refuge and strength, an ever-present help in trouble. Therefore we will not fear . . ." (Psalm 46:1–2).

"Knowledge is an unending adventure at the edge of uncertainty"
(JACOB BRONOWSKI).

Reflection: As a past editor in the Bible department of a large Christian publishing house, I'm aware that the "rules" don't require an ellipsis at the end of a Bible quote. But in this case, those three little dots practically insisted I include them. When it comes to the opening of Psalm 46, there's just no good cutoff point.

For almost a decade, this psalm has held for me an unshakable association: It's the passage on which my church's evening service on 9/11/01 was based. I don't know what situation the sons of Korah had in mind when they composed this song, but it has afforded comfort to God's people for countless generations.

Once again, God's faithfulness comes to the fore, this time as we jump into the activities of another year. In the words of Dan Millman, "Faith means living with uncertainty—feeling your way through life, letting your heart guide you like a lantern in the dark." As a Christian I resonate with his observation, with the one qualification that it's the Spirit who guides my heart.

If we're going to face the year ahead with confidence, we as Christians need to acknowledge God as our refuge and strength in trouble and uncertainty.

Prayer Prompt: Does the prospect of uncertain possibilities stimulate you or make you cringe?

G*odly woman,*

BE FAITH-FULL BECAUSE HE IS FAITHFUL.

$\mathcal{T}$he variable that matters

Verses: "The mystery that has been kept hidden for ages and generations . . . is now disclosed to the Lord's people. To them God has chosen to make known among the Gentiles the glorious riches of this mystery, which is Christ in you, the hope of glory" (Colossians 1:26–27).

"Hope is the dream of a soul awake"
(FRENCH PROVERB).

Reflection: Sometimes we're tempted to wring our hands at the sorry state of this old world. The troubles all around and within us make us want to shrug our shoulders (maybe while wringing our hands) and give up. Truth is, human history is winding down. Our Earth is, figuratively speaking, beginning to creak on its axes. But what we're missing in this picture is the variable of hope: what Paul refers to here as the "hope of glory."

Do you ever try to imagine life—your life—once the new heavens and the new earth have been ushered in? This initial phase of eternity is, after all, less than a blip in comparison to what lies ahead for us. Still, time-locked as we are, we bemoan our present troubles. But have you paused to consider the benefit, indeed the privilege, of being a New Testament (new covenant) believer?

God in his infinite wisdom and grace saw fit to place you on the far side of the revelation of the mystery that had been hidden for ages and generations. And you may be sure his choice for you wasn't random. How does this truth change your perspective?

Prayer Prompt: What practical difference does hope make in your life?

odly woman,
DON'T MISS THE HOPE OF GLORY.

$\mathcal{D}$istributing hope

Verses: "Comfort, comfort my people, says your God. Speak tenderly to Jerusalem, and proclaim to her that her hard service has been completed, that her sin has been paid for" (Isaiah 40:1–2).

"Without God there is for mankind no purpose, no goal, no hope,
only a wavering future, an eternal dread of every darkness"
(JEAN PAUL).

Reflection: Yes, Isaiah's words were situational, pertaining to the people of Judah and spoken by God through his prophet within a specific context. But these words send a shiver up and down our spines too. The term "my people" has come to include all of God's new covenant children. In that sense the call for Isaiah to comfort God's people reverberates in our ears. It's our call too.

As made clear by Paul (see yesterday's passage), God wants us, his children, to go beyond comforting one another; he has chosen us to "make known among the Gentiles the glorious riches of this mystery." How many of those lost ones "out there" are people of God who have yet to enter the fold? The larger world is in dire need of comfort too, and the hope Isaiah could only envision is real and functional in our day.

If there's one thing this world needs, it's hope. It's a commodity in very short supply among billions. If you've grown up in possession of hope, you may find it hard to imagine facing the future (this unfolding year, even) without it.

The problem with hope's "scarcity" has nothing to do with availability: Hope is accessible in infinite supply, and it grows exponentially as it's doled out. It's the distribution channel that needs our attention.

Prayer Prompt: In what practical, hands-on ways can you distribute this priceless resource today and every day as the year progresses?

$\mathcal{G}$*odly woman,*
THIS HOPE IS YOURS—AND THERE'S ENOUGH TO GO AROUND.

$\mathcal{F}$ield of diamonds

Verse: "For God, who said, 'Let light shine out of darkness,' made his light shine in our hearts to give us the light of the knowledge of God's glory displayed in the face of Christ" (2 Corinthians 4:6).

"There are two ways of spreading light; to be the candle or the mirror that reflects it" (EDITH WHARTON).

Reflection: If you live in the snow belt, you'll relate to an undisturbed blanket of white that sparkles like a field of diamonds when illuminated by headlights. As unlikely as this may seem, that's your heart and mine—under the searchlight of God's grace. It's what his gaze takes in when he sees us, redeemed and washed clean by the blood of the Lamb. Those pinpricks of light are what the world sees, too, as Christ's kingdom representatives intersperse to infiltrate the darkness around us.

The operational principle behind that light shining in our hearts is, of course, the fact that its original source is external. Our own light, though real, reflects Christ's.

For that wintry white landscape to twinkle requires a contrasting background: In the words of Arlo Guthrie, "You can't have a light without a dark to stick it in." Oh, this world has plenty of darkness. "No matter how fast light travels," notes Terry Pratchett, "it finds the darkness has always got there first, and is waiting for it."

What will you do to penetrate the blackness that defines life for so many?

Prayer Prompt: Ask the Spirit where he would have you shine you light today.

odly woman,

HE SEES IN YOU A PRISTINE HEART.

$\mathcal{T}$he season for increase

Verses: "Preach the word; be prepared in season and out of season; correct, rebuke and encourage—with great patience and careful instruction. For the time will come when people will not put up with sound doctrine" (2 Timothy 4:2–3).

"I do not pray for success, I ask for faithfulness"
(MOTHER TERESA).

Reflection: What "seasons" did Paul have in mind here? Was he referring to opportune times? Receptive periods? Whether or not we're engaged in "professional" ministry—and whether or not we "preach" the Word (probably best not, if that isn't our calling)—we can all relate to spiritual winters or, to use what to me is an opposite image, dry spells, times in which the Spirit seems latent in terms of the effectiveness of our sharing and service.

Whether our intended recipients/beneficiaries are our spouse, our kids, our coworkers, our neighbors, our students, or anyone else, we at times feel the need to question ourselves: *Am I doing something wrong? Something different from before?*

It's so easy during those periods to lose sight of who's in charge of the outcomes. God asks for our faithfulness, plain and simple. Not our annual reports, quarterly projections, or detailed strategies. How many missionaries haven't toiled for decades in a given field with only a handful of converts to show for their labor—only to have the Spirit select the season for an incredible increase!

God asks for our faithfulness, but in order to be faith-full we first need to be faith-filled. As reported in Luke 17:5, "The apostles said to the Lord, 'Increase our faith!'" We can do no better than to add our voices to this call . . . and then to keep on working, "with great patience and careful instruction."

Prayer Prompt: In what season are you when it comes to your own ministry and service?

$\mathcal{G}$*odly woman,*
HE WANTS YOUR FAITHFULNESS.

What kind of anxious?

Verses: "They all wept as they embraced him and kissed him. What grieved them most was [Paul's] statement that they would never see his face again" (Acts 20:37–38).

"Together forever, never apart. Maybe in distance but never at heart" (AUTHOR UNKNOWN).

Reflection: Have you ever taken comfort, as I have, in the realization that you're "sharing" an extensive weather/storm system with loved ones who may be several states away? Or simply that you're viewing the reflected light from the same sun or moon, even though the hours between you are varying its presentation in the sky?

I've only experienced real homesickness once in my life, at summer camp (fortunately in company with my sister) when I was in the fourth grade. For an entire week I carried in the forefront of my mind a picture of a tiny island containing one structure—my house. Perhaps only an hour away, I ached to transcend that distance.

My dad, born the youngest of seven and now in his eighties, is experiencing the progressive loss of his siblings. With the exception of my mom (my second mom, as you'll see from tomorrow's meditation), all of the spouses are gone. One brother and one sister remain here in Grand Rapids, both in frail health. Dad is facing the increasing likelihood of having to wait till the far side of death to embrace them again. Grief, I'm coming to recognize, for the elderly is progressive too, with losses coming incrementally but inevitably. Already for me at fifty-nine, the gradual process of weaning myself from earthly relationships has begun, as aunts and uncles, not to mention some friends and many fellow church members, have one by one joined the lineup for that passage.

As our earthly futures and quality of life diminish, homesickness gradually shifts its direction. The beauty for us as Christians is that it's often God's face we yearn most to see.

Prayer Prompt: How do you view your eventual passage to heaven? Does the prospect make you anxious—anxious as in anxiety, or as in anticipation?

odly woman,

THERE'S NO SUCH THING AS TEMPORARY ON THE OTHER SIDE.

⒯he figures of time

Verses: "There is a time for everything, and a season for every activity under the heavens: a time to be born and a time to die" (Ecclesiastes 3:1–2).

"A circle is the reflection of eternity. It has no beginning and it has no end—and if you put several circles over each other, then you get a spiral" (MAYNARD JAMES KEENAN).

Reflection: January 8 has for many years called up poignant and ambivalent associations for me—my mom's death anniversary at the age of thirty-five (I was eleven) and my new mom's birthday, celebrated just a year later on the same date. As I reflect on these overlapping associations, I'm picking up a unique perspective on the passage of time, particularly from God's infinite perspective.

As each year circles back to its beginning and surges into a new one, time begins to overwrap itself. It reminds me of the painstaking "figures" Olympic ice skaters used to perform, slowly navigating, for example, a circle or figure eight with the goal of having their blade precisely follow the arc of the line already marked on the ice.

As the years continue to make their circuit, joy overlays sorrow and vice versa. Human experience ebbs and flows, waxes and wanes, and the circle gradually picks up new generational players and drops others.

Perhaps January 8 comes at a good time for me, so early in the year. What comparable ironies cause you to reflect on God's providential timing?

Prayer Prompt: Think back on your lifetime of joys and sorrows, ups and downs—all of the situational and generational contrasts from Ecclesiastes 3. How has God remained constant through it all?

⒢odly woman,

YOUR TIMES ARE IN HIS HANDS.

$\mathscr{A}$nd we know . . .

Verse: *"And* we know that in all things God works for the good of those who love him, who have been called according to his purpose" (Romans 8:28, emphasis added).

"Perhaps the way you or I hold up under suffering may be
instrumental in the conversion of someone who in turn brings up
his family in the fear of the Lord" (D. A. CARSON).

Reflection: I love the conjunction *and* at the beginning of this verse. In my mind these words would lose something if we didn't append them to some (usually adverse) experience, either in anticipation of God's blessing or in hindsight. I suppose that in a way I'm reading that *and* as a *but . . .*

When I was eleven Dad hired a housekeeper/caregiver for his dying wife and five children. Ester, a lovely Hispanic lady with an alcoholic husband and four kids, grew close to Mom, and she accepted the Lord during those few months in our home.

A decade or so ago she made contact with my two siblings still in California. My sister Terri learned then that Ester and her husband Cecil had together entered the ministry. In a phone call some forty-five years after the fact, Terri filled me in on her memory of that morning Mom died. After the ambulance and the rest of us had departed, five-year-old Terri, alone with Ester, experienced a meltdown.

Ester laid her hands on Terri's head and prayed over her (she confided in the adult Terri that this had been her first ever attempt at prayer). Terri remembers being suffused by peace—an outcome not lost on either of them. God worked a quiet, understated miracle that morning in the lives of a young woman at loose ends and a lonely and bewildered little girl.

My reflections on Ester in no way minimize our loss. But in God's grace, our personal loss resulted in eternal gain for a family we would never otherwise have known.

Prayer Prompt: When has God blessed you or someone else through a difficult experience?

odly woman,
LOSS AND GAIN ARE RELATIVE.

$\mathcal{K}$ind of serious

Verses: "In your teaching show integrity, seriousness and soundness of speech that cannot be condemned" (Titus 2:7–8).

"The kindest word in all the world is the unkind word, unsaid"
(AUTHOR UNKNOWN).

Reflection: A few days ago my granddaughter Adelyn, Annabelle (our canine family member), and I were on our way home from preschool when we experienced an encounter with another vehicle. I could see before we passed the side street that the fast-approaching car wouldn't manage to stop on the sheer ice. The teenaged driver was profusely apologetic. It was a good learning experience, I assured him at some point during the next half hour, on the unexpected aspects of winter driving.

I had managed to pull into a driveway, where Addie and I stood shivering until a preschool mom with a daughter in Addie's class happened by and offered Addie shelter in her van before bringing us home. Addie was absolutely quiet until we entered my condo. I waited a day and then broached the question whether she had felt afraid or upset. Her answer was winsome: "No, just kind of serious."

There's a lot in life that calls for solemnity, isn't there? Looking back, I'm grateful that the Spirit checked my response so that Addie didn't have to see a reaction of anger or extreme frustration. How much better for a four-year-old to deal with a rumpled fender than a grandma's ruffled feathers! Paul's words to Titus in the above verses apply to any of us who find ourselves in a teaching role. Integrity, seriousness, and soundness of speech: A child can encounter some pretty somber situations and come through intact as long as the attitude and speech of the adults they love "cannot be condemned."

Prayer Prompt: Over what issue do you find it difficult to maintain your integrity, seriousness (as opposed to unrestrained anger), and soundness of speech?

$\mathcal{G}$odly woman,
DON'T LET YOUR SPEECH CONDEMN YOU OR THE CHRIST YOU SERVE.

$\mathcal{D}$isregarded entities?

Verse: "So God created mankind in his own image, in the image of God he created them; male and female he created them" (Genesis 1:27).

"God does not love us because we are valuable; we are valuable because He loves us" (MARTIN LUTHER).

Reflection: I was browsing a tax form recently when I was stopped in my visual "tracks" by a sentence beginning something like "If you are a disregarded entity . . ." This was my first exposure to that disconcerting term, which immediately called to mind the unfortunate Tom Hanks character in the movie *The Terminal*.

Curious, I pulled it up on the Internet. I now know that this descriptor refers to "a business entity that chooses to be disregarded as separate from the business owner for federal tax purposes." Well, OK . . . sort of. Still, the phrase takes me aback.

A saying popular a couple of decades ago still speaks: "God doesn't make junk." Oh, there's plenty of junk around. But it's manmade (or should I say human-made?). Human beings, though tragically sin-marred, have never been castoffs in God's sight. For my part, I'm going to renew my efforts to view all people through his eyes.

"When you say a situation or a person is hopeless," notes Charles L. Allen, "you are slamming the door in the face of God." If God has yet to give up on any of those "marginal" others populating the planet alongside me, I as a caring Christian have no business doing so either. Two words to expunge from my vocabulary when it comes to human beings: *disregarded* and *entity*.

Prayer Prompt: Think about someone you view as substandard, second-class, even a "mistake." Pause for a moment to picture God loving her. Then pray for her well-being.

odly woman,

GOD CREATED NO SECONDARY IMAGE BEARERS.

The everlasting instant

Verse: "God is love. Whoever lives in love lives in God, and God in them" (1 John 4:16).

> *"The way of paradoxes is the way of truth. To test Reality we must see it on the tightrope. When the Verities become acrobats we can judge them"* (OSCAR WILDE).

Reflection: The presentation of Jesus Christ in the New Testament is rich in paradox—full of seemingly opposing truths. In this case John's wordplay on the preposition *in* highlights the reality of the believer being *in* the same Christ whose Spirit lives *in* him or her.

In the nineteenth century Søren Kierkegaard addressed the issue of biblical paradox, noting the many simultaneous but seemingly contradictory truths that define our faith: "The paradox in Christian truth is invariably due to the fact that it is the truth that exists for God. The standard of measure and the end is superhuman; and there is only one relationship possible: faith." Precisely because this kind of mystery is beyond our reach, it isn't our business to figure it all out.

I appreciate the lyrics of a song authored by Sylvia Dunston, showcasing the ironies intrinsic to the mystery of Christ. Take a few moments to prayerfully consider the implications of these two verses:

> "You, Lord, are both Lamb and Shepherd.
> You, Lord, are both prince and slave.
> You, peace-maker and sword-bringer
>   of the way you took and gave.
> You, the everlasting instant;
> You, whom we both scorn and crave."

> Worthy is our earthly Jesus!
> Worthy is our cosmic Christ!
> Worthy your defeat and vict'ry.
> Worthy still your peace and strife.
> You, the everlasting instant;
> You, who are our death and life."

Prayer Prompt: Who is Jesus Christ to you? What characteristics do you most highly treasure?

Godly woman,
FIND SECURITY IN THE CHRIST IN YOU.

$\mathscr{S}$urprised by pain?

Verse: "Dear friends, do not be surprised at the fiery ordeal that has come on you to test you, as though something strange were happening to you. But rejoice inasmuch as you participate in the sufferings of Christ, so that you may be overjoyed when his glory is revealed" (1 Peter 4:12).

"He who does not know Christ does not know God hidden in suffering" (MARTIN LUTHER).

Reflection: My daughter Khristina's cat Baby Girl (the name just sort of happened) sleeps on my bed, and I enjoy her company. She's a sweet kitty, but I began months ago to notice an irritating behavior. Whenever I get up during the night to use the bathroom, she rises with me, nipping my bare toes as I make my way down the hall.

It occurred to me only recently that Baby Girl is doing me a favor. Somehow knowing that my night vision isn't on a par with hers (she's evidently watched me stumble and grope for furniture), she's taken it upon herself to guide me to my destination. As soon as I make the turn she trots off toward the kitchen for a snack. Mission accomplished.

Peter counsels us in the verse above not to be surprised by our participation in Christ's sufferings. It occurs to me that those sufferings, like Baby Girl's smarting bites, don't always come in the form of fiery trials. In fact, they can be pretty subtle. Nor are we to view them as something strange, like I did those annoying nibbles.

God doesn't tempt us (see James 1:13), but he does test. That isn't strange either. His Word is replete with examples (for two biblical instances with opposite results, think of Abraham responding to the call to sacrifice his son and of Peter denying his Lord).

BTW, has it ever occurred to you—in the midst of real life, while you're undergoing annoyances or sufferings in Christ's name—to rejoice over (not just in spite of) them? That's a perspective worth bearing in mind.

Prayer Prompt: Acknowledge some ways in which you've suffered for Christ, some tests he's put you through. Drawing a blank? Consider asking him about it.

odly woman,

SUFFERING FOR CHRIST CONFIRMS YOU AS HIS OWN.

𝒯he God of life

Verses: "Now choose life, so that you and your children may live and that you may love the Lord your God, listen to his voice, and hold fast to him. For the Lord is your life" (Deuteronomy 30:19–20).

"You can see God from anywhere if your mind is set to love and obey Him" (AIDEN WILSON TOZER).

Reflection: We can only conclude from these verses (if we were in doubt) that God is pro-life. We're quick with our buy-in on God loving and valuing life, but how often do we think of him as *being* our life?

God created us for his own pleasure and praise; as such, he's our sole reason for living. He also sustains us so that our every breath, our every involuntary heartbeat, is a gift. How sad that not all of us do love, listen to, and hold fast to God.

About that matter of choosing life, Moses wasn't talking about abortion, stem cell research, euthanasia, eugenics, or any other controversial contemporary term. There are, of course, countless ways in which we can choose life. But the emphasis in Deuteronomy is solidly on obedience/disobedience, associated, respectively, with life and death.

We're uncomfortable with that kind of black-and-white distinction. But our twenty-first-century perspective on the matter doesn't negate God's equations. No, we aren't saved by our good deeds. Yet as James points out in James 2:18, we have to question faith unaccompanied by obedience to God's overarching law of love.

Prayer Prompt: What kinds of life or death choices are you making, not just in terms of healthy and ethical living but of obedience to God?

𝒢*odly woman,*

OPT FOR LIFE.

$\mathcal{N}$ot OK? Not the end!

Verse: "It was good for me to be afflicted so that I might learn your decrees" (Psalm 119:71).

> *"Evil can no more be charged upon God than darkness can be charged on the sun"* (AUTHOR UNKNOWN).

Reflection: I was surprised by the psalmist's reference to "decrees" in conjunction with suffering. I would have thought that affliction might teach me God's love, his grace, his faithfulness—but not so much his law.

Trouble comes to us in a variety of ways, not the least of which is natural consequence. And natural consequence results from disregard for natural laws or for the spiritual and social mandates encapsulated for us in the Ten Commandments and their New Testament summary. In this sense, affliction can teach me God's expectations. And his forgiveness.

As Job learned, though, there isn't necessarily (or even typically) a one-on-one correspondence between personal sin and personal suffering. The skewing of the order and balance of creation based on original sin produces hardship for all living things.

Paul alludes to natural consequence in Romans 8:20–21, where he makes the following observation: "For the creation was subjected to frustration, not by its own choice, but by the will of the one who subjected it, in the hope that the creation itself will be liberated from its bondage to decay and brought into the freedom and glory of the children of God."

What a beautiful prospect! It occurs to me that this long-awaited freedom—this stability, this harmony, this *shalom*—will coincide in the new creation with enthusiastic, universal compliance with God's decrees. I'm drawn to an anonymous quote on the subject of hardship: "Everything is okay in the end. If it's not okay, then it's not the end."

Prayer Prompt: What perspective on suffering has influenced your responses/reactions?

odly woman,
ANTICIPATE YOUR LIBERATION.

$\mathscr{A}$fraid of God?

Verse: "David was afraid of God that day and asked, 'How can I ever bring the ark of God to me?'" (1 Chronicles 13:12).

> *"Our brains are no longer conditioned for reverence and awe. We cannot imagine a Second Coming that would not be cut down to size by the televised evening news, or a Last Judgment not subject to pages of holier-than-thou second-guessing in The New York Review of Books"* (JOHN UPDIKE).

Reflection: David, the man after God's heart, was afraid of God one day. What had begun as a jubilant march to return the ark of the covenant or testimony to Jerusalem had ended in a sobering reminder of a not-often-seen side of God's nature.

As this sacred object jounced along on a cattle-drawn cart, Uzzah reached out his hand to steady it—and was struck dead for his sacrilege. Why? Because David had disregarded God's explicit instructions in Exodus 25:13–15 for carrying the ark on poles.

The God of the Bible does at times make himself fearful. Think about Korah, Dathan, and Abiram; Achan; and Ananias and Sapphira, all of whom committed sins we would count as more serious than Uzzah's reflexive action. Still, who of us, accustomed as we are to God's kindness, would have predicted the outcomes these individuals experienced?

It has been suggested that God was setting precedents at critical junctures in the lives of his people, and this does appear to have been the case. Beyond that, though, we do well to heed these warnings against a lackadaisical approach to the things of God.

There can be no doubt in the church today that forgiveness—even to the point of cheap forgiveness—is in vogue. But God may choose to surprise us again.

Prayer Prompt: What do you make of God's scary side? To what degree have you come to terms with this aspect of his nature?

$\mathscr{G}$*odly woman,*
FORGIVENESS IS FREE, BUT IT ISN'T CHEAP.

$\mathcal{I}$ntergenerational esteem

Verse: "Children's children are a crown to the aged, and parents are the pride of their children" (Proverbs 17:6).

"I have often thought what a melancholy world this would be without children, and what an inhuman world without the aged"
(SAMUEL TAYLOR COLERIDGE).

Reflection: We Boomers (just apply that to me if it doesn't fit you) are "coming of age." How typical of this generation to do it twice! We've tackled life with gusto and, despite a desire to remain engaged and active, are looking toward retirement.

Probably more than any of our predecessors, we hang our dreams on our grandchildren. Life isn't always easy for twenty-first-century kids; many depend on us, if not for sustenance at least for a good share of their upbringing and stability.

Wiling away some time with granddaughter Adelyn in a McDonald's Playland late last Saturday afternoon, I couldn't help but notice that the adults present could have organized a grandparents' club. The majority of us, I gathered from conversational snatches, were killing, or filling, time before picking up our own "kids" from work. (My daughter Khristina is currently working not one but two forty-hour minimum-wage jobs!) Boomers waiting for our Boomerang kids . . .

What bothers me most about the arrangement is the entitlement mentality characterizing so many of the young adults who rely on continued "hands-on" parenting for themselves, not to mention a kind of grandparental involvement for their offspring that looks a lot like parenting. With regard to the first clause of Solomon's observation, above, well and good—or at least real (with the exception that most of us haven't quite made it to "aged"). But what of the second? At least in our societal context, the notion of parents being the pride of their kids doesn't ring true for me.

No matter what generational group you represent (at least by default), how well does this verse apply to your situation? With your parents? Your kids? Have we lost something along the way?

Prayer Prompt: Assess your relationships with the three or even four generations surrounding you.

odly woman,

THE LORD EXPECTS INTERGENERATIONAL HONOR.

*H*emmed in by God

Verse: "I keep my eyes always on the LORD. With him at my right hand, I will not be shaken" (Psalm 16:8).

> *"Security is not the absence of danger but the presence of God, no matter what the danger"* (AUTHOR UNKNOWN).

Reflection: Keeping our "eyes" on God is a choice, as is situating anything else in our direct line of vision. When we set our sights on anything, we gravitate in that direction, like it or not. When I was a kid, I was instructed not to look in the direction of high-beam headlamps from an approaching vehicle. They would, so the warning went, draw me toward them. I've never been able to verify this—but then I suppose I've never quite dared experiment.

A summary of Israel's history in Nehemiah includes the following: "But they were disobedient and rebelled against you; they turned their backs on your law" (Nehemiah 9:26). *Hmmm.* Sounds like the good stuff I look or walk away from is significant too. But God doesn't let me go that easily.

In the words of David in Psalm 139:5–6: "You hem me in behind and before. . . . Such knowledge is too wonderful for me" (I love the unexpected reaction in that second clause!). The more negative imagery in Job 13:27 makes a similar point, as Job protests God's close scrutiny of his ways: "You fasten my feet in shackles; you keep close watch on all my paths by putting marks on the soles of my feet." The reference seems to be to the Babylonian equivalent of a parolee on a tether; the ancient code of Hammurabi called for marking the bottoms of slaves' feet, presumably as a tracking device.

The fact is that God doesn't manipulate us or demand our obedience. But he does mark us as his own. What better reminder of the importance of setting him before us in terms of our decision making?

Prayer Prompt: Do you at times resent God's knowledge of your ways and whereabouts?

*G*odly woman,
TRAIN YOUR SIGHTS ON HIM.

$\mathscr{W}$hatever is admirable

Verse: "Finally, brothers and sisters, whatever is true, whatever is noble, whatever is right, whatever is pure, whatever is lovely, whatever is admirable—if anything is excellent or praiseworthy—think about such things" (Philippians 4:8).

> *"Your own mind is a sacred enclosure into which nothing harmful*
> *can enter except by your permission"* (RALPH WALDO EMERSON).

Reflection: What difference do our thoughts make? Presuming we're disciplined people, do they in any real way affect our actions? Our attitudes? I've always been a bit of an armchair thrill seeker when it comes to scary movies, although my chill tolerance has declined with maturity—or is that age? For a period during my twenties I was indiscriminate about the *kind* of scary movies I watched (including some with demonic plot lines).

(Reading the wrong book can be the same issue. In the words of John Kenneth Galbraith, "A bad book is the worse that it cannot repent. It has not been the devil's policy to keep the masses of mankind in ignorance; but finding that they will read, he is doing all in his power to poison their books.")

The "problem"—or blessing—for me after such unsettling exposure was that my conscience became over time increasingly ill-at-ease after I had allowed myself to view films with questionable premises. Those were the nights when I went to bed not only scared but alienated from God and embarrassed to seek his comfort. After inviting the devil into my apartment, I reasoned, I deserved whatever out-of-character thoughts preoccupied my mind and peopled my dreams.

In the words of Watchman Nee, "When a Christian does not repel the thoughts which originate with evil spirits he affords them a base for working."

The truth is that we don't have to look hard to find excellent and praiseworthy influencers on which to hang our thoughts. And this makes all the difference in the quality of our Christian lives.

Prayer Prompt: Are "outside" thought influencers of one kind or another an issue for you?

odly woman,

HANG YOUR THOUGHTS ON EXCELLENCE.

$\mathcal{G}$uidance gone bad

Verse: "Plans are established by seeking advice; so if you wage war, obtain guidance" (Proverbs 20:18).

"Advice is what we ask for when we already know the answer but wish we didn't" (ERICA JONG).

Reflection: When it comes to seeking guidance, there are definite pitfalls to avoid. One has to do with the reason we're asking. If our goal is corroboration of a preconceived plan, we're going to continue soliciting advice until or as long as we hear exactly what we want.

A case in point: Israel's King Ahab and Judah's Jehoshaphat were considering a joint attack on Aram (see 1 Kings 22:1–28). Four hundred false prophets and the same number of green lights later, Jehoshaphat asked whether at least one *godly* prophet might be available. Ahab's peevish response: "There is still one prophet through whom we can inquire of the LORD, but I hate him because he never prophesies anything good about me" (verse 8).

I did the same thing during my ten-year-wait for a second adoption. As though expressing my desire would place it in the forefront of God's mind, I solicited endless validation of my already formulated plan. I remember how devastated I was when a coworker informed me over coffee that another child wasn't within God's will for me (both of us in that situation were seriously misguided).

Guidance can go bad for several obvious reasons, among them: The asker may seek only "yes men" (or women); the advisers may be so carried away by the emotional undercurrent of the moment that the result is group think run amuck; or, as in my case, an individual may presume to speak on God's behalf.

"One cool judgment," noted President Woodrow Wilson, "is worth a thousand hasty counsels. The thing to do is to supply light and not heat." Sounds to me like advice worthy of Proverbs 20:18. Works well for waging peace too!

Prayer Prompt: What guidance have you sought recently? Are you looking for advice now?

$\mathcal{G}$*odly woman,*

SEEK GODLY COUNSEL.

The authentic why

Verse: "In your hearts revere Christ as Lord. Always be prepared to give an answer to everyone who asks you to give the reason for the hope that you have. But do this with gentleness and respect" (1 Peter 3:15).

"We are all in the gutter, but some of us are looking at the stars"
(OSCAR WILDE).

Reflection: If someone asks the reason for your *hope*, you can be pretty sure they want it—the hope, that is. This is heart language, not an invitation to an intellectual argument. The question may come out sounding quite different, something like *How come you're not worried?* or *How can you be so calm at a time like this?*

Even if the asker knows nothing of your Christian faith, he or she may well be grasping for a safety net. Arguments that do arise may be an attempt to overcome objections the individual has heard before and wants to move beyond.

As Peter cautions, this answer (the why of your hope) requires forethought. It doesn't have to be particularly well worded (although it's important to cover the basics of the gospel message), but it does need to be experiential and heartfelt.

As Friedrich Nietzsche pointed out, "He who has a why to live for can bear almost any how." If there's one critical shortage in our world today, it's precisely that: an authentic, believable *why*.

Prayer Prompt: Have you thought through your answer? Does it ring true for you?

Godly woman,
BE READY TO EXPLAIN YOUR HOPE.

$\mathcal{G}$od's perspective on affliction

Verse: God "does not willingly bring affliction or grief to anyone" (Lamentations 3:33).

> *"God's plans are being accomplished despite, yes, even through, tragedies. And they are tragedies. He considers them so. He loathes the wickedness, misery and destruction itself—but he has determined to steer what he hates to accomplish what he loves. If God didn't control evil, the result would be evil uncontrolled"* (STEVEN ESTES).

Reflection: The first, prose chapter of the book of Job provides us with a unique insight into at least one of the origins of personal "misfortune" in our world. Unlike the all-knowing God, Job's know-it-all friends were convinced that Job had committed some egregious sin, for which God was meting out his just deserts. The truth is that while God does discipline his children, he never does so to even a score.

The prophet Ezekiel sheds additional light on the above Verse: "Do I take any pleasure in the death of the wicked? declares the Sovereign LORD. Rather, am I not pleased when they turn from their ways and live?" (Ezekiel 18:23).

And Isaiah, speaking of the new heavens and the new earth, hints at God's grief over the sad realities of life in the here and now: "Never again will there be in it an infant who lives but a few days, or an old man who does not live out his years. . . . No longer will they build houses and others live in them. . . . They will not labor in vain nor will they bear children doomed to misfortune" (Isaiah 65:20, 22–23). How contemporary these scenarios. Who of us can't relate to specific examples of any or all of them? But do we ever pause to recognize that such events, whether they affect God's children or other human beings, are contrary to his will?

In his very next breath Isaiah provides us with a beautiful assurance about prayer: "Before they call I will answer; while they are still speaking I will hear" (verse 24). God bemoans the lingering effects of sin in his world just as much as we do. No, much more. Because only he knows how different life could be.

Prayer Prompt: What comfort do you take from Isaiah's words about prayer?

$\mathcal{G}$odly woman,
HE ISN'T OUT TO EVEN A SCORE.

*S*ongs in the night

Verse: "Where is God my Maker, who gives songs in the night?" (Job 35:10).

"Music that gentler on the spirit lies,
Than tired eyelids upon tired eyes."
—ALFRED, LORD TENNYSON

Reflection: "When I lie down I think, 'How long before I get up?' The night drags on, and I toss till dawn" (Job 7:4). I chuckled when I read this verse just now (although I know this was no laughing matter for Job); it's 4:32 a.m., and I've been writing for two hours because I couldn't sleep. I knew when I went to bed that this would be a problem. It's one of those unfinished business issues when finishing the business (in this case this devotional manuscript) will take a good deal longer than the hours in one day. Khristina and Annabelle (her dog), who for whatever reason last night opted to sleep on the couch in my office (er, living room) are both snoring gently only feet away from me, but the power of suggestion isn't phasing me.

"By day the LORD directs his love, at night his song is with me—a prayer to the God of my life" (Psalm 42:8). Sounds like one of the sons of Korah (joint authors of this psalm) was up too. The context tells me that his situation was tough, that the song that was with him that night was one of comfort.

I can relate. Shortly before Mom died when I was eleven, someone gave Dad a record album with a title something like "Songs of Comfort." The group went by the no-nonsense name of Sixteen Singing Men and had a barbershop sound. For weeks I looked forward every night to going to bed—not so much to sleep as to savor that hopeful Christian music.

I'm not in need of comfort this morning (more like needing to pull back my internal engine from a rev to an idle). But the memory of that album is pleasant. I can hear it in my mind right now, as though every note is imprinted there. Next time I'm in need of nighttime comfort, I'll have to remind myself to remember a few of those songs.

Prayer Prompt: Think back on a song or hymn that has meant a great deal to you. If appropriate, sing it back to God. Or thank him for having blessed you with it.

odly woman,
REMEMBER *YOUR* SONGS IN THE NIGHT.

$\mathcal{S}$erene ambition?

Verses: "Make it your ambition to lead a quiet life: You should mind your own business and work with your hands, just as we told you, so that your daily life may win the respect of outsiders and so that you will not be dependent on anybody" (1 Thessalonians 4:11–12).

> *"Apart from God every activity is merely a passing whiff of insignificance"* (ALFRED NORTH WHITEHEAD).

Reflection: "Laziness," so says Jules Renard, "is nothing more than the habit of resting before you get tired." In light of the emphasis of so many of us Christian women on work ethic, this may not be a temptation for you. And Paul's choice of the word "ambition" sounds anything but passive.

Many of us cringe inwardly, in fact, at the thought of depending on anyone. And that's OK, as long as our independence doesn't serve for us as a source of false pride. Or as long as we remember and acknowledge that God isn't just anybody.

In Psalm 16 David reflects on his secure lot, acknowledging, "The boundary lines have fallen for me in pleasant places; surely I have a delightful inheritance" (verse 6). He goes on to clarify that he isn't talking about coincidence or good fortune: "I keep my eyes always on the LORD. With him at my right hand, I will not be shaken" (verse 8; see also the meditation for January 18).

We as believing women do well to aspire to a lifestyle that will win the respect of a watching world—and reflect our absolute dependency on God.

Prayer Prompt: Does your work ethic compromise your trust?

$\mathcal{G}$ *odly woman,*
DEPEND ON HIM.

$\mathcal{H}$ow much?

Verse: "You, God, are my God, earnestly I seek you; I thirst for you, my whole being longs for you, in a dry and parched land where there is no water" (Psalm 63:1).

> *"[T]he God who pursues those who deny him interrupted my existence, he captured my soul with raw love. Two decades later, God's tangible friendship still amazes me"* (ALICIA BRITT CHOLE).

Reflection: I was entering the store a couple of weeks ago when I was surprised by a plaintive announcement from Adelyn, seated facing me in the front of the cart: "Grandma, sometimes I want you." Moved, I was quick to declare my mutual feeling.

When Khristina and I allow my granddaughter the privilege of sharing my queen-size bed, I almost invariably feel during the night her little hand reaching over to touch my arm and her toes to feel for my leg. Her breathing deepens after those confirming touches. Addie has had some difficult experiences in her short life, but this past year with Mom and Grandma has gone a long way toward restoring her security.

David's words in Psalm 63:1 are so full of passion that they make me squirm. Because I can't help but ask myself, *Do I want God that much?* Or, assured that I already "have" him, am I taking his presence in my life totally for granted? Does my soul reach out for him in the night, just to make sure he's there?

An anonymous quote speaks to me: "To love is to risk not being loved in return. To hope is to risk pain. To try is to risk failure, but risk must be taken because the greatest hazard in life is to risk nothing." Little ones like Addie take the risks; they have to, for survival. We who are more sophisticated and less dependent are also more inclined to weigh the pros and cons before giving of ourselves in a relationship. Perhaps my question needs to change: *If I weren't so sure of God, how badly would I want him?*

Prayer Prompt: Try to resolve that question in your heart and mind before coming before God in gratitude.

odly woman,

THIRST FOR HIM.

$\mathscr{F}$orward, march . . .

Verses: "When I brought your ancestors out of Egypt . . . I gave them this command: Obey me, and I will be your God and you will be my people. Walk in obedience to all I command you, that it may go well with you. But they did not listen or pay attention . . . . They went backward and not forward" (Jeremiah 7:22–24).

"I am a slow walker, but I never walk backwards"
(ABRAHAM LINCOLN).

Reflection: How much thought do we as Christians give to our sanctification (according to my dictionary, "the state of growing in divine grace as a result of Christian commitment after baptism or conversion")? If you're like me, not much. We take it on faith that we've been justified (made right with God) through the atoning death and resurrection of our Savior and Lord Jesus Christ. That was a once-for-all-time occurrence, a historical happening that changed the course of human history for all who would believe.

But we too easily view our growth in grace as a given, a phenomenon in the life of the believer orchestrated from the divine end—if we think about it at all. We see sanctification as a theological truth; a big word to learn (if our background is doctrinally inclined); a mysterious, guaranteed reality— but hardly a real-life, day-to-day operative force in our lives.

Assessing our degree of sanctification can be slippery, like taking pride in our humility. But each of us, looking back over a span of time, should at least be able to see a steady, if slow, improvement in the evidences of Christian grace in our life. If we detect slippage, it's time for a reality check.

I like John Piper's "take" on this issue: "Assurance of salvation is a precious thing, so precious and so necessary that we dare not dilute it with feelings of safety apart from transformed lives." Or, in the words of Leighton Ford, "God loves us the way we are, but too much to leave us that way."

Prayer Prompt: Ask God to show you those areas in your Christian life in which you're making progress—as well as any that may be lagging.

$\mathscr{G}$*odly woman,*
YOU'RE A WORK IN PROGRESS.

*Y*our shining temple

Verses: "Do you not know that your bodies are temples of the Holy Spirit, who is in you, whom you have received from God? You are not your own; you were bought at a price. Therefore honor God with your bodies" (1 Corinthians 6:19–20).

> *"Nursing is an art: and if it is to be made an art, it requires*
> *an exclusive devotion as hard a preparation, as any painter's or*
> *sculptor's work; for what is the having to do with dead canvas or*
> *dead marble, compared with having to do with the living body, the*
> *temple of God's spirit? It is one of the Fine Arts: I had almost said,*
> *the finest of Fine Arts"* (FLORENCE NIGHTINGALE).

Reflection: A year or so ago my then three-year-old granddaughter Adelyn and I were goofing off when she reverted momentarily to a serious tone, chiding, "Don't poke my tummy, Granna. That's where Jesus is."

Addie had it right in terms of the importance of God's Spirit within her. Her little body, like yours and mine and that of every other daughter or son of God, is a sacred, shining temple and needs to be treated as such.

What that means for you may be a little different from what it means for Addie or me or that other temple down the street or at your side. But we do well to keep the realization of God's indwelling presence in the forefront of our minds and hearts. When we do that, our response to encroaching temptation or danger will be immediate and instinctual.

Prayer Prompt: Identify the temptations with which you struggle the most, especially those that directly affect your body. Then, before praying for the power to resist, visualize your body as the holy temple it is.

odly woman,
YOU'RE HIS TEMPLE.

𝒲atchers

Verse: "Watch your life and doctrine closely. Persevere in them, because if you do, you will save both yourself and your hearers" (1 Timothy 4:16).

"I call the mind free . . . which does not content itself with a passive or hereditary faith" (WILLIAM ELLERY CHANNING).

Reflection: Adelyn and I awoke together to the alarm this morning (Khristina had already left for work), but I allowed myself the unaccustomed pleasure of hitting the snooze button. Addie didn't snooze. Ten minutes later she met me at my bed with a couple of scientific observations: "Granna, did you know that water turns hair brown?" (she's a blonde) and "Water is invisible, like gas" (I think "transparent" is what she was getting at). I soon discovered that she had "washed" her hair in the sink with liquid soap (no rinsing). A good reminder for me of the need for continual vigilance in terms of my granddaughter's activities.

Paul's words to Timothy in the above verse remind me of a much more important kind of vigilance for me as a believing woman—that of my own life and doctrine. No, I'm not a pastor like Timothy, not in the public eye in the way he was. But I pass off this difference far too glibly if I picture myself slipping off the hook on that basis. The fact is that I, like Timothy, do have "hearers"—an audience that both sees and hears my public life and judges me, and my Savior and Lord, accordingly. Bottom line: I need to watch myself, at least in part because others are watching me.

Has it ever occurred to you that your personal vigilance can indeed affect others, including others you might not know or dream are paying attention?

Prayer Prompt: Take a quick inventory of the people who may have observed you publicly so far today, or yesterday, if the day is young. What words or actions in particular may have made an impression in one way or another?

𝒢odly woman,

BE VIGILANT—IT MATTERS!

ℐlippage

Verse: "The LORD makes firm the steps of the one who delights in him; though he may stumble, he will not fall, for the LORD upholds him with his hand" (Psalm 37:23).

"Do not look where you fell, but where you slipped"
(AFRICAN PROVERB).

Reflection: What's the difference in our Christian life between stumbling, or slipping, and falling? It's a matter of degree. It's all about checking ourselves, with the Spirit's prodding, or allowing him to check us, depending on how we look at his intervention in our lives.

David in Psalm 37 may have been talking about physical protection. Either way, how comforting to envision the Lord there beside us to grab our hand when we slip or stumble.

"Black ice" is an unpleasant reality during the frigid months in a climate like Michigan's. Adelyn relies on me to hold her hand, but I could easily pull her down with me if I go. That's not a problem for me when I'm with my God.

I like that proverb about looking where you slipped; chances are that if you don't pay attention you'll go down again in the same spot. If you're wise you'll throw a little salt on that treacherous area or deliberately walk in the snow to avoid the less forgiving ice. Temptation is a lot like that. Once our footing starts to go, whether or not we manage to right ourselves, we can be that much more vulnerable the next time we venture that way. It may not be the ice at all but a tree root, a crack in the sidewalk, whatever. But the likelihood is that we'll become less vigilant over time.

The doxology at the end of Jude (verses 24–25) always gives me chills (the good kind): "To him who is able to keep you from stumbling and to present you before his glorious presence without fault and with great joy—to the only God our Savior be glory, majesty, power and authority, through Jesus Christ our Lord, before all ages, now and forevermore! Amen."

Prayer Prompt: In what areas are you prone to slippage?

odly woman,
GRASP HIS HAND.

ℳoose in praise?

Verse: "The LORD is my strength and my shield . . . . My heart leaps for joy, and with my song I praise him" (Psalm 28:7).

"Of all the wonders of nature, a tree in summer is perhaps the most remarkable; with the possible exception of a moose singing 'Embraceable You' in spats" (WOODY ALLEN).

Reflection: While not my favorite month, I'll have to say that January has its charms. I was delighted this morning watching Annabelle, my daughter Khristina's lab-mix puppy, reveling in the fluffy snow. She snorted and snuffled in the white stuff, licked it, and slid down the driveway chasing a divot of grass she had pulled from underneath it. Her treasure!

I remember years ago enjoying an anecdote in the *Reader's Digest* about moose in the wild. The author, deep in the woods, claimed to have spotted a number of them above an incline leading to a frozen-over lake. One at a time, he reported, they took position, made their way down the incline, and slid on the ice. The action appeared to be deliberate and, well, fun! Like kids taking turns at a water slide or skiers lining up for a run.

When I stop to think about it, what does Annabelle do besides eat, drink, sleep, eliminate, bark, chew, slobber—and play? (In an effort to be positive, I'm leaving "ruin my condo" off the list. Hopefully she's almost past that stage, and her chew function covers it pretty well.)

How, I ask myself, can I observe the sheer abandon of frolicking animals without seeing their Maker—and learning something valuable about his character? Jesus once told the Pharisees that if his disciples were to squelch their exuberant praise the very stones would cry out (see Luke 19:40). Annabelle does that too. As do the moose—whether or not they have anyone but an appreciative God as their audience.

Prayer Prompt: When have the actions of God's nonhuman creatures inspired you to praise?

Godly woman,
DON'T LEAVE HIS PRAISE TO THE ANIMALS . . . OR THE STONES.

*P*roducing wealth

Verse: "But remember the LORD your God, for it is he who gives you the ability to produce wealth" (Deuteronomy 8:18).

"Work while you have the light. You are responsible for the talent
that has been entrusted to you" (HENRI-FRÉDÉRIC AMIEL).

Reflection: Notice what this verse doesn't say: that humans don't produce wealth. We don't, of course, do so on our own. It goes without saying that we can't accomplish anything without the ability to do so.

But we don't necessarily follow through on anything just because we're capable. *Who wouldn't want to be well off?* you might ask. That's a fair question. But producing wealth, as egotistical as that goal may sound to the Christian woman, generally requires focused effort.

I would expect a reflection on this verse to concentrate on stewardship of financial resources. On acknowledging, perhaps specifically at W2 time, the true source of our income and on doing what we can to give back to God, and others in his name, on the basis of love and gratitude. But other stewardship categories come into play here—those of time, talent, and opportunity, for example.

When God gives us an ability, he expects us to use it. Jesus' parable of the talents (as in money; it's referred to as the parable of the bags of gold in the 2010 NIV revision) in Matthew 25:14–30 may catch us slightly off guard. But we do well to remember, at tax time as always, that the possession of wealth doesn't have to induce guilt in us as Christians. The real issues are twofold: how we view our financial resources and how we manage them. I suppose that does come back around to financial stewardship.

Prayer Prompt: Do you see your God-given ability to produce wealth as a kingdom opportunity?

odly woman,

EXERCISE YOUR GIFTS. THEN USE THE PROCEEDS WELL.

$\mathcal{T}$he repentant God

Verses: "'I have seen these people,' the LORD said to Moses, 'and they are a stiff-necked people. Now leave me alone so that my anger may burn against them and that I may destroy them. Then I will make you into a great nation'" (Exodus 32:9–10).

> *"Among the attributes of God, although they are equal, mercy shines with even more brilliance than justice"*
> (MIGUEL DE CERVANTES).

Reflection: Did God really mean what he said here to Moses? If we're honest with ourselves, this statement strikes us as shortsighted, grumpy, and—well, er, un-Godlike. OK. The thought is out on the table. What *do* we do with the "repentant" God of the Old Testament, the God who is portrayed not as expressing remorse over any wrongdoing but as regretting his own loving-kindness and long-suffering?

Are these sentiments (for lack of a better, less human term) coming at the junction between God's mercy and his justice, from the intersection between the two "sides" of his nature some view as diametrically opposed?

The answer is, of course, that we don't know. There's so much in the Bible that has to be taken at face value, as fodder for our reflection, without the hope of resolution this side of the consummation of salvation history.

Listen to the psalmist Asaph on this issue: "Time after time [God] restrained his anger and did not stir up his full wrath. He remembered that they were but flesh, a passing breeze that does not return" (Psalm 78:38–39). Perhaps our best and only appropriate response is gratitude for the triumph of grace.

Prayer Prompt: How do you deal with the Bible's "hard sayings"—its head scratchers and seemingly unsolvable mysteries?

$\mathcal{G}$*odly woman,*

THANK HIM FOR HIS GRACE AND RESTRAINT.

The one God loves

Verse: "Lord, the one you love is sick" (John 11:3).

"The best practical advice I can give to the present generation is to practice the virtue which the Christians call love"
(BERTRAND RUSSELL).

Reflection: This brief verse is such a beautiful understatement. Its seven single-syllable words, at least when rendered in the English language, carry a cadence that sets it apart. The reference is to Jesus' good friend Lazarus. But it could apply at various times to any one of us.

I'm reminded of a stanza from a well-loved "Jesus song": "Jesus loves me, loves me still, when I'm very weak and ill. From his shining throne on high comes to watch me where I lie." Fifty-some years ago the first-grade class of the Christian school I attended sent a handmade card to me, their classmate hospitalized with nephritis, with those lyrics written out on it.

I've carried vague regrets for that same half-century plus about declining to play Candyland in the pediatric playroom with a younger boy from my church who later died of leukemia. It's funny how those twinges can stay with us.

Who in your world is sick today? Yourself? A loved one? A fellow church member? An acquaintance? Someone not quite an acquaintance? If it's you, take comfort in this brief verse. If it's someone else, what can you do, today, to reflect Christ's love for this other one whom he loves? Send a card or flowers? Call or pay a visit? Offer to run an errand or bring dinner? Play a game of Candyland? Don't let the impulse pass you by.

Prayer Prompt: How can you, today, represent Jesus to some hurting person?

odly woman,
EXERCISE GOD'S LOVE.

$\mathscr{S}$taggering around in God's shoes

Verse: "The LORD reigns, he is robed in majesty; the LORD is robed in majesty and armed with strength; indeed, the world is established, firm and secure" (Psalm 93:1).

"God does not suffer presumption in anyone but himself"
(HERODOTUS).

Reflection: It takes a while for little kids to get a handle on size differentiation. Several years ago my granddaughter Becky, then about three or four, was playing with Barbie dolls on my living room floor. Her little brother Tavis, finding his dad's size 13 loafers nearby, proudly stood a Ken doll in those big shoes, evidently unfazed by the proportional discrepancy.

As ridiculous at that looked, I can't help but compare it to the futility of human beings presuming to transplant themselves into God's big "shoes." In big and small ways, this happens all the time—even for us as Christians. The irony is that we stumble or shuffle along, completely oblivious to the incongruity of the situation.

"You," David acknowledges to God, "have delivered me from death and my feet from stumbling, that I may walk before God in the light of life" (Psalm 56:13). David may have stumbled before making this declaration, but we can be pretty sure he wasn't staggering around in God's gigantic footwear. If the shoe fits . . .

Prayer Prompt: In what ways do you try to control your circumstances?

$\mathscr{G}$*odly woman,*
LET GOD BE GOD.

$\mathcal{B}$eyond endurance

Verses: "We do not want you to be uninformed, brothers and sisters, about the troubles we experienced in the province of Asia. We were under great pressure, far beyond our ability to endure, so that we despaired of life itself. Indeed, we felt we had received the sentence of death. But this happened that we might not rely on ourselves but on God, who raises the dead" (2 Corinthians 1:8–9).

> *"Not everyone can be trusted with suffering. Not everyone can endure a fiery ordeal. So the Master scrutinizes the jewels and carefully selects those which can bear the refining"*
> (JONI EARECKSON TADA).

Reflection: When we reach the end of our ability to endure, we can be under no illusion. It's then that we know that God takes over. "What is to give light," observed Viktor Frankl, "must endure burning."

Burning, we know, doesn't merely injure; it destroys and consumes, leaving behind a heap of smoldering ashes. If and when we rise from that, we do so as those reborn by the Spirit. Fire also refines and purifies, bringing out the best in us, showcasing our true, new mettle, recharged and aglow with the Spirit's power.

That sounds great, you may protest, *but let's get real. I'm certainly no Paul. And when did I experience trouble like that?* The point is that you *did* get real when you died to your old nature and experienced spiritual rebirth.

Your burning may not have been as dramatic as Paul's, but God saw to it that the new creation that's you has the Spirit-empowered ability to be authentic, a light to those who observe or, better yet, get to know you.

Prayer Prompt: What practical difference does your spiritual rebirth make in your attitudes and actions? In what ways do you function as light to those around you?

odly woman,

A NEW YOU HAS RISEN.

ℛeal or virtual?

Verse: "He who fashioned and made the earth, he founded it; he did not create it to be empty, but formed it to be inhabited" (Isaiah 45:18).

"I must confess that I've never trusted the Web. I've always seen it as a coward's tool. Where does it live? How do you hold it personally responsible? Can you put a distributed network of fiber-optic cable 'on notice'? And is it male or female? In other words, can I challenge it to a fight?" (STEPHEN COLBERT).

Reflection: My daughter Angela, who joined our family through adoption at the age of nearly ten, finds herself burned out at twenty-eight. So much so that she has opted out. Not into the active, high-risk addictions of her past; she's quite safe and sedentary. But she's addicted nonetheless—to a "virtual [Internet] universe." Personal hygiene, changes of clothing, eating, and sleep all happen for her haphazardly.

Angie's only schedule revolves around the times her fellow players and their avatars (the word means "incarnation in human form") are expected to be "on." She plies her laptop eighteen hours a night (this requires a stretch into daylight at both ends), and she's hardly alone. She and her Internet cohorts sometimes lapse into "drama" and make concessions for "real life," but they scorn both terms.

But what about the real world? I feel myself compelled to ask, the world God created for us to inhabit? (I'm aware that I'm stretching Isaiah's words beyond his reference to the holy land, "empty" as it was during the exile. But I trust that I'm grasping a principle, evident already in Genesis 1 as the earth moves from "empty" to populated.) If life on this side of sin is so intolerable for some, what does God want the rest of us to do about it? (I don't have a particular answer in mind, by the way.) Heavy questions for a devotional meditation, but when has God retreated from shaking his people?

Prayer Prompt: Intercede this morning for that individual on your heart who is opting in one way or another against engagement with God's world.

𝒢odly woman,
LIVING ENTAILS MORE THAN BREATHING.

$\mathcal{S}$ecurity

Verse: "Whoever loves money never has enough; whoever loves wealth is never satisfied with their income" (Ecclesiastes 5:10).

"The more we depend on God the more dependable we find He is"
(CLIFF RICHARD).

Reflection: "I have seventeen moneys!" announced Adelyn, opening her purse to display her trove. It occurs to me that, beyond her collecting the stuff as she would anything else, coins mean virtually nothing to this trusting little one. Her security is wholly elsewhere. *Can I say the same about myself,* I can't help but ask—*all of the time?*

The answer to the second part of this question has to be no. Living as I do primarily on a monthly disability income, based on my chronic fatigue syndrome and fibromyalgia, I'll have to confess that the first half of the month, when most of the bills come due, can be problematic. My payments are taken automatically from my bank account, and I too often find it necessary to hedge and finagle when time and resources put on their joint monthly squeeze. Somehow it all works, but I can put in plenty of worry equity to "make it happen."

Back, then, to the first part of the question: *Can I say the same about myself—that my security is wholly elsewhere?* I've already negated the "wholly," but if I take the question without that qualifier I'm surprised at the answer. Because I think it's yes. Do you ever assume you're going to come up short every time you assess yourself against the standard of God's law and expectation? I'm not sure we have to. And my guess is that you're a lot like me on this one.

If you've been a believer for as far back as you can remember, as I have, you may find it difficult to imagine *not* being secure in God, your strength. In some sense that's so basic that it almost defines us—or should. It may well be true that security in our status (finances included) and satisfaction with our income are two different matters. Dwelling on the positive side of that comparison, what a comfort to know that my needs will always be met!

Prayer Prompt: Before approaching God in prayer, take some time to assess both your security and your satisfaction quotients.

odly woman,
REST SECURE IN HIM.

$\mathcal{T}$he aroma of Christ

Verses: "Thanks be to God, who always leads us as captives in Christ's triumphal procession and uses us to spread the aroma of the knowledge of him everywhere. For we are to God the pleasing aroma of Christ among those who are being saved and those who are perishing" (2 Corinthians 2:14–15).

"Behave so the aroma of your actions may enhance the general sweetness of the atmosphere" (HENRY DAVID THOREAU).

Reflection: A succinct observation by the late Congregationalist preacher Henry Ward Beecher reminds me of Paul's challenge in the above verses: "A man ought to carry himself in the world as an orange tree would if it could walk up and down in the garden, swinging perfume from every little censer it holds up to the air." Having grown up across from an orange grove in Southern California, I resonate with Beecher's simile.

Oddly enough, though, when I think about that grove my first association is of the smudge pots the owner would light to protect the fruit on chilly winter nights. I don't recall a smell from those pots, but I do recollect awakening to blackened nostrils and a house blanketed indoors by a fine layer of silt. Yikes! That's definitely not the association I want the world to make with me or my church.

I need to ask myself: What kind of aroma wafts from me through my neighborhood? What bouquet does the world whiff from my fruit when I return home from worship, hopefully ready to engage with others? Do my lifestyle, character, and integrity attract not only "those who are being saved" but also, and especially, "those who are perishing"?

I want to make certain not to ignore two significant little words from verse 15: "to God." Yes, the aroma picked up by others matters enormously. But according to Paul the ultimate recipient of the sweet smell of Christ at work in the world in God.

Prayer Prompt: Pray that Isaiah 55:12 may describe you and your congregation as you disburse from worship: "You will go out in joy and be led forth in peace; the mountains and hills will burst into song before you, and all the trees of the field will clap their hands."

$\mathcal{G}$*odly woman,*
DISTILL HIS FRAGRANCE.

Our keeping God

Verses: "The LORD bless you and keep you; the LORD make his face shine on you and be gracious to you; the LORD turn his face toward you and give you peace" (Numbers 6:24–26).

> *"If you hoard a thing for yourself, it will turn into spiritual dry rot,*
> *as the manna did when it was hoarded"* (OSWALD CHAMBERS).

Reflection: It's been nearly four years since I "lost" my three oldest grand-children, then four, five, and six years old—nearly four years since their troubled custodial dad dragged them for the last time out of my reach, only to lose them permanently to an out-of-state child welfare agency.

As the family had drifted in and out of homelessness (my daughter was no longer in the picture), they had repeatedly found refuge with me for months at a time, sometimes unannounced. And I had done all I could to love those little ones and provide for their spiritual nurture.

The last time Walter, Becky, and Tavis spent a weekend in my home, little Tavis approached me with a solemn proposition: *"Gramma, please keep me!"* I told him I wanted to, that the decision wasn't mine. All the right stuff. But it wasn't enough.

The fact is that we as humans don't own one another. "Our" kids are placed with us in trust; God entrusts to us as his representatives the job of raising them to know him, the One to whom they really belong. Last I heard, my grandkids were in the process of pre-adoptive visits with a Christian family.

I, for my part, trust that they'll remember me and that we'll one day reunite. In the meantime, I pray that *God will keep them*—even though I can't—enfolded securely in his peace. Who do you know and love who needs that peace, that keeping presence? God longs to respond to your plea.

Prayer Prompt: Is there a situation in your life or on your heart that seems too "big"—possibly even too hopeless or complicated—for prayer? Take it to God.

odly woman,
YOU SERVE A KEEPING GOD.

$\mathcal{T}$hinking hard

Verse: "The wicked are waiting to destroy me, but I will ponder your statutes" (Psalm 119:95).

> *"Only when the clamor of the outside world is silenced will you be able to hear the deeper vibration. Listen carefully"*
> (SARAH BAN BREATHNACH).

Reflection: The Bible doesn't fill us in on the authorship of this psalm, but we have to be impressed with 176 verses on the subject of God's commands, precepts, laws, and statutes. As new covenant believing women who've been freed from the strictures of the Old Testament law (which we still strive to keep on the basis of love and gratitude to God), we rejoice in the triumph of grace.

The above verse takes me aback, though. Given the apparent immediacy of the writer's predicament, I wouldn't have expected him to be in the pondering mode. Yet his juxtaposition of the two clauses alerts me that they're closely related. Wisdom, to be gleaned from God's law, was just what this author needed.

Victor Hugo offers a cogent reminder of the importance for the Christian life of time spent in reflection: "One is not idle because one is absorbed. There is both visible and invisible labor. To contemplate is to toil, to think is to do. The crossed arms work, the clasped hands act. The eyes upturned to Heaven are an act of creation."

Prayer Prompt: About what issue are you working hard at thinking? Have you invited God to participate with you in the process?

$\mathcal{G}$*odly woman,*

PRAY, REFLECT, AND TRUST.

$\mathcal{A}$udacious dreams, contingent plans

Verse: "Many are the plans in a person's heart, but it is the LORD's purpose that prevails" (Proverbs 19:21).

"God's gifts put man's best dreams to shame"
(ELIZABETH BARRETT BROWNING).

Reflection: A cryptic observation from an unknown source catches my eye in this Black History Month: "Martin Luther King said 'I have a dream,' not 'I have a plan.'" Certainly we Christians plan ahead. We'd be irresponsible if we didn't. But it's easy for us to forget one thing: "There is no wisdom, no insight, no plan that can succeed against the LORD" (Proverbs 21:30).

We might be tempted to ask why God *wouldn't* endorse and facilitate a good, godly human plan. (*"Godly human"*: Now there's an interesting juxtaposition of adjectives! The irony is that I didn't even notice until I reread the sentence I had just keyed!) In response to that question, we can't assume that God *won't* help our plans succeed. He certainly isn't working at cross purposes with his well-intentioned daughters, especially when his righteousness and glory are our goal. But time-bound he is not!

The book of Hebrews isn't the easiest reading, but I'm intrigued by the final words of its well-known "hall of faith" chapter: "These were all commended for their faith, yet none of them received what had been promised, since God had planned something better for us so that only together with us would they be made perfect" (Hebrews 11:39–40). Talk about delayed gratification!

Like Dr. King, we need to dream big things for God, especially when it comes to righting injustice. We need to do our best to plan, too—within the framework of our acknowledgment that the master plan, with its timetable, is his alone.

Prayer Prompt: What big, audacious dream motivates you in your Christian life?

odly woman,

DREAM BIG—AND PLAN CONDITIONALLY.

The secret

Verse: "I have learned the secret of being content in any and every situation" (Philippians 4:12).

"Who is the wealthiest? He who is content with the least"
(SOCRATES).

Reflection: To what extent are you controlled by the before and after of your life? On what do you base your worth? If what comes to mind are past accomplishments or future goals (your pedigree or your perceived potential), you aren't seeing yourself as God does. On another front, if you're allowing your net worth to determine your personal value, you could be setting yourself up for a serious fall.

How would you assess your contentment quotient? Little kids are for the most part happy, and a good share of the credit goes to the fact that they're totally present in the present, absolutely engaged with the chunk of life in which they find themselves at any given moment.

The truth is that we adults aren't going to be satisfied in the here and now unless we have an internal core of contentment to carry around with us. We will indeed be at the mercy of circumstances—including the financial—if this is absent or depleted, if we have to rebuild or replenish our satisfaction supply on a continual, situational basis.

How "well" are you keeping the secret? This one's meant to be shared!

Prayer Prompt: What criteria are you using to assess your worth? Pause to recognize your infinite value in God's eyes.

Godly woman,
YOU'RE HIS CHERISHED DAUGHTER.

$\mathcal{G}$ainful employment?

Verse: "Whatever your hand finds to do, do it with all your might" (Ecclesiastes 9:10).

"The person who is waiting for something to turn up might start with their shirt sleeves" (GARTH HENRICHS).

Reflection: I don't know whether this anomaly is isolated to West Michigan, but recently a low-budget marketing ploy has become prevalent here. Drive a few miles down one particular east-west corridor during business hours, and you'll observe a number of employees I refer to as "wavers." This time of year they're clad in hoodies and winter gear, over which they've thrown some outlandish outfit: Statue of Liberty and Uncle Sam look-alikes are big during tax time.

Whatever they hawk, these mascots typically waggle signs. Not long ago I waited at a stoplight adjacent to a waver. This skinny boy with the oversized glasses, pale complexion, and receded chin had every mark of the nerd. But he was putting on a remarkable break-dancing performance for the entertainment of his temporarily captive audience. At least a decade behind the times, he still managed to elicit subdued smiles from some otherwise preoccupied motorists.

Whenever I encounter the verse above, I can't help but cycle back to the facetious version my dad shared with me when I was a kid: "Whatsoever thou puttest forth thy hand to do, give it thy dog-gonedest!"

I've come to appreciate this visible subset of the West Michigan workforce engaged in negligibly gainful employment. Thanks, those of you who are Christian wavers, for performing your duties for God's glory and to the best of your ability.

For my part, I'll dignify you created-in-the-image workers with a smile and nod. And I'll put forth my hand with an authentic, unapologetic wave of acknowledgment.

Prayer Prompt: Pray for underemployed and barely employed workers in a difficult economy who still give their best.

odly woman,

HONOR OTHER WORKERS.

$\mathcal{P}$re-consummation living

Verses: "Scripture foresaw that God would justify the Gentiles by faith, and announced the gospel in advance to Abraham: 'All nations will be blessed through you.' So those who rely on faith are blessed along with Abraham, the man of faith" (Galatians 3:8–9).

> *"If thou sin, the word of God is thy adversary. It is the adversary of thy will till it become the author of thy salvation"* (AUGUSTINE).

Reflection: The good news of the gospel permeates Scripture. The promise of a Savior is first announced in Adam and Eve's hearing to the serpent in Genesis 3:15: "And I will put enmity between you and the woman, and between your offspring and hers; he will crush your head, and you will strike his heel."

The head crushing began at the cross and was completed at the empty tomb. And as Satan well knows, his continued heel-striking ability is a temporary concession.

If the Bible, with its sixty-six strikingly different books, seems disjointed to you, consider this: God's Book, from beginning to end, is entirely thematic, the story of the fall and rise of the human race, recounted in four distinct steps: creation, fall, redemption, and consummation.

We're privileged to be living post-redemption/pre-consummation. The final fulfillment of the same promise heard by the first human couple still awaits us.

Prayer Prompt: Thank God for the simple, clear, and consistent message of his Word.

$\mathcal{G}$odly woman,
THE FINAL FULFILLMENT AWAITS YOU.

*J*ustifying the means?

Verses: "Abraham replied, 'I said to myself, "There is surely no fear of God in this place, and they will kill me because of my wife." Besides, she really is my sister, the daughter of my father though not of my mother. . . . And when God had me wander from my father's household, I said to her, "This is how you can show your love to me: Everywhere we go, say of me, 'He is my brother'"'" (Genesis 20:11–13).

"It is best to avoid the beginnings of evil" (HENRY DAVID THOREAU).

Reflection: Talk about rationalizing! When have you eased yourself off the hook for a lie based on the fact that, in some convoluted way, it could be argued to be true? Worse yet, when have you asked someone else to prove their love or loyalty by backing you up in a deception?

Abraham's motive of saving his and Sarah's necks may have been understandable, if not commendable, but his method—as pointed out by the ungodly but still ethical Abimelek (see verses 9–10)—most definitely was not.

What token of love will you offer someone this Valentine's Day? Sure, it's a sentimental holiday, but can we say "I love you" too often? Today is as good a time as any to assess how we go about showing our love.

If we're ever tempted to ask the object of our affection to cover for us, tell a lie or half truth for our sake, or keep a guilty secret on our behalf, we'd better think carefully about whose well-being is on our heart.

Prayer Prompt: Have you ever asked a loved one to do something questionable on your behalf?

odly woman,

HONESTY IS THE *ONLY* MEANS TO A GOOD END.

Godlikeness

Verse: "Dear friends, now we are children of God, and what we will be has not yet been made known. But we know that when Christ appears, we shall be like him, for we shall see him as he is" (1 John 3:2).

"Only God is love, and for this love to be fully realized self must step aside. And not only do we not need a self to love God, but for the same reason we do not need a mind to know him, for that in us which knows God, is God" (BERNADETTE ROBERTS).

Reflection: How amazing already now to be a daughter of the living God! But for me the real wow factor of the verse above lies in John's concession that we don't yet know what, or who, we'll one day become. We don't yet know because we wouldn't understand; we wouldn't understand because we aren't yet prepared to handle such knowledge.

We Christians understand that we'll one day be like God, although it isn't clear to what degree. It occurred to me recently that this intriguing possibility, dangled before the first woman by the serpent at the dawn of history (see Genesis 3:5), was the basis for humanity's fall into sin. (I can't help but wonder why one particular aspect of Godlikeness, "knowing good and evil," so appealed to Eve, who until the moment of succumbing had possessed the ability not to sin.)

As I reflect on this packed verse, I wonder about other things: How is seeing God as he is a prerequisite for becoming like him? And why aren't we more anxious to find out?

Prayer Prompt: Daughter of God, what will it take for you to really look forward to your final condition?

Godly woman,
BE WOWED BY YOUR ETERNAL STATUS.

*S*tatus-quo sinning

Verse: "Give, and it will be given to you. A good measure, pressed down, shaken together and running over, will be poured into your lap" (Luke 6:38).

> *"Are right and wrong convertible terms, dependent upon popular opinion?"* (WILLIAM LLOYD GARRISON).

Reflection: We've all read the disclaimer on a cereal box: "This product is sold by weight, not by volume." The intent, of course, is to assure us that we've gotten all the cornflakes we paid for. But food packagers have no trouble finding other ways to dupe us. A popular current ploy is to maintain the price while reducing the size and weight of the box. Truth is, we expect to be cheated. And we get weary of having to be wary.

But let's be honest, at least with ourselves: We (and this includes us as Christians) expect fully as much to get away with cheating. How do we cheat others (individuals, employers, the government, or God) in small—and "expected"—ways? Personal Internet or copier use from the office? Declining to report cash income? Skimping on our tithe? The possibilities are endless.

It's amazing how human beings throughout history have rationalized status-quo wrongdoing. From slavery to infanticide (of whatever form) to racism to unquestioned nationalism, people have always been quick to fall into step with that vaguely defined but always present "everybody." If it's sanctioned, it's sacred, seems to be the validation.

What we fail to recognize is that God isn't fooled. Whether the issue for us involves taking or giving, Jesus assures us in the verse above that we'll be repaid in kind. That's good to know. But this can never be our primary motivator for honest dealings with God and others. We can do no better than to ask ourselves in each situation whose honor is at stake.

Prayer Prompt: For what sin that "everybody's doing" do you as an individual need forgiveness?

odly woman.
IF IT'S WRONG, BE THE EXCEPTION.

Chasing the wind

Verse: "Better one handful with tranquility than two handfuls with toil and chasing after the wind" (Ecclesiastes 4:6).

"I have held many things in my hands, and have lost them all;
but whatever I have placed in God's hands, that I still possess"
(MARTIN LUTHER).

Reflection: Not to be outdone by the Teacher of Ecclesiastes, I have my own handfuls with toil / chasing-after-the-wind-story. When I was in my twenties, my company paid out quarterly bonuses, and on this particular Friday mine was *big*—I'm talking $200 plus (in the 1970s). We had enjoyed a potluck at work the same day. Stopping at the bank's drive-through window after work, I accepted my loot in an open paper sleeve, not bothering to secure it in my purse.

Upon arrival at my apartment parking lot that blustery evening, I made an attempt to lug in everything, including the bag of potluck paraphernalia, in one trip. As the wind tore at me, I must have inadvertently relaxed my grip on that paper sleeve. Finding myself in a tornado of flying bills, I made the decision to deposit my load in the corridor before proceeding back to chase the wind. Needless to say, there was nary a greenback in sight.

This unlikely story goes on, with four people searching into the wee hours along what seemed to be miles of chain-link fence within the private confines of the llama ranch across the street, part of the time assisted by a searchlight from a police cruiser. (We did manage to retrieve about half of those twenties!)

In the decades since then I've learned tranquility, and on my disability income I now have to be satisfied with a single monthly handful. I will say that it feels good in these more mellow days to trust God with the finances. (And the debit card is SO much easier!)

Prayer Prompt: Is your situation more like a handful with tranquility or two handfuls with toil?

Godly woman,
SATISFY YOURSELF WITH THE HANDFUL—WITH TRUST.

*F*ound wanting?

Verse: "Greet Apelles, whose fidelity to Christ has stood the test" (Romans 16:10).

> *"God does not want us to do extraordinary things; He wants us to do ordinary things extraordinarily well"* (BISHOP GORE).

Reflection: This verse wouldn't stand out for me if I hadn't learned that Apelles was a common name for a slave in the imperial Roman household. Paul states so matter-of-factly that this individual of lowly human status had nonetheless won God's "seal of approval."

I can't help but contrast this with King Belshazzar, supreme ruler of another great earthly dynasty, who, we read, was weighed by God "on the scales and found wanting" (Daniel 5:27).

The obvious takeaway, that earthly status means nothing to God, is significant. But what I find more startling, based on the example of the Persian king, is that God evidently tests every individual, whether or not that person is one of "his own."

Based on my identity as a Christ follower, I do expect a much more rigorous test. In Jesus' own words, "From everyone who has been given much, much will be demanded; and from the one who has been entrusted with much, much more will be asked" (Luke 12:48).

"Never forget," cautions Kathryn Hulme, "that God tests his real friends more severely than the lukewarm ones." Or, we can only assume, than the uncommitted or ungodly.

Prayer Prompt: How might you determine whether or not your own fidelity to Christ "stands the test"?

odly woman,
STRIVE FOR HIS APPROVAL.

The limit

Verses: "Job replied to the LORD: 'I know that you can do all things; no purpose of yours can be thwarted. You asked, "Who is this that obscures my plans without knowledge?" Surely I spoke of things I did not understand, things too wonderful for me to know'" (Job 42:2–3).

> *"Can a mortal ask questions which God finds unanswerable? Quite easily, I should think. All nonsense questions are unanswerable"*
>
> (C. S. LEWIS).

Reflection: "I have night vision, like a cat" (*Adelyn, preparing to advance down the basement stairs in the semi-dark*).
"I can see a little bit too, but I'm going to turn on the light. I don't want us to fall."
"Big ladies do fall sometimes. You should get a trampoline so you can get more bouncy!"

From babyhood on we humans are prone to problem solving. We're hardwired by God to be that way, innovative and inventive. But there's a limit, and it's when we attempt to resolve those issues that should be left to God—to probe beyond where he wants us to go—that we run into trouble.

Whether the issue for you revolves around scientific advances involving life and death, prophecy, the demonic, interpreting God's will, or something else, it's true that the limits get blurred sometimes. The field of ethics is all about defining those shadowy lines. In the words of Paul, "For now we see only a reflection as in a mirror; then we shall see face to face. Now I know in part; then I shall know fully, even as I am fully known" (1 Corinthians 13:23).

I can see a little bit, but I'm going to walk in the light. I don't want to fall.

Prayer Prompt: Ask God to reveal any areas that spark your interest but may be off limits to you as a Christian.

Godly woman,

HE HAS REVEALED WHAT YOU NEED TO KNOW.

$\mathcal{T}$he choice

Verse: "He who seeks good finds goodwill, but evil comes to him who searches for it" (Proverbs 11:27).

> *"All maxims have their antagonist maxims; proverbs should be sold in pairs, a single one being but a half truth"* (WILLIAM MATHEWS).

Reflection: Little Adelyn likes to append a caveat to her sage observations about life (dog behavior is a recent case in point): "Some do and some don't." Sort of covers the gamut of possibilities, doesn't it?

The proverbs of Solomon, beginning in Proverbs 10, are a lot like that. Almost singsong in their cadence, these contrasting clauses, one after another, cover both sides of any given issue. Some do and some don't. Some are and some aren't.

This wise man's conclusions may strike us as a little too predictable, a bit too cut and dried for our modern sensibilities. Where our minds look immediately for exceptions, those of the ancients sought out generalities.

One thing is certain: Each of us has a critical choice to make, and there are no nuances, degrees, loopholes, or caveats. The choice is one or the other, and so is the consequence (no exceptions, no generalities). This choice and its consequences are spelled out repeatedly throughout Scripture; there can be no mistaking either one. Deuteronomy 30:19 expresses both in three words: "Now choose life." The truth is that some will and some won't. Have you made your decision?

Prayer Prompt: If this issue has been resolved between you and God, thank him. If not, don't put it off another day.

odly woman,
THERE ARE ONLY TWO OPTIONS.

$\mathcal{R}$eliable boundaries

Verse: "It was you who set all the boundaries of the earth; you made both summer and winter" (Psalm 74:17).

"Winter dies into the spring, to be born again in the autumn"
(MARCHE BLUMENBERG).

Reflection: Two weeks ago we experienced the "storm of the decade," with preschool closed on a Monday morning. Then last week two gusty days in the fifties marked the first time this year the thermometer has inched above freezing. Adelyn was convinced of the arrival of summer, despite my attempts at explaining the phenomenon of unseasonable temperatures. Not surprisingly, winter returned with a vengeance yesterday afternoon, dropping ice over several inches of snow.

Addie awoke early this morning, another Monday, wanting to check out the news for weather and school-closing information. I had already received a recorded phone message about the school's closure, but she was insistent: "No, I want to see if *summer* is closed" (I assume she meant cancelled).

The electricity went off at this point in my reflection. Now, three hours later, I'm bundled over an end table near the living room window, making use of whatever shard of light is trickling in from beneath the drawn shade—a buffer of sorts against a moaning, intrusive wind.

How glad I am that our God is both a promise keeper and a boundary setter. I can't say I wouldn't relish a hot cup of coffee right about now, or take comfort in an ability to use the phone or open the garage door to liberate the car. But how much more do I appreciate the freeing knowledge of a faithful Father who not only isn't going to forego summer this year but who won't forget Addie and myself despite my laughable feeling of isolation.

Well, alright! As though on cue, the lights and heat just kicked back on. "God is so nice to us!" exclaimed Addie as we hugged. Yup—to put it mildly. Praise the Lord!

Prayer Prompt: For which God-imposed boundaries are you thankful?

$\mathcal{G}$odly woman,
HIS CHARACTER DEFINES RELIABILITY.

*O*ur busy God?

Verse: "Does he who fashioned the ear not hear? Does he who formed the eye not see?" (Psalm 94:9).

"An infinite God can give all of Himself to each of His children.
He does not distribute Himself that each may have a part, but to
each one He gives all of Himself as fully as if there were no others"
(A. W. TOZER).

Reflection: There's a word for the imagery in the above verse—*anthropomorphism*. It has to do with attributing humanlike qualities to God (or to some other nonhuman creature or entity). Sounds a little backward in the case of God, but when we stop to think about it, why not? If we're created in his image, then all of our qualities, from senses to emotions, derive from and reflect back on him. These qualities are godly, or at least have the potential to be used in that way.

Still, we sometimes question whether God really can, or chooses to, hear or see us. We long for his attention but fear that our timing may be off. Maybe we should wait for a more opportune moment. What with earthquakes, terrorism strikes, spreading oil in the Gulf (I wrote this pre-cap), and two deaths this past week in our congregation alone, he's pretty busy right now.

What we fail to recognize is that the concept of busyness doesn't apply to God, who established time itself as a concession to our inability to understand reality from his perspective. The only reason for time," quipped Albert Einstein, "is so that everything doesn't happen at once." The fact is that God has nothing "better" to do right now than to sit and chat with you.

Prayer Prompt: Thank God for his undivided attention. He has all the time in the world to dialogue with you, and now is as good a time as any

odly woman,
HE'S NEVER TOO BUSY FOR YOU.

*T*oxic spills

Verses: "Do not betray another's confidence, or the one who hears it may shame you and the charge against you will stand" (Proverbs 25:9–10).

"Betrayal does that—betrays the betrayer" (ERICA JONG).

Reflection: I'm struck again and again as I reflect on the book of Proverbs by the contemporary feel of so many of its observations. Human nature is a constant that unifies human history.

I recently caught myself fanning the flame of conflict between two acquaintances by betraying confidences in both directions. My "She said . . ." messages felt at the time like honest clarifications, but my guilt became so unbearable that I confessed what I'd been doing to the party I knew better, resolving with regard to the other to resist the temptation to intervene in a dispute that wasn't mine. If we think we're mediating, we do well to reality-check our motivation; we might just be meddling.

Benjamin Franklin, a writer of proverbs in his own right, made an observation that seems pertinent here: "The heart of a fool is in his mouth, but the mouth of a wise man is in his heart." And Jesus himself made a direct connection between the heart and the mouth: "For the mouth speaks what the heart is full of" (Matthew 12:34).

If my running at the mouth is the consequence of an overfull heart, I'm wise to monitor my heart's content. A periodic junk dump will benefit myself and others—and hopefully prevent toxic spillover in the future.

Prayer Prompt: What role have you played in others' quarrels?

*G*odly woman,

IF NOT INVITED, DON'T GO THERE. IF INVITED, TREAD CAREFULLY.

$\mathscr{S}$puttering candles

Verse: "A bruised reed he will not break, and a smoldering wick he will not snuff out" (Isaiah 42:3).

"God has not called us to see through each other, but to see each other through" (AUTHOR UNKNOWN).

Reflection: Isaiah's moving words about the coming servant of the Lord afford tremendous comfort still today. When a candle sputters because its flame is drowning in molten wax, the easiest course of action is to blow it out. How often don't we expect just that in our dealings with other people?

You've most likely heard the now clichéd expression that the church is the only institution that shoots its wounded. Not wanting to debate the validity of this observation, I mention it only to make a point about Christ's perspective on our treatment of fellow Christians who are vulnerable, compromised, damaged, or who simply disappoint us.

One of my favorite songs as a very little child had lyrics that went like this: "Jesus bids us shine with a clear, pure light, like a little candle burning in the night. In this world of darkness we must shine, you in your small corner and I in mine." While I wondered at the time what the corners were all about ("Go stand in the corner" didn't have a positive connotation), I got the general idea.

I realize today, though, that I need to do more than shine Christ's candle into the dark recesses around me: I need to use my flame to rekindle others'. "A candle loses nothing," notes James Keller, "by lighting another candle."

Prayer Prompt: Are you more interested in snuffing out the sputtering candle of that fellow believer you dislike or in reigniting it?

odly woman,

REVIVE A GASPING FLAME.

*W*hy in the world?

Verse: "I am not ashamed of the gospel, because it is the power of God that brings salvation to everyone who believes" (Romans 1:16).

> *"The Holy Spirit can't save saints or seats. If we don't know any non-Christians, how can we introduce them to the Savior?"*
> (PAUL LITTLE).

Reflection: Why in the world are we Christians often sheepish, apologetic, or silent when it comes to proclaiming and living out our Christian faith? My guess is that the "in the world" part of the question has a lot to do with its answer. There's something about fitting in that compels us—and about being different that often repels us.

A couple of generations ago Christians from my denomination related to the catchphrase of being "in this world but not of it." While this fit well with Paul's language in Romans 8, it encouraged a "holy" withdrawal from society that too often served to weaken and even negate their testimony.

I wonder whether a more pertinent goal might be deliberate involvement in this world (we're here for a purpose, after all) without being *into* this world. Without an active participation in life we can have no real impact for Christ.

"I have come," announced Jesus, "that [you] may have life, and have it to the full" (John 10:10).

Prayer Prompt: How invested are you in the full life Jesus came to offer—not just for yourself but for those hurting others as well?

*G*odly woman,

BE FULLY PRESENT WHERE HE HAS PLACED YOU.

*H*ow did he know?

Verses: "My witness is in heaven; my advocate is on high. My intercessor is my friend as my eyes pour out tears to God" (Job 16:19–20).

"Surely God would not have created such a being as man, with an ability to grasp the infinite, to exist only for a day! No, no, man was made for immortality" (ABRAHAM LINCOLN).

Reflection: While Job was right on in his assessment that he had an intercessor before God, I'm mystified as to how he could have known this. And I'm blown away by his assertion that this intercessor was his friend. To our knowledge this early God-fearer lacked any hint of the existence of God the Son or God the Spirit.

A few chapters later on this Old Testament figure (who, scholars believe, probably lived around the time of Abraham or one of the later patriarchs) said something even more startling: "I know that my redeemer lives, and that in the end he will stand on the earth. And after my skin has been destroyed, yet in my flesh I will see God" (Job 19:25–26).

Old Testament believers spoke of Sheol, a less-than-heavenly place of the dead, but there's little evidence that they had any concept beyond that of eternal life. So how did Job know? These questions will, of course, have to remain unanswered for the time being, but we can stand amazed at the faith of this ancient, suffering saint.

Prayer Prompt: How might you have responded to Job's situation, knowing only what he did? Or possessing the knowledge you're privileged to enjoy?

odly woman,

THANK GOD FOR HAVING SHARED THE MYSTERY.

$\mathcal{S}$haken . . . or secure?

Verses: "With [God] at my right hand, I will not be shaken. Therefore my heart is glad and my tongue rejoices; my body also will rest secure" (Psalm 16:8–9).

"If we don't come apart, we will come apart" (VANCE HAVNER).

Reflection: Esther ("Etty") Hillesum, a Jewish woman who died in 1943 in the Auschwitz prison camp, wrote letters and diaries between 1941 and 1943 that describe life in Amsterdam during the German occupation.

I don't imagine that city in Holland during those years to have been a secure setting for a young Jewish woman. Yet the following quote from her pen grabs my attention: "Sometimes the most important thing in a whole day is the rest we take between two deep breaths, or the turning inwards in prayer for five short minutes."

The words *shaken* and *secure* (verses above) are mutually exclusive. The truth is that, as long as I'm rattled, I can't possibly get any rest—at least not of a rest-orative variety. And my body (it's interesting here that David singles out the physical) will inevitably suffer for it.

David's words in verse 8 (see also my meditation for January 18) remind me that God takes the initiative of positioning himself at my right hand. With him stationed there, I'm unshakable! When it comes to rest, quality matters even more than quantity. And quality rest is defined by the rest we take in God.

Prayer Prompt: What does resting in God mean for you?

$\mathcal{G}$odly woman,
SEEK REPOSE IN HIM.

$\mathcal{M}$y kingdom go

Verse: "He must become greater; I must become less" (John 3:30).

"It is the nature of the ego to take, and the nature of the spirit to share" (ANONYMOUS PROVERB).

Reflection: I resonate with the above proverb—if and only if "spirit" is capped. I have a hard time separating my ego and my own spirit (my spirit sans the influence of the Holy Spirit). I can't imagine an unredeemed human spirit acting opposite a human ego, nor do I view it as naturally inclined toward sharing. Even with the Spirit's help I have to work at it. How about you?

I have to acknowledge, though, that Paul's words in Romans 8 contradict my "take" on this issue. Listen: "Those who live according to the flesh have their minds set on what the flesh desires; but those who live in accordance with the Spirit have their minds set on what the Spirit desires" (verse 5). I don't want to get caught up in semantics here (ego, spirit, mind), but Paul makes it clear that it is in fact in the nature of the redeemed spirit to share. Wow! What a concept—both enabling and ennobling! Do we as Christian women dare to believe it rings true for us? More to the point: Do we live as though it does?

In the words of Alan Redpath, "Before we can pray, 'Lord, Thy Kingdom come,' we must be willing to pray, 'My Kingdom go.'" If we allow the Spirit to grow within us, to take charge of our desires, inclinations, and actions, others will take notice, both of our selves and of the Christ shining through us.

Prayer Prompt: Ask for the power and grace to surrender your agenda and to live out your Spirit enablement.

odly woman,

YOU'RE EMPOWERED IN HIS STRENGTH.

$\mathscr{L}$eap Year

Verse: "The mind governed by the flesh is hostile to God; it does not submit to God's law, nor can it do so" (Romans 8:7).

> *"The most incomprehensible thing about the world is that it is at all comprehensible"* (ALBERT EINSTEIN).

Reflection: Leap Year sounds to me more like a lag than a leap. To my mind, jumping forward in the spring to Daylight Savings Time fits the "leap" concept more logically. Ever wonder why God worked things out so we'd have to throw in, every four years, a February 29 comprised of four accumulated six-hour periods? Does it strike you as counterintuitive that the God of perfect order would leave us with a "remainder" when we divide up years and seasons? Sounds like a slight oops, doesn't it?

No, I don't have the answer, in case you were waiting. But neither am I ready to discount God or write him off for an apparent mistake. People do that all the time. Their standards for God (whether or not they believe in him) are high, as well they should be.

But when we begin with the premise that God doesn't exist or doesn't have it all together, we're going to end up "proving" our point in one way or another. I don't know about you, but when it comes to Leap Year (or any other aspect of the mystery that's God), I'm willing to wait for the answer.

Prayer Prompt: Do you ever ask to be convinced of God's existence, power, or authority? What role does doubt play in your Christian life?

$\mathscr{G}$*odly woman,*

HE'LL TRANSCEND YOUR UNDERESTIMATION.

That mad?

Verse: "God said to Jonah, 'Is it right for you to be angry about the plant?' 'It is,' he said. 'And I'm so angry I wish I were dead'" (Jonah 4:9).

"Hanging onto resentment is like letting someone you despise live rent-free in your head" (ANN LANDERS).

Reflection: I've always been fascinated by the book of Jonah, but chapter 4, which may seem anticlimactic after the most amazing fish story ever, interests me the most. For one thing, this book is a cliff-hanger, ending with a tantalizingly unanswered question posed by God. Sure, the question is intended to be rhetorical, but we're not advised one way or the other on Jonah's buy-in.

What truly intrigues me about this chapter, though, is the dialogue around the verse above. How, I ask myself, could a man so amazingly rescued from death so soon afterward express a desire to die based on rage over a withered shade plant?

The underlying source of Jonah's anger was, we know, his disapproval over God's willingness to offer the Ninevites, Israel's sworn enemies, an opportunity to repent. Like Jonah, when we allow ourselves to react with disproportionate fury over some petty complaint, we're probably nursing resentment over a wholly unrelated issue.

How much better to take that concern to God, rather than allowing ourselves to lash out inappropriately at him or at others we love.

Prayer Prompt: Over what underlying issue are you doing a slow simmer?

odly woman,

ROOT OUT BITTERNESS FROM YOUR HEART.

$\mathcal{P}$referring one another

Verses: "Do nothing out of selfish ambition or vain conceit. Rather, in humility value others above yourselves, not looking to your own interests but each of you to the interests of others" (Philippians 2:3–4).

"True strength lies in submission which permits one to dedicate his life, through devotion, to something beyond himself"
(HENRY MILLER).

Reflection: It's one thing—while certainly not an easy one—to love our neighbors as we love ourselves (Matthew 19:19). *So what's this now?* we might protest were we encountering the above verses for the first time. Is Paul trying to trump Jesus' mandate by asking us to value others more highly than we value ourselves?

The fact is that Paul wasn't calling Christians to a false or neurotic humility. Nor was he attempting to squelch in us any vestiges of self-esteem. Far from it, Paul understood the tremendous worth God sees in each of us.

Listen: "He chose us in [Christ] before the creation of the world to be holy and blameless in his sight. In love he predestined us for adoption to sonship [in our case "daughter-ship"?] through Jesus Christ, in accordance with his pleasure and will" (Ephesians 1:4–5). And Paul goes on. Do these sound like the words of someone who's asking you to grovel?

In Romans 12:10 Paul directs us as Christians to be devoted to one another, to honor each other above ourselves. He's talking about a deliberate decision to treat fellow believers preferentially, a choice to mutually submit to one another on the basis of our love and gratitude for the free gift of salvation we share.

Prayer Prompt: How is the principle of mutual submission playing out in your Christian life?

$\mathcal{G}$*odly woman,*
SUBMIT TO OTHER BELIEVERS IN LOVE.

$\mathcal{F}$alling backward into grace

Verse: "He tends his flock like a shepherd: He gathers the lambs in his arms and carries them close to his heart; he gently leads those that have young" (Isaiah 40:11)

"When prayer is at its highest . . . we lean back in His everlasting arms and feel the serenity of perfect security in Him"
(WILLIAM BARCLAY).

Reflection: That afternoon of March 3, 2007—the last of my thirty-one-year employment—remains seared in my memory. A "regular" work day was interrupted by a call to the human resources department—a call that shattered my world by the abruptness of the change, and by its lack of closure. I still dream on variations of the theme, some terrifying and others restorative.

My tenure at a Christian publishing house had been fulfilling. To my frustration, though, much of the last decade had been a challenge in light of physical limitations due to chronic fatigue syndrome and fibromyalgia. Periodic hour-long naps behind the locked door of the sick room, along with difficulty concentrating and thinking proactively, caused me to question my effectiveness and the legitimacy of my position. And traumatic family situations were gobbling up my dwindling energy reserves.

I look back now and wonder how I ever managed to hold a job and still keep all the other "balls in the air." I do remember that it was with difficulty. From the time Khristina had returned to work after her maternity leave I had found it necessary to leave work early every day to meet the bus, remove Addie from Khris's carrying harness, and take the baby home for the evening. On too many nights I found myself crawling into bed, exhausted, as early as 6:00.

I had known for too long that I could no longer pull my load and had been haunted by guilt. So much so that I almost found it a relief to have been "found out" and released. That perception was at least mostly false, but it's amazing how mental exhaustion can skew our perception.

That life change was something I would never have initiated—something I would have resisted, "kicking and screaming," had I had any option. But through the redeemed vision of hindsight I can see clearly that my tumble into the unthinkable was in reality a falling backward into grace.

Prayer Prompt: When has the "worst-case" scenario proven to be a blessing in your life?

odly woman,

BASK IN HIS GRACE.

ℱor my good

Verses: "Now listen, you who say, 'Today or tomorrow we will go to this or that city, spend a year there, carry on business and make money.' Why, you do not even know what will happen tomorrow. . . . Instead, you ought to say, 'If it is the Lord's will, we will live and do this or that'" (James 4:13–15).

"Having given us the package, do you think God will deny us the ribbon?" (OSWALD C. HOFFMAN).

Reflection: I'll have to confess that I get hung up on the words "your will be done." This important clause—or at least its spirit—is fundamental to my prayer life. But I too often use it to negate the force of a request I've just made. I throw in the equivalent to a reluctant "nevertheless, your will be done," implying my willingness to settle for a negative response, or no apparent response at all. It's easy for me to view these four little words as an ultimate, divine "catch-22."

It's a little like asking God to act "for my own good" (sounds like a punishment, doesn't it?), as opposed to "for my good." C. S. Lewis voiced this pitfall as follows: "We're not necessarily doubting that God will do the best for us; we are wondering how painful the best will turn out to be."

What I fail to recognize is that God delights in filling my requests, so long as they aren't opposed to the spirit of his will. Yes, he knows what's going to happen (that's his foreknowledge, not his will), but he doesn't orchestrate or ordain every detail. There may be multiple paths I can take at a given time, all within the scope of his purpose for me.

When I pray that God's will be done, I'm acknowledging that even my "best laid" plans are contingent on his larger purposes. That's a good thing to keep in mind before I get too confident. Paul's familiar refrain, which I never tire of quoting, puts it all in perspective: "And we know that in all things God works for the good of those who love him, who have been called according to his purpose" (Romans 8:28).

Prayer Prompt: In what area(s) of life might you be viewing God's will as a potential impediment?

𝒢odly woman,

TRUST HIS GOODNESS.

*K*indness

Verse: "A kindhearted woman gains respect, but ruthless men gain only wealth" (Proverbs 11:16).

"Criticism, like rain, should be gentle enough to nourish a man's growth without destroying his roots" (FRANK A. CLARK).

Reflection: "Be who you are and say what you feel," advises Dr. Seuss, "because those who mind don't matter, and those who matter, don't mind." Although I get a chuckle from his quip, I'll have to say I strongly disagree with this philosophy, prevalent as it is in our world. There are situations, of course, in which withholding the truth constitutes a lie, but this doesn't apply when tact overrides observing aloud what doesn't need to be articulated.

When my extroverted daughter Amanda was three, I took her to a restaurant. Pausing at a booth en route to our own, she solemnly addressed the white-bearded gent seated there: "You look like a *mean* man!" Oops!

Incredibly to me, a friend of my daughter Angie was raised by his parents with two hard-and-fast principles: State the truth (or, I suppose, what you perceive to be the truth), and never apologize (for this or anything else). Another oops, as far as I'm concerned. At the very least, it isn't the Christian way.

Like so many proverbs, the pithy nugget in the verse above contrasts apparent opposites. Focusing as a Christian woman on the first clause, what better gift can I offer than kindness—and what better return can I desire than respect?

There are times when kindness calls for confronting a hard truth. But this principle more often dictates overlooking a fault.

Prayer Prompt: Are there difficult realities you need to address with a loved one? Imperfections you need to accept with tact and grace?

odly woman,
CHOOSE KINDNESS.

$\mathcal{A}$voiding the shadows

Verse: "Every good and perfect gift is from above, coming down from the Father of the heavenly lights, who does not change like shifting shadows" (James 1:17).

"When we are unhurried and wise, we perceive that only great and worthy things have any permanent and absolute existence, that petty fears and petty pleasures are but the shadow of the reality"
(HENRY DAVID THOREAU).

Reflection: A Maori proverb reads like this: "Turn your face to the sun and the shadows fall behind you." If our sights are set on the stationary God, we won't notice life's shifting shadows—because they'll play out their delusional antics behind our backs. Those gray shadow lands are the stuff of Satan, and he'd love nothing better than to draw our attention to them.

If you'll bear with me in a slightly changed metaphor, one of my favorite scenes in winter is the brilliance of an orange sky accentuating the skeletal outlines of barren trees. It is, of course, unrealistic and undesirable for us as Christians to be so God-focused that we miss, or dismiss, the world around us. But God puts that in perspective too, relegating it to a foreground of one-dimensional blackness, behind which God's presence and glory shine all the more strikingly. There remains an incredible beauty in the starkness of those asymmetrical silhouettes, a loveliness I can appreciate in perspective when my gaze is trained beyond them.

The day is coming when God will redeem shadows and silhouettes, rendering them a part of the glory of a renewed and integrated Eden—a gift that will indeed be good and perfect.

Prayer Prompt: Do you find yourself distracted from God by the stuff of life?

$\mathcal{G}$odly woman,
SET YOUR SIGHTS ON HIM.

$\mathcal{A}$ good start

Verse: "Start children off on the way they should go, and even when they are old they will not turn from it" (Proverbs 22:6).

> *"When I was this many" (holding up three fingers), "I was*
> *scared of the carwash. When I was a kid I was scared"*
> (ADELYN HUISJEN, AGE FOUR).

Reflection: How quickly kids today grow up! And a lot of this, for good or ill, is our own doing. I heard the observation years ago that eleven is the ideal childhood age. Old enough, I suppose, for some independent thinking and action, while young enough to dream big. I remember clearly that eleven was the age at which I made the hard decision to pass on asking for a baby doll for Christmas. Relinquishing dolls isn't, of course, a rite of passage for every maturing girl. But it amazes me today when I hear of girls "outgrowing" this phase at three or four.

This past Christmas Khristina and I discussed the pros and cons of a computer-related gift for Addie. Although Khris preferred a more traditional Christmas—and I generally view anything electronic as too impersonal to enjoy giving—I surprised myself by being the one to express the concern that my granddaughter might get "behind" her classmates.

I can't help but wonder whether parents today are emphasizing competence at the expense of character. We all agree that those early, "formative" years are critical, but critical for what? If character formation comes first, which I believe it must, competency can follow—even if it comes a little more slowly . . . as it did way back when I was a kid.

Prayer Prompt: What are you doing to encourage character development in the kids in your life?

odly woman,
CHARACTER COUNTS.

God's records

Verse: "Record my misery; list my tears on your scroll—are they not in your record?" (Psalm 56:8).

"God invented forgiving as a remedy for a past that not even he could change and not even he could forget. His way of forgiving is a model for our forgiving" (LEWIS B. SMEDES).

Reflection: The Bible tells us in various contexts that God keeps records. David's question, above, is rhetorical—the answer implied and unquestioned. The psalmist refers elsewhere to the impossibility of counting God's thoughts on his behalf (Psalm 139:17–18). And Jesus reminded his disciples that "Even the very hairs of your head are all numbered" (Matthew 10:30).

We know from Revelation 3:5 that God maintains a log referred to there as the book of life. What exactly does it take to make this list of overcomers? Not sinless perfection: "If you, LORD, kept a record of sins, LORD, who could stand?" (Psalm 130:3). Last Friday I enjoyed the opportunity of visiting a veterinarian's office with Adelyn's preschool class. The doctor showed a series of novel animal x-rays, including one of a snake in the process of digesting a mouse. When questioned how she got the x-ray, she explained that she had filmed it through the cloth bag holding the snake. Her intention was to keep the animal as immobile as possible, but my thoughts naturally turned to the relief of keeping that "evil" in check. Job confirmed the psalmist's assurance in Psalm 130, above, that our sins won't appear on some divine tic sheet: "Surely . . . you will count my steps but not keep track of my sin. My offenses will be sealed up in a bag" (Job 14:16–17). *Whew!*

We as new covenant believers have a much greater assurance than either David or Job that God *doesn't* keep track of our sins. Why? Because they're gone. Expunged. Our slates have been washed clean by the blood of the Lamb.

Prayer Prompt: What comfort do you glean from the records God does—and doesn't—maintain?

Godly woman,

TO USE AN ANALOGY BEFORE IT ENTIRELY LOSES CURRENCY,

YOU'RE IN THE BOOK.

*C*rocus

Verses: "The desert and the parched land will be glad; the wilderness will rejoice and blossom. Like the crocus, it will burst into bloom" (Isaiah 35:1–2).

"Paradise is exactly like where you are right now . . . only much, much better" (LAURIE ANDERSON).

Reflection: Here in Michigan the crocus is an early harbinger of spring. This hardy, often sun-hued flower can sustain some weather reversals, but unseasonal balmy weather can coax out its blossoms prematurely. As any Midwesterner can attest, springtime in this part of the world comes in fits and starts—including some false starts.

Charles Dickens describes this in-between time with precision: "It was one of those March days when the sun shines hot and the wind blows cold: when it is summer in the light, and winter in the shade." Or, in the words of poet Lilja Rogers,

"First a howling blizzard woke us,
Then the rain came down to soak us,
And now before the eye can focus—
Crocus."

Isaiah in the verses above was describing a day in which there will be no unsung natural casualties. I appreciate Nathaniel Hawthorne's take on this issue: "Our Creator would never have made such lovely days, and have given us the deep hearts to enjoy them, . . . unless we were meant to be immortal."

Prayer Prompt: Train your thoughts beyond the fragility of nature to the new earth to come.

odly woman,
HE CREATED YOU IMMORTAL.

No "—ish" to it!

Verse: "All wrongdoing is sin" (1 John 5:17).

"When you rationalize, you do just that. You make rational lies"
(AUTHOR UNKNOWN).

Reflection: Adelyn and I had a brief conversation this morning on the difference between "pink" and "pinkish" (her question). Distinctions like this are fun and harmless—as long as we steer clear of adjectives (or coined adjectives) like "wrong" and "wrongish."

I grew up learning that there's no such thing as a "little white lie." But are there other "little white" wrongs? How easy it is for us, from childhood on, to rationalize "minor" infringements of God's law. Jesus addressed this issue with regard to two other specific sins by equating lust with adultery and hatred with murder (Matthew 5:21-22, 27-28)—connections that come much closer to being ouches for any of us!

The context of the verse from 1 John, above, is difficult, well beyond the scope of this meditation. But these four short words do legitimately stand on their own. Wrong is wrong. Sin is sin. "It ain't no sin if you crack a few laws now and then," quipped Mae West, "just so long as you don't break any." *Beep! Wrong!*

For a helpful exercise, consider each of the remaining seven commandments, looking for any "little white" loopholes that come to your mind. You might be surprised at how often the concept of "wrongish" colors our perceptions. There are no "whitish" infractions, either. If we keep our minds on the spirit and summary of God's law, as expressed by Jesus in Matthew 22:37-39, we won't go far afield.

Prayer Prompt: Consider your standards on obedience to God's law. How closely do they match its demands—in letter and in spirit?

Godly woman,
MAKE NO MISTAKE: SIN IS SIN.

$\mathcal{H}$umiliated

Verses: "David said to Michal . . . 'I will celebrate before the LORD. I will become even more undignified than this, and I will be humiliated in my own eyes'" (2 Samuel 6:21–22).

"We're not very accepting of people who act strangely"
(CHESTER BROWN).

Reflection: The ark of the covenant or testimony, captured earlier by the Philistines, had been retrieved by Israel. David was on a joyous mission: to return this sacred object to the Jerusalem tabernacle. He didn't travel incognito. It seems that "all the king's men"—thirty thousand, to be exact—accompanied him for this less than stealthy operation.

David was outrageously happy, and his particular brand of enthusiasm was raucous and untamed. David wore a linen ephod, a close-fitting, sleeveless pullover of hip length, maximizing freedom of movement as he leaped and danced and bellowed his way forward.

Enter Michal. Well, not exactly *enter*. David's wife chose to observe the spectacle from behind the shadow of a palace window. How did she react to her husband's unrestrained display? Verse 16 minces no words: Michal "despised him in her heart."

With regard to the actions and indiscretions of others, we have a choice: We can assume the Michal role, or we can expect the best in people. When we relax, expecting others to like and accept us (and our loved ones or companions) exactly as we are, we'll more than likely discover that this is exactly what happens.

Prayer Prompt: Ever feel humiliated by the actions of someone close to you, perhaps especially in a worship setting? Ask yourself how God responds to their exuberant style.

odly woman,
ACCEPT OTHERS AS HE DOES.

*W*ho would you disown?

Verse: "Whatever you did not do for one of the least of these, you did not do for me" (Matthew 25:45).

"The rate at which a person can mature is directly proportional to the embarrassment he can tolerate" (DOUGLAS ENGELBART).

Reflection: Going a little further with yesterday's meditation, a number of my young adult memories center around the emotions of embarrassment and self-consciousness. Many of these situations, like that involving David and Michal, involved perceived loss of face over the actions of someone else. One incident stands out. Since no one else involved is living, I feel free to share it.

My aunt decided it would be good for twenty-something me and my schizophrenic younger cousin to do lunch and spend time together at the mall. We began the afternoon at IHOP. During the meal Mary discovered at intervals a need for ketchup and water, each of which set her to calling out loudly and repeatedly from our corner booth.

From there we proceeded across the parking lot to the mall, where she sat hunched over near a fountain in the center aisle, inhaling a dozen doughnuts while I stood well off to the side, mortified. Draped in my fragile self-image, I couldn't bring myself to recall or model God's unconditional love for Mary, his created-in-the-image daughter!

Prayer Prompt: Who do you know whom you'd just as soon disown in public? What about God's words in Matthew 25:41: "Depart from me . . ." (implication: "I never knew you")?

*G**odly woman**,*

TOLERATE OTHERS' IDIOSYNCRASIES. GOD DOES.

𝓛oss and gain

Verses: "Whatever were gains to me I now consider loss for the sake of Christ. What is more, I consider everything a loss because of the surpassing worth of knowing Christ Jesus my Lord, for whose sake I have lost all things" (Philippians 3:7–8).

> *"People lose people, we lose things in our life as we're constantly growing and changing. That's what life is is change, and a lot of that is loss. It's what you gain from that loss that makes life"*
> (THOMAS JANE).

Reflection: As a language-loving kid, I valued "big" words. It took a long time to convince myself that little words stand proudly on their own. Take *loss*, as an example (you may prefer not to). None of us fails to "get it"; fact is, we know precisely when we've lost it and what "it" is.

The antonyms vary: We can lose or find, lose or win, lose or gain, lose or profit. And the synonyms for *loss* are many: defeat, misplacement, bereavement—even declining to grasp some opportunity.

My life has in many ways been full of loss. In its adult phase, much of that loss has been, if not self-inflicted or invited, at least not particularly well warded off. The "problem" hasn't been carelessness or inattention as much as a deliberate lack of risk avoidance.

Nor do I regret the risks I've chosen, particularly in the area of special needs adoption. No risk, no gain. Speaking of which, gain has also become a significant reality for me, in many cases because I've chosen for it to be so. I look for gain and seldom have to look too hard.

Ideally, it's like that in our Christian lives too. Loss and gain have everything to do with two life-changing "p" words: *priorities* and *perspective*.

Prayer Prompt: What significant losses and gains have you experienced? Consider this question again, specifically with relation to your life in Christ.

odly woman,
GUARD WELL YOUR PRIORITIES AND PERSPECTIVE.

$\mathcal{E}$arly loss

Verse: "Precious in the sight of the Lord is the death of his faithful servants" (Psalm 116:15).

"Some babies do die" (ADELYN HUISJEN, AGE FOUR).

Reflection: Kids understand the finality of death from a surprisingly early age. And their grief can be as deep as that of any adult. Little ones may (or so we're told) be incapable of abstract thought, but they do mull things over and come to whatever conclusions they require to make sense of a confusing world.

Several years ago my then four-year-old grandson Tavis stood by my side on a Sunday morning helping me greet congregational members as they filed in to church. A young couple came in with a stroller, in which lay a premature infant. The baby's eyelids appeared stretched, and he lay absolutely still. That night at bedtime Tavis found the courage to ask the burning question: "Grandma, was that baby dead?"

It used to bother me that fairy tales (and Bible stories, not that we're talking apples to apples) make no apology for tragedy. The truth is that kids need to experience loss, whether in their own lives or vicariously, through the lives of others. They need it to develop into compassionate adults. They need it to learn about bouncing back; at this naturally resilient age, the lesson may come more easily. They need the experience of loss to learn about grace—and about heaven.

Prayer Prompt: How have your own earliest experiences of loss affected your life?

$\mathcal{G}$odly woman,
GUIDE LITTLE ONES THROUGH LOSS.

*H*eart condition

Verse: "I will remove from you your heart of stone and give you a heart of flesh" (Ezekiel 36:26).

> *"Everyone recognizes that Stephen was Spirit-filled when he was performing wonders. Yet, he was just as Spirit-filled when he was being stoned to death"* (LEONARD RAVENHILL).

Reflection: Friedrich Nietzsche described the kingdom of heaven as "a condition of the heart—not something that comes 'upon the earth' or 'after death.'" Not only is God's kingdom immaterial, borderless, and timeless, but it permeates human life and history in the same way that yeast pervades, works upon, and expands a lump of dough.

That slab of dough starts out as inert, cold, and insensible as a stone. But God's kingdom swells, inflates, and spreads out precisely through once-petrified hearts that have been activated by the Spirit. Its leaven swells to other hearts, bringing about a chain reaction of life and sensitivity where once was death.

I'm reminded of the vision of the valley of dead bones in the chapter of Ezekiel to follow the above quote. I shiver when the bones come together with their rattling sound. The prophet recalls in Ezekiel 37:8, "I looked, and tendons and flesh appeared on them and skin covered them, but there was no breath in them"—an illusion of life, with apparently animate but non-animated bodies.

But God moves on in his vision to the prophet: "Then you, my people, will know that I am the LORD, when I open your graves and bring you up from them. I will put my Spirit in you and you will live" (Ezekiel 37:13–14).

Prayer Prompt: Thank God for the role of the Spirit in the steady advance of the kingdom.

odly woman,

BE OPEN TO THE SPIRIT'S MOVEMENT IN AND THROUGH YOU.

$\mathcal{R}$ainbow citings

Verses: "Whenever I bring clouds over the earth and the rainbow appears in the clouds, I will remember my covenant between me and you" (Genesis 9:14–15).

"The soul would have no rainbow had the eyes no tears"
(JOHN VANCE).

Reflection: That day I "lost" my job of thirty-one years (see my meditation of March 3), Khristina, needing to run some errands, had driven me to work, planning to pick me up afterward. As it was deemed necessary early in the afternoon, after my visit to human resources, for me to leave the building immediately, under escort (company policy for all displacements), the human resources director drove me home.

Moments before I stepped from her car into an icy downpour, I realized not only that my daughter wasn't home but that my house key was out with her. Neither of us owning a cell phone, I found myself huddled on my back steps, hiding from the imagined stares of neighbors and adding my tears to the drilling rain.

Twenty minutes passed before the misery of numb fingers and the thorough drenching convinced me that another approach to this bizarre situation was in order. My next-door neighbor—a single mom like myself—was at work. But her son, an unemployed construction worker who had just moved back home, and her teenage daughter, home sick from school, welcomed my unannounced visit with no apparent surprise. The next two hours, spent getting to know them in their warm living room, were unaccountably pleasant. As the three of us laughed and shared, it occurred to me with a stab of surprise that life wasn't about to end.

No, there was no physical rainbow on that wet and chilly March afternoon. Nor do the two verses above, articulating God's ancient covenant with Noah, fit the context of my circumstances in any direct way. But see a rainbow I did, not only that afternoon but the following day and in the months and years to follow.

Prayer Prompt: Think back to that time when you were so devastated you were certain life as you knew it just had to end. How long did it take to spot the rainbow?

$\mathcal{G}$*odly woman,*
TRUST HIS HEART.

The interminable instant

Verse: "Is this the city that was called the perfection of beauty, the joy of the whole earth?" (Lamentations 2:15).

"If I find in myself a desire which no experience in this world
can satisfy, the most probable explanation is that I was made for
another world" (C. S. LEWIS).

Reflection: When I was about thirteen I devoted serious attention to coming up with the perfect sentence for the beginning of a great novel. (Years later, I encountered the same behavior in an adult character in Albert Camus's classic novel *The Plague. Are there more of us?* I wondered.)

This continuously evolving sentence was a still frame. I never planned a plot. Movement of any kind would have been a letdown.

It had some great words, that sentence—*vivacious, animated, rapt* (I think *azure* was in there too). I was just starting to get into words, and I was describing the perfect girl, lying motionless on a hillside, gazing, enraptured, at wildflowers. (Which is funny because I don't personally have a lot of patience with flowers.)

What I was trying to grasp, I recognize now, was that "perfection of beauty" spoken of in Lamentations 2:15. I wanted that beauty to last for an interminable instant (notice from the past tense "was called" in the verse above that Jerusalem's beauty wasn't lasting either).

Isn't that precisely what our innate longing for eternity is all about?

Prayer Prompt: In what ways does your desire for eternal perfection manifest itself?

odly woman,

LONG FOR THE PERFECTION TO COME.

$\mathscr{C}$onscience impairment

Verse: "When you sin against [people] . . . and wound their weak conscience, you sin against Christ" (1 Corinthians 8:12).

"Conscience is what hurts when everything else feels so good"
(AUTHOR UNKNOWN).

Reflection: I recently ran across a journal entry detailing a conversation I'd had a few years into my middle daughter's adoption with a Christian pediatrician and fellow adoptive parent. Angie's behavior had been especially problematic prior to our visit. As he and I had discussed, there were likely multiple contributing factors, including ADHD, past abuse, adoptive issues, and problems with conscience development. It's difficult, he noted, to find much literature on this last subject, as conscience is basically a Christian concept.

Angie, we agreed, was an enigma in this area, contrasting moral fragility with a childlike faith. I had recently disciplined her for skipping a day of school, sending her to bed early that evening. She'd complained about this measure, which I had insisted was necessary, either as a "memory enhancer" or as a "conscience enhancer." Which of the two, I asked her, applied? Her response was immediate: She knew right from wrong, and she also remembered. She had a conscience, but it was hard for her to follow it.

This tied in exactly with what the doctor had suspected. Angie's problem with impulse control was making it hard for her to take the right path when immediate gratification could otherwise be obtained. Because consequential thinking came hard for her, she needed a Jiminy Cricket on her shoulder.

If the lack of a healthy conscience can be genetically linked, I asked—or even if it's the tragic result of circumstances beyond a person's control—won't God make allowances? Revisiting this question now, I come back to a reluctant answer of no, but I also realize that morality is one of the most complex issues with which any thinking person must grapple. What a comfort to approach this question as a Christian, trusting God's fairness and knowing that his "logic" is on a plane infinitely higher than mine.

Prayer Prompt: Consider thanking God for your healthy, functional conscience.

$\mathscr{G}$*odly woman,*
TRUST HIS FAIRNESS.

$\mathcal{C}$ustomer compassion

Verse: "This is what the LORD Almighty said: 'Administer true justice; show mercy and compassion to one another'" (Zechariah 7:9).

"The first responsibility of a leader is to define reality. The last is to say thank you. In between, the leader is a servant" (MAX DEPREE).

Reflection: Every once in a while an unexpected television moment strikes the fancy of my daughter Khristina and me. A few years ago we caught a commercial for a local auto transmission service. Sprinkled among the typical adjectives was a surprise: This company touted itself as "compassionate"—an association with auto repair that struck us both as ludicrous.

But in the final analysis, why not? Why limit our sincere emotion to life's private moments? Or our caring for its more poignant and memorable encounters? What does it mean to be truly human—and more especially Christian—all the time?

What is your line of work? Does it by its nature "force" you to draw the line in terms of the depth or quality of your dealings with people? You may not have the ability to bend rules, but what would it take for you to transmit concern for an individual in financial or other dis-ease?

This past weekend I spotted a rusted car being towed from a McDonald's parking lot. In the front seat of the wrecker the driver and the stranded motorist appeared to be sharing a joke. I couldn't help but notice the lettering on the door of the wrecker: Brother Love's Towing Service.

Prayer Prompt: If your work puts you in touch with the public, in what ways do you reflect God's love?

odly woman,

CARING IS ALWAYS APPROPRIATE.

*L*onging for what?

Verses: "Like a slave longing for the evening shadows, or a hired laborer waiting eagerly to be paid, so I have been allotted months of futility, and nights of misery have been assigned to me" (Job 7:2–3).

> *"It's spring fever. . . . And when you've got it, you want—oh, you don't quite know what it is you do want, but it just fairly makes your heart ache, you want it so!"* (MARK TWAIN).

Reflection: "Granna, how big is the temp'ature?"
                   "It's about 38."
                   "Wow! That's a lot of degrees."

Well, it is and it isn't. If one month of the year tends to try my patience, it's often March. To be honest, I don't expect anything but inclement weather in January and February (I've always thought there should be such a thing as "clement" weather). But the very hope of warmth tickles my fancy enough to make the continuing cold seem exasperating and interminable. I just this evening bristled when the weather man predicted temperatures in the thirties for the entire eight-day forecast. It's technically spring, or just about. And at this time of year I want to get technical.

Do you know that feeling of being all revved up with no reason to burn rubber? Of experiencing an adrenaline rush for no apparent reason right when bedtime looms, followed by the promise of another mundane day of same old same old? What do you do with that kind of unchanneled internal energy? Do you lie awake, at first counting the hours till morning and finally (when you remember you have nothing in the near future to be excited about) counting the hours of missed sleep? As Mark Twain puts it, you want something so badly your heart aches . . . ; you just can't pinpoint what it is.

That kind of frustration characterizes the human psyche—because God engineered us that way. We pine for fulfillment, closure, for "it" to be buttoned up and beautiful—whatever "it" is. Whether it's the eight-day forecast or a season of life that's dragging for you, know that he has better things in store.

Prayer Prompt: For what do you yearn, both in the shorter term and in the long?

*G*odly *woman,*
HE KNOWS YOUR LONGINGS, AND HE CARES.

The wonder season

Verses: "See! The winter is past; the rains are over and gone. Flowers appear on the earth; the season for singing has come" (Song of Songs 2:11–12).

"Springtime is the land awakening. The
March winds are the morning yawn"
(QUOTED BY LEWIS GRIZZARD IN *KATHY SUE LOUDERMILK, I LOVE YOU*).

Reflection: "Spring," reflects Virgil A. Kraft, "shows what God can do with a drab and dirty world." If you haven't seen evidence of this by now, on this first official day of the season, you're in for a particularly concentrated display of beauty this year. In the words of Ellis Peters, "Every spring is the only spring—a perpetual astonishment."

Spring is the only one of the four seasons I long for with a barely contained impatience. While the coming of each of the other three seasons punctuates the year in its own way, calling to mind upcoming annual benchmarks and prompting changes in lifestyle, clothing, maintenance, and activities, only springtime, "the season for singing," draws out my breath in a "We finally made it!" exhalation of relief.

Whether your spring song this year is in acknowledgment of God's faithfulness or in anticipation of his annual promise keeping, prepare to thank him for this season of wonder.

Prayer Prompt: Does the discipline of having to wait for springtime accentuate its thrill for you?

Godly woman,
IT'S TIME TO SING!

Your children's peace

Verse: "All your children will be taught by the LORD, and great will be their peace" (Isaiah 54:13).

> *"A child needs both to be hugged and unhugged. The hug lets her know she is valuable. The unhug lets her know that she is viable"*
> (POLLY BERRIEN BERENDS).

Reflection: Those of us growing up in the era of siblings sharing double beds learned valuable lessons in tolerance. *Or not.* I, for one, was ruthless with my slightly older sister, Debbie, who had a tendency in sleep to encroach on my side of the invisible mid-mattress line. Prior to sleep, though, we were compatible bed partners.

Dad had constructed a shelving unit that hung above our headboard. The back side of its curlicue frame served as a repository for wads of ABC (already-been-chewed) gum. On a typical night, Debbie and I would settle into bed, propped against our pillows, select promising wads, and chew and giggle contentedly for a while. There was no taste whatsoever in those rubbery relics, but the very act of chewing seemed a luxury. Our parents tolerated the none-too-smothered outbursts for a predictable amount of time, but my most precious recollection of a nighttime ritual focuses on that period between beginning to settle down and the coming of sleep.

Our room also included a blackboard, hung on the wall beyond the foot end of our bed. Mom and Dad would come into our room together to pray with us, after which Dad would write something special on the board—a message (sometimes funny, sometimes spiritual, sometimes sentimental) to set the tone for the night and catch our eyes again in the morning. Just one of many ways in which he and Mom shared their faith—and their peace—on a regular basis.

Dad also utilized the blackboard, as well as the edge of our bed, for a much-loved talk after a punishment. If he took seriously Ephesians 6:1–3, he was fully as conscious of verse 4: "Fathers, do not exasperate your children; instead, bring them up in the training and instruction of the Lord." I was raised by Christian parents with love, responsibility, and trust—a combination for which I'll be forever thankful.

Prayer Prompt: Have you done all within your power to share your faith and your testimony—your peace—with your family?

Godly woman,

PASS THE PEACE.

*D*ependable emotions

Verse: "May the God of hope fill you with all joy and peace as you trust in him" (Romans 15:13).

> *"Joy is the flag you fly when the Prince of Peace is in residence within your heart"* (WILFRED PETERSON).

Reflection: We Christians live with emotional realities that are anything but fleeting, unreliable, or opportunistic. In fact, they override, underlie, and coexist with all our other feelings, and we can depend on them to be there all the time.

The first is joy. Unlike happiness, joy isn't situational, seasonal, or evidence of a sunny disposition. It springs from a faithful, impenetrable geyser. We know its source intimately, and we can do nothing to clog the line or dam the flow.

Joy is present in the life of a committed Christian in and through—though not necessarily because of—any circumstances. Might we legitimately state that true joy is a state of mind and heart known *only* to the believer?

Closely aligned with joy in the Christian life is contentment (akin to "peace" in the above verse)—a well-kept secret in our acquisitive, grasping society. Like joy, contentment is deep and constant, unfazed by situational ups and downs. If our Christian joy is an ever-springing geyser, our contentment is the bottomless well from which it draws.

Prayer Prompt: Gauge your joy/contentment quotient on a one-to-ten scale. If either is lacking, explore what you can do, with God's help, to raise the level.

odly woman,

REVEL IN JOY AND BASK IN CONTENTMENT.

$\mathcal{T}$he summary

Verses: "Love the Lord your God with all your heart and with all your soul and with all your mind and with all your strength.' The second [commandment] is this: 'Love your neighbor as yourself.' There is no commandment greater than these" (Mark 12:30–31).

"We come to love not by finding a perfect person, but by learning to see an imperfect person perfectly" (ANONYMOUS).

Reflection: I failed to understand for many years that we as new covenant (New Testament) believers are no longer bound to the letter of the Ten Commandments. Far from easing ourselves off the hook, though, we find ourselves pointed instead toward Jesus' incisive summary.

Loving God above all and our neighbors as we love ourselves: The "rules" may be more succinct, but they're far more demanding. Why? Because they call on us to do what God asks, as encapsulated in the Ten Commandments, not from artificial constraint but from pure, internalized motivations.

"Freed" from the specifics of the Old Testament commandments, we find ourselves pleased to keep God's commands anyway, on the basis of overflowing love and gratitude. It goes without saying that we're far from perfect. But as true believers, each situated at some unique point along the sanctification spectrum, we must assume that at the very least we're inching forward.

Prayer Prompt: Assess your motivation for obedience to God's law. Is that law written on your heart?

$\mathcal{G}$odly woman,
PREFER HIS LAW.

Who died?

Verse: "We preach Christ crucified: a stumbling block to Jews and foolishness to Gentiles, but to those whom God has called, both Jews and Greeks, Christ the power of God and the wisdom of God" (1 Corinthians 1:23).

> *"If the resurrection did not take place, then Christianity is a false religion. If it did take place, then Christ is God and the Christian faith is absolute truth"* (HENRY MORRIS).

Reflection: "Look, Granna. I made a cross. God died on a cross."
"Jesus did die on a cross for us. And then what happened?"
"Then he went alive again."

He did indeed! Hallelujah! Jesus didn't die as God, but had he not had a divine nature, and had he not been raised in his human nature, his death would have been nothing more than a tragic miscarriage of justice. The issue couldn't be more important; it stands as the crux of human history. In the words of Paul, "If Christ has not been raised, your faith is futile; you are still in your sins. Then those also who have fallen asleep in Christ are lost. If only for this life we have hope in Christ, we are of all people most to be pitied" (1 Corinthians 15:17–19).

"God is dead!" insists a group of pessimistic skeptics. "God *isn't* dead," his Easter people can and must proclaim. What did die on the cross with the human Jesus, though, is our sin nature. Once again in the words of Paul, "Now if we died with Christ, we believe that we will also live with him. For we know that since Christ was raised from the dead, he cannot die again; death no longer has mastery over him. The death he died, he died to sin once for all; but the life he lives, he lives to God" (Romans 6:8–10).

No, God didn't die on the cross. Jesus, the God-Man, died in our stead in his human nature, taking upon himself as the only sinless human being the punishment for all of us. The Father allowed the Son to vicariously atone for the sins of all of his brothers and sisters. And the Son consented. But he "went alive again." Hallelujah!

Prayer Prompt: Thank God for the implications of Jesus' death and resurrection, for you and for all who will believe. Then ask for the courage to proclaim the truth.

odly woman,

SPREAD THE NEWS.

$\mathcal{D}$arkness before dawn

Verses: "You must no longer live as the Gentiles do, in the futility of their thinking. They are darkened in their understanding and separated from the life of God" (Ephesians 4:17–18).

"Lives in eternity's sun rise" (WILLIAM BLAKE).

Reflection: "The cradle rocks above an abyss, and common sense tells us that our existence is but a brief crack of light between two eternities of darkness." This tragic quote from Vladimir Nabokov, a twentieth-century Russian-American novelist, reveals that secular thinkers may share Paul's perspective in the verses above—at least on the issue of futile thinking.

But when it comes to spiritual realities, common sense doesn't rule the day. If pressed for our own light/darkness analogy, we as Christian women would more likely picture this earthly life as the darkness before the light. Dark-light-dark versus dark-light: Given the eternal implications, which one will most people prefer? If, that is, they can get beyond their darkened understanding.

Rabindranath Tagore, the Bengali poet, artist, musician, and playwright whose career spanned the nineteenth and twentieth centuries, spent his lifetime exploring the indwelling presence of God—sadly, from a spiritual-ist, not a Christian, perspective. The quote to follow still sounds "right on" to our ears: "Death is not extinguishing the light; it is only putting out the lamp because the dawn has come."

How blessed we are to be able to flesh out Tagore's statement based on the truth of salvation. The world around us longs for the beam of light we alone, as representatives of Christ, are able to shed.

Prayer Prompt: What non-Christian friend or acquaintance might welcome your insight into the things of God?

$\mathcal{G}$odly woman,
LEAD OTHERS TO THE LIGHT.

$\mathcal{T}$he wild card

Verses "When the LORD restored the fortunes of Zion . . . [o]ur mouths were filled with laughter, our tongues with songs of joy" (Psalm 126:1–2).

"I have never understood why it should be considered derogatory to the Creator to suppose that he has a sense of humour" (WILLIAM RALPH INGE).

Reflection: During my junior year at a Christian college decades ago I found myself intimidated by my assertive suitemates. Sometime during the course of that year I realized I had changed my sleeping position. I would invariably awaken with my hand held over my mouth. At that most vulnerable time of the day, when I couldn't consciously rein in the true me lurking beneath the façade, I was holding it in physically.

Most of us do our best to maximize our public persona. But the wild card within us, the one we try so carefully to obscure somewhere within the deck God has handed us, is too often the aspect of our selves we'd just as soon deny—our emotions.

Basic to your theology is undoubtedly the knowledge that you're a unique creation, formed in God's own image. Sin, of course, is the variable separating you from Jesus as he lived out his life on Earth. Have you ever wondered what his days were like? Was he bland? Passive? Imperturbable and impenetrable? Hardly! We're talking about the man of endless compassion, who wept at the grave of his friend, vented his wrath in the temple courtyard and agonized with his Father in Gethsemane. Nor is the Father depicted in Scripture as impassive. We're told that God personifies love, that he was grieved, that he changed his mind, and that he was angry enough to cut off his people. And the Holy Spirit groans as he intercedes for us with the Father.

God knows all about your emotions—and delights in them. In fact, he deliberately (even with a chuckle?) created the right-brained side of each of us. It's exactly as he wanted it—a mirror image of himself! And he wants you, like himself, to feel, to express . . . and at times to vent.

Prayer Prompt: Consider the emotional expression that bothers you most about yourself. Ask God to help you accept and work with this manifestation of you.

odly woman,

HE DOESN'T WANT YOU TO QUASH YOUR EMOTIONS.

*P*riceless, pricey love

Verse: "How priceless is your unfailing love!" (Psalm 36:7).

"Grace and gratitude belong together like heaven and earth.
Gratitude evokes grace like the voice and echo. Gratitude follows
grace as thunder follows lightning" (KARL BARTH).

Reflection: God's love is priceless, but it comes to us free of charge. We have only to receive and accept it. Sure, we offer him our lives, but the transaction isn't based on some divine barter system. We do so purely on the basis of love and gratitude.

And we have everything to gain. God offers his love freely, but its distribution to humankind was anything but free. From the divine side, that priceless love was inconceivably pricey.

The Bible is full of the principles of good stewardship, but it also gives startling evidence that God isn't opposed to extravagance in worship: "A woman came with an alabaster jar of very expensive perfume, made of pure nard. She broke the jar and poured the perfume on [Jesus'] head. Some of those present were saying indignantly to one another, 'Why this waste of perfume? It could have been sold for more than a year's wages and the money given to the poor.' . . . 'Leave her alone,' said Jesus. 'Why are you bothering her? She has done a beautiful thing for me'" (Mark 14:3–6).

There's no such thing as an excess of appreciation.

Prayer Prompt: Above and beyond your service, how do you proclaim your gratitude to God?

*G**odly woman,**
HIS LOVE IS INVALUABLE.

$\mathcal{T}$he household

Verses: "Teach slaves to be subject to their masters in everything, to try to please them, not to talk back to them, and not to steal from them, but to show that they can be fully trusted, so that in every way they will make the teaching about God our Savior attractive" (Titus 2:9–10).

> *"Command that in no way there be in your household any*
> *who make strife, discord or divisions in the hostel, but all*
> *shall be of one accord, of one will as of one heart and one soul*
> (ROBERT GROSSETESTE, THIRTEENTH-CENTURY ENGLISH BISHOP).

Reflection: It's difficult for us as twenty-first-century Christian women to relate to Paul's messages to slaves. While our mindset immediately focuses on the injustices of slavery (and we don't want to downplay the inequalities in Paul's day), we may not recognize the different societal role played by this institution at that time than in recent centuries in the West.

Slavery was intrinsic to the culture in the Roman Empire, and it didn't necessarily connote all of the negatives we attribute to it. Paul made frequent reference to "households," a term that encompassed both family and other residents of the home, most often slaves. His brief letter to Philemon, owner of the runaway slave Onesimus, provides a telling picture of New Testament slavery, alluding to its upsides and downsides.

What catches my attention in Titus 2:10 is Paul's call to *slaves* to make the teaching of God attractive, primarily through their attitudes and behavior. We oversimplify this verse and others like it when we substitute "employees" for "slaves."

No, we can't put ourselves in the sandals of a New Testament slave (assuming they wore them); that cultural gap is just too wide. But we can take note of God's expectation for his children, in whatever circumstances we find ourselves.

Prayer Prompt: What presentation of the gospel do those around you glean from your outlook and conduct?

odly woman,

ATTRACT OTHERS TO THE GOSPEL.

$\mathcal{G}$reat physician

Verse: "Heal me, LORD, and I will be healed; save me and I will be saved, for you are the one I praise" (Jeremiah 17:14).

"Surgeons must be very careful
When they take the knife!
Underneath their fine incisions
Stirs the Culprit—Life!"

—EMILY DICKINSON

Reflection: Several years ago I asked my grandson Tavis, then three, "Who made you?" His response was immediate and assured; he'd evidently thought this one through: "A docker." While this unexpected reply took me aback, I had to concede that, at least in a certain sense, Tavis was right.

Jesus had this to say to the Pharisees, whom he overheard asking his disciples why he deigned to eat with tax collectors and sinners: "It is not the healthy who need a doctor, but the sick" (Matthew 9:12). It goes without saying that the terms *sickness* and *health* encompass the spiritual dimension of our lives fully as much as the physical, emotional, and mental. And what a comfort to know that our Maker (the One who knows our "workings" inside and out) is also our Great Physician.

If you've been privileged to develop over time a relationship with a primary care doctor, or even a specialist, think about the qualities you admire in him or her. Then take a moment to ask yourself in what condition you would be, body and soul, if you hadn't been fashioned by the caring "hands" of an internist!

Prayer Prompt: Of what kind of healing do you stand in need?

$\mathcal{G}$ *odly woman,*
PRAISE YOUR HEALER.

Advice or guidance?

Verse: "Trust in him at all times, O people; pour out your hearts to him" (Psalm 62:8).

"It is certain that before we call upon God He is willing and ready to help us because—where comes the desire to pray? Does it not come from the Holy Spirit? . . . [I]f we are patient and able to continue to pray—that, in and of itself, is a token that God has heard already and has given you the grace to continue to turn to Him" (JOHN CALVIN).

Reflection: My desire for a second daughter formed almost immediately following Amanda's placement. My mother was adventurous enough to debate the issue, which we did endlessly, for several years, any time I could formulate an excuse to broach the subject. The talking, to Mom and others (see my meditation of January 20), to some extent met a need in me, as though this substitute for action might draw the outcome nearer. My arguments, won or lost, were not with people who had a hand in the outcome, but I tracked small victories in drawing support to my side.

When Amanda was eleven I reluctantly canceled my long-term application. My parents, cool to the idea of a second adoption from the beginning, had counseled me to enjoy life, take trips with Amanda, and purchase more things. For six months I tried to follow this course, but I was desolate. I finally mustered the courage to call the agency about the possibility of reinstating myself. To my relief, my application was still on file, and no questions were asked.

That six-month period of "limbo" had changed me drastically. I no longer sought advice concerning this basic direction in my life—nor am I quick to do so today. I felt compelled to seek the course I was on and ready to relax and allow myself to be led. My impatience was as keen as ever, but anticipation now crowded out devastation. I began to plan for an event that was going to happen.

Sometimes God does reveal his will for us through the advice of others. But in other situations his Spirit works directly in our hearts, compelling us forward on a given course.

Prayer Prompt: Are you relying on human advice rather than seeking divine guidance?

odly woman,

ALLOW HIM TO GUIDE YOU IN HIS WAY.

$\mathcal{F}$oolishness

Verse: "Even fools are thought wise if they keep silent, and discerning if they hold their tongues" (Proverbs 17:28).

> *"April 1. This is the day upon which we are reminded of what we are on the other three hundred and sixty-four"* (MARK TWAIN).

Reflection: The Bible contains plenty of fodder for the Fool's Day, doesn't it? The Old Testament, and the book of Proverbs in particular, is full of references to wisdom and foolishness. With regard to the verse above, my dad used to quote a similar adage: "Keep silent and be thought a fool. Open your mouth and remove all doubt."

My association with this verse may not be precisely what the author had in mind, but it is the point at which his words hit me between the eyes. I see myself as a bit of an anomaly on the silence/talking spectrum. Naturally shy in a social setting, I'm tempted, possibly on the basis of nervous anxiety, to monopolize a more formal, small-group discussions. Too often I "use" the time during which others are speaking to formulate my own insights, which I'm then anxious to share.

You might find it instructive to scan a chapter or two of Proverbs for some verses that convict you (on whatever subject and at whatever level). Stop when you reach one that gives you an ouch, even if it's only a little one. There's something in this book for each of us. In what areas are you tempted to "play the fool"?

Prayer Prompt: Ask God for the wisdom to correct that area of imbalance in your life.

$\mathcal{G}$*odly woman,*
UNCOVER AND SEEK TO ELIMINATE THOSE BLIND SPOTS.

$\mathcal{P}$riorities

Verse: "Seek first his kingdom and his righteousness, and all these things will be given to you as well" (Matthew 6:33).

"Of all the things Christ wants for us, loving Him and focusing our attention on Him are the most important" (CHARLES STANLEY).

Reflection: I must have been only two, but a fleeting memory from almost sixty years ago lingers in the recesses of my mind. My dolly was missing an arm, and my parents used this as a basis for taking their three preschoolers on an outing to a doll hospital in Los Angeles, two hours from home. The problem was that I/we somehow forgot the doll! My memory of this long-ago incident may be seriously flawed, but I've retained a twinge of guilt over a lesson learned. A foolish little story, yes. I chuckle when I think about my parents' good intentions juxtaposed against the busyness of getting three little ones dressed and fed and pottied/diapered and stowed in the car. At the very least we had a family outing.

Still, the subject of priorities is one with which we all struggle. Jesus' words on worry that form the context of the verse above assure us that he'll provide shelter and sustenance, and we believe that. But do we really believe he'll bother with the nitty-gritty specifics that preoccupy our overtaxed brains? That if we leave these minor issues with him he'll free us up to concentrate on the truly significant things?

How often aren't the nagging irritants that prevent us from seeking God and his righteousness based on the most niggling concerns? In the words of Robert Service, "Be master of your petty annoyances and conserve your energies for the big, worthwhile things. It isn't the mountain ahead that wears you out—it's the grain of sand in your shoe." I agree, with the exception that we as believing women are to leave those petty annoyances in the hands of our Master, trusting that he'll "give them to us as well." How true for each of us as we make our often lurching and stumbling way through life. Only two big, audacious, worthwhile things deserve our primary attention: Christ's kingdom and his righteousness.

Prayer Prompt: What's preventing you from seeking God with an unclouded mind and heart?

odly woman,

CONSIDER HIS KINGDOM AND RIGHTEOUSNESS, AND LEAVE

THE REST WITH HIM.

$\mathcal{C}$onstancy

Verse: "Jesus Christ is the same yesterday and today and forever" (Hebrews 13:8).

"Every creature is continually becoming. It is changeable, constantly striving, seeks rest and satisfaction, and finds this rest in God, in him alone, for only he is pure being and no becoming. Hence, in Scripture God is often called the Rock"
(HERMAN BAVINCK).

Reflection: We humans long for constancy (beyond, that is, constant change). Nearly all of the skills my mom meticulously taught me as a child are long since obsolete; nor did my formal education, which ended in 1973, come close to adequately preparing me for life in today's world.

Kudos to those much older than myself who have kept up with technology to the point of being comfortable with the Internet; e-mail; online banking and shopping; the complexities of cars, TVs, cell phones, and computers—and the list goes on . . . and on. Change during the life span of an older person living today has outpaced that of all previous centuries and millennia of human history combined.

It's no wonder many employers no longer value seniority: An aging worker who has kept up to the best of her ability can too often be replaced by a young person with the same qualifications, along with energy, innovation, and optimism to spare. I know—I've been there! Life, while often more exciting than in the past, can hardly boast consistency.

Except, that is, for our lives as Christians. Worship styles, evangelistic approaches, emphases, and the like can and need to change; they've changed throughout church history. Even theology is refreshed by new insights, often the result of societal changes that bring to light new issues.

But if we're seeing a change in Jesus, there's something wrong with our organs of sight. He alone embodies that elusive constant for which the world is groping.

Prayer Prompt: How are you doing at sharing the changeless Christ?

$\mathcal{G}$odly woman,
HOLD FAST TO CHRIST.

"*N*obody cares"

Verse: "I say to God my Rock, 'Why have you forgotten me?'" (Psalm 42:9).

"God loves each of us as if there were only one of us" (AUGUSTINE).

Reflection: Have you ever noticed the many wistful and wishful phrases spoken by God's Old Testament people? Two-word expressions like "If only . . . ," "Oh, that . . . ," and "How long . . . ?" recur again and again. We can just about hear the sighs, can't we? From that point it takes only a small step to the classic human lament of "nobody cares": "Look and see, there is no one at my right hand; no one is concerned for me. I have no refuge; no one cares for my life" (Psalm 142:4).

In the New Testament, practical Martha confronted the Savior with a variation on this theme: "Don't you care that my sister has left me to do the work by myself?" (Luke 10:40). And Jesus' disciples cried out as the waves threatened to swamp their little boat, "Don't you care if we drown?" (Mark 4:38).

How tempting it is for us during difficult times to write God off, to view him as aloof, unapproachable, preoccupied. I know I've been there, though thankfully not too often. When I think back to my state of mind at such times, I recall my principal emotion to have been anger.

Anger, of course, isn't wrong in itself; it has its place. But a word to the wise: When we as Christian women allow ourselves to indulge our anger against our Creator/Father, we become . . . well, aloof, unapproachable, and preoccupied. Is it any wonder we don't see him then?

Prayer Prompt: Make it a point to resolve any anger or bitterness that's getting in the way of your relationships with God and others.

odly woman,
HE CARES.

$\mathcal{A}$n Easter people

Verses: "Our citizenship is in heaven. And we eagerly await a Savior from there, the Lord Jesus Christ, who, by the power than enables him to bring everything under his control, will transform our lowly bodies so that they will be like his glorious body" (Philippians 3:20–21).

> *"Grace is but glory begun, and glory is but grace perfected"*
> (JONATHAN EDWARDS).

Reflection: "Good morning, Addie."

"Morning, Granna."

"Guess what? We can say Happy Easter to each other today!"

"Yeah!"

"We could say it to other people too. We could say it to people at church."

"No—I can't" (*dejected*).

"How come?"

"Because I'm shy at people."

"I'm shy too. But being shy doesn't mean you can't talk. It just means you might not want to."

"Oh . . . Yea . . . . Hey, I know what. I could talk in Spanish. *Uno, dos . . .* " (*Adelyn at three knows a handful of Spanish words from TV*).

And so began our Easter morning. Easter isn't primarily about the circle of life or the reawakening of nature, although these realities fit in well with the theme of new life in Christ. What Christ did in conquering sin and death is all about renewal and transformation: of our lowly bodies and of the heavens and Earth too, although we don't yet fully realize these changes.

What physical inhibitions or disabilities—from shyness to migraines to bipolar disorder to diabetes to paralysis—hamper you? For what minor or major transformations do you long with regard to your resurrection body?

Prayer Prompt: Take those areas of perceived personal deficiency to God, asking specifically for a measure even now of his renewal—or of serenity and acceptance.

$\mathcal{G}$odly woman,

WE'RE AN EASTER PEOPLE.

Bunny's reclamation

Verse: "Praise be to the God and Father of our Lord Jesus Christ! In his great mercy he has given us new birth into a living hope through the resurrection of Jesus Christ from the dead" (1 Peter 1:3).

"We are to be re-made. All the rabbit in us is to disappear—and then, surprisingly, we shall find underneath it all a thing we have never imagined: . . . strong, radiant, wise, beautiful, and drenched in joy" (C. S. LEWIS).

Reflection: She began life as a two-and-a-half-foot-tall Kmart Easter bunny, purchased on a whim as a spring spruce-up. But sometime during the course of a difficult year for my daughter Khristina and little Adelyn, she morphed into Addie's "best friend" and inseparable companion. In the meantime she suffered serious deterioration, becoming Addie's personal velveteen rabbit.

Then one day three-year-old Addie forced Bunny's fused metal spine into a sitting position, and the skeleton snapped at the waist. "Is it time to introduce death?" Khris wondered aloud. I thought so, but she fought the notion.

Hammer and screwdriver in hand, my resourceful daughter managed to drill new holes through the metal backbone cylinder, and a much shortened but still viable Bunny emerged. Bunny had experienced a resurrection.

The application to our own resurrection is ridiculously forced, but the analogy did come to my mind, unbidden, on the night of Bunny's reclamation. Perhaps it's the impenetrable gap between the two restorations that so inspires my wonder!

Prayer Prompt: Before going to God, reflect on the meaning of your own coming resurrection of body and soul.

odly woman,
YOU'VE BEEN REDEEMED AND RECLAIMED.

Rejuvenation

Verses: "[God] says to the snow, 'Fall on the earth.' . . . The tempest comes out from its chamber, the cold from the driving winds. The breath of God produces ice, and the broad waters become frozen" (Job 37:6, 9–10).

"Our Lord has written the promise of resurrection, not in books alone, but in every leaf in springtime" (MARTIN LUTHER).

Reflection: A few years ago our pastor used a sermon illustration that has stuck with me: On the morning of the first snow the previous year (which coincided with Thanksgiving), he was leaving church when he spotted a rare flock of snow geese flying south in their "V" formation. Several months later, on the first warm spring day (which happened to be the morning after Easter), he spied another flock en route to points north. Could've been the same geese . . . Who knows?

What we do know is that God controls the times and seasons, coordinating animal migrations with shifting weather patterns. On Thanksgiving we recall his blessings through the prior year's growing season. And what better time than Easter—Resurrection Sunday—to celebrate the unfailing annual rejuvenation of all things living!

Look around and marvel at the reinvigoration of life taking place. What special meaning does the springtime (and more especially Eastertide) have for you as a Christian woman?

Prayer Prompt: Thank God for his Easter blessings, available to you every day throughout this life and beyond.

Godly woman,
HE CONTROLS YOUR TIMES AND SEASONS.

$\mathcal{R}$esponsible *to*

Verse: "I don't know [where Abel is]. . . . Am I my brother's keeper?" (Genesis 4:9).

"The gospel does not make us like Adam in his innocence—it makes us like Christ, in all the perfection of His reflection of God"
(SINCLAIR FERGUSON).

Reflection: What three words roll off the human tongue more easily than "That's not fair!"? From the time we as toddlers begin interacting with our peers to the point when our focus shifts back to the more action- and option-filled days of our past, some variation of this theme too often dominates our thoughts.

If you're not so familiar with the story of the first murder that you can't experience a shiver when you read it, ask yourself which jolts you more: the act itself or Cain's cavalier—perhaps even sarcastic—response, above, when God broaches the subject of Abel's whereabouts.

No, we're not, under ordinary circumstances, our brothers' or sisters' "keepers" in the sense of being responsible *for* them. We're correctly taught from early childhood on that we're responsible for ourselves, that we can't control what anybody else says or does. But aren't we—especially once we've aligned ourselves with Christ—definitely others' "keepers" when it comes to looking out for their well-being (being responsible *to* them)?

Trevor Huddleston expressed this beautifully: "My responsibility is always and everywhere the same: to see in my brother more even than the personality and manhood that are his. My task is always and everywhere the same: to see Christ himself."

Prayer Prompt: How seriously are you taking your responsibility to promote others' welfare?

odly woman,

LOOK FOR CHRIST'S IMAGE IN YOURSELF AND OTHERS.

The mark

Verse: "My punishment is more than I can bear" (Genesis 4:13).

"As the grace grows nearer my theology is growing strangely simple,
and it begins and ends with Christ as the only Savior of the lost"
(HENRY BENJAMIN WHIPPLE).

Reflection: Getting back to yesterday's reflection, we may ask ourselves to what extent Cain understood the ramifications of his action. Abel was likely the first homicide victim, but was his the first human death? At the least, Cain must have understood that he was inflicting dire injury. How biting the irony of Cain's response to God's just consequence: "My punishment is more than I can bear. . . . Whoever finds me *will kill me*" (verses 13–14, emphasis added).

God provided Cain with a pledge of protection and a mark of ownership (verse 15). Pay attention to that mark: It's the same one that appears on the forehead of every baptized believer—the sign and seal of God's limitless grace (see 2 Corinthians 1:21–22).

No, God doesn't let us off the hook any more than he did Cain. Instead, he offered a scapegoat: his own Lamb to bear the brunt of his just verdict against all sinners. In grace he acquits us, allowing us to walk away scot-free. Jesus Christ bore on behalf of all of us a punishment infinitely harsher than Cain could ever have imagined.

There are no strings attached, but there is a responsibility that the liberated and enabled sinner embraces in gratitude: to spread his glory throughout a world dying for grace. Yes, our core theology is simple, but hardly simplistic and certainly not strange. Thank God for the gift of Jesus Christ, the only Savior of the lost.

Prayer Prompt: To what extent have you internalized this central truth of God's Word?

Godly woman,
YOU'VE BEEN MARKED AS HIS OWN.

ℬait and switch

Verses: "Laban had two daughters; the name of the older was Leah, and the name of the younger was Rachel. Leah had weak eyes, but Rachel had a lovely figure and was beautiful. Jacob was in love with Rachel" (Genesis 29:16–18).

"The finite is annihilated in the presence of the infinite, and becomes a pure nothing. So our spirit before God, so our justice before divine justice" (BLAISE PASCAL).

Reflection: The relatives back home weren't God-fearers, but Isaac sent his son back to the old home place: "Take a wife for yourself there, from among the daughters of Laban, your mother's brother" (Genesis 28:1–2). But the deceiver Jacob ended up being conned by an equally conniving uncle into doing more than taking *a* wife from Laban's family: Within the course of just over a week he married, for good or ill, *both* of them: the homely and the comely.

The contrast in Genesis 29 couldn't be more pronounced. Verse 20 tells us in lilting cadence (at least in English) that "Jacob served seven years to get Rachel, but they seemed like only a few days to him because of his love for her." But verse 25 breathes in blunt staccato his shock and dismay following the consummation of the marriage: "When morning came, there was Leah!" Ouch! Talk about a bait and switch!

The conflicts to follow in Jacob's family are a direct link in the working out of salvation history. Still, I can't help but wonder *why* God allowed this to happen . . .

Prayer Prompt: Do you ever wonder about God's fairness, even when a seemingly negative circumstance results in long-term good (see Genesis 50:19–21)? If so, take it to him now.

odly woman,
HIS WAYS ARE INFINITELY HIGHER.

The favorite

Verses: "Do we still have any share in the inheritance of our father's estate? . . . Not only has he sold us, but he has used up what was paid for us" (Genesis 31:14–15).

"As for me, I love all of my children equally, but for different reasons" (LYN LOMASI).

Reflection: Leah entered marriage with no illusions about her father Laban's disappointment in her. For him to pawn off this unappealing liability on her lovesick cousin was an outrage. But convention dictated that the older marry first.

We're told that Leah's pregnancy resulted from God's concern for her unloved state. She named her son Reuben, "'because the LORD has seen my misery. Surely my husband will love me now'" (Genesis 29:32).

But no. Chapter 30:1–24 tragicomically reports the race for sons between the rival sisters. When Rachel at last gave birth, her immediate words were "'God has taken away my disgrace. . . . May the LORD add to me *another son*'" (verses 23–24, emphasis added). Both sisters felt cheated, not only in terms of their frantic sprint for their husband's affections but in light of their father's low estimation of their worth.

Fast-forwarding to the present, never be fooled: Kids know their relative value in the eyes of their parents. If this is an issue in your family, don't allow it to escalate any further. Christian families aren't immune from the consequences of favoritism.

Prayer Prompt: Whether approaching God as parent or child, share with him whatever intergenerational conflict, jealousy, or preferential treatment divides your family.

Godly woman,
HE HAS NO FAVORITES.

*L*iving post-resurrection

Verses: "Since, then, you have been raised with Christ, set your hearts on things above, where Christ is, seated at the right hand of God. Set your minds on things above, not on earthly things. For you died, and your life is now hidden with Christ in God. When Christ, who is your life, appears, then you also will appear with him in glory" (Colossians 3:1–4).

"The life of Jesus is bracketed by two impossibilities: 'a virgin's womb and an empty tomb.' Jesus entered our world through a door marked 'No Entrance' and left through a door marked 'No Exit'"
(PETER LARSON).

Reflection: Even we as Christians in some sense fear death. This world, for all its pain, is still the only thing we know. And we've grown attached.

What we fail to realize, and what Paul points out, above, in two short clauses ("you died" and "you have been raised," in inverse order) is that our real death and resurrection to new life are *behind* us. The death of our old self occurred when we received and accepted new life in Christ.

What a comfort to know that our life (our eternal life, which we're already now living) is hidden with Christ in God. That doesn't mean that we're invisible to the world—quite the opposite. Nor is Paul calling us to be otherworldly.

Our security in Christ is precisely what the world needs, and we're here to share. God isn't asking us to bury our heads in the sand like an ostrich, with an attitude of "Let me know when it's all over." He wants us to get in step with the Spirit, asking, "What can I do to help?"

Prayer Prompt: How actively are you sharing the secret of your security?

odly woman.
SHARE THE GOOD NEWS.

$\mathcal{T}$he right home

Verse: "I will provide a place for my people Israel and will plant them so that they can have a home of their own and no longer be disturbed" (2 Samuel 7:10).

"Home is any four walls that enclose the right person"
(HELEN ROWLAND).

Reflection: Praying at bedtime one evening several months after moving in with me, Khristina thanked the Lord that she was no longer living in her former home, "where I was like a child kidnapped." The clause stunned me with its precision, epitomizing the helplessness of the moved child. Both Khristina and Angie disliked and distrusted their case workers, who alone they viewed as the agents of change in their lives, for good or ill.

Khrissy knew that her first placement was not in a "good home" [her words], but her social worker in her mind failed to make this obvious deduction. Her favorite placement had been in her first foster home (Angie's experience was similar), and she would like to have stayed. But powerful adults had other ideas.

"Before I moved in with you," Khrissy confided in me at one point during that first year, "I didn't know there was love in the world." Either the four walls enclosing my daughter-to-be weren't the right walls, or she wasn't the right person to be in them.

Any place can be home if the right mix of people inhabits it. I recently edited a devotional manuscript written by a military wife, who wrote about the lengthy succession of residences that had served over the years as home to her family. She had worked hard in every case for a homey feel, but the variable that mattered was the people, not the location, the architecture, the style, the size, or the building materials.

Prayer Prompt: What makes your home "right" for you and those others who live there? What touches might you add, aesthetically, emotionally, or spiritually?

$\mathcal{G}$odly woman,
MAKE THE MOST OF THE HOME HE HAS PROVIDED.

Not the loudest girl

Verse: "The quiet words of the wise are more to be heeded than the shouts of a ruler of fools" (Ecclesiastes 9:17).

"There are many fine things which we cannot say if we have to shout" (HENRY DAVID THOREAU).

Reflection: "Is the TV too loud for you, Granna?"
"No, it's fine for me."
"It's too loud for me. I'm not the loudest girl."

I couldn't help but chuckle at this flash of self-perception. Nothing profound, but Adelyn at four is coming to discover some of the nuances of who she is. It's my hope that my reserved but perceptive granddaughter will continue to grow in her unpretentious wisdom.

The truth is, though, that quiet people tend to fade into the background in a world that values the assertive, the vocal, the outspoken. The Teacher of Ecclesiastes discovered this to be true of his generation. The verses just prior to the one above tell a fascinating but little-known story: "There was once a small city with only a few people in it. And a powerful king came against it, surrounded it and built huge siege works against it. Now there lived in that city a man poor but wise, and he saved the city by his wisdom." So far, so good. But the Teacher presses on: "But nobody remembered that poor man. So I said, 'Wisdom is better than strength.' But the poor man's wisdom is despised, and his words are no longer heeded" (verses 14–16).

A sobering story, part of the Teacher's lineup of evidence in support of his theory of life's futility—without God, that is (check out the author's wrap-up in Ecclesiastes 12:13–14). Ah! There's the serendipity. Our self-perception is so often based on the wrong audience. Only one spectator really matters, and he does indeed hear and heed the whispers, and even the unspoken thoughts, of the quiet wise. Truth is, I'm not the loudest person either. What a blessing to know that, with God, there are no wallflowers. None of us can ever be lost in the crowd.

Prayer Prompt: To what degree is your self-concept based on comparison with others? Pause to consider as realistically as possible God's perspective on you.

odly woman,
BE TRUE TO THE YOU HE INTENDED.

$\mathcal{U}$p or down?

Verse: "You heavens above, rain down my righteousness; let the clouds shower it down. Let the earth open wide, let salvation spring up, let righteousness flourish with it" (Isaiah 45:8).

> *"If every call to Christ and His righteousness is a call to suffering,*
> *the converse is equally [true]—every call to suffering is a*
> *call to Christ, a promotion, an invitation to come up higher"*
> (CHARLES BENT).

Reflection: I'm intrigued by the up-and-down imagery in this verse, in terms of what comes down from heaven and what leaps up to meet it. Not knowing what Isaiah had in mind, I can't verify that my associations capture his point.

(It's the same way for me with much contemporary poetry: If I'm not sure I get the point, I figure it's probably good stuff. Since I don't care to work that hard, I avoid modern poetry. You too?) Anyway, it makes perfect sense that the heavens rain down righteousness. It definitely doesn't come from here, right? Or does it?

Salvation, too, comes from heaven, but in light of Jesus' human nature and sojourn on Earth it also springs up from down here. That's a big part of the wonder of it. Further, the righteousness that made possible that salvation now rises heavenward from those of us who identify ourselves with Christ's name.

In the words of Romans 1:17, "For in the gospel the righteousness of God is revealed—a righteousness that is by faith from first to last, just as it is written: 'The righteous will live by faith.'" What an opportunity we have to share in—and spread abroad—Christ's goodness!

Prayer Prompt: What does sharing in Christ's righteousness mean to you?

$\mathcal{G}$odly woman,

LET YOUR RIGHTEOUSNESS RISE TO MEET HIM.

ℛecord keeping

Verse: Love "does not dishonor others, it is not self-seeking, it is not easily angered, it keeps no record of wrongs" (1 Corinthians 13:5).

"Forgiveness is not an occasional act. It is a permanent attitude"
(ANN LANDERS).

Reflection: If we keep no record of wrongs, it follows that we'll keep no record of the number of times we have to forgive wrongs. This meshes with Jesus' point in his response to Peter's misguided question, "Lord, how many times shall I forgive my brother or sister who sins against me? Up to seven times?" (see Matthew 18:21–22).

Perhaps the operative words in Peter's query are "brother or sister." As William Blake observed, "It is easier to forgive an enemy than to forgive a friend."

There can be no doubt that our friends and relatives hold an extraordinary degree of power to hurt us. We are, after all, emotionally invested in them, and they in us. Paul isn't talking here about the "wounds from a friend" that "can be trusted" (Proverbs 27:6)—those hurts intended for our healing, inflicted with the best of intentions by those who care enough to be honest.

No, the wounds he refers to here are *wrongs*. Forgiveness is a choice, a choice that may have to begin unaccompanied by parallel feelings. By the grace of God, they'll come later. In the words of Lewis Smedes, "You will know that forgiveness has begun when you recall those who hurt you and feel the power to wish them well."

Prayer Prompt: What brother or sister would benefit from your deletion of a record?

odly woman.
LET THE RESENTMENT GO.

*O*nly the best?

Verse: "You, LORD, you are our Father. We are the clay, you are the potter; we are all the work of your hand" (Isaiah 64:8).

"The perfect is the enemy of the good" (VOLTAIRE).

Reflection: From my kindergarten days on, I dreamed of making books. Undaunted by my status as a pre-reader, I devoted myself in those early days to drawing sequential pictures, gradually progressing to stories with words.

Sometime after Mom's death, when I was eleven, I riffled through the box she had saved over the years of my attempts at drawing and writing. I recall being at a stage of continuously wanting to trash the past and start over with life (the self-talk was always along the lines of "From this moment on I'll be kinder, more grown up, thinner, *perfect*").

In this ruthless mode and with no adult supervision, I decided to throw out everything in that box I deemed to be below my sixth-grade standard—which, not surprisingly, turned out to be everything!

I'd love nothing better today than to catch a glimpse of those early works. Older and wiser (or at least more forgiving), I'm "perfectly" content today to be the particular jar of clay God had in mind when he fashioned me.

"Use what talent you possess," urged Henry Van Dyke, going on, "The woods would be very silent if no birds sang except those that sang best."

Prayer Prompt: How satisfied are you with the design and functionality the Potter gave you?

G odly woman,

USE YOUR GIFTS; DON'T COMPARE THEM.

$\mathcal{M}$elding pot

Verse: "Above all, love each other deeply, because love covers over a multitude of sins" (1 Peter 4:8).

"After expectations come acceptance" (KELA PRICE).

Reflection: I like the word *meld*—coined as a combination of *melt* and *weld* but saying much more than either one. If you've ever been in a position of blending a family, you know just what I mean. Joining two individuals (and their extended families) in a marriage involves the same process.

The melding process for my own family ran into some difficulties after the third child moved in. Interestingly, the problem, which was short-lived, occurred between the oldest and the youngest, with the middle child functioning comfortably with her sisters on both sides.

A rift developed soon after Khristina's arrival between her and Amanda. I chuckle now at the memory of fourteen-year-old Amanda leaning over Angie during the pastoral prayer one Sunday morning to announce in a loud whisper, "Mom, I don't think Khristina's going to work out!"

Khristina did in fact "work out," and relationships among my three daughters are going as well as I can expect, given their markedly different backgrounds and characteristics. In the words of Kela Price (whom I've also quoted above), "It is possible to successfully blend a family. It depends on how and when you start and what you put into the blender." I heartily concur, pointing out that her principle applies just as well to birth families.

We can't expect our children to produce qualities we don't first inject into our family blender by example, instruction, admonition, and nurture. Nor can we expect them to exercise tolerance and compassion, let alone love, in a vacuum. The quality of the ingredients makes all the difference in the blend. Expressed in another way by Josh Billings, "To bring up a child in the way he should go, travel that way yourself once in a while."

Prayer Prompt: If your family relationships are lacking in terms of love and acceptance, ask yourself how liberal you've been with those ingredients.

odly woman,

YOU WON'T GET OUT WHAT YOU DON'T PUT IN.

*S*et in a family

Verse: "God sets the lonely in families" (Psalm 68:6).

"The bond that links your true family is not one of blood, but of respect and joy in each other's life. Rarely do members of one family grow up under the same roof" (RICHARD BACH).

Reflection: We've heard it said that life can be "lonely at the top." But God, seated at the pinnacle of authority, has not only surrounded himself with saints and angels but has seen fit to relate to *himself* within the intimacy of a Godhead made up of three distinct persons.

From God's concern for Adam in Eden ("It is not good for the man to be alone" [Genesis 2:18]) to Jesus' attention to the void in the lives of his mother and beloved disciple ("Woman, here is your son. . . . Here is your mother" [John 19:26–27]) to the Spirit's indwelling presence in the hearts of Christians ("I will ask the Father, and he will give you another advocate to help you and be with you forever" [John 14:16]), God has always demonstrated concern for the lonely.

Our world as a whole is characterized by insecurity and isolation. While I would be quick to qualify Richard Bach's statement, above, arguing that many family members *do* grow up under the same roof, we can hardly deny that many other adults and children find solace in meaningful relationships outside the family construct that has offered safe boundaries for centuries. From singles sharing household expenses to live-in relationships to group homes to same sex "marriages" to gangs to cults to foster families, adults and children desperately seek to fulfill their God-given need to "belong" to other people.

God's Word provides encouragement as we grope our way through the maze of the "new morality" and the breakdown of the family values that have shored us up for so long. Provided a particular living arrangement does not constitute sin as defined in the Bible, we as Christians do well to support and accept those of his children whose "families" happen to be nontraditional.

Prayer Prompt: Intercede for someone you know whose lifestyle may be less than desirable or outside God's design. Pray also for an inclusive attitude toward that household whose members are seeking to serve him from within a unique or unconventional setting.

G odly woman,

TOLERATE AND SEEK TO UNDERSTAND.

$\mathscr{I}$nside information

Verse: "Overhearing what [the messengers] said, Jesus told him, 'Don't be afraid; just believe'" (Mark 5:36).

> *"Perhaps God brings us to the end of our resources so we can discover the vastness of His"* (NEIL ANDERSON).

Reflection: Jesus' words to the distraught father immediately after the death of Jairus's daughter surprise me. I would have expected our Lord to refer to an emotion other than fear in addressing the devastated dad. Probably not "Don't cry" (from Jesus' tears at the tomb of Lazarus, I know that he wasn't the "Buck up and take it like a man" type). Maybe an expression of commiseration, not including "Don't" anything.

The opening clause of this verse is easy to pass over. But in the economy of Scripture—perhaps especially in Mark's sparsely worded Gospel—every word counts. In light of this clue, we might want to preface Jesus' words with something like "You didn't just hear that." (It's interesting to note, BTW, that a textual footnote for this verse in the 2010 revised NIV translation suggests "ignoring" as an alternative to "overhearing.")

Of course Jairus would have been scared prior to his daughter's death. Encouragement to "just believe" would have made sense then too. What Jairus didn't know is that the Healer's words were appropriate from Jesus' perspective.

Jesus wasn't speaking prior to the girl's death; he was addressing her father just before her resurrection! No matter what you're facing, Jesus is telling you the same thing he told Jairus. He isn't being crass or clueless; he just has inside information. Don't be scared. Trust him!

Prayer Prompt: When have you jumped to a negative conclusion, only to be surprised by God?

odly woman.
JUST BELIEVE.

$\mathcal{O}$pen up!

Verse: "I am the LORD your God, who brought you up out of Egypt. Open wide your mouth and I will fill it" (Psalm 81:10).

"God keeps giving Himself as long as we bring that into which He can pour Himself" (ALEXANDER MACLAREN).

Reflection: I love the passivity (humanly speaking) of this verse. Since appreciating passivity seems a little odd, I'll turn that around: I love the active role God takes in providing for our needs. We need only to be available for dinner and to refrain from clamping our mouth shut.

I don't doubt, either, that God would like us to be clear on the identity of our breadwinner. Several years ago I was moved to put a portion of Psalm 81 to rhyme for kids. Two of the four verses go like this:

I feed my baby sister
and tell her, "Open wide!"
And when I open up my heart
you pour your love inside!

You hold your hand out to me—
with good things from above.
You fill me with my favorite foods
and feed my soul with love.

Prayer Prompt: Which of your needs is God providing without any "help" from you? Maybe rephrasing that question would be more effective: For which of your needs does God rely on your assistance?

$\mathcal{G}$odly woman,
OPEN WIDE YOUR MOUTH AND HEART FOR HIM TO FILL.

*W*isted twords

Verse: "He who searches our hearts knows the mind of the Spirit, because the Spirit intercedes for God's people in accordance with the will of God" (Romans 8:27).

"Has it ever struck you that the vast majority of the will of God for your life has already been revealed in the Bible? That is a crucial thing to grasp?" (PAUL LITTLE).

Reflection: "I know that you believe you understood what you think I said," quips Robert McCloskey, "but I'm not sure you realize that what you heard is not what I meant." As most of us have learned at some point, one of the basic components of effective listening is repeating back to the speaker what we've just heard her say to make sure we caught the gist.

This is a problem with prayer too. Not only do we not know what to say, but we tend not to give it much thought, rattling something off and assuring ourselves that God will get the idea.

God has a desired outcome my petitions must achieve (correspondence with his will) if I'm to expect an affirmative answer. Thankfully for short-sighted me, I'm comforted by the assurance that he won't willy-nilly grant whatever I ask.

Paul's word choice, above, with regard to "hearts" and "mind" is interesting. My mind isn't always defogged (verse 26 says that I don't know what I should pray), but the Spirit's is. No, the Spirit doesn't change my prayer, but he does straighten out my wisted twords—er, make that twisted words—and translate them directly to God from their source—my heart.

Stephen Crotts has an interesting take on this issue: "God has editing rights over our prayers. He will . . . edit them, correct them, bring them in line with His will and then hand them back to us to be resubmitted." I agree to some extent, with one "edit" (comes naturally for me, I guess): The Spirit eliminates a step by doing the resubmission himself. We can trust him.

Prayer Prompt: Do you ever feel "dyslexic" in prayer? Have you thanked the Spirit for rewording?

odly woman,

HIS SPIRIT INTERCEDES FOR YOU.

&xtended family

Verse: "This is his command: to believe in the name of his Son, Jesus Christ, and to love one another as he commanded us" (1 John 3:23).

"In the total expanse of human life there is not a single square inch of which the Christ, who alone is sovereign, does not declare, 'That is mine!'" (ABRAHAM KUYPER).

Reflection: The ancient African proverb "It takes a village to raise a child" has become clichéd, in part due to Hillary Rodham Clinton's controversial 1996 release *It Takes a Village*, in which the then-first lady advocated government and societal involvement in raising our nation's young.

Few would disagree that a strong familial community is an essential umbrella for a healthily functioning family. But there's an unbridgeable, qualitative difference between membership in a brotherhood and sisterhood of believers and affiliation with any other group. When we join a church, we identify ourselves with Christ's overarching, insoluble family.

My tradition practices infant baptism (yours may dedicate infants). The doctrinal perspectives and implications underlying these traditions are, of course, different. But a point of commonality is that these little ones, declared to be Christ's own, are returned to the arms of the earthly parents God has appointed, along with the rest of his church, as their trustees.

Parents, along with the assembled body, make promises. The words I hear at the close of the sacrament never fail to resonate with me: "I hereby declare that [infant's name] has been received into Christ's church through baptism. May God help all of us to keep the promises we have just made."

Prayer Prompt: What is your role and responsibility with relation to your congregation's children?

odly woman,

BE AN ACTIVE CHURCH FAMILY MEMBER.

𝒯he borrowed tool

Verse: "As one of [the prophets] was cutting down a tree, the iron ax-head fell into the water. 'Oh no, my lord!' he cried out. 'It was borrowed!'" (2 Kings 6:5).

"People see God every day, they just don't recognize him"
(PEARL BAILEY).

Reflection: If you were already familiar with this story, have you ever asked yourself how it made the cut for inclusion in God's Word? Yes, a miracle was performed: Elisha threw a stick into the water, causing an iron axhead accidently lost in the Jordan River to resurface and float so it could be lifted out.

The crux of the issue: The tool had been borrowed. We find this less than gripping account sandwiched between the healing of the Syrian army commander Naaman and the blinding of the entire Aramean army. *So what?* we want to ask. Or *and . . . ?* (raising our eyebrows and circling both hands in a gesture of waiting for some spectacular finale).

Yet this understated slice of life can afford us comfort missing from either of the political/military dramas surrounding it. Who of us wouldn't be unsettled by the loss of a neighbor's on-loan tool or a fender bender in a borrowed vehicle?

Speaking of lifting (skim ahead in that chapter to verse 7), Peter instructs us: "Humble yourselves, therefore, under God's mighty hand, that he may lift you up in due time. Cast all your anxiety on him because he cares for you" (1 Peter 5:6–7).

Prayer Prompt: What would it take for you to regain the childlike trust to take *all* your needs to God?

odly woman,
YOU SERVE A DETAIL-ORIENTED GOD.

$\mathcal{T}$he schmooze

Verse: "Many curry favor with a ruler, and everyone is the friend of one who gives gifts" (Proverbs 19:6).

> *"Don't come into the presence of God to impress Him with something He gave you!"* (T. D. JAKES).

Reflection: *Schmooze*—one of those delightful words that rolls off the tongue with the suave sophistication it suggests. Pronounce it slowly and note your facial expression at the end. You look so . . . French!

Seriously, though, this isn't a word you pronounce often. Because it isn't supposed to exist. It did come up, though, in a conversation I overheard from the backseat of a van riding home a few years ago in the wee hours from an out-of-town business meeting. A certain amount of ingratiation was expected of this female coworker. Not for upward mobility so much as for maintaining hard-earned status. Possibly even for job security.

The beauty of your relationship with God is that he sees through—and discounts—a schmooze. Look at the contrast between the posturing prayer of the Pharisee and the humble entreaty of the tax collector in Luke 18:9–14. Jesus' summary of the parable leaves no doubt as to his attitude about brownnosing: "All those who exalt themselves will be humbled, and those who humble themselves will be exalted" (Luke 18:14).

Isn't it refreshing to approach this VID (Very Important Deity) with everything—all your doubts and insecurities and guilt—hanging out like a baggy sweatshirt? So settle in, tuck your bare feet underneath you, and talk with him—straight.

Prayer Prompt: Do you find it necessary or natural to schmooze God?

$\mathcal{G}$odly woman,

GOD WANTS YOU—AS IN *YOURSELF*.

"You're the one"

Verse: "The LORD sent Nathan to David. When he came to him, he said, 'There were two men in a certain town, one rich and the other poor . . .'" (2 Samuel 12:1).

"You are only what you are when no one is looking"
(ROBERT C. EDWARDS).

Reflection: "The fact of storytelling hints at a fundamental human unease, hints at human imperfection," reflects Ben Okri. "Where there is perfection there is no story to tell." An effective story requires a protagonist (the good guy), an antagonist (the guy who antagonizes the good guy), and a crisis. Take most any riveting Bible story, and you've got these elements.

With regard to the short story at the beginning of 2 Samuel 12, I wonder whether God gave his prophet the story with which to implicate David. One thing we know for sure: God loves stories! The Bible constitutes one grand story, and Jesus relied on parables for much of his teaching.

I can't help but admire Nathan's skill. The prophet's emphatic "You are the man!" (verse 7) reverberates in our ears. The same line (substitute "that person" to drive this home) could be affixed to every parable.

It's so comfortable to ease ourselves off the hook as we recognize other people we know in these deceptively simple stories. But that "fundamental human unease" is intended to afflict each one of us. If we're willing to take a closer look, *we're there* in every case. Ask God for the courage to point the finger in your own direction when you engage with a biblical parable.

Prayer Prompt: Try putting yourself in the place of the rich man in Nathan's story.

odly woman,
HE'S SPEAKING TO *YOU.*

$\mathcal{T}$he struggle?

Verse: "For our struggle is not against flesh and blood, but against the rulers, against the authorities, against the powers of this dark world and against the spiritual forces of evil in this dark world" (Ephesians 6:12).

"Take care of your life and the Lord will take care of your death"
(GEORGE WHITEFIELD).

Reflection: Adelyn and I were discussing the lyrics of "Michael, Row the Boat Ashore." Since she has tended to sing this immediately following a verse of "There Was a Man Named Michael Finnegan," I came to the conclusion that she was confusing two Michaels.

The conversation naturally turned to death, at which point my granddaughter made an astounding statement: "Grandma, when I die you'll have to stay in the house while I fight the bad people." It occurred to me with a start that this courageous little girl equated death with murder and wanted to shelter her grandma when this fate confronted her.

Addie and I went on to discuss the beauty of dying in the Lord. Many sick people, I informed her, die in bed surrounded by their loved ones and ready to be welcomed by God and his angels. She and I sometimes pray "Now I Lay Me Down to Sleep" at bedtime, but I've been reluctant to expose her to the lyrics "If I should die before I wake . . ." It occurs to me now that "pray[ing] the Lord my soul to take" is both realistic and comforting. If I leave my granddaughter in the dark about the beauty of death for the believer, she'll fill in the mental gaps with much more sinister thoughts.

Speaking of sinister, Paul minced no words as he addressed the Ephesians in the verse above. While I'm aware that he was speaking of the struggle of Christians, I can't help but wonder just what the nonbeliever faces as he or she encounters death. There's certainly much evil on the loose in this dark world. Praise God that we can look forward to slipping into his welcoming embrace when our time comes. Make sure to let your kids know . . .

Prayer Prompt: How do you feel about your own coming death? That of your loved ones in the Lord?

$\mathcal{G}$odly woman,

CHRIST'S SACRIFICE HAS ELIMINATED THE STRUGGLE.

$\mathscr{S}$elective vision

Verses: "Open my eyes that I may see wonderful things in your law. I am a stranger on earth; do not hide your commands from me" (Psalm 119:18–19).

"The only thing worse than being blind is having sight but no vision" (HELEN KELLER).

Reflection: Selective vision is one of the interesting facts of human life. We all suffer—or benefit—from it, as the case may be. A few miles from my home stands a row of three connected, department-store-sized storefronts, all of which have been vacant for as long as I can remember (it's been at least fifteen years since I became acquainted with the area, and I'll have to say that nobody seems to notice). This lengthy and increasingly dilapidated structure, which sits on the far side of an extensive parking lot, away from the thoroughfare that runs alongside, is anchored on one end by a tiny beauty salon, the only open business. On the street side, though, has mushroomed a row of fast-food establishments and other franchise businesses, all of which seem to be bustling. If we all "agree" not to see the eyesore, seems to be the consensus, we can go about business as usual.

Psalm 119:18 approaches God's law from a somewhat surprising perspective: The psalmist asks God to open his eyes not to the reality of God's law but to its wonder (perhaps we could say to its beauty). No, God doesn't deliberately hide his commands from us (verse 19), but so many do fail to "see" them. The apostle Paul tells us in Romans 8:7 that "the mind governed by the flesh is hostile to God; it does not submit to God's law, nor can it do so. Those who are in the realm of the flesh cannot please God." That's pretty sobering stuff. For those so blinded business as usual will have disastrous eternal consequences.

But what of us whose minds are not governed by the flesh? Let's go back a verse to Romans 8:6: "The mind governed by the Spirit is life and peace." If you and I fail to see the wonderful things in God's law—and we know he hasn't hidden them from us—it may be that we're failing to get past a selective-vision problem.

Prayer Prompt: In what ways might deliberate blindness be a problem in your Christian life?

odly woman,

ASK HIM TO OPEN YOUR EYES.

Heads or tails?

Verse: "The LORD will make you the head, not the tail. If you pay attention to the commands of the LORD your God that I give you this day and carefully follow them, you will always be at the top, never at the bottom" (Deuteronomy 28:13).

"Nothing is so boring as having to keep up a deception"
(EDWARD V. LUCAS).

Reflection: I once heard about a species of snake that protects itself by a unique camouflage system: convincing facial markings on its tail end. Obviously, a serpent's line of defense lies in its head. No matter how sleek its body line, its ability to maneuver its front end (its "top," not its "bottom") is critical. Any living, non-plant creature in a real way "is" its head, or its ability to use it.

To add context to these verses, the Israelites were poised to enter the Land of Promise. But they were intimidated. Still, God demanded obedience. He doles out daily challenges for us too—and gives us the heads—and the hands—to accomplish what he calls us to do, for his glory and for the growth of his kingdom.

What is he asking of you today? Will you lift your head in recognition of your high calling as a believer or flick your tail with its counterfeit markings in the hope that others will "buy" a fake persona? The choice is yours.

Prayer Prompt: Identify what God is asking of you today, this year, and beyond.

Godly woman,
ONLY OBEY . . .

𝓛oving strength

Verses: "Be on your guard; stand firm in the faith; be courageous; be strong. Do everything in love" (1 Corinthians 16:13–14).

> *"Love takes off masks that we fear we cannot live without and know we cannot live within"* (JAMES BALDWIN).

Reflection: *Grandma (to dog):* "Get down, Annabelle. My lap's all full. *Sit!*"
Addie (to dog, jumping to a standing position on my leg): "Stand up for Jesus, Annabelle!"
(Annabelle, sitting, wags tail harder.)
Grandma (to Addie): "You're very silly."
Addie (flattered): "Thank you!"

That chuckle from last night got me to thinking about standing up for the faith. I first considered this issue, I suppose, as a little girl singing those bewildering lyrics from "The B-I-B-L-E": "I stand alone on the Word of God." Standing on a Bible didn't strike me as respectful, but this was just one of so many adult mysteries I had to take in stride.

Seriously, though, what strikes me in the above passage isn't so much Paul's hard-hitting, no-nonsense words in verse 13 as their understated appendage in verse 14. Strength from a New Testament perspective *is* all about love, isn't it?

Prayer Prompt: What situations in your life call for strength grounded in love?

odly woman,

FIND STRENGTH IN HIS LOVE.

𝒰nforgotten gesture

Verse: "Dear children, let us not love with words or speech but with actions and in truth" (1 John 3:18).

"Any good therefore that I can do, or any kindness I can show to another creature, let me do it now. Let me not defer it, for I shall not pass this way again" (STEPHEN GRELLET).

Reflection: I grew up in something of a Dutch Reformed enclave in Redlands, California. A highlight of each spring was our Christian school's Holland Festival. Nearly everyone, from grandparents to babies, donned traditional Dutch costumes, some complete with wooden shoes.

There were booths; a kitchen-turned-restaurant with mouthwatering ethnic specialties; and classrooms displaying bonsai and cactus gardens and other contest entries. In the afternoon the kids put on an outdoor program, at the end of which grades K–9 belted out "Wilhelmus" (the Dutch national anthem) and "God Bless America."

The evening finale was an auction, and the last item for bidding was the same every year: a doll donated by the Sunshine Circle (a group of high-school girls from church), complete with a wardrobe of hand-sewn and (depending on the doll) store-bought fashions.

Mom had been the leader of this group in the years just prior to her death, and the girls missed her. Whoever bought the coveted doll that spring (a life-sized baby that year) brought it to our house afterward to present to five-year-old Terri.

(As an aside, I learned after writing this that the tradition goes on. A cousin who had just attended this annual gala mentioned on Facebook that she used to think the "Dutch Festival" was a national holiday!) At any rate, Terri and I recently reminisced online, forty-nine years after the fact, about this unforgotten gesture on the part of a caring church member.

Prayer Prompt: What act of love from a fellow believer has touched you?

𝒢odly woman,
NEVER UNDERESTIMATE LOVE'S POWER.

In all these things

Verse: "In all these things we are more than conquerors through him who loved us" (Romans 8:37).

> *"Prosperity is the blessing of the Old Testament; Adversity is the*
> *blessing of the New"* (FRANCIS BACON).

Reflection: What does it mean to be more than a conqueror? Is there something more ultimate? Or is this expression, at least in Paul's mind, the superlative extraordinaire?

If an uninitiated someone were to read this verse out of context, her interest might be piqued by the undefined "In all these things." What antecedents for *these* might we expect from a natural perspective?

Of one thing we can be certain: They wouldn't match Paul's list, either in content or in spirit. *Trouble, hardship, persecution, famine, nakedness, danger,* and *sword? Come again?* Nor does Paul state that once we've overcome these negatives we'll be more than conquerors by comparison. No, the apostle says—and means—*in* all these things.

As Christian women who understand the New Testament's counterintuitive economy, we're neither surprised—nor, regrettably, particularly intrigued—by these oh-so-familiar words. Yet we're wise to ask ourselves how well they define our concept of personal reality.

Prayer Prompt: In what hardships are you a conqueror—and beyond?

odly woman,

YOU SHARE IN CHRIST'S VICTORY.

$\mathcal{I}$nopportune service

Verse: "Each one should use whatever gift you have received to serve others, as faithful stewards of God's grace in its various forms" (1 Peter 4:10).

"To help a friend in need is easy, but to give him your time is not always opportune" (CHARLIE CHAPLIN).

Reflection: Over a period of eleven years I adopted three special-needs daughters. Did I do so in service to God? Only secondarily; my principal motivation was a love for kids and a desire to parent.

Today, though, the Spirit is calling me to a more mundane phase of family service. I'm all too aware that, at least at times, I act in grudging obedience to his calls—which come to me over the phone, generally at inopportune times.

Due to the loss nearly four years ago of a longtime editorial position with a Christian publisher and ongoing physical struggles, I find myself in my late fifties working from home as a freelance editor and writer. Not only my kids but some of their friends as well have depended on me to meet transportation and other needs.

How do I respond to the Spirit's intermittent calls? Too often with martyr-like sighs and meaningful looks that shout "Can't you see I'm busy serving the Lord?"

I'm making an effort to be more cheerfully available for those blocks of time spent in the interest of someone else's errand. And I can see positives: For example, some of our conversations en route to a destination seem to have been of value. (Have you ever noticed that people open up more easily side by side than face-to-face?)

This phase of my Christian service is neither glam nor stimulating, but it does appear to be one of God's purposes for this passage of my life.

Prayer Prompt: To what aspect of Christian service is the Spirit calling you at this time?

$\mathcal{G}$odly woman,
YOU'RE GIFTED FOR HIS SERVICE.

*E*motional intelligence

Verses: "I took the wine and gave it to the king. I had not been sad in his presence before, so the king asked me, 'Why does your face look so sad when you are not ill? This can be nothing but sadness of heart.' I was very much afraid" (Nehemiah 2:1–2).

> "YOU, who created me, who created vulnerability, can see
> me for me and not flee, and not GASP and not belittle. But
> you welcome it, vulnerability! The real stuff, the raw stuff, the
> hidden things. And He refines it to what it should be. No front,
> no façade and complete nakedness before Him is of no regret"
> (NADINE HAWTHORNE).

Reflection: I'm intrigued by these verses in Nehemiah. It would appear that the deadpan affect of the diplomat has been around for as long as diplomacy itself. Then again, maybe the expectation was more the schmooze than the inscrutable poker face. At any rate, the possible consequences of Nehemiah's hint of honest emotion terrified him.

One of the qualities of an effective leader is "emotional intelligence"— the instinct or ability to reveal enough emotion to gain support while not so much as to suggest weakness. What about the emotional intelligence of the Christian leader—or of any of us as Christ's representatives on Earth?

Wouldn't the same Jesus who wept at Lazarus's grave advocate vulnerability for us? Not the wearing of our emotions on our sleeve but the willingness and courage to show appropriate, authentic feeling? In the words of Paul, "For Christ's sake, I delight in weaknesses, in insults, in hardships, in persecutions, in difficulties. For when I am weak, then I am strong" (2 Corinthians 12:10).

Prayer Prompt: What have you found to be the right degree of openness for you?

odly woman,
MODEL JESUS' VULNERABILITY.

God's signs

Verses: "And God said, 'Let there be lights in the vault of the sky to separate the day from the night, and let them serve as signs to mark sacred times, and days and years, and let them be lights in the vault of the sky to give light on the earth.' And it was so" (Genesis 1:14–15).

> *"I want to know how God created this world. I am not interested in this or that phenomenon, in the spectrum of this or that element. I want to know His thoughts; the rest are details"* (ALBERT EINSTEIN).

Reflection: The creation is incredibly sophisticated. And that very much includes the human mind. God built enough clues into his creative work to guide people from the earliest days to delineate days and nights, seasons and years. He created us with the ingenuity to interpret the nuances of his work.

The animal world is amazingly sensitive to nature's clues, knowing instinctively when to mate, nest, gather, migrate, and return. Human beings, on the other hand, don't come equipped with instinct—because we don't need it. God allows us to try and err and try and fail and try again until we get it right.

Scientific endeavor is anything but contrary to the working out of our faith. It has everything to do with developing the incredible potential God has engineered into our brains. Nor is God trying to trick us with false leads built into the creation schema.

Many of the world's great scientists are dedicated Christians intent on piecing together more and more of the intricate puzzle God has laid out for us to decipher.

Prayer Prompt: Do you view science as God's invitation to exercise our own creative potential?

Godly woman,
NO ONE WILL PROVE GOD WRONG.

𝒯rigs

Verse: "To the weak I became weak, to win the weak. I have become all things to all people so that by all possible means I might save some" (1 Corinthians 9:22).

"Ours is the age of substitutes: instead of language, we have jargon; instead of principles, slogans, and instead of genuine ideas, bright ideas" (ERIC BENTLEY).

Reflection: "Your blood work was fine. Your trigs are up a little, but we can regulate that."

"OK. Thanks. . . . What are trigs?"

"I don't know. If you need to find out, I'll have to get you in contact with . . ."

I don't recall the term she used in this unlikely exchange, but as soon as I hung up "triglycerides" popped into my mind. Duh! If there's one generalization we can make about speech in our day, it's that it's all about shortcuts—abbreviations, acronyms, and idioms. Daunting for anyone struggling with ESL, isn't it?

The Christian vocabulary has its own lingo, much of which has been around for a long time. For those of us who grew up with it, it isn't striking, but think of how it must confuse the newbie. My tradition doesn't use the term "born again," but we do refer to Christian "rebirth" (means the same thing, but to the uninitiated it must sound like reincarnation). Similarly, an unbeliever who isn't in the know is going to think "Christian walk" smacks more of 'tude than it sounds like "sojourn." Doctrinal terms specific to certain traditions (think "Spirit baptism" or "the rapture") leave people scratching their heads, and even terms like "unregenerate" or "sanctification" mean absolutely nothing to anyone who's "out of the loop."

If you engage in spiritual discussions outside "the fold" (and I hope we all do), do you adjust your speech patterns to suit?

How are your trigs, by the way?

Prayer Prompt: Pray for the Spirit's clarity when you explain your faith.

odly woman,

SHARE YOUR FAITH IN WORDS THAT COMMUNICATE.

*E*xercising hope

Verse: "There is surely a future hope for you, and your hope will not be cut off" (Proverbs 23:18).

"Depression is the inability to construct a future" (ROLLO MAY).

Reflection: Aren't you glad it isn't up to us as Christians to structure our future? The fact is that a good deal of the time we not only don't know what we want or need but don't or can't go after it. For many of us it isn't a matter of idealistic plans and unattainable dreams but of an inability to conceive or maintain high hopes. Status-quo thinking, inertia, habit, lethargy, apathy, intimidation—no matter what name we use, our resistance to exertion or change can be the strongest motivating (or non-motivating!) force in our lives, leaving us to wallow in the same ole same ole till we find ourselves first dejected and then in despair.

How ironic that we as Christian women, who on the basis of our status live with an unshakable hope, are still subject to depression. Giving ourselves the benefit of the doubt, it's hard to conceive of an unimaginably glorious future.

In my case, depression was an issue of young adulthood, gradually alleviated through the mellowing process of maturity. Without conscious awareness of the change, I at some point crossed an invisible line between pessimism and optimism. With many it's the other way around: Languor and disillusionment can increase with advancing age, in inverse proportion to a perception of diminishing possibilities for earthly fulfillment.

We Westerners put a lot of emphasis on feeling—and feeling requires energy that can be hard to summon when we're already at a low point. If depression is or has been a problem for you, have you considered *exercising* your hope? You can claim God's sure promise of a future hope, and do so regularly, without any pressure to arouse accompanying feeling. Quiet assurance can sustain us even when we can't sustain an emotional high.

Prayer Prompt: No matter how you feel about your eternal future, claim God's guarantee of a hope that won't disappoint.

*G**odly woman,***

HOPE ISN'T JUST A FEELING.

"Dear Mom . . ."

Verse: "The sayings of King Lemuel—an inspired utterance his mother taught him" (Proverbs 31:1).

"A mother understands what a child does not say"
(AUTHOR UNKNOWN).

Reflection: We didn't spend a lot on Mother's Day this year—Adelyn and I—but it was definitely her thoughts that counted. I entered the dollar store with an open mind in terms of what this preschooler would select. Ten dollars later we headed for the checkout, the bottom of our cart littered with a variety of Addie's choices, from a pair of tiny glass slippers (she's big on all things princess) to a sprig of artificial flowers.

The $ .40 card was as generic as anything from the heart of an almost four-year-old can be. In the car, I handed Addie a pen and asked her to "write" on it a "Dear Mom . . . Love, Addie" note. She chose to dictate aloud from the car seat as she expressed her sentiments with squiggly lines on the envelope: "Dear Mom, I like you. You're my best friend. Well, except for Olivia and Jaman [daycare playmates]. Love, Addie."

Throughout history moms have held a prominent place in many hearts; the Bible is representative of this—from Timothy, Paul's son in the faith (I delight to note in his case the importance of *Grandma!*), to the unidentified King Lemuel of Proverbs.

Motherhood is a unique, God-ordained institution. If you call someone Mom or respond to the word yourself, make sure this year to make the most of Mother's Day.

Prayer Prompt: Thank God for the influence of your mom. If you're playing this role, appreciate and take seriously the privilege and responsibility that are yours.

odly woman,
HE HONORS MOMS.

The only one?

Verse: "'I have been very zealous for the LORD God Almighty. The Israelites have rejected your covenant, torn down your altars, and put your prophets to death with the sword. I am the only one left, and now they are trying to kill me too'" (1 Kings 19:14).

"If things go wrong, don't go with them" (ROGER BABSON).

Reflection: The story of Elijah's burnout following the stunning victory for the Lord at Mount Carmel is so human, isn't it? Whether our letdown comes after building up to a high point or stepping up to a crisis, we all know too well that "There's nowhere to go but down" kind of dejection.

For me as a child this devastation would invariably hit the day out-of-state cousins left our home after a visit. As desolate in my lows as I was exuberant in my highs, I was the kind of kid who expected and experienced the best with no mental prep for the aftermath.

My Elijah-likeness extended also to my tendency to exaggerate the bleakness. Elijah was wrong in his estimate of the number of God-fearers left in Israel. And God set him straight in the most forthright manner: "Yet I reserve seven thousand in Israel—all whose knees have not bowed down to Baal and whose mouths have not kissed him" (1 Kings 19:18).

Have you ever been so fired up for the Lord that you burned out, thinking he had forgotten his own cause? A quote from an unidentified author resonates with me: "For peace of mind, resign as general manager of the universe."

Prayer Prompt: If you're easily let down—even way down, take that tendency to God.

Godly woman,

HE WON'T ALLOW HIS KINGDOM TO FALL.

𝒫lanet Huisjen

Verse: "The life of mortals is like grass, they flourish like a flower of the field; the wind blows over it and it is gone, and its place remembers it no more" (Psalm 103:15–16).

"We are tomorrow's past" (MARY WEBB).

Reflection: I learned this week, somewhat by accident, of the existence of a main-belt asteroid bearing the impressive moniker "17022 Huisjen." This "planet" was discovered in 1999 by a fourth or fifth cousin of mine bearing the name Martin Huisjen (I didn't know of his existence either).

While I was amused by this fun factoid, my daughter Khristina was delighted, facetiously texting her birth sister and making copies of the information from the Internet to show off at work. She quipped something like the following to her birth sister: "You may have been adopted into a rich family, but mine is famous." Well, OK, taking some major liberties with that word.

Family trees are fun, but the truth is that most of the names are just names. My dad's information dates back to the period prior to Hollanders using last names, and the only information I have about any of them is that one ancestor died after being kicked by his horse. For some reason this unfortunate fact seemed pertinent enough to pass along through the generations. There had to have been a lot more to this guy, but his place remembers him no more.

Psalm 147:4 alerts me that the Lord "determines the number of the stars and calls them each by name"! How amazing to acknowledge that the Creator is intimately acquainted with asteroid 17022 Huisjen—as well as with his own daughter, Donna Huisjen. And that he'll still remember, love, and know me intimately ages after no one else cares.

Prayer Prompt: Do you find yourself more disheartened by the transience of life or overcome by the reality of your existence as God's eternal daughter?

odly woman,

HE NEVER FORGETS.

*T*hose beautiful people

Verse: "Those who look to him are radiant; their faces are never covered with shame" (Psalm 34:5).

"God loves us the way we are, but too much to leave us that way"
(LEIGHTON FORD).

Reflection: A highlight of my childhood world was the arrival in the mail of the Sears catalog. This meant that the old one would be passed along to me. For a few days my free time would be spent on the floor with scissors and flour/water paste, creating a paper-doll world—typically a whole congregation, consisting of multiple families with first and last names and ages of children jotted on the backs of the dolls. It seemed only natural for life to revolve around the church family.

The people in my churches were always beautiful—at least as beautiful as the models chosen by Sears. My own congregation isn't bound by the artificial restrictions imposed by the mid-twentieth-century Sears "wish book," notably including a lack of dads and grandparents. But I did at times in my early adult life view myself as an outsider—a fake—an unattached single woman with her share of problems and challenges camouflaged at church within a world of "beautiful people," most surrounded in my eyes by loving family members. I learned later on that we are in reality a company of forgiven sinners, in various stages of sanctification.

Ironically, I've come full circle. When I glance around me now on a Sunday morning, I again see a gathering of beautiful people, of people lovely (especially, I'm sure, in the eyes of the Beholder they've come to worship) in the most inclusive sense. It's the loveliness that radiates from an open, smiling face.

Prayer Prompt: Might your congregation feel a little off-putting to the stranger? Pray that you, in your reflection of Christ, may be at the very least a people inviting investigation.

*G**odly woman,***

SMILE—YOU'VE BEEN FORGIVEN.

Faltering lips

Verse: "Moses said to the LORD, 'Since I speak with faltering lips, why would Pharaoh listen to me?'" (Exodus 6:30).

"Speech happens to not be his language" (MADAME DE STAEL).

Reflection: Not to sound presumptuous, but I can relate to Moses' complaint/excuse. For a little more than forty years (sounds symbolic, doesn't it?), I've struggled with a speech problem.

One day, while waiting on a customer at the dry cleaners where I worked during my senior year of high school, I found my words coming out in disconnected, strangled bursts. Stringing together specific consonant/vowel combinations, like the one in the first syllable of "hello," proved particularly difficult, emerging from my constricted throat like a sob.

My older sister developed the same problem a year or so later, and we both learned to adapt our vocabulary to what we could and couldn't say (she, for example, can successfully answer the phone with "This is Debbie").

We didn't see doctors much in those days, and Debbie diagnosed us years later from a *Reader's Digest* article on spasmodic dysphonia, a condition based on an involuntary slamming together and stiffening of the vocal cords.

By the time I gained the courage to mention this to my doctor (I had from the beginning considered the problem humiliating and hopeless), I'd gone through many debilitating years. Both Debbie and I are now on medication that has helped tremendously.

I'm no longer as embarrassed by my at times strangulated speech as I used to be, and I've learned that God can still use me, as he did Moses. Maybe I, like Paul, needed a thorn in the flesh to keep me humble in his service (see 2 Corinthians 12:7).

Prayer Prompt: What deficiency or disability hampers you? How is God helping you overcome it? Or work around it? How is he blessing you through it?

odly woman,

HE'LL HELP YOU PREVAIL.

$\mathcal{A}$ different kind of flesh

Verses: "Not all flesh is the same: People have one kind of flesh, animals have another, birds another and fish another" (1 Corinthians 15:39).

"Many years ago when an adored dog died, a great friend, a bishop, said to me, 'You must always remember that, as far as the Bible is concerned, God only threw the humans out of Paradise'"
(AUTHOR UNKNOWN).

Reflection: A typical feline, Baby Girl is rather sure of herself when it comes to navigating "difficult" household terrain. She enjoys jumping onto the narrow shelf that fronts the sliding glass doors of my wide china hutch, opening the door on one side, sashaying through my dense collection of glass and porcelain bells, and emerging, [bells] unscathed, from the other end. She leaves the doors open just wide enough to let me know that she has once again successfully made the trip. And so there!

Annabelle, on the other hand, is the epitome of endearing clumsiness. How many times hasn't she nearly thrown me off balance by hitting the outside/back of my leg, just behind the knee, in an attempt to run past me? Typical canine? I'll give her the benefit of the doubt on that one.

Granted, Paul's point in the above verse fits within a context. But the reality of the different kinds of flesh still stands. Why, I ask myself, did God go to the trouble of creating such an endless and fascinating menagerie of animals? At least in part to praise his name. "The wild animals honor me, the jackals and the owls," proclaims God through Isaiah in Isaiah 43:20. Domesticated ones too, I can't help but think—the cats and the dogs. The book of Job includes some wonderfully humorous animal anecdotes. What you may not realize is that these quotes are from *God*. If in doubt, check out the following delightful surprises (Job 39:5, 7, 13, 17–18; 41:1, 5). What a unique perspective on creation, straight from the lips of the Master Artist.

Prayer Prompt: When has the endearment of an animal moved your thoughts toward God?

Godly woman,
JOIN WITH ALL CREATION IN HIS PRAISE.

*E*nd . . . or beginning?

Verse: "The end of a matter is better than its beginning, and patience is better than pride" (Ecclesiastes 7:8).

> *"The world is round and the place which may seem like the end*
> *may also be only the beginning"* (IVY BAKER PRIEST).

Reflection: An anonymous quote has it that "what the caterpillar calls the end of the world, the master calls a butterfly." I don't know which "master" is intended, but the Master of metamorphosis certainly knows—and controls—that outcome.

In all fairness the Old Testament, and particularly the book of Proverbs, includes several verses that speak of the "end" in terms as negative as the Teacher of Ecclesiastes is positive. Negative natural consequences can be quite predictable, but that isn't my point here.

When have you had to wait patiently for a good outcome in what you perceived to be an almost entirely negative situation? My own thoughts move immediately to my job loss (a situation in which I did almost immediately identify God's hand), but also to my loss of contact with my three cherished grandchildren (whom I still grieve despite my bittersweet gratitude for the report of their adoption into a Christian home).

September 11, 2001 seemed like "the end" for many Americans, and some unforeseen and permanent lifestyle changes did result (ditto for the recent severe recession). But do we as Christian women view these upshots as "downers" or as Spirit-orchestrated correctives? It's all a matter of outlook.

Prayer Prompt: What unwelcome and seemingly disastrous events have changed your life? Are you able to see and appreciate his goodness in and through, or at least in spite of, them?

odly woman,
HIS ACTIONS ARE NEVER RANDOM.

$\mathcal{G}$uarded speech

Verse: "Sin is not ended by multiplying words, but the prudent hold their tongues" (Proverbs 10:19).

"For attractive lips, speak words of kindness" (AUDREY HEPBURN).

Reflection: We live in an age of verbal overload, but I'll have to concede some positive results. As a word lover, I appreciate publisher- and magazine-imposed word-count restrictions that force me to hone and tone my writing. Down to a certain point, the shorter and more pointed the better. People lack the time to plow through unnecessary verbiage.

As many of us know from office and other work-front experience, résumés are limited to a single page, and meeting notes and memos in the "executive" style call for bulleted synopses. Acronyms and abbreviations characterize communication, both written and verbal.

Sadly, though, a large percentage of "speech" still falls into the category of drivel. Young people (and older) wile away hours connected to phones or computers, speaking audibly or texting. Grammar, punctuation, and spelling rules are nixed as too slow for stream-of-consciousness chatter.

While most words in and of themselves are neutral, the Bible warns us repeatedly about the untamed human tongue. On those occasions when you find yourself having a lot to say, how frequently do you regret some of it?

Prayer Prompt: Ask for insight into the potential pitfalls of unguarded speech.

$\mathcal{G}$*odly woman,*

CHOOSE STONES CAREFULLY FROM YOUR STREAM OF CONSCIOUSNESS.

$\mathscr{I}$gnorance

Verse: "He is able to deal gently with those who are ignorant and are going astray, since he himself is subject to weakness" (Hebrews 5:2).

> *"Stupidity is the deliberate cultivation of ignorance"*
> (WILLIAM GADDIS).

Reflection: The reference to "he" in the above verse isn't to Jesus, as we might at first suppose without a context, but to "every [other] high priest." Despite the comforting tone of these words, I'll have to say that there's nothing more aggravating to me than the person who knowingly and willingly fosters ignorance, who simply doesn't want to know about anything that might challenge her preconceived beliefs.

Dr. Martin Luther King Jr. had something to say about this kind of deliberate head burying: "Nothing in the world is more dangerous than a sincere ignorance and conscientious stupidity." No doubt Dr. King wasn't equating the two. The ignorant or uninformed person may be anything but stupid. But a combination of the two, particularly in a Christian, can be lethal.

The issue of non-deliberate ignorance, when it comes to the things of God, is a thorny one. We simply don't know this side of eternity how God will deal with those who have never heard the good news of the gospel, who were raised in sincerity in other religions, or who have died in infancy.

Of one thing, though, we can be certain: Our own great high priest, Jesus Christ, not only can but *will* deal gently and fairly with those who have gone astray on the basis of unintentional ignorance.

Prayer Prompt: Does it trouble you not to know the answers to questions about the spiritually uninitiated? Can you trust God to make all things right?

odly woman,

TRUST HIS JUDGMENT AND FAIRNESS (REMEMBERING THAT FAIR DOESN'T NECESSARILY MEAN EQUAL).

$\mathcal{F}$ull of overcoming

Verse: "Do not be overcome by evil, but overcome evil with good" (Romans 12:21).

> *"Although the world is full of suffering, it is also full of the overcoming of it"* (HELEN KELLER).

Reflection: At first glance there seems to be a qualitative difference between the evil that's done to us by other people and that which God allows Satan to bring directly to bear on our situation. But from the larger perspective we see that our suffering comes down to the continuing presence of evil in this sad world.

I've always been amazed by the ability of Helen Keller to overcome absolute darkness and silence in the way she did. In light of my own passion for the written word, I'm perhaps most impressed by her sensitive and lucid writing style, her ability to capitalize on fine nuances to make her point in the most memorable and impactful way. Much of the credit, of course, goes to her equally amazing teacher.

Anne Sullivan's own challenges with eyesight contributed greatly to her empathy, patience, and instinct for knowing where to begin. And the same can be said for any of us whose lives have in one way or another been touched by evil (that would, of course, be all of us). There's a difference between sympathy (feeling sorry for someone) and empathy (feeling sorrow—or joy, or whatever the emotion—along with or alongside someone else). It takes suffering for us to understand another's experience with evil.

Listen to Paul's words in 2 Corinthians 1:3–4: "Praise be to the God and Father of our Lord Jesus Christ, the Father of compassion and the God of all comfort, who comforts us in all our troubles, so that we can comfort those in any trouble with the comfort we ourselves receive from God." What a marvelous insight on the up side of pain! As believing women, let's be ready to move beyond suffering and evil to help fill our world with its overcoming!

Prayer Prompt: Ask God to show you what suffering in your life has uniquely equipped you to come alongside a sister or brother in Christ.

$\mathcal{G}$*odly woman,*

SHARE YOUR OVERCOMING.

*W*ell-kept secret?

Verse: "I have learned the secret of being content in any and every situation" (Philippians 4:12).

"Do not spoil what you have by desiring what you have not;
remember that what you have now was once among the things you
only hoped for" (EPICURUS).

Reflection: As a teenager in a house bursting with family (there were nine of us), I learned a wardrobe technique that stood me in good stead through high school and well into college and the decade of my twenties. "Closet shopping," as I liked to call it, can take various forms, from mixing and matching new combinations to stashing away some items for a period of time until we get over our boredom with them or they come back in style. For the adolescent me, this activity involved rooting through our well-stocked hall closet for a pattern (all four of us "girls" could adapt the same size), fabric, thread, and "notions" (zippers, buttons, snaps, hooks and eyes, bias tape, lace, and the like).

Much of the fabric had been purchased at ridiculously low sale prices (like $ .29/yard for a cotton print), and there was generally enough "material" for whatever option we chose (each pattern offered variations). When I got the yen for something new, all I needed was a little time, ingenuity (not that my youthful creations were all that spectacular), and motivation.

To say the least, times have changed; I gave up sewing decades ago. But I still look back with some fondness on that aspect of my earlier "material"-istic satisfaction.

What adaptations have taught you a secret or two about contentment? Whether born of desire or necessity, how much gratification have you derived from your distinctive method of achieving a goal?

Prayer Prompt: How close do you come to resonating with Paul's statement?

odly woman,
DO YOU KNOW—AND SHARE—THE SECRET?

$\mathscr{C}$omparison

Verse: "For who makes you different from anyone else? What do you have that you did not receive? And if you did receive it, why do you boast as though you did not? (1 Corinthians 4:7).

"We should not judge people by their peak of excellence; but by
the distance they have traveled from the point where they started"
(HENRY WARD BEECHER).

Reflection: Beecher's insightful observation, above, applies as much to our perception of our self as of anyone else. Perhaps particularly when it comes to the often cut-throat world of work, it's probably safe to say that competition has never been stronger than it is today. We humans peak at so many different elevations, and comparison with others can become a never-ending story.

How high do we have to climb before we can be content with our selves—just the way God made us? At what point do we let go of our felt need to surpass others to just embrace the prospect of meeting or surpassing our own expectations? I recognize that the emphasis in the marketplace on "career pathing" tends to denigrate the woman who would be content in her current position for the duration of her working "lifetime." But is there anything intrinsically wrong with that kind of satisfaction?

For those of us who are striving, by the grace of God, to increase in Christ-likeness, nothing else matters anyway. "Not many of you were wise by human standards," Paul reminds the Corinthian Christians, "not many were influential; not many were of noble birth. But God chose the foolish things of the world to shame the wise; God chose the weak things of the world to shame the strong. He chose the lowly things of this world and the despised things—and the things that are not—to nullify the things that are, so that no one may boast before him" (1 Corinthians 1:26–29).

Prayer Prompt: How satisfied are you with your self and your status? In what areas are you striving to better yourself—and why?

$\mathscr{G}$odly woman,

HE CHOSE AND EQUIPS YOU!

God's eternal purpose

Verses: "Join with me in suffering for the gospel, by the power of God. He has saved us and called us to a holy life—not because of anything we have done but because of his own purpose and grace" (2 Timothy 1:8–9).

"All men should strive to learn before they die, what they are running from, and to, and why" (JAMES THURBER).

Reflection: Several years ago I heard a speaker explain in this way the difference between *cause* and *purpose*: Cause has to do with the past and asks Why? Purpose has to do with the future and asks What for?

The word *cause* doesn't appear often in Scripture. When it does, the context generally has to do with the impetus for sinning or tempting someone else to sin. In the words of Jesus, "If your eye causes you to stumble, gouge it out and throw it away" (Matthew 18:9). Understanding why I've slipped can help prevent a repeat. Jesus was, of course, using hyperbole.

If something on the TV or Internet "causes" (or tempts) me to sin, my first recourse is to turn it off. If a more extreme measure proves necessary, I'm wise to cancel the service.

God's Word throughout is much more interested in purpose than in cause. In fact, God's eternal purpose is central to the Bible's ongoing story.

When I'm caught, or catch myself, in sin, I do well to figure out what triggered my misstep. But I won't get far in my Christian life if I fail to move beyond the *why* of my lapses to the *what for* of a holy life. The positive motivations of love and gratitude will be infinitely more effective than all the preventative measures in the world.

Prayer Prompt: How much thought do you give to the purpose behind Christ-like living?

odly woman,

FOCUS ON THE *WHAT FOR.*

$\mathcal{P}$recaution

Verse: "The prudent see danger and take refuge, but the simple keep going and pay the penalty" (Proverbs 22:3).

"A danger foreseen is half avoided" (PROVERB).

Reflection: Driving home from work years ago, I was approaching an intersection when I noticed other drivers slowing to a bewildered stop. It was then that I saw it—the older model pickup from the cross street, backing slowing into the shared roadway against the red light from my right. The driver, a shaggy, panting mutt with front paws slung over the wheel, seemed to make eye contact with me as the truck proceeded, slow motion, into the intersection.

The thunk of metal on metal was inevitable, thankfully causing little damage. Upon turning the corner, I found myself face-to-face with a sweating, arm-pumping man, charging down the middle of my lane after his runaway ride.

That anecdote from years back was funny—until last year when I drove up to the office of a client to pick up a freelance editorial assignment. The reception desk being only steps from my idling car, I left three-year-old Adelyn strapped in her car seat while I ran in. By the time I returned only seconds later, my granddaughter was behind the wheel, exploring—too engrossed with possibilities to make eye contact with her momentarily panicked grandma.

How different the context of a scene similar enough in my mind to trigger a flashback! It's all about perspective, isn't it?

Prayer Prompt: In what ways are you courting unnecessary danger (as opposed to tolerating potentially productive risk) in your life?

$\mathcal{G}$*odly woman,*
REMAIN ALERT.

$\mathcal{L}$eaping like calves

Verse: "For you who revere my name, the sun of righteousness will rise with healing in its rays. And you will go out and frolic like well-fed calves" (Malachi 4:2).

"If you have no joy, there's a leak in your Christianity somewhere"
(BILLY SUNDAY).

Reflection: What a delightful image! Have you ever actually watched a cavorting calf? You might think you were witnessing a bad case of bovine ADHD. Human kids act similarly. Position yourself outside an elementary school as it disgorges its kids. You can't fail to miss a common behavior: They *run*. Almost all of them. Whether they have to traverse ten steps to the bus queue or the two blocks home.

When was the last time you leaped? When did you dance like Tevye in *Fiddler on the Roof* or like David returning the ark of the covenant/testimony to Jerusalem? (1 Chronicles 15:28–29; see my meditation for March 11). *Not!?*

Well, then, David in Psalm 28 describes a dance you might sound more doable: "My heart leaps for joy, and with my song I praise [the LORD]" (verse 7). That works for me, but I also want my joy over God's healing presence to have a public component.

How do you express your jubilation over the restoration you've experienced?

Prayer Prompt: Before thanking God for his healing and redemption, envision the release of dancing before him without inhibition.

odly woman,

FIND WHAT WORKS FOR YOU TO EXPRESS YOUR JOY.

My sister, my friend

Verse: "Accept one another, then, just as Christ accepted you, in order to bring praise to God" (Romans 15:7).

> *"Disability is a matter of perception. If you can do just one thing well, you're needed by someone"* (MARTINA NAVRATILOVA).

Reflection: It's easy to write off people who don't "have what it takes" in life. I was surprised by how nervous I felt the first night of my commitment, two years ago, to function as a mentor to a disabled "friend" as part of a church ministry program. *How do I talk to these people?* I asked myself, approaching a clot of friends, some wheelchair bound, others wearing helmets or grimacing with facial contortions.

What a difference time makes. When I attend meetings today, I look forward to the group camaraderie. Whether touching base before the meeting, singing to rhythm instruments, applauding soloists (including those limited to unintelligible noises), sharing prayer requests, reenacting Bible stories, working on crafts, or playing bingo, we experience mutual blessing. No holds are barred in terms of communication, and group laughs are contagious.

Linda, my wheelchair-bound mentee, is approximately my age. Highly opinionated on many issues, she gets excited when I wear "blocks" (fabric with a geometric pattern) and is never without a plush snake around her neck to ward off bugs or rowdy friends.

Linda recalls and shares the context of when and how she learned each hymn or gospel song. She gets down about her seizures or her brother's cancer, but when something strikes her as funny her chortles are heartfelt. Linda is my friend, my sister in Christ.

Prayer Prompt: What criteria do you use to assess the "value" of other people?

Godly woman,
EACH OF US IS EVERYTHING TO HIM.

$\mathcal{B}$ack to your people

Verses: "Then Naomi said to her two daughters-in-law, 'Go back, each of you, to your mother's home. . . .' Then she kissed them goodbye and they wept aloud" (Ruth 1:8–9).

"How far you go in life depends on your being tender with the young, compassionate with the aged, sympathetic with the striving and tolerant of the weak and strong. Because someday in life you will have been all of these" (GEORGE WASHINGTON CARVER).

Reflection: Some time ago I had occasion to converse with a smartly dressed Bosnian sales associate. She was amazed at the number of American young people setting up independent housekeeping. In her country, unmarried adults remain in their birth homes for a lifetime. Multigenerational households are common.

This is becoming increasingly true in the United States as well. "Blending" may include sons- or daughters-in-law (sometimes with kids from previous relationships), as well as family members from up to four generations. (In my case the household has included—repeatedly for months at a time—an ex-son-in-law, his girlfriend, her son, and my three grandchildren [at times four children under age four].) This phenomenon is cyclical in American culture, with an upsweep whenever the economy trends downward.

The word *family* is fluid in the current English vocabulary. It's a displaced term, seeking definition in the midst of flux and shakedown.

If you (singular or plural), like me, are juggling the challenges of a multigenerational blended household, particularly if you're at the center, feeling a need to choreograph the whole complicated dance, you can do no better than to remain close to your heavenly Father, your true patriarch and enabler. Your well-being is closer to his heart than you can imagine.

Prayer Prompt: Make your own or another intergenerational or otherwise blended family the focus of your prayer.

odly woman,
BE OPEN TO INTERGENERATIONAL DEPENDENCY.

Risk and reward

Verses: "I have been constantly on the move. I have been in danger from rivers, in danger from bandits, in danger from my fellow Jews. . . . For Christ's sake, I delight in weaknesses, in insults, in hardships, in persecutions, in difficulties. For when I am weak, then I am strong" (2 Corinthians 11:26; 12:10).

> *"Come to the edge. We might fall. Come to the edge. It's too high! Come to the edge! And they came, and he pushed . . . and they flew"* (CHRISTOPHER LOGUE).

Reflection: Many of us can relate to that millisecond of terror when we release a toddler for his first solo flight in a "big" swing. Is his diaper-clad rear end too far back? Will he remember to clutch both chains with those pudgy fingers, and will he be strong enough to hold on?

If my time frame is correct for this memory, during the spring after Mom's death an aunt on her side invited us older kids to join some extended family overnight at a California mountain lodge. Dad, the fire prevention officer, rightly assessing the old house as a firetrap, at first reneged on the overnight promise but later relented.

But a more obvious danger—not to mention a strong allure—beckoned from the yard. A swing, suspended by long, thick ropes, dangled from the branch of a tall tree near the end of a precipitous drop-off to the road.

Repeated flights on that swing turned out to be the epitome of thrill—a thrill I would never have experienced had I calculated the risks and avoided the danger.

Prayer Prompt: What risks have you been willing to take, particularly in terms of your Christian service? What rewards have you—or others—experienced as a direct result?

Godly woman,

DON'T MISTAKE YOUR BOUNDARIES WITH THE PERIMETER OF YOUR COMFORT ZONE.

$\mathcal{S}$cattering the seed

Verse: "The wind blows wherever it pleases. You hear its sound, but you cannot tell where it comes from or where it is going. So it is with everyone born of the Spirit" (John 3:8).

"I believe in the surprises of the Holy Spirit" (L. J. SUENENS).

Reflection: Come May in our "neck o' the woods" we cycle rapidly through two mini seasons in terms of output from the sky. Long about midmonth we experience a perfect storm of maple-tree whirlybirds, reminding me of thousands of little parachutists landing from hovering copters. Annabelle, Khristina's lab-mix puppy, loves nothing better than to chase and pounce as the wind carries and then drops phalanxes of these intruders in sudden, lurching swirls.

We experience a short respite before the cottonwoods become active, coordinating with the wind to blow white fuzzies into my yard until the junction of lawn and driveway looks like the beginnings of a snowdrift. The lake in front of my condo becomes covered with these weightless floaties, its placid surface looking like a table top in need of dusting. The winds are wasteful in terms of scattering nature's seed, but scatter it they do.

In Jesus' words in the verse above, the Spirit behaves in much the same way as the wind in terms of scattering the "seeds" of regeneration and renewal. The Holy Spirit works sovereignly and with a less than predictable pattern, but his efforts are anything but willy-nilly.

Come May in Christ's church, we commemorate the season of Pentecost. Let's pause to appreciate together the mighty, productive wind of the Spirit.

Prayer Prompt: Thank the Lord for the tireless working of his Spirit.

odly woman,

NEVER UNDERESTIMATE THE HOLY SPIRIT.

*W*ith all your heart

Verses: "Whatever you do, work at it with all your heart, as working for the Lord, not for human masters. . . . It is the Lord Christ you are serving" (Colossians 3:23–24).

"Efficiency is doing things right; effectiveness is doing the right things" (PETER DRUCKER).

Reflection: Many people dislike busywork, the upside being that it prevents us on occasion from having to think too hard or too "big picture." From my perspective mundane tasks can be a welcome reprieve. As an editor I'm often content to breeze along in a copyedit mode (correcting sentence structure, grammar, punctuation, etc., as it flows by me), as opposed to tackling a macro or content edit, which involves evaluating the integrity, logic, and organization of a manuscript.

All of us work at a variety of tasks, and some of us require more or less stimulation than others. Even if your job is high-energy and calls for creative, proactive thinking, the chances are you still spend time filling out reports—or filling up the dishwasher.

Even if you dislike repetitive work, are you willing, for Christ's sake, to put your heart into it? Are you willing to volunteer for some mundane task in his service? In terms of their kingdom value, he doesn't differentiate among the services you render in his name.

Prayer Prompt: How much excitement, incentive, and reward to do require in your work? Are you willing at times to forego this stimulation in the interest of service?

G odly woman,

WORK WHOLEHEARTEDLY—NO MATTER WHAT THE TASK AT HAND.

"*I* heard that story 'afore!'"

Verses: "These commandments that I give you today are to be on your hearts. Impress them on your children. Talk about them when you sit at home and when you walk along the road, when you lie down and when you get up" (Deuteronomy 6:6–7).

> *"Children can tell you what Channel 7 says, but not what Matthew 7 says"* (LEONARD RAVENHILL).

Reflection: I'll have to admit to being less than consistent in reading Bible stories to Adelyn. On a recent Sunday morning the story of baby Moses was covered in the three-year-old class. The paper came home with Addie, and I picked it up a few days later. As I launched into the reading, she interrupted in an excited squeal, *"Granna, I heard that story 'afore!"*

Recognition of this simple narrative had touched a chord in Addie, and her response in turn fingered me. How could I overlook the importance of weaving these essential stories into the formation of her character? They won't get there by osmosis. I recall a poignant story, shared by an adoption social worker, of a teen mom who asked in perfect innocence of her one-year-old, "When will she know her ABCs?"

This incident with Addie served for me as a gentle reminder of the importance of equipping the rising generation with the stories on which our faith is founded and grounded. The competing voices in today's fraying society make the need for faith training that much more urgent.

Lyrics from a song we sing in our church come back to me: "How will they know, unless we tell them so?"

Prayer Prompt: Before approaching God, reflect on the inestimable gift of his Word.

odly woman.

PLAY A ROLE IN THE TELLING.

Coming or going?

Verses: "The LORD will keep you from all harm—he will watch over your life; the LORD will watch over your coming and going both now and forevermore" (Psalm 121:7–8).

*"We live longer than our forefathers; but we suffer more from
a thousand artificial anxieties and cares. They fatigued only
the muscles, we exhaust the finer strength of the nerves"*
(EDWARD GEORGE BULWER-LYTTON).

Reflection: "I'm so busy I don't know half the time whether I'm coming or going." Have you ever stated this or something similar? It's my guess that most of us can relate to the experience of being so preoccupied behind the wheel that we either take a familiar route that doesn't lead to where we're intending to go or arrive at our intended destination with little recall of the process.

Stress, while potentially healthful for us (if nothing else, it kicks in the flight or fight response when appropriate), can also be decidedly detrimental to our health. I don't view anxiety so much as a manifestation of God's image in me as a mechanism by which I, as a limited human being in a sinful world, react to evil.

How comforting to know that God doesn't stress out. That he can separate me in the first place from the harm I would otherwise need to fight or flee. That he'll keep track of my coming and going, as well as the details of my route, even when my brain seizes up. And that he'll keep on doing it forever!

Prayer Prompt: In what ways is negative stress affecting your life?

Godly woman,
RELINQUISH THE STRESSING AND BASK IN HIS BLESSING.

*G*od's braille

Verse: "Do your best to present yourself to God as one approved, a worker who does not need to be ashamed and who correctly handles the word of truth" (2 Timothy 2:15).

"The longer the teabag sits in the cup, the stronger the tea.
The more God's word saturates our minds, the clearer our
grasp on what's important to him and the stronger our prayers"
(STEVEN ESTES).

Reflection: "You cannot help but learn more as you take the world into your hands," reflects John Updike. "Take it up reverently, for it is an old piece of clay, with millions of thumbprints on it." Archaeologists know the importance of careful handling of the earth in a dig. Once evidence from the past has been damaged or destroyed, it goes without saying that it can never be recovered.

In similar fashion, we're responsible for reverent and proper handling of God's Word. We have so much to learn as we take up that Word in our hands. It too is old, fingerprinted by millions of others before and alongside us. And it, too, requires reverential treatment.

More importantly, it occurs to me that we're running our hands over God's own fingerprints as we thumb the pages of his Word. Going back to the John Updike quote, it's the same way with the world. Yes, it bears the image of millions of human prints. More to the point, though, the universe formed by God's own fingers lies at our disposal. Whether we're taking in God's general, natural revelation or his special, written revelation, we're running our fingertips, like a sightless person using Braille, over his prints, hoping to learn everything we can.

Prayer Prompt: How anxious are you to learn more and more as you study God's Word and world?

odly woman,
APPRECIATE HIS REVELATION.

$\mathcal{S}$acred sensibilities

Verse: "Be careful, however, that the exercise of your rights does not become a stumbling block to the weak" (1 Corinthians 8:9).

"Being offended is a natural consequence of leaving the house"
(FRAN LEBOWITZ).

Reflection: The book of fairy tales I gave Adelyn last Christmas looks and feels like her Bible story book. When I offered last night to read her a story, she picked it up, announcing, "This one—my Bible." I reminded her that this particular book contained fairy tales, to which she insisted, "Yup, my Bible, my princess Bible." An endorsement on the cover of one of Khristina's dog books refers to the work as something like "the Bible of dog care"; my dictionary does allow for "bible" to be applied to any authoritative publication.

I have trouble with that personally, much as I do with my daughter Angie's decision as a young adult to go by Angel. Another minor item on my personal squirm list: Popular at work a few years back was the phrase "It's not a hill to die on" (meaning that compromise on the issue was possible). Too close to Golgotha/Calvary for my comfort.

About what biblical terminology are you sensitive? Referring to something held dear as "sacred"? To a difficult situation as "a living hell"? I doubt there's anything inherently wrong with any of these terms. The issue has everything to do with our own sensibilities or those of our listeners.

The behavioral habits and tolerances of Christians vary widely. If you're aware that your words or behaviors are ruffling another believer's sensibilities, are you willing to accommodate, even if only in their presence?

Prayer Prompt: What fellow believer might you be offending in some way? Are you more inclined to flaunt your freedom or to treat the issue with tact and understanding?

$\mathcal{G}$*odly woman,*
EXERCISE YOUR LIBERTY WITH CARE AND CARING.

Above circumstances

*F*OR THE MONTH of June I invite you to share with me what I'm calling "Thirty Biblical Health and Beauty Tips." There's no myrrh, perfume, or cosmetics involved; the beauty we seek is of a different sort entirely: "Charm is deceptive, and beauty is fleeting; but a woman who fears the LORD is to be praised" (Proverbs 31:30).

Verse: "She is clothed with strength and dignity; she can laugh at the days to come" (Proverbs 31:25).

> *"Laughter is the closest thing to the grace of God"* (KARL BARTH).

Reflection: 1. LIVE ABOVE CIRCUMSTANCES. The description of the "wife of noble character" in Proverbs 31 is both enlightening and inspiring. It would seem that the twentieth-century Superwoman (or its somewhat more realistic twenty-first-century equivalent) has been around since time immemorial. Verses 30 and 31 climax this memorable ending to the book of Proverbs, and the centrality of fearing the Lord in this "beauty regimen" comes through clearly.

The verse above, however, particularly catches my eye, as well as my fancy. What kind of laughter would "become" this noble wife? Not the scorn of a woman hardened to grim realities.

Perhaps a capacity for delight in spite of situational ups and downs is more what the writer had in mind. The ability to live and laugh graciously, under God and above the flux of circumstances: Now there's a beautiful thing!

Prayer Prompt: What do honoring God and living above anxiety have in common?

Godly woman,
LIVE UNDER GOD, NOT THE WEATHER OR OTHER VARIABLES.

$\mathcal{B}$ought at a price

Verses: "You are not your own; you were bought at a price. Therefore honor God with your bodies" (1 Corinthians 6:19–20).

"Beauty, unaccompanied by virtue, is as a flower without perfume"
(ANONYMOUS PROVERB).

Reflection: 2. REMEMBER WHERE YOUR BEAUTY CAME FROM. Honor God with it. If there's one thing in this world that belongs to you, it's your body, right? Depending on your degree of comfort in your skin, you might wish you could auction it off to the first bidder.

But slow down there, says Paul. The truth is that your body isn't yours at all. Not only that, but you'll live in that body—in its redeemed (Christ-purchased) and transformed state—after the resurrection through all eternity. The body God has assigned to you is intrinsic to the package that is you.

Paul's mandate in verse 20, above, has to do with sexual behavior as it affects us physically, but the principle of honoring God with our bodies encompasses other areas as well: health, well-being, nourishment, conditioning, cleanliness, modesty, appropriateness, and presentability, to name only a few.

Through his atoning death Jesus Christ has purchased all of you (all, that is, of you in the singular).

Prayer Prompt: As an image bearer of your Creator, what responsibilities do you have with regard to your physicality?

Godly woman,
HONOR HIM FOR AND WITH YOUR BODY.

$\mathcal{M}$utual submission

Verse: "Wives, submit yourselves to your own husbands as you do to the Lord" (Ephesians 5:22).

> *"Submission is like a dance. If you have ever seen a partner*
> *dance then you know there can be only one leader. If they both*
> *try to lead they step all over each other and they do not flow. . . .*
> *Ephesians 5 tells us to respect our husbands. We need to respect*
> *them enough to allow them to lead us in this dance of life"*
> (ANGELA AT REFRESH MY SOUL BLOG).

Reflection: 3. HONOR YOUR HUSBAND. Many women today bristle at this business of honoring one's husband, to the point that some brides opt to scratch honor and submission from their vows. While it's true that not all men are honor*able* or even safe, God's will for us isn't thereby altered.

There is, of course, a subtle difference between honor and submission. In a certain sense the first is an attitude of heart, a respect for the other's position, while the second is a voluntary action. We can, for example, respect the station of someone who is acting in defiance of God's law even as we, in good conscience, choose not to obey them.

A lot of words to cover the exception! What Paul had in mind was the norm for Christian marriage. Paul was advocating mutuality, mandating from the guys' side: "However, each one of you also must love his wife as he loves himself" (verse 33). Mutual submission is a natural outgrowth of mutual love. It's also the root of a beautiful marriage.

I'm drawn to an anonymous quote on the subject of a well-functioning marital relationship: "You make me happier than I ever thought I could be and if you let me I will spend the rest of my life trying to make you feel the same way."

Prayer Prompt: Do you find that your love makes you want to submit? To your husband, if you're married? To God?

odly woman,

SUBMIT TO GOD AND TO YOUR SPOUSE.

*N*ot so fast!

Verse: "Marriage should be honored by all, and the marriage bed kept pure" (Hebrews 13:4).

> *"He that but looketh on a plate of ham and eggs to lust after it hath already committed breakfast with it in his heart"* (C. S. LEWIS).

Reflection: 4. KEEP THOSE BED LINENS SPOTLESS. God takes adultery very seriously, so seriously that this sin warranted the death penalty for his biblical people. Even so, it's easy for most of us to pass right over the seventh commandment, as we do the sixth (on murder). We glibly mark these off with a mental "n/a" before moving on to stealing and lying, which are much more likely at some level to apply to us.

Hold it right there! says God. In Jesus' words, "Anyone who looks at a woman lustfully has already committed adultery with her in his heart" (Matthew 5:28; change a noun and switch two pronouns to apply Christ's words to yourself as a woman). In the same way, our Lord had just equated hatred with murder (verse 21–22).

God isn't trying to trap us in a catch-22. Adultery of the heart is a deadly serious matter. More than ever before, a particularly insidious form of adultery (and fornication) is taking place in the privacy of the homes and hearts of believing women around the globe.

How easy it is for us as Christians to convince ourselves that we're hurting no one as we first dabble and then immerse ourselves in Internet porn. Like it or not, this sin has become epidemic in Christian circles.

Prayer Prompt: At what level are you guilty of breaking the seventh commandment?

*G*odly woman,

FLEE FROM SEXUAL TEMPTATION.

$\mathcal{M}$otherhood

Verse: "Her children arise and call her blessed" (Proverbs 31:28).

"The phrase 'working mother' is redundant" (JANE SELLMAN).

Reflection: 5. TAKE MOTHERHOOD SERIOUSLY. It's a sacred calling from God. In a world where making a living consumes so much of us, it's easy to feel guilty about a lack of time and energy expenditure on our kids. The fact is, though, that being the recipients of our undivided attention isn't their greatest need.

An observation by Mother Teresa rings true for me: "Love begins at home, and it is not how much we do . . . but how much love we put in that action." The wife and mom of Proverbs 31 was busy too, using artificial illumination, as we do, at both ends of the dark/light cycle. (It took years, BTW, for me as a kid to figure out that "both ends" in that saying refers to the darkness and not the candle!)

My guess is that the biggest difference between motherhood in our day and motherhood in most previous generations is that so much of our energy is expended in isolation from our children. When we are together, we need to do all we can to maximize the quality of our interaction. Reciprocal giving, accepting, and sharing are mutually satisfying and effective.

It has been observed that kids are never more serious than when they're playing—preparing for adulthood, trying on roles. Along the same lines, what child doesn't love being a helper? From baking cookies to folding towels to feeding the dog to "tightening" a screw, little ones relish working alongside a parent.

My own stay-at-home mom taught me all kinds of skills in my very early years. In many cases technology matured much faster than I did (I don't, for example, spend any time dampening and rolling men's hankies for ironing). But those early moments with a mom who died when I was eleven remain dear to me. They're a big part of how I remember her love. And those memories are indeed beautiful.

Prayer Prompt: How do you interact most meaningfully with your children of whatever age?

odly woman,
DON'T UNDERESTIMATE YOUR INFLUENCE.

ℋonoring Mom and Dad

Verses: "'Honor your father and mother'—which is the first commandment with a promise—'so that it may go well with you and that you may enjoy long life on the earth'" (Ephesians 6:2–3).

> *"There was no respect for youth when I was young, and now that I am old, there is no respect for age—I missed it coming and going"*
> (J. B. PRIESTLY).

Reflection: 6. HONOR YOUR OWN MOM AND DAD. For years the logical side of me wondered about this commandment with a promise—a promise with so many tragic exceptions. In fact, it wasn't until several years ago that it was explained to me that the book of Proverbs is about general principles, not hard-and-fast rules.

(I had the same problem with David's observation in Psalm 37:25: "I was young and now I am old, yet I have never seen the righteous forsaken or their children begging bread." *"Come on, David,"* I wanted to argue. *"Never?"* Biblical writers simply weren't concerned about closing up those exception loopholes.)

It occurs to me that, if you as an adult are still honoring your mom and dad, they've been blessed with a degree of longevity. On a purely genetic basis, it's quite possible that you will be too. It's also probable that, if you're still honoring your parents, life has gone reasonably well for you and for them. At least there hasn't been a generational rift—or the need for one. If your spiritual ancestry includes your parents, do you treasure that legacy?

Prayer Prompt: What's the quality of your relationship with your parents, if they're still living? What are you teaching your kids in this regard? Do you view generational honor as beautiful, as God does?

𝒢odly woman,

HOLD IN ESTEEM THE PARENTS HE CHOSE FOR YOU.

$\mathcal{M}$arital romance

Verse: "'How beautiful you are, my darling! Oh, how beautiful! Your eyes are doves'" (Song of Songs 1:15).

"If a June night could talk, it would probably boast it invented romance" (BERN WILLIAMS).

Reflection: 7. KEEP THE SPARK OF ROMANCE ALIVE. While we thrill to the imagery in, for example, Psalms and Isaiah, most of us find it difficult to relate to the writing style of Song of Songs. Have you actually, or recently, read this stuff?

Do you find it a little hard to keep a straight face when the lover (that's him) informs the beloved (her) that her teeth are like a flock of sheep or her nose like the tower of Lebanon? Strange similes aside, Song of Songs is, at its essence, a beautiful and uninhibited expression of the sensual love between husband and wife.

Unmarried as I am, I feel under-qualified to write on this subject. But this aspect of the well-being of a married couple is too essential to pass over. (I'm also taking Paul, an outspoken single on the marriage issue, as a kind of precedent!)

The infatuation of energetic young love fades, eventually giving way to the more mellow satisfaction of comfortable companionship. (Don't just assume, though, that your husband is too old for romancing.)

I suspect, though, that the danger lies not so much in youth or old age as in those middle years when couples become overextended, too preoccupied to show their love romantically or too complacent to see the need for it. Midlife crises don't "just happen." And it's up to each partner to do everything possible to ensure that they don't happen at all.

Prayer Prompt: On a romantic level, are you taking too much for granted in your marriage?

odly woman,

ROMANCE IS HIS GIFT FOR YOUR MARRIAGE—EVEN AFTER THE WEDDING.

Cows of Bashan

Verse: "Hear this word, you cows of Bashan on Mount Samaria, you women who oppress the poor and crush the needy and say to your husbands, 'Bring us some drinks!'" (Amos 4:1).

"None are so empty as those who are full of themselves"
(BENJAMIN WHICHCOTE).

Reflection: 8. CURB YOUR DESIRES AND CHECK YOUR DEMANDS. Can't you just picture a field of ample-bodied cows, contentedly chewing their cuds, the scene punctuated by an occasional, protracted *moooo*? This bovine imagery is comical to us.

But the picture could just as well apply to pampered women in any age. The point to me (if I can legitimately divorce the imagery from the intended metaphor for Israel) is that selfish and beautiful don't sit well together.

My daughter Khristina at one point worked for a foreign-born restaurateur who clucked his tongue to signify a desire to have his drink replenished. While his female relatives responded quickly enough, it took the American-born servers more time to "hear" him.

Gender aside, he, too, reminds me of a cow of Bashan. Amos's picture, above, seems too extreme to be taken seriously. But we do well to ask ourselves how a cow of Bashan might look and act in our day.

Prayer Prompt: Ask yourself seriously whether this picture of a spoiled or selfish woman in any way applies to you.

Godly woman,
PRACTICE SELFLESSNESS.

𝒫lip plop

Verses: "A quarrelsome wife is like the dripping of a leaky roof in a rainstorm; restraining her is like restraining the wind or grasping oil with the hand" (Proverbs 27:15–16).

> *"Three things drive a man outdoors; smoke, a leaking roof and a scolding wife"* (PROVERB).

Reflection: 9. AVOID NAGGING. Not to be overly graphic, but if you've ever been around a female cat in heat (as I have recently, for the first time), you know the definition of an annoying sound. The proverb above, which points out another obnoxious category of sound, comes from Solomon. We can bet that, with one thousand wives and concubines, this husband knew whereof he spoke. One faultfinding wife can generally be enough to turn away or tune out a husband.

Whether the issues fall within the "Honey do" or "Honey don't" category, the upshot is the same: Honey don't wanna hear it. Beyond that, nagging is by its nature counterproductive. In extreme cases it's been known to cause deafness.

If this scenario sounds familiar, chances are your husband has a completely different perspective than you do on the subject. Why not take the time to listen to his side?

The following quote from Guillermo Mordillo seems to me at least tangentially relevant: "After God created the world, He made man and woman. Then, to keep the whole thing from collapsing, He invented humor."

Prayer Prompt: If you even suspect that nagging may be an issue in your marriage, talk to your husband before taking it to God.

odly woman,

AVOID THE URGE TO NAG.

*M*oving on

Verse: "Better to live on a corner of the roof than share a house with a quarrelsome wife" (Proverbs 21:9).

"A happy marriage is the union of two good forgivers"
(ROBERT QUILLEN).

Reflection: 10. INVITE YOUR HUBBY DOWN FROM THE ROOF BEFORE HE TAKES A NASTY FALL. It may be that I'm reading too much into this verse. At face value it reiterates the issue of the badgering wife of yesterday. But a husband on the roof reminds me of a husband in the doghouse—or on the couch. The situation sounds a little more serious.

If you've ever found yourself in the position of having to deal with a spouse's marital indiscretion—or some other serious issue, like criminal activity or a porn, gambling, or substance addiction—you know what alienation is all about. But consider this: While the forced isolation you're free to bring about by imposing an unrelenting guilt trip may give you some smug satisfaction, it will do nothing to mend the rift.

It's quite conceivable that a relationship that has survived such upheaval may emerge the stronger and more beautiful for it. A new level of appreciation, an unwillingness to take the good for granted, may go a long way toward cementing your bond.

What it takes is forgiveness, unconditional and final. You can't move on while you're stuck in the past.

Prayer Prompt: Is a lack of forgiveness on your part standing between you and your husband?

*G*odly woman,
CONSIDER WELL THE IMPLICATIONS OF YOUR VOWS.

$\mathcal{T}$he "lived in" house

Verse: "The wise woman builds her house, but with her own hands the foolish one tears hers down" (Proverbs 14:1).

"Marrying is easy, it's housework that's hard" (PROVERB).

Reflection: 11. DON'T NEGLECT HOMEMAKING. "Like plowing," observes Letty Cottin Pogrebin, "housework makes the ground ready for the germination of family life. The kids will not invite a teacher home if beer cans litter the living room. The family isn't likely to have breakfast together if somebody didn't remember to buy eggs, milk, or muffins."

Any house can be a home, but that transition is never automatic or a foregone conclusion. I've been surprised over the years by how many male coworkers have confided to me that they wish their wives kept a neater, cleaner house.

The euphemism "lived in" can reflect that comfortable human touch difficult to achieve through an interior decorator—or a state of unrelenting turmoil. When it comes to stressors, clutter can be a major offender— enough to keep a frustrated spouse away from home.

The fact is that our home building has a lot to do with our homemaking. If your husband is stumbling over toys or riffling through overflowing stacks in quest of the bank statement, it may be time to adopt new habits.

Prayer Prompt: Is the situation at your house under—or out of—control?

odly woman,
PURSUE ORDER IN ALL ASPECTS OF LIFE.

Which temptation?

Verses: "Do not be wise in your own eyes; fear the Lord and shun evil. This will bring health to your body and nourishment to your bones" (Proverbs 3:7–8).

"Whatever we have of this world in our hands, our care must be to keep it out of our hearts, lest it come between us and Christ"
(MATTHEW HENRY).

Reflection: 12. AVOID PRIDE AND OVERINDULGENCE. It's interesting to me that the first woman sought to achieve wisdom (along with nourishment and aesthetic pleasure) *through* blatant disobedience to God: "When the woman saw that the fruit of the tree was *good for food* and *pleasing to the eye*, and also *desirable for gaining wisdom*, she took some and ate it" (Genesis 3:6, emphasis added).

In what contexts do we, like Eve, disregard godly living in order to unwisely acquire or enjoy something that in itself may be either good or neutral? Answers, of course, will be as varied as we are.

With regard to nourishment, we might be tempted to overdo a good thing or to satisfy our palates at the expense of our own physical well-being or that of someone else. Ditto aesthetic pleasure, especially when sexuality is a part of the picture. Food, drink, and worldly goods (including clothing and beauty aids) can all be enjoyed to excess, tempting us in the directions of addiction, idolatry, and vanity. And our desire for worldly wisdom can be just as insatiable, leading us toward arrogance and a false sense of independence from God.

Prayer Prompt: Of the three facets of temptation Eve faced, which is most alluring to you?

Godly woman,

DON'T INVITE THE BAD BY DABBLING IN AN UNHEALTHY OR UNGODLY
WAY WITH THE GOOD OR NEUTRAL.

$\mathcal{G}$ood cheer

Verse: "A cheerful heart is good medicine, but a crushed spirit dries up the bones" (Proverbs 17:22).

> *"Nobody says you must laugh, but a sense of humor can help you overlook the unattractive, tolerate the unpleasant, cope with the unexpected, and smile throughout the day"* (ANN LANDERS).

Reflection: 13. MAINTAIN A POSITIVE OUTLOOK. I've heard it said that a small child laughs an average of once every four minutes. That's a lot of endorphins released into those little brains, a lot of cushion against the inevitable pain of life. "At the height of laughter," says Jean Houston, "the universe is flung into a kaleidoscope of new possibilities." And Bill Cosby has this to say on the subject: "Through humor, you can soften some of the worst blows that life delivers. And once you find laughter, no matter how painful your situation might be, you can survive it."

It's difficult to maintain a negative outlook around merriment. Even if we don't know the context of the joke, a hearty laugh can be enough to make us smile or chuckle along. "A happy heart makes the face cheerful," notes Solomon in Proverbs 15:13. And a cheerful face is invariably beautiful.

When my mom first became sick years ago, Dad found it necessary to interview applicants for the position of "housekeeper." Not surprisingly, he was discouraged by the parade of candidates. I remember his comment after one interview that the woman's face would crack if she smiled. An impressionable eleven-year-old, I envisioned a slow but inexorable breakdown of collagen, culminating in her features imploding in on themselves. I was both impressed and relieved that Dad could see this coming.

There can be no doubt about it: A crushed spirit dries up the bones.

Prayer Prompt: Are you drawn more by attractive facial features or by a contagious smile?

odly woman,
LET OTHERS CATCH YOUR HAPPINESS.

$\mathcal{L}$aughing along

Verse: "Sarah said, 'God has brought me laughter, and everyone who hears about this will laugh with me'" (Genesis 21:6).

"Even if there is nothing to laugh about, laugh on credit"
(AUTHOR UNKNOWN).

Reflection: 14. LOL. For those of you who aren't texting savvy, that's "laugh out loud." The truth is that not all laughter is equal. Sarah's laughter of incredulous delight at Isaac's birth is such a refreshing contrast to her earlier, cynical laughter on overhearing God's "far-fetched" promise of a son. Can't you just see the years (and quite possibly the tears) falling from her careworn face as she lifts her voice in hilarity?

I've had an experience that reminds me of Sarah's, an experience that, in an understated way, seemed fully as miraculous. I began adopting children in the early 1980s, a decade in which the state of Michigan was reluctant to terminate birth-parental rights. A full ten years passed between my adoption of three-year-old Amanda and that of her sister Angela, then almost ten, a decade that passed for me with agonizing slowness. But the adoption of my second daughter involved for me a serendipity—a "coincidence" that seemed beyond belief.

I arrived at work one morning unaccountably excited, certain the long-awaited event was imminent. My observations to this effect to a coworker were interrupted by my first phone call of the morning, pulling me reluctantly back into my familiar round of "hurry up and wait." As we've all experienced at one time or another, it's hard to be all revved up with nowhere to go—hard to calibrate our exuberance for something we're sure is going to happen . . . sometime! I still get chills, though, when I remember that call: My social worker was on the line, advising me that a nine-year-old was "waiting for me."

I had guiltily reminded myself more than once during my less-than-patient wait of Sarah and Abraham's work-around, through Hagar, with regard to God's promise. Now, in contrast, I was able on a personal level to share in the laughter of Sarah.

Prayer Prompt: With what "improbable" blessing has God thrilled you? Have you remembered to thank him, then or lately?

$\mathcal{G}$*odly woman,*

HE DELIGHTS IN SURPRISING YOU.

*I*ntravenous strength

Verse: "In repentance and rest is your salvation, in quietness and trust is your strength" (Isaiah 30:15).

> *"Everything that slows us down and forces patience, everything*
> *that sets us back into the slow circles of nature, is a help.*
> *Gardening is an instrument of grace"* (MAY SARTON).

Reflection: 15. GET ADEQUATE REST. The passive imagery in the above verse strikes me at first as counterintuitive. I might have expected something more along the lines of "in proactivity and vigilance is your salvation; in conditioning and preparation is your strength."

The point, though, isn't that we're saved by our repentance and rest or that our strength lies in our passivity or trust. Repentance, rest, quietness, and trust all describe the modus operandi of the Christian, but we can and must take this stance because our salvation and strength come from an outside source. We're passive recipients of salvation and borrowers of strength. In much the same way that a person stranded on an ice floe must lie absolutely still, relying on outside intervention for rescue, so we need to give up our struggle to lend God unneeded assistance.

Rest and quiet are beautiful by-products of the salvation and strength we enjoy for the asking, based upon—but not merited by—our repentance from our sins and absolute trust in the finished work of Jesus Christ. God is the proactive force behind our salvation, the ever vigilant One whose eyes never close or wander, the all-powerful Savior and author of our redemption.

Prayer Prompt: Before approaching God with words, make a deliberate effort to divest yourself of anxiety and to lean completely on—or better yet *into*—his strength.

odly woman,

REST IN HIM.

$\mathscr{E}$arly to rise

Verses: "As a door turns on its hinges, so a sluggard turns on his bed" (Proverbs 26:14–15).

"My only hobby is laziness, which naturally rules out all others"
(GRANNI NAZZANO).

Reflection: 16. BE AN EARLY RISER. For a year following my college graduation I shared an apartment with three other girls. Over the holidays a student friend of one of my apartment mates requested permission to spend her Christmas break with us. Having finished the semester with some incompletes, she prepared us to expect that she would be working nonstop on papers. In reality, though, she managed to keep herself in a state of almost continuous slumber for two weeks. For obvious reasons I didn't get to know her well, but an observation by Watchman Nee seems to me to address the situation: "How often laziness and emotional distaste for work join to employ physical fatigue as a cover-up."

Not all instances of laziness or procrastination are this pronounced, of course, nor is there necessarily a serious physical, mental, or emotional issue involved. In the words of Peter Marshall, "Most of us know perfectly well what we ought to do; our trouble is that we do not want to do it."

The truth is that an early start to the day has a good chance of being a good start. On the other hand, there's nothing quite like running late from the get-go to introduce a harried day of running, late. In the words of Richard Whately, "Lose an hour in the morning, and you will spend all day looking for it."

Time spent enjoying a sunrise, listening to the twittering of birds, communing with God, breakfasting with loved ones, enjoying a quiet cup of coffee, running or exercising, walking the dog . . . you know what puts you in the frame of mind to maximize your day.

Prayer Prompt: At what time of day are you at your best? What time are you giving to God?

$\mathscr{G}$odly woman,
BEGIN EACH DAY WELL.

*E*very green plant

Verses: "Daniel then said to the guard, . . . 'Give us nothing but vegetables to eat.' . . . At the end of the ten days they looked healthier and better nourished than any of the young men who ate the royal food" (Daniel 1:11–12, 15).

> *"A vegetable garden in the beginning looks so promising and then after all little by little it grows nothing but vegetables, nothing, nothing but vegetables"* (GERTRUDE STEIN).

Reflection: 17. EAT YOUR VEGGIES. Then God said, "To . . . everything that has the breath of life in it . . . I give every green plant for food" (Genesis 1:30). Much to my personal relief, God in his mercy did later relent (see Genesis 9:3), incorporating the meat group into the human diet.

I clearly recall my mortification in kindergarten, where I was reduced to tears by my inability to swallow an increasingly large mouthful of the carrot Mom had sent along with me for my midmorning snack. (This was a *real* carrot, the large, misshapen kind that has to be peeled and can be nibbled from the sides to expose the greenish core.)

Don't get me wrong: I'm not veggie adverse so much as veggie indifferent (although I do favor carrot cake). For the most part, this food group just doesn't call out to me. In the words of Will Rogers, "An onion can make people cry, but there has never been a vegetable invented that can make them laugh." Or this from Doug Larson: "Life expectancy would grow by leaps and bounds if green vegetables smelled as good as bacon."

So here you have it: the closest I can come to an honest meditation on this (for me) troublesome nutritional principle. Hopefully it's less a stumbling block for a healthy you!

Prayer Prompt: Which of the Bible's clearly defined health principles poses the most difficulty for you?

odly woman,

ACCEPT AND USE WELL HIS NUTRITIONAL GIFTS.

*F*amily style

Verse: "Better a small serving of vegetables with love than a fattened calf with hatred" (Proverbs 15:17).

> *"Never argue at the dinner table, for the one who is not hungry always gets the best of the argument"* (RICHARD WHATELY).

Reflection: 18. AVOID MEALTIME SQUABBLES. In all fairness to the vegetable, meat was a luxury in the Israelite diet. But whether a family was eating in luxury or in poverty, Solomon's point was that love and togetherness are the mealtime factors that count. He was able to take it for granted that families sat down and ate together.

Novelist F. Scott Fitzgerald had this to say about discord within a family (a universal truth already in Solomon's day): "Family quarrels are bitter things. They don't go by any rules. They're not like aches or wounds; they're more like splits in the skin that won't heal because there's not enough material."

Whether the fare is fast-food pizza, grilled cheese sandwiches, or serious meat and potatoes (and other veggies), the opportunity afforded in the evening for family members to face one another around and across a table can go a long way toward cementing cohesion, respect, and understanding.

As an addendum, one of the by-products of real family dinners is the passing along of manners, whether in terms of table etiquette or of basic civilities. This principle goes beyond a cursory mouthing of the right words to statements that require empathy, emotional investment, and simple human kindness. "In some families," reflects Margaret Laurence, "*please* is described as the magic word. In our house, however, it was *sorry.*"

Prayer Prompt: In what context does your family commune together? Is God included?

Godly woman,

SHARED MEALTIMES BRING LOVED ONES TOGETHER.

*E*xercise as a fringe benefit

Verse: "[Ruth] came into the field and has remained here from morning till now, except for a short rest in the shelter" (Ruth 2:7).

"Honest labour bears a lovely face" (THOMAS DEKKER).

Reflection: 19. GET YOUR EXERCISE. Until modern times exercise for the sake of exercise was both unnecessary and nonexistent. Imagine walking wherever you went, often in swirling dust and blistering temperatures, clothed in ankle-length garments, and—I'll have to say it—without deodorant.

No need for weight-pumping power walks; much of the time you'd be toting a water jug or armloads of prickly hay anyway. Still, Ruth's outstanding work ethic was enough to attract the attention and admiration both of Boaz and of his field foreman.

"Concentrate all your thoughts on the work at hand," advised Alexander Graham Bell. "The sun's rays do not burn until brought to a focus."

I've long wondered how outdoor laborers bear up under climatic extremes but suspect that the answer has to do with involvement in the work itself. I assume that the construction worker or gardener who enjoys the work is able to focus on dreams and goals in much the same way I do when engrossed in editing or writing.

Prayer Prompt: Are you blessed with an ability to integrate meaningful exercise with purpose?

odly woman,

YOUR WORK ETHIC MATTERS.

ℒifelong learning

Verses: Solomon "spoke three thousand proverbs and his songs numbered a thousand and five. He spoke about plant life, from the cedar of Lebanon to the hyssop that grows out of walls. He also spoke about animals and birds, reptiles and fish" (1 Kings 4:32–33).

> *"There are no uninteresting things, there are only uninterested people"* (G. K. CHESTERTON).

Reflection: 20. EXERCISE YOUR MIND TOO. "The world," quipped Bertrand Russell, "is full of magical things patiently waiting for our wits to grow sharper." And I've always appreciated Christopher Plummer's quip in *The Sound of Music* that he suffered from "a deplorable lack of curiosity."

If we're honest with ourselves, many of us have that problem. My dad and his two brothers (no doubt his four sisters as well), none of them college educated, spent their lives learning all they could—for the sheer pleasure of it. I've always admired that in them.

Sadly, my own high school and college days were so devoted to earning grades that I avoided overtaxing my brain with extraneous learning. My daughter Khristina, on the other hand, who has accumulated by fits and starts a few semesters of community college, dreamed in her less work-focused days of mastering foreign languages and has dabbled in interests from architecture to trigonometry to mythology to Russian history.

I've long held the notion that our accumulated knowledge falls into the broader category of "things we can't take with us into the next phase of eternity." For a long time, consciously or otherwise, I believe I went so far as to devalue knowledge on that basis. But I'm no longer so sure. One way or another, I have no doubt that God encourages both our curiosity and our active inquiry.

Prayer Prompt: In what areas of knowledge are you still growing? Are you growing in wisdom?

𝒢odly woman,
YOU CAN NEVER LEARN TOO MUCH.

The race

Verses: "Let us throw off everything that hinders and the sin that so easily entangles, and let us run with perseverance the race marked out for us. Let us fix our eyes on Jesus" (Hebrews 12:1–2).

"In the confrontation between the stream and the rock, the stream always wins. Not through strength, but through persistence"
(H. JACKSON BROWN).

Reflection: 21. EXERCISE PATIENCE. The above quote, like the fable of the tortoise and the hare, reminds us that plodding often gets us farther in life's long run than intermittent sprinting. It's easy for women in this hectic world—a world in which the need to multitask can force us to function in a series of disjointed fits and starts—to suffer from a kind of self-inflicted ADHD that allows us to do little more than dabble and stab at life. A perfectionist at heart, I've spent most of my adulthood trying to find that delicate balance between doing it well and getting it done.

Oh, I'm persistent all right, but it's not always the kind of persistence that characterizes patience. I'm vulnerable to repeated frustration as life's jarring pace interrupts the flow for which I long.

So how do we maintain the poise of patience, that imperturbable calm we all recognize as beautiful and healthful when we see it? Most biblical references to patience have more to do with endurance in the face of trial than with negotiating irritations and interruptions, but both are intrinsic to Christ-likeness. And the second may well be the more difficult. Think of Jesus' response to disruptions and intrusions. We don't read about sighs or grudging resignation. Our Lord was fully present all of the time, ready to embrace the teachable or opportune moment.

In the verses above the author to the Hebrews touches, I believe, on the variable that matters: keeping our eyes on Jesus. With our Savior and Lord as our focus, our priorities will fall into place as they align with his.

Prayer Prompt: Do you struggle more with patience or with persistence? What would it take for you, with the Spirit's help, to synchronize the two?

odly woman,
LOOK BOTH AHEAD AND UP.

$\mathcal{A}$ beautiful heart

Verse: "The LORD does not look at the things people look at. People look at the outward appearance, but the LORD looks at the heart" (1 Samuel 16:7).

"God sees hearts as we see faces" (GEORGE HERBERT).

Reflection: 22. BE HEART SMART. An anonymous saying has it that if you have a song of faith in your heart, it will be "heard" by the look on your face. If that's true, our outward appearance reflects to others what God is already seeing/hearing in our heart.

No, there's no automatic face-lift involved here. But clear, sparkling eyes and lips turned more upward than downward will give a lift both to you and to all others you may encounter.

A benediction found in Numbers twice mentions God's face: "The LORD make his face shine on you and be gracious to you; the LORD turn his face toward you and give you peace" (6:25–26). And Exodus 34:29 tells us what happened to Moses as the result of speaking to God "face to face": "When Moses came down from Mount Sinai . . . , he was not aware that his face was radiant because he had spoken with the LORD." In Moses' case, the luminosity was so extreme the people were afraid to look at him.

What about us as Christ's representatives? Is the wonder of having been with the Lord reflected in the clarity of your gaze and the brightness of your smile? And if you are indeed smiling, is your heart where your mouth is?

Prayer Prompt: What do your expression and carriage tell others about your heart's condition?

$\mathcal{G}$*odly woman,*

YOUR FACE REFLECTS YOUR HEART.

$\mathcal{R}$eflected beauty

Verses: "Your beauty should not come from outward adornment. . . . Rather, it should be that of your inner self, the unfading beauty of a gentle and quiet spirit, which is of great worth in God's sight" (1 Peter 3:3–4).

"Not being beautiful was the true blessing. Not being beautiful forced me to develop my inner resources. The pretty girl has a handicap to overcome" (GOLDA MEIR).

Reflection: 23. CONCENTRATE ON YOUR INNER BEAUTY REGIMEN. I tend to be unfair to unusually attractive people—especially other women. They're suspect to me, "guilty" in my mind of snobbery and haughtiness until proven otherwise. Even when I see shining through them a gentle and quiet spirit, I'm wary of them, waiting for the biting remark, ungracious action, or evidence of superficiality I just know is coming. For a person like this to develop a beautiful inner spirit may in fact require an extra measure of grace; they do have a hurdle to overcome.

I don't know, of course, where you stand on the outer beauty spectrum. My physical asset is soft, expressive eyes, but other than that I've never seen myself as attractive. A younger, slimmer, tanner, and prettier cousin of mine looked me up and down at one point during my late teen years and made an observation intended, I think, as a compliment: "You're really not *that* ugly!" Sorry—didn't work! Why else would I remember it forty years later?

Pause for a moment to take inventory of the people who matter most in your life. Chances are they vary widely in terms of physical features. But if they're believers, my guess is that they share in common a reflection of the beauty of Jesus Christ, manifested through their demeanor, attitudes, words, and actions. Where do you stand—honestly—on the inner beauty spectrum?

Prayer Prompt: What makes you attractive to others? What kind of attractiveness do you seek?

odly woman,
HE VALUES A GENTLE SPIRIT.

$\mathcal{N}$ose ring

Verse: "Like a gold ring in a pig's snout is a beautiful woman who shows no discretion" (Proverbs 11:22).

> *"Temperance is moderation in the things that are good and total abstinence from the things that are foul"* (FRANCES E. WILLARD).

Reflection: 24. MAKE MODERATION YOUR MANTRA. Thomas Fuller, a seventeenth-century English clergyman, historian, and prolific author, had this to say about overindulgence: "Venture not to the utmost bounds of even lawful pleasures; the limits of good and evil join." Now there's some advice worthy in any age of a second look and thought.

My daughter Angie and I had occasion yesterday to spend some idle time in the lobby of our city's courthouse. Always curious, I enjoy the human aspect of a waiting area. While we were chatting, an attractive young woman in her twenties strutted in, clad in a scanty outfit that shouted "Look at me."

Angie and I exchanged a glance, asking each other how anyone could enter a courthouse in such attire—as did nearly everyone else around us. Nor was the ridiculous exhibition lost on the three middle-aged male court employees sitting around the security check area.

We were doubly shocked to realize shortly afterward that this attention-seeker was a court employee. This woman, who could have turned some appreciative heads, opted instead to call attention to the ring in her snout.

Prayer Prompt: In what areas is indulgence or indiscretion an issue for you?

$\mathcal{G}$odly woman,
PRACTICE MODERATION.

$\mathscr{B}$eautiful feet

Verse: "How beautiful on the mountains are the feet of those who bring good news, who proclaim peace, who bring good tidings, who proclaim salvation" (Isaiah 52:7).

"Go the extra mile. It's never crowded" (AUTHOR UNKNOWN).

Reflection: 25. KEEP UP THOSE PEDICURES. The imagery in the above verse was evidently familiar to God's people (note the similar wording in Nahum 1:15). I don't know what kind of good news either prophet had in mind with this analogy, but I am aware that fleet-footed messengers were regularly dispatched in Old Testament days to announce the outcome of a battle (see the gripping—and sobering—story told in 2 Samuel 1:1–16).

I can't help but contrast the image of beautiful feet with "feet that are quick to rush into evil" from Proverbs 6:18 (one of the seven things the Lord hates) or feet that are "swift to shed blood" (part of Paul's description of unregenerate people; see Romans 3:15).

On the positive side, I'm reminded of some beautiful Gospel imagery: John the Baptist's declaration of unworthiness to untie the thongs of Jesus' sandals (Luke 3:16); the sinful woman anointing Jesus' feet, first with her tears and then with expensive perfume (Luke 7:36–38); and Jesus kneeling to wash his disciples' grungy feet (John 13:1–17).

I find it instructive to consider both the vulnerability and the vital role of an individual's feet in ancient times. How effectively are you finishing the race Jesus has given you, "the task of testifying to the good news of God's grace" (Acts 20:24)?

Prayer Prompt: What in particular makes your feet, or their function, beautiful to God?

odly woman,
BE QUICK TO DO GOOD.

$\mathcal{H}$elping hands

Verses: "In Joppa there was a disciple named Tabitha . . . ; she was always doing good and helping the poor. . . . All the widows stood around [Peter], crying and showing him the robes and other clothing that Dorcas [aka Tabitha] had made while she was still with them" (Acts 9:36, 39).

"I'd help the homeless but I don't know where they live"
(SEEN ON BUMPER STICKER)

Reflection: 26. MIND YOUR MANICURES. Keep those hands busy with beauty. About a year ago I attended the funeral of an aunt, my dad's sister. On display at the funeral home were samples of her beautiful knitting projects—literally the work of a lifetime. Over a period of decades Aunt Mina had been in the loveliest sense a Dorcas for the poor in Grand Rapids, donating literally thousands of hand-knitted mittens, stocking caps, and scarves for inner-city children. And the Spirit sees to it that the kingdom is equipped with many quiet, faithful servants like her.

It can be easy for us to dismiss any felt responsibility for service (as opposed to financial donations) on the basis that we're lacking in skill. But the truth is that all of us have abilities that, if not marketable, are useful for the kingdom. "I am only one," declared Edward Everett Hale, "but I am one. I cannot do everything, but I can do something. And I will not let what I cannot do interfere with what I can do." This same early American author, historian, and clergyman is also quoted as inviting God's people to "Look up and not down. Look forward and not back. Look out and not in, and lend a hand."

A Swedish proverb has it that "The best place to find a helping hand is at the end of your own arm." What will you put forth your hand to do for the Lord?

Prayer Prompt: How are your hands extensions of Christ's on behalf of others?

$\mathcal{G}$odly woman,
DEVOTE YOURSELF TO HIS SERVICE.

ℱor such a time as this

Verse: "The king was attracted to Esther more than to any of the other women, and she won his favor and approval" (Esther 2:17). "If I have found favor with you, Your Majesty, and if it pleases you, grant me my life—this is my petition. And spare my people—this is my request" (Esther 7:3).

"Availability is better than ability for God" (AUTHOR UNKNOWN).

Reflection: 27. DON'T LET BEAUTY GO TO YOUR HEAD. Keep it down there in your heart where it belongs. "People are like stained-glass windows," reflects Elisabeth Kübler-Ross. "They sparkle and shine when the light is out, but when the darkness sets in their true beauty is revealed only if there is light from within."

How fitting for Esther: "When Esther's words were reported to Mordecai, he sent back this answer: 'Do not think that because you are in the king's house you alone of all the Jews will escape. For if you remain silent at this time, relief and deliverance for the Jews will arise from another place . . . . And who knows but that you have come to royal position for such a time as this?' Then Esther sent this reply to Mordecai: ' . . . I will go to the king, even though it is against the law. And if I perish, I perish'" (Esther 4:12–16).

Outstanding physical beauty may not be your (or my) doorway to influence, but God grants ample opportunity for each of us to accomplish good in his name. When have you found yourself "in the right place at the right time," as Esther was, in terms of the prospect of performing a service for God? Did you, like Esther, rise willingly to the occasion?

Prayer Prompt: Assess both the opportunities for good God has opened for you and your current level of response.

odly woman,

FOR WHAT OPPORTUNITY MIGHT HE BE PREPARING YOU?

$\mathcal{A}$ wordless heart

Verses: "But you, dear friends, by building yourselves up in your most holy faith and praying in the Holy Spirit, keep yourselves in God's love as you wait for the mercy of our Lord Jesus Christ to bring you to eternal life" (Jude 20–21).

> *"I strain toward God; God strains toward me. I ache for God; God aches for me. Prayer is mutual yearning, mutual straining, mutual aching"* (MACRINA WIEDERKEHR).

Reflection: 28. MAINTAIN A VIBRANT PRAYER LIFE. Even for "practiced" Christians, prayer can be an elusive discipline. Jesus' disciples had the same problem, as reflected in their request, "Lord, teach us to pray" (Luke 11:1).

It's helpful for me to recognize that prayer isn't a performance, a chore, or for that matter, an *action* at all—it isn't something we need to learn or know how to *do*. Private prayer in particular is as passive as it is active, because it's reciprocal, an alternating current. We aren't responsible to focus in on our wording or to make sure we incorporate a list of required elements. In fact, a prayer that includes intervals of reflection or even of mind wandering can free us up to hear God's voice.

"God speaks in the silence of the heart," notes Mother Teresa. "Listening is the beginning of prayer." John Bunyan reinforces this thought, pointing out that "When you pray, rather let your heart be without words than your words without heart."

Is it possible, I wonder, to commune with God without labeling the exchange a prayer? My hunch, believing sister, is that you and I do it all the time.

Prayer Prompt: How reciprocal is your prayer life? Do you consider fellowshipping with God to be an accountability or a privilege?

$\mathcal{G}$odly woman,

PRAYER ISN'T JUST TALK.

*E*ager students

Verses: "The Bereans . . . received the message with great eagerness and examined the Scriptures every day to see if what Paul said was true. As a result, many of them believed, as did also a number of prominent Greek women and many Greek men" (Acts 17:11–12).

> *"Oh, to be bathed in a text of Scripture, and to let it be*
> *sucked up in your very soul, till it saturates your heart!"*
> (CHARLES HADDON SPURGEON).

Reflection: 29. KNOW YOUR BIBLE. A well-known Anglican evangelist from eighteenth-century England, George Whitefield had this to say about Bible readership in his generation: "God has condescended to become an author, and yet people will not read his writings. There are very few that ever gave this Book of God, the grand charter of salvation, one fair reading through." How sobering—and how contemporary sounding!

It's tempting for us to "take" our doses of Bible in measured and minimal daily spoonfuls (an RDA mentality), contenting ourselves with sermons and out-of-context verses. The Spirit doesn't cram the Word down our throats, but our well-being, not to mention our witness, is directly affected by our willingness to drink deeply from the well God has provided.

(BTW, did you happen to catch Paul's reference to "a number of prominent Greek women"—*before* the "many Greek men"? Paul must have been impressed with these ladies!)

Prayer Prompt: How much of God's revelation is "enough" for you? Are you thriving, or barely getting by?

odly woman,
HIS WORD IS ONE OF HIS BEST GIFTS.

The stakes

Verses: "[The older women] can urge the younger women to love their husbands and children, to be self-controlled and pure, to be busy at home, to be kind, and to be subject to their husbands, so that no one will malign the word of God" (Titus 2:4–5).

"Some people, no matter how old they get, never lose their beauty; they merely move it from their faces into their hearts"
(MARTIN BUXBAUM).

Reflection: 30. PASS IT ON. So far throughout the month of June we've considered together 29 biblical health and beauty secrets. What we didn't discuss are the stakes: Incredibly, Paul points out here that God's very reputation depends on our inner beauty, as reflected through our attitudes and actions. That's the kind of beauty that mellows with age, like a fine wine or a piece of driftwood sculpted by repeated exposure to the tides.

Marie Stopes captured something of this reality: "You can take no credit for beauty at sixteen. But if you are beautiful at sixty, it will be your soul's own doing." No, this author doesn't credit God for his sanctifying work, but she does, at least in my reading, catch something of Paul's point when he enjoins us to "continue to work out your salvation with fear and trembling, for it is God who works in you to will and to act in order to fulfill his good purpose" (Philippians 2:12–13).

I'm not quite sixty (well, almost fifty-nine). Sure, I'm noticing a collagen breakdown, but hopefully my growth in grace is the more evident change.

If you're younger, are you modeling yourself after a mature Christian in the process of graceful aging? If you're in the modeling position, how seriously are you taking Paul's charge?

Prayer Prompt: Before going to God, take a few moments to consider Paul's remarks to Titus, above (for balance, you might also want to read verses 1 and 2). Are you surprised by the stakes of godly living?

Godly woman,

GUARD WELL HIS REPUTATION.

$\mathcal{P}$erfect in Christ

Verses: "Who can discern their own errors? Forgive my hidden faults. Keep your servant also from willful sins; may they not rule over me" (Psalm 19:12–13).

> *"The command 'Be ye perfect' is not idealistic gas. Nor is it a*
> *command to do the impossible. He said (in the Bible) that we were*
> *'gods' and he is going to make good his words. He will make us*
> *into a god or goddess, a dazzling, radiant, immortal creature . . .*
> *a bright stainless mirror which reflects back to God perfectly"*
> (C. S. LEWIS).

Reflection: I learned about them as a kid—sins of omission and sins of commission, the good stuff we omit doing and the bad stuff we commit by doing. But I never realized before today that this distinction is covered in the Bible in two consecutive verses. David nuances this in a slightly different way, referring to sins that are hidden even from ourselves (the good stuff we omit—or the bad stuff we do—without even recognizing it) and those sins we willfully commit.

There's a qualitative difference between sinning (an inevitable part of the human condition, the debt for which Jesus Christ has already paid for those who love him) and deliberately living in sin (a choice that will separate us eternally from God if we fail to repent). The "perfection" of which the New Testament speaks is, I believe, possible for the believer in terms of the second category.

The author of the book of Hebrews says of our Lord that "by one sacrifice he has made perfect forever those who are being made holy" (Hebrews 10:14). Our perfection through Jesus' once-for-all sacrifice is vicarious in the sense that, once we receive and accept our atonement, our slate is wiped clean in God's eyes.

But being made holy (our sanctification) is an ongoing process by which we draw closer and closer to God and move steadily farther from our old lives of sin. If we as forgiven sinners are allowing sin to rule over us, we do well to double-check our status.

Prayer Prompt: What sin in your life comes closest to controlling you?

odly woman,
BE SURE OF YOUR STATUS.

What more can he say?

Verse: "And these are but the outer fringe of his works; how faint the whisper we hear of him! Who then can understand the thunder of his power?" (Job 26:14).

"I love to think of nature as an unlimited broadcasting station through which God speaks to us every hour if we will only tune in"
(GEORGE WASHINGTON CARVER).

Reflection: Yes, the whisper of God's power was faint in the days of Job. He and others, attuned to the wonders of nature as the ancients were, noted the signs and were in awe. They had no question who was in control but were frustrated by their lack of information about him.

David echoed Job's wonder at the forces at work in nature: "The heavens declare the glory of God; the skies proclaim the work of his hands. . . . They have no speech, they use no words; no sound is heard from them" (Psalm 19:1, 3).

Job and David, whose writings have been recorded in consecutive books of the Bible, actually lived many generations apart. And David understood a great deal more of God than Job had. The whisper had become audible to him through the voices of prophets like Nathan, the Old Testament Scriptures then available, and the history of God's people.

If David lived with an audible voice, we're privileged to hear a shout! In the words of an old hymn, "What more can he say than to you he has said, to you who for refuge to Jesus have fled?"

Prayer Prompt: Consider and thank God for his self-revelation through his Word and Spirit, as well as through his world.

Godly woman,

HOLD IN AWE THE GOD WHO HAS IN LOVE SEEN FIT TO REVEAL HIMSELF.

$\mathcal{T}$he real thing

Verses: "If you hold to my teaching, you are really my disciples. Then you will know the truth, and the truth will set you free" (John 8:31–32).

"Where I found truth, there found I my God, who is the truth itself" (AUGUSTINE).

Reflection: An unrelenting demand, particularly with regard to today's younger generations, is that life be *real*. This gets a little complicated in a postmodern society, where truth is seen as indefinite and personal, not to mention fluctuating even in terms of the individual. But the felt need is potent nonetheless.

Nearly two thousand years ago Pontius Pilate ruefully asked the same question that falls from the lips of cynics today: "What is truth?" (John 18:38). Pilate's question was rhetorical, expecting a shrug denoting hopeless relativity.

Most of us remember the long-running Coca-Cola jingle that went like this: "It's the real thing in the back of your mind. What you're hoping to find is the real thing." This demand for authenticity goes far beyond Coke, of course. And for many the hope could be defined more strongly, as a yearning, even a compulsion to scrabble their way down to life's most basic common denominator. There's more than a little desperation in that quest.

During the mid-twentieth Ralph W. Sockman identified that illusive real thing altogether differently: "When the dictators and opportunists are gone, the cross will still stand before us and something in us will say, That is the real thing." How blessed we are to share this life-changing insight!

Prayer Prompt: Do those around you view you as authentic—the real thing, the genuine article? Are they right in their assessment?

odly woman,
LIFE AND TRUTH PIVOT AROUND THE CROSS.

$\mathcal{F}$reedom—to or from?

Verse: "'I have the right to do anything,' you say—but not everything is beneficial. 'I have the right to do anything'—but I will not be mastered by anything" (1 Corinthians 6:12).

> *"What is the essence of America? Finding and maintaining that*
> *perfect, delicate balance between freedom 'to' and freedom 'from'"*
> (MARILYN VOS SAVANT).

Reflection: Not *everything* is permissible for us as Christians—or as Americans—but we in the West do live with unprecedented liberties, not the least of which is the privilege of practicing our faith unimpeded. Another delicate balance is that between my own liberty and that of my neighbor.

"Liberty means responsibility," pointed out George Bernard Shaw, going on, "That is why most men dread it." Living with liberties—and more particularly living with liberties *under God*—doesn't allow me to live thoughtlessly or mechanically; it requires me to make daily choices that may at times call for massive doses of care and grace.

I need to go further than refraining from stepping on my neighbor's toes in the exercise of my freedom; I need to avoid elbowing my way in front of her in my effort to maximize my opportunities or cutting off his source of light by planting myself in his way.

Living as a Christian in a free society places restrictions on me that go far beyond the law of the land. This privilege requires of me a deliberate and voluntary obedience to God's law, as summarized by Jesus in Mark 12:30–31. No one, least of all Jesus, claimed this would be easy. In the words of Bernard Baruch, "The greatest blessing of our democracy is freedom. But in the last analysis, our only freedom is the freedom to discipline ourselves."

Prayer Prompt: How might your practice of freedom be limiting someone else's opportunity?

$\mathcal{G}$odly woman,
EXERCISE YOUR FREEDOM RESPONSIBLY.

The merciful

Verses: "You prepare a table before me in the presence of my enemies. You anoint my head with oil; my cup overflows" (Psalm 23:5). "Blessed are the merciful, for they will be shown mercy" (Matthew 5:7).

"We are cups, constantly and quietly being filled. The trick is,
knowing how to tip ourselves over and let the beautiful stuff out"
(RAY BRADBURY).

Reflection: Several years ago I wrote a series of rhymed children's poems based on the Beatitudes. This one caught my eye this morning, and I believe that it's as appropriate for us as adult Christian women as it is for kids. Simplicity is never a detriment when it comes to the truths of God's Word.

> My cup is full of Jesus' love,
> so full it overflows.
> But there's another kind of full
> that grows and grows and grows!
>
> That kind of full is merciful.
> That's how I want to be.
> For when I'm merciful
> I'm full of caring, and it's free!
>
> It's free to me (from God);
> his pipeline never will run dry.
> And so it's free from me to you.
> There's always a supply.
>
> I feel as though I'll burst
> if I don't give it all away.
> It's like a spring that bubbles up
> inside my heart each day!

Prayer Prompt: Do these words ring true for you on a personal level?

Godly woman,
NEVER STINT ON DISTRIBUTING MERCY; GOD DOESN'T.

$\mathcal{W}$hose finger?

Verses: "How great is God—beyond our understanding! . . . He fills his hands with lightning and commands it to strike its mark" (Job 36:26, 32).

"God's fingers can touch nothing but to mold it into loveliness"
(GEORGE MACDONALD).

Reflection: An ancient Chinese proverb has it that "when a finger points to the moon the imbecile looks at the finger." While there's certainly truth to that, I would counter based on the above verse that it depends on whose finger we're talking about.

I think I can honestly state that, whenever I gaze upon natural beauty, my thoughts turn to God. We whose lives are centered on the "foolishness of God" simply see the created order that way.

God once told Moses, "There is a place near me where you may stand on a rock. When my glory passes by, I will put you in a cleft in the rock and cover you with my hand until I have passed by. Then I will remove my hand and you will see my back; but my face must not be seen" (Exodus 33:21–23). Much as we preserve our retinas by resisting the urge to gaze directly into a solar eclipse, God shields us from the devastating effects of full-on exposure to his splendor. That isn't to say it won't come.

David stated in Psalm 27:4, "One thing I ask from the LORD, this only do I seek: that I may dwell in the house of the LORD all the days of my life, to gaze on the beauty of the LORD and to seek him in his temple." David didn't fully grasp the implications of his wish, but we'll share with him in its fulfillment.

Prayer Prompt: To what, or whom, do your thoughts turn when you're exposed to grandeur?

$\mathcal{G}$*odly woman,*
DON'T LET HIS GLORY PASS YOU BY!

$\mathscr{S}$tones—or gems?

Verse: "The kingdom of heaven is like treasure hidden in a field. When a man found it, he hid it again, and then in his joy went and sold all he had and bought that field" (Matthew 13:44).

"Contentment is a pearl of great price, and whoever procures it at the expense of ten thousand desires makes a wise and happy purchase" (JOHN BALGUY).

Reflection: I'll have to admit that I've always had a problem with Jesus' words in the verse above. In my mind the motivation to buy that field with its carefully concealed treasure seems suspect. But Jesus wasn't talking about deception. His point was about priorities, about the single-minded pursuit of the one and only treasure that counts. About joy in the Lord and, if I'm not reading too much into the verse, about joy's partner, contentment.

The June following Mom's death, when I was eleven, Dad drove us four older kids to Michigan to spend the summer with aunts, uncles, and cousins. A vivid memory from that special summer was a trip taken with an aunt and uncle up North along the coast of Lake Superior.

The highlight for me was Agawa Bay, a lovely beach covered with multicolored, tide-washed stones that I took, based on the name of the place, to be agates. For the two days we camped there I was in ecstasy, wandering nonstop along this private field of dreams making sure I selected *the* twelve loveliest gemstones—twelve to accommodate the slots in the egg carton my aunt had emptied for my trove.

I later colored the carton, glued the stones in place, and labeled the box "real agats from Agoa Bay." This treasure made its way back to California with me on the train and remained stored in our basement for several years. Those two beachcombing days brought me a sense of joy and contentment I'll never forget.

Prayer Prompt: How contented are you in your Christian life, regardless of your degree of luxury?

odly woman,
LUXURIATE IN CONTENTMENT.

What's in your heart?

Verse: "The word is very near you; it is in your mouth and in your heart so you may obey it" (Deuteronomy 30:14).

"The word of God hidden in the heart is a stubborn voice to suppress" (BILLY GRAHAM).

Reflection: What would it mean for you to "hide" God's Word in your heart (Psalm 119:11)? What kind of hiding place would your heart make? It's deep and impenetrable, if you want to keep its content classified. But it's also close and dear—as vital, involuntary, and unfailing as your next breath or thrusting pulse. "Hiding" something there should be just the opposite of stuffing it into your subconscious.

By the time a thought has made it to our lips, it can indeed be hard to suppress. But the thoughts that bubble up to the surface generally reflect the condition of our heart. David expressed this in Psalm 37:30–31: "The mouths of the righteous utter wisdom, and their tongues speak what is just. The law of their God is in their hearts."

So how hidden are God's words when they're residing in your heart and mouth? Hopefully, not very. Cherished? Absolutely. They're a source of delight, like a kicking fetus secure in its sac but forcefully expressing its desire to emerge.

God once asked the prophet Ezekiel to eat a scroll, then to go and speak its words to Israel (see Ezekiel 3:1). Talk about internalization!

Prayer Prompt: Pray that God will help you cherish his Word, to make it a vital part of who you are from the inside out.

Godly woman,

MANAGE YOUR HEART; YOUR LIPS WILL FOLLOW SUIT.

$\mathcal{U}$ntil . . . ?

Verse: "I am with you and will watch over you wherever you go, and I will bring you back to this land. I will not leave you until I have done what I have promised you" (Genesis 28:15).

> *"In place of our exhaustion and spiritual fatigue, God will give us rest. All He asks is that we come to Him . . . that we spend a while thinking about Him, meditating on Him, talking to Him, listening in silence, occupying ourselves with Him—totally and thoroughly lost in the hiding place of His presence"* (CHARLES SWINDOLL).

Reflection: The interactions between God and his early Old Testament saints were so refreshingly personal. These individuals didn't, after all, enjoy the ever-present treasure of God's Word or Spirit (at least not in the same way we do today).

God was with Jacob every millisecond of every day, but I wonder how much of that reality Jacob comprehended. God conceded to his limited grasp by speaking in terms he could understand: "I will not leave you *until* I have done what I have promised." How reassuring does that sound to you? Would he depart afterward?

Hundreds of years passed before Moses addressed the Israelites shortly before his death, assuring them that the Lord "will *never* leave you nor forsake you" (Deuteronomy 31:6, emphasis added). The author of Hebrews quotes Moses directly: "Keep your lives free from the love of money and be content with what you have, because God has said, 'Never will I leave you; never will I forsake you.' So we say with confidence, 'The Lord is my helper; I will not be afraid. What can mere mortals do to me?'" (Hebrews 13:5–6).

Now *that's* a comforting prospect.

Prayer Prompt: What comfort does this promise of God afford you? Be specific in your prayer.

odly woman,
YOU NEVER WALK ALONE.

*L*avish blessing

Verses: "The heavens are yours, and yours also the earth; you founded the world and all that is in it. . . . Your arm is endowed with power" (Psalm 89:11, 13).

"Where, except in uncreated light, can the darkness be drowned?"
(C. S. LEWIS).

Reflection: Typical, I think, of children growing up today, Adelyn is quite aware of energy use and misuse. One evening last week, noticing the sun still up long after bedtime, she came to me with an observation: "God is wasting power." I did my best to explain the difference between God's inexhaustible energy supply and our own.

It's laughable, of course, to compare the power of a light bulb to the "wattage" of the sun. More to the point for me, though, is that God isn't sparing with his natural illumination, despite the dark times that supply other necessities of life, like quiet and sleep and rain and heat relief. While no climate is ideal, and some areas of the world are more compatible with human life than others, I can only observe that, on the whole, our God is profligate with his natural blessings.

As a matter of fact, God is generous with all of his blessings, isn't he? He doesn't operate from a shortage mentality as we often do; the idea of shortage is incompatible with who he is. No, God operates in every way on the basis of infinity. We know all too well, of course, that not all of our resources on Earth are here in infinite supply. That's the very reason we teach the upcoming generations to ration and recycle. But despite the gloom and doom forecasts of some environmentalists, we also know that God will not abandon this world or allow its destruction before the day he has ordained for that event—after which he'll usher in the new one.

Prayer Prompt: With which blessings in your life has God been particularly lavish?

*G*odly woman,

WHEN IT COMES TO THE ENVIRONMENT, HE WANTS YOUR CONCERN,

NOT YOUR ANGST.

$\mathcal{G}$race for today

Verse: "Therefore do not worry about tomorrow, for tomorrow will worry about itself. Each day has enough trouble of its own" (Matthew 6:34).

"God never built a Christian strong enough to carry today's duties and tomorrow's anxieties piled on top of them"
(THEODORE LEDYARD CUYLER).

Reflection: "The thing about family disasters, muses Robert Brault, "is that you never have to wait long before the next one puts the previous one into perspective." Looking back over the hectic years of raising three daughters alone, I must concede some doubt that the agency made the best decision in matching three such needy children with a single mother employed full-time outside the home.

School vacations were particularly difficult, with Amanda already in her early teens when the younger girls joined our family: "old" enough to scare off any potential babysitters but far from able to manage two challenging sisters on her own. We lived at the time in a mobile home park filled with unsupervised kids, all of whom seem to gravitate to the alluring chaos of our home. Not surprisingly, "situation" followed situation, too many ending in disasters or near disasters.

I occasionally still learn from one of the girls about some event or another that would have totally frazzled me had I known about it at the time. Perhaps God was shielding me from overload. I sometimes wonder what I could have done differently, but this kind of second-guessing is both unproductive and futile.

It's far too late to worry about yesterday and absolutely useless to worry about tomorrow. As my dad used to counsel the young adult me, "Live in day-tight compartments." Each day has enough trouble of its own—and just enough grace!

Prayer Prompt: What problems are you facing *today*?

odly woman,
LEAVE TOMORROW'S TROUBLE THERE; IT WILL WAIT FOR YOU.

*G*od's sweet time

Verse: "Before the mountains were born or you brought forth the whole world, from everlasting to everlasting you are God" (Psalm 90:2).

"To get all there is out of living, we must employ our time wisely, never being in too much of a hurry to stop and sip life, but never losing our sense of the enormous value of a minute"
(ROBERT UPDEGRAFF).

Reflection: "In the presence of eternity," reflects Robert Green Ingersoll, "the mountains are as transient as the clouds." It's fascinating, isn't it, to watch a fast-moving, ominous gray "sky" scape pushing forward as though in a rush to erase the blue (or vice versa). Or even a time-lapse television view of darkness giving way to light or of a storm riding in.

What you've never viewed, though, is a non-simulated, time-lapse vision of a mountain eroding away to nothing. It happens, but not within a human life span.

As Moses reminds us only two verses following the above quote, "A thousand years in your sight are like a day that has just gone by, or like a watch in the night." Moses knew a lot about the sometimes inchmeal passage of time. As a young fugitive who had been raised as royalty, he vegged in the desert for forty years watching the slow movements of sheep. Later on he endured another forty-year span of suspended motion in another wilderness, waiting for God's punishment of his people to run its course.

You and I get antsy when the car or computer in front of us has a less than instantaneous start-up. No wonder communing with God comes so hard for us.

Prayer Prompt: What would it take for you to build some productive downtime into today?

*G*odly woman,

"GIVE" HIM TIME; IT'S HIS ANYWAY.

$\mathcal{S}$trength to strength

Verses: "Blessed are those whose strength is in you, whose hearts are set on pilgrimage. . . . They go from strength to strength, till each appears before God in Zion" (Psalm 84:5, 7).

> *"We can never obey God in our own strength, but we can always trust Him to provide the strength we need"* (WARREN WIERSBE).

Reflection: Have you ever noticed that, despite the slower pace of summer, the world fairly pulsates on a hot day? The air seems to throb around us, and the pavement swims before our eyes. Summer is an intense time of year. In its own way, it's no time for sissies.

The adult me has a low tolerance for heat and humidity. I recall with amazement a much younger version of myself, flying barefooted over the sidewalk in the baking California sun, seeking those oases of grass to momentarily sooth my sizzling soles.

What I don't recollect is ever finding it too hot to play outside. What was I thinking? In midsummer today I equate going from strength to strength with lunging from my air-conditioned car to my air-conditioned condo.

It's inevitable that each of us will find ourselves at times somewhere between strength and strength, somewhere on the ebb side of rejuvenation. At such times it helps to recall that the oases that dot the roadway to God are connected by the sinews of his strength.

Wherever we stand along the path, we're "in" that strength. Our strength, as the psalmist points out, is in God. And we know that his strength is in us.

Prayer Prompt: What does movement from strength to strength mean for you?

odly woman,

TRAVEL IN HIS STRENGTH.

*R*eading the signs

Verses: "When the south wind blows, you say, 'It's going to be hot,' and it is. Hypocrites! You know how to interpret the appearance of the earth and the sky. How is it that you don't know how to interpret this present time?" (Luke 12:55–56).

> *"The apostolic church thought more about the Second Coming of Jesus Christ than about death and heaven. The early Christians were looking, not for a cleft in the ground called a grave but for a cleavage in the sky called Glory"* (ALEXANDER MACLAREN).

Reflection: I rely on the meteorologist for my weather expectations, only to be surprised when I've missed the news and a drastic change catches me unaware. I'll call out to a neighbor "Beautiful morning, isn't it?" and get met with "So far. Too bad it's going to storm [heat up, turn humid, blizzard, or whatever]." With an agreeable nod, I'll second the motion, adding something inane like "We'd better enjoy it while we can."

The religious leaders in Jesus' day were equally clueless about the "heat" that was building. Hopefully we're more attuned to the spiritually charged atmosphere in our day. Christians seem to entrench themselves in one of two positions: insisting that we're living in the end times or pointing out that God hasn't disclosed the day or the hour—or the generation, century, or millennium.

Both are true, of course, which is precisely why we need to be on continual alert.

Prayer Prompt: How prepared are you for Jesus' second coming?

*G*odly woman,

HE'S COMING BACK.

𝒰nexpected

Verse: "I waited patiently for the LORD; he turned to me and heard my cry" (Psalm 40:1).

> *"However many blessings we expect from God, His infinite*
> *liberality will always exceed all our wishes and our thoughts"*
> (JOHN CALVIN).

Reflection: If Angie's adoption was painstakingly slow in coming (see my meditation of June 14), Khristina's was instantaneous. So certain was I that two daughters were my "limit" that I avoided reflecting on the unthinkable. The spring after Angie's arrival, our family of three traveled to Colorado to visit my parents. During an errand Mom casually, and to my astonishment, broached the subject: Did I think I would adopt again? My response echoed my surprise at this unexpected parental "permission," but I couldn't wait to return home to call my agency.

I did so almost apologetically, explaining that I would appreciate being held in a back-of-mind status in case the right situation came along (I wanted to be sensitive to the fact that other families were now ahead of me in terms of waiting "equity"). It did—two weeks after my phone call! Angie had been the product of a disrupted adoption, an experience Khristina at almost seven was about to undergo. That made me the most experienced swimmer in the agency's waiting pool!

I'm reminded of Hannah's angst in waiting for the birth of a son she probably never expected to see (see 1 Samuel 1). But listen to a little-known verse referring to the time *after* Hannah had dedicated her miracle child to God's service: "And the LORD was gracious to Hannah; she gave birth to three sons and two daughters. Meanwhile, the boy Samuel grew up in the presence of the LORD" (1 Samuel 2:21).

When have you longed and prayed for some particular blessing, only to be blessed with so much more very soon afterward?

Prayer Prompt: Identify a blessing for which you prayed long and hard. What about those others that were absolutely unexpected?

odly woman,
APPRECIATE HIS BONUSES.

"*I*'m sorry"

Verse: "Fools mock at making amends for sin, but goodwill is found among the upright" (Proverbs 14:9).

"Love means saying 'I look at it differently' instead of 'You're wrong'" (ANONYMOUS).

Reflection: It's surprising how many people I've run into who make it a point never to apologize. A male friend of one of my daughters is like that; he also believes, based on his upbringing, in telling it like it is (whether or not "it" really has to be stated). I couldn't disagree more strongly with the premise of the 1970s film *Love Story*: "Love means never having to say you're sorry." I can't imagine such an approach doing anything to enhance the quality of a relationship, short-term or long. To the contrary, a willingness to apologize is of the very essence of love.

As every kid can attest, however, apology under duress (typically with a glare in the eye or, as we become more sophisticated, an *I could care less* aloofness) can be worse than no apology at all. "A stiff apology," points out Gilbert K. Chesterton, "is a second insult. . . . The injured party does not want to be compensated because he has been wronged; he wants to be healed because he has been hurt."

Those two short words *I'm sorry* are solidly within the territory of the heart. Any situation calling for them deserves from us as Christians the caution *Fragile; handle with care*—not to mention with prayer.

Prayer Prompt: Is there someone who would benefit from your apology?

Godly woman,

YOU, WITH THE SPIRIT'S HELP, HAVE THE POWER TO MAKE
THAT SITUATION BETTER.

Assurance, yea or nay

Verse: "Those who live in accordance with the Spirit have their minds set on what the Spirit desires" (Romans 8:5).

"There are four ways God answers prayer: No, not yet; No, I love you too much; Yes, I thought you'd never ask; Yes, and here's more"
(ANNE LEWIS).

Reflection: In my June 14 meditation I shared my experience of a serendipitous phone call—far too timely to be coincidental—which I took to be the Spirit's confirmation that Angie's adoption would be "right" for me. By the same token, I'm convinced that the Spirit on another occasion gave me a firm no to an equally cherished dream, again on the basis of a phone call.

In May of 2007 I sold my house after almost a year on the market. I had just walked through the front door after making an offer on my condo when the phone rang. An out-of-state social worker advised me that my three oldest grandchildren—Angie's sons and daughter—had been removed from their dad's custody. Would I consider guardianship?

If I've ever experienced ambivalence, it was at that moment. The condo purchase rendered the addition of three children to my household an impossibility. Before their unexpected departure from my home (see my meditation of February 8), I had naively assumed that I would in effect raise them. Now, when the offer came, I had to acknowledge what I had known all along: Not only were my age and situation not conducive to taking on very needy four, five, and six year olds, but I was in no way physically or emotionally equipped to follow that long-cherished dream.

I'm not one to take any coincidence as a message from God. For example, just this morning I heard a touching story from a fellow grandma waiting in the school hallway with me for a preschooler. Her son and daughter-in-law, she told me, shared a birthday. When they began dating, the two moms both realized that the couple had been born in the same hospital room on the same day. What fun! But a sign that they should marry? Hardly. So how can we know when the Spirit wants to tell us something? Not an easy question. But I can say that those two life-altering phone calls spoke to my heart.

Prayer Prompt: When has the Spirit convinced your heart of the "right" course to take?

odly woman,
ACCEPT HIS ANSWERS.

$\mathcal{S}$hibboleth

Verses: "Whenever a survivor of Ephraim said, 'Let me cross over,' the men of Gilead asked him, 'Are you an Ephraimite?' If he replied, 'No,' they said, 'All right, say "Shibboleth."' If he said, 'Sibboleth,' because he could not pronounce the word correctly, they seized him and killed him" (Judges 12:5–6).

> *"The devil doesn't persecute those who aren't making a godly difference in the world"* (PAUL CHAPPELL).

Reflection: Being recognized as a Christian is more comfortable for us in some contexts than in others. Here in the West any discomfort we may feel is primarily a matter of our natural human desire to blend in, to be accepted as one of the group.

In many parts of our world, though, the stakes are much higher. Just as being identified as an Ephraimite in the Judges 12 story meant certain death, or being branded a Galilean could have meant trouble for Peter on the night of Jesus' betrayal and arrest (see Matthew 26:73), so identification with Christ in many locations and situations around the globe carries devastating consequences.

Christians don't speak with a distinctive inflection, but we as believing women *are* often identified by our speech. It's interesting to me that when Paul encouraged young Timothy to set an example for the believers (1 Timothy 4:12), he mentioned speech first, before life, love, faith, and purity.

What is it that gives you away?

Prayer Prompt: How readily does your speech declare your affiliation with Christ—no matter what the topic of conversation? What difference does this identification make in your life?

$\mathcal{G}$odly woman,

PROCLAIM CHRIST—WHETHER OR NOT YOU'RE TALKING ABOUT HIM.

$\mathcal{W}$aiting for . . .

Verses: "See how the farmer waits for the land to yield its valuable crop, patiently waiting for the autumn and spring rains. You too, be patient and stand firm" (James 5:7–8).

"The key to everything is patience. You get the chicken by hatching the egg. Not by smashing it" (ARNOLD H. GLASGOW).

Reflection: "Walking" my daughter's eight-month-old lab-mix pup in the heat of the day is an exercise in patience. (I'd probably say "our" pup if I weren't so frustrated.) Annabelle, who can lurch me along with bursts of exuberance when it's cool, becomes an avid sunbather at midday in July.

She'll meander along for a short while, sniffing the ground with her whole body, after which she'll plop down on the asphalt or grass, nest her head on her paws, and look up at me with those beseeching, soulful eyes.

At times she'll roll until I scratch her belly, but I believe she could lie there, contented, for the duration. Disliking open-ended durations, I break into a slow fume. A watching neighbor called out a day or two ago, "That dog's like a mule, isn't she?"

I recognize that I can be accused of taking the above verses out of context. OK, I've already accused myself, but I just couldn't resist. In my own way I too am waiting for autumn. But the biblical message on which I'm rightly focusing is the call for patience—even, and especially, when it's "hot."

While I'm at it, I can't resist carrying the analogy one step further. When it comes to Annabelle, standing firm along with my patience isn't a bad idea.

Prayer Prompt: What minor frustrations tend to try your patience?

odly woman,
FLEX YOUR PATIENCE.

*D*rinking from the well

Verse: "The LORD will guide you always; he will satisfy your needs in a sun-scorched land and will strengthen your frame. You will be like a well-watered garden, like a spring whose waters never fail" (Isaiah 58:11).

"The insatiable thirst for everything which lies beyond, and which life reveals, is the most living proof of our immortality"
(CHARLES BAUDELAIRE).

Reflection: I resonate with tinder-dry, sun-scorched land much more from my growing up days in Southern California than from my current experience in Michigan's more frequently waterlogged climate. Still, when the rains ease up here for even a little while during the hot months, there can within a short time be a whole lot of shriveling going on. It's amazing how quickly the landscape can transform from lush to withered.

I'm fortunate, given my low heat tolerance, not only to live in this relatively mild climate (our temperatures, summer and winter, are moderated by the Great Lakes) but to enjoy the creature comforts afforded by condo living.

Did you know that if you wait to drink until you're thirsty, you're already dehydrated? This principle applies to spiritual hydration as well. No matter where you find yourself, or in what season of life, you do well to discipline yourself to drink daily, and deeply, from the Water of Life. Your spirit will indeed be "like a well-watered garden, like a spring whose waters never fail." I think I'll just go and get myself a glass of water . . .

Prayer Prompt: How's your "heat tolerance" when it comes to life's challenges?

*G*odly *woman,*
DRINK DEEPLY.

$\mathcal{T}$he debt

Verse: "Let no debt remain outstanding, except the continuing debt to love one another, for whoever loves others has fulfilled the law" (Romans 13:8).

"One can pay back the loan of gold, but one dies forever in debt to those who are kind" (MALAYAN PROVERB).

Reflection: We as Christian women are accustomed to revolving debt. But the idea of a debt that's designed—without ulterior motive on the part of the creditor—to be permanent eludes our mindset.

It's clear that our association with debt fails to encompass Paul's intended point. To begin with, we're playing a dangerous mind game if we suppose we can do anything in the direction of repaying God for his blessings. Oh, it would put our minds at ease if we could work off the smallest fraction of our "balance due."

But what can we offer the God who has everything? Are we viewing ourselves, consciously or otherwise, as equal to our benefactor? What we owe God, and by extension those others he loves, is a debt of *gratitude*, and that's something else altogether.

What comparable situation comes to mind? None at all? Isn't that precisely why Paul singled out this debt as qualitatively, if not quantitatively, unlike any other?

Prayer Prompt: What role does love play in your gifts of gratitude to the Lord?

odly woman,

LOVE WITHOUT CONDITION OR RESERVATION, JUST AS HE LOVES YOU.

$\mathcal{N}$othing but the best

Verse: "I am the LORD your God, who teaches you what is best for you, who directs you in the way you should go" (Isaiah 48:17).

"Good, better, best. Never let it rest. 'Til your good is better and your better is best" (ST. JEROME).

Reflection: It's interesting to note in the above verse that God doesn't say he gives us what is best. He wants to, but he doesn't take the automatic approach. Instead, he teaches us to identify and go after the good (or, better yet, the best!). On a practical level, how does this occur?

Have you ever pursued something you believed to be good in itself—or at least neutral—but found yourself thwarted at every turn? Maybe you wanted to be a foreign missionary, but your house didn't sell, you couldn't garner financial support, or a family member developed a chronic illness that required medical attention closer to home. Sometimes the issue is one of timing, attitude, or both.

God's implied "no" may really be a "not yet," but, like Sarah and Abraham with Hagar, you insist on helping him do it your way. God didn't allow me to do that with my second adoption, for which I waited ten years. That isn't to say I didn't try to sidestep his will (I explored several unlikely and expensive adopt-quick schemes).

In my case, it was only when I let go of the reins, along with my developing bitterness, that he gave me exactly the "best" I'd been seeking. It turned out to be a difficult best, and I needed every ounce of added maturity those ten years had afforded.

Prayer Prompt: In what ways is God directing you at this juncture in your life? Are you accepting his answers without trying to prod him along?

$\mathcal{G}$odly woman,
FOLLOW THE LEADER.

*H*appiness, ~~health~~, holiness

Verses: "Just as he who called you is holy, so be holy in all you do; for it is written: 'Be holy, because I am holy'" (1 Peter 1:15–16).

> *"Man's chief and highest end is to glorify God, and fully to enjoy him forever"* (WESTMINSTER LARGER CATECHISM).

Reflection: In the well-recognized words of Pastor Rick Warren of California's Saddleback Church, "It's not about you." God could have created the first two people without the capacity to sin. But what pleasure could he have taken in the praise of robots?

It's precisely because of the human ability to fall, exercised so early on in human history, that the holiness of redeemed saints means so much to the Creator. It's helpful for us to remember that our holiness—based on the renewed faculty of Christians to choose on a situational basis not to sin—while glorifying to God, doesn't impress him. In the words of A. W. Tozer, "Although God wants His people to be holy as He is holy, He does not deal with us according to the degree of our holiness but according to the abundance of His mercy."

Oswald Chambers hones our perspective on this issue still further: "The destined end of man is not happiness, nor health, but holiness. God's one aim is the production of saints. He is not an eternal blessing machine for men; he did not come to save men out of pity; he came to save men because he had created them to be holy."

Prayer Prompt: What emphasis do you place on holiness in living out your Christian life?

odly woman,

HE CREATED YOU FOR HIS GLORY, AS A REFLECTION BACK
TO HIMSELF OF HIS OWN HOLINESS.

$\mathcal{H}$ope to hope

Verse: "'I know the plans I have for you,' declares the Lord, 'plans to prosper you and not to harm you, plans to give you hope and a future'" (Jeremiah 29:11).

> *"We must accept finite disappointment, but never lose infinite hope"* (MARTIN LUTHER KING JR.).

Reflection: There are those verses, particularly in the Old Testament, that God's people seem to discover in tandem. Think back to the emphasis a few years ago on the prayer of Jabez (see 1 Chronicles 4:10). Jeremiah 29:11 is, I think, one of those gems that captured the imagination of the church—and of myself—several years ago. I marveled when I "first" read these words, wondering how I could have been a believer for so long without realizing that this gem was tucked away in God's Word, patiently waiting to be mined.

I recognize, of course, that these words are tied to a context. But as with so many Scripture promises, I feel justified in "grandfathering" myself in. Why? Because I'm convinced that this is a statement not just of God's intentions for the exiled Jewish people but of his modus operandi with all of his children.

"The natural flights of the human mind," noted Samuel Johnson, "are not from pleasure to pleasure but from hope to hope." Nothing, from my perspective, could be truer. Pleasures tend to be shallow, elusive, fleeting, and overrated. Not so with hope. A hope only becomes brighter as I polish it up and gaze at life in its glow.

Plans, hope, future. Whether we adapt Jeremiah's words corporately, to Christ's church, or individually, as we Westerners are so fond of doing, they deliver a punch that thrills our souls. How could we begin to endure life's disappointments outside the context of such hope?

Prayer Prompt: What hopes, both finite and infinite, secure your future?

Godly woman,
HOPE MAKES ETERNITY WORTH THE WAIT.

$\mathscr{A}$n old friend

Verse: "Do not forsake your friend or a friend of your family" (Proverbs 27:10).

"It takes a long time to grow an old friend" (JOHN LEONARD).

Reflection: Many friendships tend to be seasonal, matters of expediency, proximity, or temporarily shared activities or life experiences. Oh, we would be more than happy to run into one of these old friends (there are *old* friends and then there are *old friends*) on the street, might enjoy some light chitchat or catching up, but to pick up where we left of?—likely not. Either our circumstances have changed or we have or both.

We grow in and out of relationships throughout our lives. This is especially true when one party moves on in life or when two individuals grow at different rates.

True friendship doesn't depend on convenience, coincidence, commonality, or circumstances. True friendship is a constant that transcends change, and that's precisely what makes it so precious in an uncertain world.

Even so, as the verse above suggests, such relationships need to be tended and cultivated. I failed to do that with a best friend whose company I had enjoyed in church and neighborhood and school from our church nursery days through high school. She and I and another mutual friend from those early years struck up an e-mail relationship ten or fifteen years ago. I knew she had struggled through bouts of cancer but wasn't aware until a "chance" conversation at a funeral several months ago that she had passed away after we had once again drifted apart and lost touch. Jeannie peoples my dreams these days with some regularity. If only I had made more of an effort to treasure our re-acquaintance!

Prayer Prompt: Who are your old friends, your tried and true friends? Thank God for each one individually.

odly woman,

CULTIVATE FRIENDSHIPS.

ℋere and gone?

Verses: "The life of mortals is like grass, they flourish like a flower of the field; the wind blows over it, and it is gone, and its place remembers it no more" (Psalm 103:15–16).

"Life is eternal; and love is immortal; and death is only a horizon; and a horizon is nothing save the limit of our sight" (R. W. RAYMOND).

Reflection: It occurs to me that I "used" these verses already in my May 10 reflection. "Used" (the term sounds so crass), but hardly exhausted! What a tribute to the wealth of God's Word that its words can withstand endless scrutiny while still inviting new insight. Whether our approach is a fly-by, a deep dive, or a long gaze at cruising altitude, we can never begin to diminish the possible angles of approach to its truths. And this without taking into account the horizon temporarily limiting our sight (see quote above)!

Getting back to Psalm 103, an anonymous quote from the Native American Crowfoot tribe echoes David's sentiments: "What is life? It is the flash of a firefly in the night. It is the breath of a buffalo in the wintertime. It is the little shadow which runs across the grass and loses itself in the sunset."

This same lament, in one form or another, has risen from every culture and tribe in every era since the world began. But it isn't, as we know so well, the whole story. If you've been a Christian for all or most of your life, as I have, have you ever paused to imagine what it must be like to face the certainty of death without the certainty of life? How might you be tempted to live if you were convinced that it didn't really matter anyway?

We don't know whether David expected an afterlife, but he did at least trust in God to be with his descendants for as long as they remembered him. Listen as he goes on in verse 17: "But from everlasting to everlasting the LORD's love is with those who fear him, and his righteousness with their children's children."

The world around us is crying out for our assurance. And we can't just assume the unchurched masses have rejected the message. Could it be they've never heard . . . ?

Prayer Prompt: Ask God to lead you to one person with whom to share your assurance.

𝒢odly woman,
LIVE AS THOUGH IT MATTERS.

$\mathcal{T}$he antidote

Verses: "Do not be anxious about anything, but in every situation, by prayer and petition, with thanksgiving, present your requests to God. And the peace of God, which transcends all understanding, will guard your hearts and your minds in Christ Jesus" (Philippians 4:6–7).

> *"Anxiety is a thin stream of fear trickling through the mind. If encouraged, it cuts a channel into which all other thoughts are drained"* (ARTHUR SOMERS ROCHE).

Reflection: Every morning I swallow an anti-anxiety pill. It was pre-scribed decades ago for my spasmodic dysphonia (vocal disorder), but I've noticed lately that if I miss a dose I become "unaccountably" stressed out. Possibly more so now, four years after the beginning of my home-based employment, than in those relentless years of juggling full-time employment with other responsibilities. So what, I ask myself, is the problem? Am I getting rusty? Spoiled? Out of touch?

My sense is that the answer lies in those two short verses from Philippians, above. The first summarizes my responsibility, and the second pledges God's response. Paul's reminder is timely for me today, as it is, frankly, any time I encounter his words. I can think of no more effective way to stanch that seemingly innocuous trickle of dis-ease there in the back of my mind.

I hope you can share in my relief. Take a moment right now to flex those taut shoulders and sketch a few backward circles with them in the air. Then draw a deep breath, even if there's a catch in it, and visualize releasing those anxieties with your exhalation. Only then, after you've taken these prelimi-nary steps, approach God with your petitions and your thanksgiving.

Prayer Prompt: About what are you anxious today? For what are you grateful?

odly woman,

PRAYER IS THE ANTIDOTE FOR ANXIETY.

ᴬudacious prayer

Verse: "The man said, 'Let me go, for it is daybreak.' But Jacob replied, 'I will not let you go unless you bless me'" (Genesis 32:26).

"Prayer is the only form of revolt which remains upright"
(GEORGES BERNANOS).

Reflection: I don't know about you, but I find the honesty of Jacob's relationship with God to be both refreshing and off-putting. I see the same in the book of Job, who, scholars believed, lived in roughly the same era.

Since those days we've sanded down the rough edges in our dealings with the divine. Most of us wouldn't think of demanding, preferring to beat around the bush with our requests, sprinkling our prayers with liberal repetitions of "Your will be done" that prepare us for disappointment.

Persistent, determined prayer—How far are we permitted to go? In Matthew 17:20–21 Jesus made an astounding claim about the efficacy of faith, closing with a declaration that stops us in our tracks (or would, if the words weren't so familiar): "Nothing will be impossible for you." Notice what Jesus didn't say—that nothing is impossible for *God*. He wants us to be involved. Following is a children's poem I wrote some years ago based on this passage:

Once Jesus told some people
that if they believed in him
that they could ask for anything
and that thing would be done!

He said if they believed
that they could tell a mountain tall,
"Go, throw yourself into the sea,"
and it would crouch and fall!

I tried that once. The mountain
stood up straight against the sky.
I didn't *think* that it would work.
It didn't—is *that* why?

I don't think Jesus wanted mountains
diving into seas.
But praying *can* "move mountains."
God will do hard things for me!

Prayer Prompt: Approach God with a sincere petition, deliberately refraining from watering it down. Feel free to plead—and to claim his sure promises.

ᴳodly woman,
HE CAN HANDLE YOUR HONESTY.

$\mathcal{A}$nticipating glory

Verses: "To me, to live is Christ and to die is gain. . . . I am torn between the two: I desire to depart and be with Christ, which is better by far; but it is more necessary for you that I remain in the body" (Philippians 1:21, 23–24).

"It is a very mixed blessing to be brought back from the dead"
(KURT VONNEGUT).

Reflection: "Beauty is unbearable, drives us to despair," observed Albert Camus, "offering us for a moment the glimpse of an eternity that we should like to stretch out over the whole of time." When I was in my twenties a friend of mine had a slightly older sister who had survived Hodgkin's disease. Much to my shock, my friend confided in me that her sister was, at least on some level, disappointed in her recovery. She had come close to death, had come to look forward to it, and had only reluctantly accepted the lesser consolation of continuing life in the here and now.

There have been times in my life when, generally in the throes of depression, I've thought I looked forward to the next life. Gauging those sentiments can be tricky, though. Feelings of despair or disillusionment with life as we know it don't precisely equate to anticipation of heaven.

Paul's statement, above, is full of pathos, but logic comes through as well. His desire to depart this life (his emotive side) contrasts with his acknowledgment of his earthly calling (his rational conclusion).

I doubt that many of us are truly at the point of yearning to be with Christ. On the other side of Camus's point, it's hard to look forward to perfection we can't begin to conceive.

Prayer Prompt: What are your thoughts and feelings about your eternal future?

odly woman,

MAKE THE EFFORT TO ANTICIPATE ETERNITY.

$\mathscr{I}$nundated

Verse: "Deep calls to deep in the roar of your waterfalls; all your waves and breakers have swept over me" (Psalm 42:7).

"So often we have a kind of vague, wistful longing that the promises of Jesus should be true. The only way really to enter into them is to believe them with the clutching intensity of a drowning man" (WILLIAM BARCLAY).

Reflection: I'm not sure how to interpret deep calling to deep, but the imagery is powerful nonetheless. In terms of the second clause of this verse, Jonah used similar language (check out Jonah 2:3).

I can't think of many physical situations more panic inducing than that of being underwater, unable to breathe, swirled around by breakers. I experienced this as a little girl in the Pacific Ocean; feeling as though the salt and sand were being ground into my body didn't ease my discomfort. More to the point for me, though, was the clutching anxiety I experienced during the summer following my college graduation. A shy girl, lacking in self-confidence and plagued by a vocal disorder, I felt that I was about to be inundated by a tidal wave (we didn't know the word *tsunami* then). The movie *The Poseidon Adventure*, then current, defined my desolation and fear quite accurately.

A respect for and fear of deep water seems to have been common to many Old Testament people. Raised as they were in an arid climate, many had no experience with seafaring and probably felt out of their element ("like a fish out of water"?) when confronted by "the deep."

The question for us becomes how to break free, how to replenish our oxygen supply when we're in over our heads. Whoever composed the lyrics of Psalm 42 (it's attributed to the Sons of Korah) resolved his own dilemma in closing: "Why, my soul, are you downcast? Why so disturbed within me? Put your hope in God, for I will yet praise him, my Savior and my God" (verse 11). How ready are you at times like that to claim God's promises with the clutching intensity of a near-drowning woman? The absolute assurance that you'll live to praise God yet again goes so far beyond a wistful longing to break through to the surface.

Prayer Prompt: What makes you feel inundated? Do you share the psalmist's reassurance?

$\mathscr{G}$*odly woman,*
HOPE IN HIM.

For our enjoyment

Verse: "Many, LORD my God, are the wonders you have done, the things you planned for us. None can compare with you; were I to speak and tell of your deeds, they would be too many to declare" (Psalm 40:5).

> *"Gratitude looks underneath the surface. Gratitude is not simply a form of 'positive thinking' or a technique of 'happy-ology,' but rather a deep and abiding recognition and acknowledgment that goodness exists under even the worst that life offers"*
> (RICH VINCENT).

Reflection: Our instant-gratification mentalities can blind us to that fine line between needs and wants many of us older Americans learned in childhood. Conversely, though, it may be easy for some of us to gravitate too far in the opposite direction, feeling guilty about asking God for anything pleasurable or comfortable.

We go after it all right, but that niche of life remains our own. Paul counseled the young pastor Timothy to command "those who are rich in this present world not to be arrogant nor to put their hope in wealth, which is so uncertain, but to put their hope in God, who richly provides us with everything for our enjoyment" (1 Timothy 6:17).

Wow! Did you catch that last phrase? Not "for our need" or "for our survival."

The decline of the auto industry here in Michigan has made the state's rust-belt status more noticeable lately. Recently I spotted a bumper sticker on one of those "Cash for Clunkers" could-have-beens that didn't get traded in: "Want to get rich quick? Count your blessings." In the words of Ramona C. Carroll, "Faith is putting all your eggs in God's basket, then counting your blessings before they hatch.

Prayer Prompt: Before approaching God in gratitude, count and even write down ten blessings God seems to have provided solely for your enjoyment.

odly woman,
HE DELIGHTS IN PLEASING YOU.

Being nice to God

Verse: "You shall not misuse the name of the Lord your God, for the Lord will not hold anyone guiltless who misuses his name" (Exodus 20:7).

"Vulgarity is the garlic in the salad of life" (CYRIL CONNOLLY).

Reflection: Little Adelyn has become quite sensitive to misuse of the Lord's name. Upon overhearing a "clean" exclamation recently, she informed me that this person was "being nice to God." I don't know where she picked it up, but the last couple of days she's been trying on a new expression: "Oh, my gorgeous!" I can't help but chuckle, but it works for me!

The English language is incredibly deep and rich; I've loved it since I was a kid. So it never ceases to amaze me that so many desire to water it down by sprinkling nearly everything they say with the same handful of crude or sacrilegious expletives.

And it isn't just Americans. Years ago, during a stint in customer service, I was in conversation with a woman from the UK with a "to die for" British accent. Upon informing her of a delay in her shipment, she responded with a beautifully inflected *"Ooow, [expletive]!"*

Who, I ask myself, are such people trying to impress? I can't help but observe that the mainstream acceptability of their word choice shouts mediocrity more than it does rebellion.

Prayer Prompt: Is vulgarity or profanity a temptation for you?

Godly woman,

REVERE HIS NAME AND RESPECT HIS CREATION.

*P*ayback

Verse: "Make sure that nobody pays back wrong for wrong, but always strive to do what is good for each other and for everyone else" (1 Thessalonians 5:15).

"Never look down on anybody unless you're helping him up"
(JESSE JACKSON).

Reflection: It sounds uncharacteristic of Paul to tell us to *strive*—to try—to do anything. The "make sure" in the first clause sounds much more like what I would expect from this driven man with the high standards. So why might we be less than successful in our attempts at kindness?

It's possible to be rebuffed, ignored, or written off to the extent that we can't get close enough to treat a person *any* which way. Another possibility is that we just can't muster the grace to override our negative feelings, whether for a fellow believer or for someone else who has either wronged us or just likes to crawl up there under our skin.

"Kindness can become its own motive," points out Eric Hoffer. "We are made kind by being kind." But the underlying incentive for us as Christians goes much deeper: We're kind in response to Christ's kindness.

To quote Paul once again, "Consider therefore the kindness and sternness of God, sternness to those who fell, but kindness to you, provided that you continue in his kindness" (Romans 11:22).

Prayer Prompt: To whom are you finding it especially difficult to extend kindness?

odly woman,

IMITATE YOUR LORD, WITH EACH OTHER AND EVERYONE ELSE.

Running on empty

Verse: "'Call me Mara, because the Almighty has made my life very bitter. I went away full, but the Lord has made my life empty'" (Ruth 1:20).

"Women are the cup from which everyone drinks; Empowerment begins with Loving and Nurturing the self first—in order to quench the thirst of those who need us" (MARIANNE GOLDWEBER).

Reflection: At eighteen Angie left home for apartment living with a boyfriend. This followed two years of regular disappearances, sometimes for days at a time. Evicted months later, the couple took up residence at an expressway rest stop—until their car was repossessed one night during dinner from the curb outside my mobile home. For lack of other options, I took them in for the two weeks before their hastily planned justice-of-the-peace wedding. I was to learn after that event that Angie was already pregnant with Walter Jr., the first of the couple's three children, born one after another within a span of a little more than two years.

Coincident with Walter and Angie's move-in, I began experiencing extreme fatigue, overall body pain, difficulties with concentration, and anxiety. Two years later I was diagnosed with chronic fatigue syndrome / fibromyalgia. My sister Terri had suffered with fibromyalgia for more than a decade, suggesting a genetic component, but both of us have also experienced significant adult trauma. I am now diabetic and dealing with a number of other physical constraints.

An optimist at heart, I find it easy to brush off and even "forget" negative past experiences. In rereading some journal entries from those difficult years, though, I'm astounded at how serious some of the situations really were (far too traumatic and personal for inclusion in a devotional manuscript).

Trying experiences take their toll on us. As Christian women, we may take pride in our resilience and positive attitude. But overcoming and negating are two quite different things. Like Naomi in the verse above, we do well in the right contexts to honestly express our feelings—including our utter depletion—both to God and to others. God won't think less of us, and others should appreciate our honesty.

Prayer Prompt: If you tend toward positivity, assess the level of honesty behind your optimism.

Godly woman,
HE APPRECIATES SINCERITY.

How I know

Verse: "If you declare with your mouth, 'Jesus is Lord,' and believe in your heart that God raised him from the dead, you will be saved" (Romans 10:9).

"The heart has its own reasons of which reason knows nothing" (BLAISE PASCAL).

Reflection: In 1963, when I was twelve, the city of Redlands, California, hosted a "Why I Believe in God" essay contest for seventh graders in *public and private schools*. Sounds pretty radical to our ears, doesn't it? Anyway, our Christian school Bible teacher (who also pastored my church) suggested ideas, which I enthusiastically copied from the board. I remember being impressed by his logic—systematic theology for the seventh grade! Not yet having encountered the crime called plagiarism, I quoted him almost word for word—and (you guessed it) won first place. I received a check for $10, which I held on to for a coming family reunion out East.

When vacation time came, we tackled the Mojave Desert at night (lack of air conditioning was a given), sliding through Beaumont and Barstow after dark and arriving in Las Vegas, that glittering nighttime wonder, around midnight. We kids weren't used to businesses being open at night, even if we were out and about, which was rare. We stopped at a gas station to service the car and stretch our legs.

It was there, in the bathroom, that I experienced a loss—one that I had to chalk up to just deserts: A couple of hours down the road from Las Vegas I realized that I had left my purse in that Sin City restroom. I had always known it: *"Your sin will find you out!"*

I chuckle now at this loss of my ill-gotten gain. But what strikes me even more about the incident is the cold theological argument that was proposed to a bunch of impressionable kids by that minister. As in all Christian school classrooms of that day, each morning began with prayer and singing. My class's favorite song was "I Serve a Risen Savior." And our favorite line, which we belted out with appropriate enthusiasm, was the finale: "You ask me how I *know* he lives: he *lives* within my heart." Not one of us needed that minister to tell us why we believed. It is now, and has always been, the witness of our lives—not our logic—that convinces. I wonder what the other kids wrote. More than that, I wonder why someone more honest didn't win . . .

Prayer Prompt: Assess why you believe in God. Then share the reason with him!

odly woman,

WHAT MAKES *YOU* SO SURE?

$\mathcal{L}$iving in the light

Verses: "You were once darkness, but now you are light in the Lord. Live as children of light . . . and find out what pleases the Lord" (Ephesians 5:8, 10).

"All I have seen teaches me to trust the Creator for all I have not seen" (RALPH WALDO EMERSON).

Reflection: A quote from C. S. Lewis recently caught my attention: "If the whole universe had no meaning, we should never have found out that it has no meaning: just as, if there were no light in the universe and therefore no creatures with eyes, we should never know it was dark."

Thanks to godly parents, I've been in the light from as far back as I can remember. But I suppose that, if I had for a time been "darkness," as Paul puts it, I wouldn't have been fully aware of the meaninglessness of my condition. Oh, I would have decried my felt hopelessness, as so many do today, but I would have had no real concept of what I was missing. The only reason I would have had an inkling of the truth is that the Creator in his grace has in fact given me eyes—and a world worth the seeing!

Those eyes make all the difference. Once again in the words of Paul, "For since the creation of the world God's invisible qualities—his eternal power and divine nature—have been clearly seen, being understood from what has been made, so that people are without excuse" (Romans 1:20).

It's up to us as Christian women to interpret and disseminate that light. As expressed by Mother Teresa, "Words which do not give the light of Christ increase the darkness."

Prayer Prompt: How effectively does your light dissipate the darkness around you?

$\mathcal{G}$*odly woman,*
USE WELL YOUR EYES OF FAITH.

*I*n all circumstances

Verses: "Rejoice always, pray continually, give thanks in all circumstances; for this is God's will for you in Christ Jesus" (1 Thessalonians 5:16–18).

"The Christian life is not a constant high. I have my moments of deep discouragement. I have to go to God in prayer with tears in my eyes, and say, 'O God, forgive me,' or 'Help me'"
(BILLY GRAHAM).

Reflection: The third clause of this imperative from Paul rides on a preposition many have misunderstood. No, we're not expected to thank God *for* all circumstances, although we may legitimately look for the silver lining in a black cloud or ask for hindsight recognition of blessing in the midst of a dark time.

Paul isn't asking us to squelch or stuff our true and natural feelings. That would not only be inauthentic but a denial of our God-endowed—and godlike—emotional makeup. No, the apostle commands us as Christian women to continue giving thanks *in* and through turbulence—to pray continually, regardless of situational upheavals.

Along the same line, we are to "rejoice always." Why? Two reasons: First and foremost, according to Paul, continual joy and thankfulness are God's will for us in Christ Jesus. Second, these character qualities are so deeply ingrained in the believer that they're below the level of perturb-ability.

James Montgomery spoke of prayer as "the Christian's vital breath, the Christian's native air." More than a manifestation of who we are, prayer *is* our identity. And so is joy.

Prayer Prompt: Reflect on the meaning and application of Paul's imperatives in these verses.

odly woman,
LIVE ABOVE AGITATION.

$\mathcal{N}$umbering my days

Verse: "Our days may come to seventy years, or eighty, if our strength endures; yet the best of them are but trouble and sorrow, for they quickly pass, and we fly away" (Psalm 90:10).

"If I'd known I was gonna live this long, I'd have taken better care of myself" (EUBIE BLAKE AT AGE 100).

Reflection: I had occasion recently to uncover a black-and-white photo of my grandma in her early sixties, an amiable old lady with wire rims, waist-length gray hair braided and bobby-pinned around her head, and a sensible print dress. Fine and good—until it occurred to me that I'm nearly fifty-nine.

We're hearing a lot these days about the increasing number of octogenarians inhabiting the planet, and there can be no doubt that a heightened awareness of health maintenance and improving health care are playing significant roles. I watched a news clip this week, however, that spoke of a recently discovered genetic marker in aging; individuals born with it are said to have a seventy percent chance of living to one hundred. The report stated that while factors like diet and exercise prolong life, they account for people living into their eighties, not beyond. Still, I can't help but wonder why so many of us are reaching this century milestone within the past decade or so . . .

Checking the context of the above verse, I'm taken aback by those that flank it: "All our days pass away under your wrath; we finish our years with a moan" and "If only we knew the power of your anger! Your wrath is as great as the fear that is your due." Heavy stuff, isn't it? I'll have to concede that the author, Moses, an old man when he wrote this psalm, had seen his share of God's anger.

Moses comes to the point in verse 12: "Teach us to number our days, that we may gain a heart of wisdom." Ah, there's the issue. How am I doing at numbering my days? At gaining that heart of wisdom? If I'm to be one of those who lives to an extreme age, what does God want me to do with those bonus years? These are questions worth pondering as I inch my way toward old age, twenty-first-century style.

Prayer Prompt: If your family history points to long life, what will you do with your later years?

$\mathcal{G}$odly woman,
NUMBER YOUR DAYS.

Facing the unthinkable

Verses: "For I am convinced that . . . [nothing] in all creation will be able to separate us from the love of God that is in Christ Jesus our Lord" (Romans 8:38–39).

"Compassion brings us to a stop, and for a moment we rise above ourselves" (MASON COOLEY).

Reflection: Each of us starts out life as an impressionable kid, naturally concerned about others' "ouwies." As we grow physically and mentally, though, we may start to shrivel up emotionally. Still, when we avoid a hurting person, it may not be because we're insensitive. We may in fact be ultrasensitive, lacking the emotional resources to face the person touched by such evil.

Years ago my neighbor's nephew and his wife flew to Central America to adopt an infant. On the way home the baby spiked a fever so high the plane had to return to the airport. The diagnosis was too grim for my mind to wrap itself around: This little one was discovered to have been born without a brain. His brain stem allowed for some reflex activity, but awareness was entirely absent. The couple proceeded to love their newborn until his death soon afterward and then to bury him as their beloved son.

How are we as Christians to respond to someone who has endured the "unthinkable"? When we encounter life's anomalies, we need to remind ourselves that *nothing* can separate God's children from his love. Buoyed by that assurance, we're called to break out of our comfort zones to empathize with and embrace those hurting siblings in Christ.

Prayer Prompt: Who in your acquaintance has endured something you'd just as soon avoid? Claim God's love, and pray for the grace and strength to come alongside the hurting person.

odly woman,

NOTHING CAN SNATCH YOU FROM HIS LOVE.

The command

Verse: "Have I not commanded you? Be strong and courageous. Do not be afraid; do not be discouraged, for the Lord your God will be with you wherever you go" (Joshua 1:9).

"No one can defeat us unless we first defeat ourselves"
(DWIGHT EISENHOWER).

Reflection: Dietrich Bonhoeffer had an interesting perspective on strength: "It is the nature, and the advantage, of strong people that they can bring out the crucial questions and form a clear opinion about them. The weak always have to decide between alternatives that are not their own."

A German Lutheran pastor and theologian, Bonhoeffer participated in the German resistance again Nazism. Arrested in 1943 and executed shortly before the end of WWII, his views on the role of Christianity in the secular world have been highly influential. Bonhoeffer used the strength of his intellect as commanded by God (ever notice that Joshua 1:9 is a command?). And he had no choice, given his circumstances, but to add courage to the exercise of his strength.

In what ways are you responding to God's call for strength and courage in the context of today's social, political, and economic climate? Has the Lord given you extraordinary, special, or particular abilities he wants you to use in his service? Or "ordinary" qualities you can channel in a kingdom direction? Has he endowed you with qualities that might designate you a strong or courageous person?

One way or the other, we can be sure that he's directing each of us to formulate and endorse clear opinions on today's crucial issues.

Prayer Prompt: If you're afraid or discouraged, ask for a renewed infusion of his strength.

Godly woman,
FLEX YOUR STRENGTH AND APPLY YOUR COURAGE TOWARD HIS CAUSE.

$\mathcal{I}$n his arms

Verse: "Even to your old age and gray hairs I am he, I am he who will sustain you. I have made you and I will carry you; I will sustain you and I will rescue you" (Isaiah 46:4).

"I am so weak that I can hardly write, I cannot read my Bible,
I cannot even pray, I can only lie still in God's arms like a little
child, and trust" (HUDSON TAYLOR).

Reflection: Our lives come full circle in terms of our need to be carried by God. We typically use the term "second childhood" with reference to a decline in mental agility, but it can refer to the physical as well. It's during our middle years, when we take our seemingly boundless strength for granted, that we most need to be reminded that we rely on God's sustaining power. That was certainly the case for me through those relentless years of raising three daughters. If I was frustrated by anything, it was usually lack of time, not strength.

"It is God who arms me with strength," enthuses David in his prime (2 Samuel 22:33), going on to boast of his physical ability to run, stand, and bend a bow. In verses 36 and 37 he cites softer examples of God's sustenance: "Your help has made me great. You provided a broad path for my feet, so that my ankles do not give way."

Sounds to me like a parent clearing the path of obstacles that might otherwise impede the lunging progress of a wobbly but enthusiastic toddler. Yes, the little one is moving beyond the need for being carried everywhere. But he is also hurtling into far greater risk. We're wise to bear in mind that God continues throughout our lives to "carry" us in different ways.

Prayer Prompt: How does your current situation affect your perspective on your need for God's strength?

odly woman,
DON'T RESIST HIS ARMS.

"*How*, Lord?"

Verse: "I will take refuge in the shadow of your wings until the disaster has passed" (Psalm 57:1).

> *"Your soul can ache, your heart can break, your confidence can shake, your smile can be fake, but your life is never a mistake"*
> (AUTHOR UNKNOWN).

Reflection: Last night Adelyn and I walked to a nearby school playground. After passing a knot of adolescent girls, I began to hear "hi's." I paid no attention, until the calls came closer. The greetings were for me.

"You look familiar," the oldest ventured. I knew we weren't acquainted, but that didn't last long. The four were sisters, ages thirteen, twelve, and ten (the youngest were twins—identical except that one suffered a severe and grotesque form of foot overgrowth syndrome). The girls were homeless, having moved in the day before, with their sick mom and her abusive boyfriend, with an acquaintance in the area. It sounded as though there were a total of eight siblings, give or take (some were related in a more tenuous sense than others).

For the next two hours I learned every sordid detail they had time to blurt out. Even after they had wandered off in the gathering dusk, two, and then all four, returned to tell me more. They showed me their "owies," including one or two scratches on the weblike feet the little one seemed anxious to show me. Was I coming back tomorrow night? Every other night?

Probably not. But I've thought about these sisters a good deal today, hoping and praying they'll find love here and there during the course of their nearly continual moving. How much tragedy, I ask myself, can little hearts handle? And how can God allow it? These questions are as contemporary as the ancient book of Job, one of my favorites (as you may have gathered from my frequent references). My, and no doubt your, only consolation in situations like this: God cares, and one day we'll understand.

Prayer Prompt: What tragic circumstances in the life of someone you know seem beyond belief?

Godly woman,

HE'LL MAKE IT RIGHT.

You who?

Verse: "You are a chosen people, a royal priesthood, a holy nation, God's special possession, that you may declare the praises of him who called you out of darkness into his wonderful light" (1 Peter 2:9).

> *"God is love. He didn't need us. But he wanted us. And that is the most amazing thing"* (RICK WARREN).

Reflection: Tavis at two was puzzled by a question repeatedly emerging from the lips of friendly adults: "How are you?" The answer to the query as my grandson heard it ("Who are you?") seemed obvious, and his response to still another obtuse grown-up was understandably tentative: "I'm Tavis. I'm a boy."

Simple questions? Perhaps. But if you stop to consider their ramifications, you might have to pause longer than Tavis did. How and who are you? These deceptively simple queries may have to be turned around to do them justice.

It's easy for us, like Tavis, to get them confused—even fused—in our minds. To what extent does *how* you are depend in your mind on *who* you are? If you and I can keep in mind Peter's definition, above, of our identity, there will be little question, circumstances notwithstanding, of how we're doing at any given (let's make that God-given) moment.

Prayer Prompt: Pause to assess the big picture of who you are in God. How does this affect your perception of your present situation?

Godly woman,

HE HAS DETERMINED YOUR *WHO*; YOUR *HOW* WILL FOLLOW.

$\mathcal{J}$ust beyond reach

Verse: "Never be lacking in zeal, but keep your spiritual fervor" (Romans 12:11).

"You cannot sustain spiritual momentum without the Holy Spirit's work" (PAUL CHAPPELL).

Reflection: I recall my journaled observations of a much younger Adelyn on the floor during "tummy time": I set her down inches from *the* toy, and her eyes brighten in anticipation. Her tentative reach falls short of the tantalizingly swinging Pooh, at which time she positions herself on hands and knees, rocking. Dropping back down, she resorts to the scooch.

Her efforts do yield results: Inch by inch she moves herself—sidewise and backward—away from her goal. As the toy is about to disappear from sight, she cranes her neck for a resigned backward glance. From that point on any entertainment is fair game.

If she has pushed herself off her blanket, scratching the carpet with eight fingernails serves as a poor second choice. It's then that Grandma relents and places her back within reach of the prize.

I can be a little like that. Moved by a worship service, I find myself on my spiritual hands and knees, craning my neck with every muscle taut, oh so near to grasping the ecstasy that will remain just beyond my human reach.

As I head away from the experience, I'm still inspired enough for a backward mental glance. Soon enough, though, I'm into the work week, "scratching out a living" (I enjoy my work too much for this to be an accurate metaphor, but you get the idea), my mind preoccupied somewhere between Sundays. Then, as "the Day" approaches (Hebrews 10:25), the Spirit gently pulls me back and deposits me within reach of the altar.

Prayer Prompt: Does your movement from worship to Monday lose something in the transition?

$\mathcal{G}$odly woman,

ASK THE SPIRIT FOR HELP MAINTAINING

MOMENTUM BETWEEN SUNDAYS.

*D*ownsizing

Verses: "Godliness with contentment is great gain. For we brought nothing into the world, and we can take nothing out of it. But if we have food and clothing, we will be content with that" (1 Timothy 6:6–8).

"The more wants we have, the further we are from God, and the nearer we approach him, the better can we dispense with everything that is not Himself" (MADAME GUYON).

Reflection: It seems I've made a breakthrough in the contentment category. Due to the sharpness not of my wits but of Annabelle's teeth, our household has been somewhat alarmingly downsized over the past six months. There are indicators, though, that our pup is settling down. As I sat down just now to write, in fact, I glanced appreciatively in her direction—just in time to catch a sizeable bite disappearing from one of my decorator pillows. It's OK this time around—I'm soon to turn fifty-nine, and this particular pillow was embroidered with the following message: "I'm not 50 something. I'm $49.95 plus tax." Actually, I had considered sending on this delicate reminder to my "kid" sister when her birthday rolls around. Oh well . . .

Taking a quick mental inventory, it occurs to me that much of our loss has ironically been in the clothing category (see quote from Paul, above)—with shoes and bras taking the biggest single hits. Yes, I've had to replace two-year-old carpet in the den with laminate, several of my chairs sport tooth marks, and Adelyn's collection of toys and stuffed animals is significantly smaller (that last casualty really needed to happen).

Last week, in the process of switching to a new insurance carrier, I experienced a self-revelation. I opted to reduce the coverage for my in-condo possessions by half. My rationale: "What more could I possibly need for the rest of my life?" I guess I can say I've finally internalized it: Everything I own is expendable. My treasure lies elsewhere.

Prayer Prompt: Focus in on one item from which you can't imagine being parted. What would it take for you to let even that go?

odly woman,

FIND IN HIM YOUR TREASURE.

$\mathcal{S}$taying home

Verse: "During Solomon's lifetime Judah and Israel, from Dan to Beersheba, lived in safety, everyone under their own vine and under their own fig tree" (1 Kings 4:25).

> *"Stay, stay at home, my heart, and rest. Home-keeping hearts are happiest"* (HENRY WADSWORTH LONGFELLOW).

Reflection: The expression "everyone under their own vine and fig tree" seems to have been Old Testament shorthand—or longhand, depending on how you look at it—for "at home and at peace" (see also Micah 4:4; Zechariah 3:10).

Vernon Joseph Baker, a United States Army Medal of Honor recipient for his actions in 1945 in Italy, together with his platoon killed twenty-six enemy soldiers and destroyed six machine gun nests, two observer posts, and four dugouts. He performed with valor far from home or peace, yet his later words tell us where his heart resided during his deployment: "Home is where the heart can laugh without shyness. Home is where the heart's tears can dry at their own pace."

Staying home may not be the most exciting thing a human can do, but it has throughout history been the choice of so many of those who have known a happy home. I'm blown away by some words I recently discovered tucked away in the Old Testament: "If a man has recently married, he must not be sent to war or have any other duty laid on him. For one year he is to be free to stay at home and bring happiness to the wife he has married" (Deuteronomy 24:5).

Wow! Talk about progressive. And we only recently thought family leave policies were cutting edge.

Prayer Prompt: To what degree do you associate home with rest and happiness?

$\mathcal{G}$odly woman,
YOUR HEART RESTS BEST AT HOME.

Temper shepherd

Verse: "Better a patient person than a warrior, one with self-control than one who takes a city" (Proverbs 16:32).

"It's very important not to lose your temper in a courtroom, or in anything else you're doing" (WARREN CHRISTOPHER).

Reflection: My granddaughter Adelyn and I like to use an old song for her bedtime prayer. You may know it: "Jesus, Tender Shepherd, Hear Me." Unfamiliar with the word "tender," though, Addie has substituted one she knows all too well. I chuckle each time I hear her solemn little voice raised in song: "Jesus, *temper shepherd*, hear me."

Addie recently went through about a month of regular tantrums. For the past several weeks she's managed to temper (the verb form of that word is ironic, isn't it?) the impulse to tantrum, seemingly on the basis of a serious talk with her mom, who herself struggles with anger management issues.

I tend to be the slow simmer type. I can take a lot, but (if you'll excuse my mixing metaphors) my eventual rising bubble can mean real trouble for whoever happens to be sitting on my last nerve. Addie and I have prayed about this issue, and I think she has it right: Jesus is more than willing to shepherd our tempers if we'll only allow him access.

Prayer Prompt: When it comes to anger, what's your typical pattern?

Godly woman,

INVITE HIM TO TEMPER YOUR TEMPER.

$\mathcal{A}$ngel visitors

Verse: "The angel of the Lord encamps around those who fear him, and he delivers them" (Psalm 34:7).

> *"The magnitude of life is overwhelming. Angels are here to help us take it peace by peace"* (LEVENDE WATERS).

Reflection: I'm not much of a camper, although I've done it often enough to connect the experience with summertime. I'm quite sure that in David's day the words *camp* and *encamp* were associated with soldiering rather than vacationing, but when I read this verse I still visualize a tent with an angel guardian on alert at the flap.

Psalm 34 holds special associations for me: My mom died at the age of thirty-five, and this psalm was her favorite.

I don't believe the Bible specifically teaches about guardian angels, but no matter. I don't need to have a personal, designated angel to enjoy God's protection, which evidently involves angelic delegates. Nor have I ever seen physical evidence of the presence of an angel, although I believe that many have.

George Elliot had this to say on the subject: "The golden moments in the stream of life rush past us and we see nothing but sand; the angels come to visit us, and we only know them when they are gone."

Prayer Prompt: What role do you understand God's angels to play in your life?

$\mathcal{G}$odly woman,

YOU'RE ENCIRCLED BY HIS SENTINELS.

$\mathcal{T}$he light in the window

Verse: "If you greet only your own people, who are you doing more than others?" (Matthew 5:47).

"Smile, it is the key that fits the lock of everybody's heart"
(ANTHONY D'ANGELO).

Reflection: When I was six years old I spent a month in the hospital with nephritis. My mom provided me with a tablet of paper and a pencil, instructing me to smile at everyone who walked into my room, drawing a smile (this was in the day before the smiley face had been invented) every time one of them smiled back. No one recognized, of course, that I was conducting a survey, but the results were quite amazing.

Do you ever walk past someone going in the opposite direction (not on an outdoor stroll, where people are more likely to exchange pleasantries, but in the aisle of a busy supermarket) and feel the urge to smile at them?

Some days my smiles are almost irrepressible (know what I mean?), but I feel the need to temper my enthusiasm with strangers, perhaps just turning up the corners of my mouth slightly, maybe just a tad more than the Mona Lisa. Most of the time they respond almost exactly in kind.

"A smile," observes Denis Waitley, "is the light in your window that tells others that there is a caring, sharing person inside." The person you smile at may need just that.

Prayer Prompt: How attuned are you to the importance of random gestures of well-wishing?

odly woman,
ACKNOWLEDGE THE STRANGER.

God's good will

Verse: "Let us then approach God's throne of grace with confidence, so that we may receive mercy and find grace to help us in our time of need" (Hebrews 4:16).

> *"I know God will not give me anything I can't handle. I just wish*
> *He didn't trust me so much"* (MOTHER TERESA).

Reflection: Already as a little child, I was instructed to avoid words like *luck* and *chance*. Many was the time I found a greeting card with a great picture, only to return it to its slot because of "Good luck" in the message. We weren't that kind of people, I knew.

Only recently have I come to recognize that, while God has indeed planned our big-picture futures, he doesn't orchestrate every detail of our lives. God foreknows but doesn't foreordain our decisions or the events— events that may be consequences of our decisions—in our lives. It's always outside his will for bad things to happen to people.

This is clear from the Bible's teaching on temptation: "When tempted, no one should say, 'God is tempting me.' For God cannot be tempted by evil, nor does he tempt anyone" (James 1:13). (The prelude to the book of Job bears this out.)

It's at that point that grace comes into play. God didn't get us into our predicament, but he does offer us a way out.

Prayer Prompt: Is there a circumstance in your life in which you particularly need God's grace?

Godly woman,

HE HAS YOUR BEST INTERESTS AT HEART.

Mack

Verse: "'The poor man had nothing except one little ewe lamb he had bought. He raised it, and it grew up with him and his children. It shared his food, drank from his cup and even slept in his arms. It was like a daughter to him" (2 Samuel 12:3).

"Be thou comforted, little dog. Thou too in resurrection shall have
a little golden tail" (MARTIN LUTHER).

Reflection: Growing up in Grand Rapids in the 1930s, my dad remembers the day his brother rescued an injured young crow in the woods. He nursed "Mack" back to health, clipped his tongue, and taught him some English, after which the crow regaled the family and neighborhood with loud ramblings. In 1935 and 1936 Grandpa worked for the government's WPA program. He spent his days digging ditches, often with Mack perched on his shoulder.

It wasn't unusual for Mack to fly off during the day, but one evening, to the family's dismay, the crow failed to return. Months later, arriving at a new job site, Grandpa was stopped in his tracks by a loud, distinctive voice. His investigation took him to a nearby backyard, where he encountered the friendly Mack in a cage, carrying on a lively monologue.

The Bible is full of references to God's concern for animals (see Jonah 4:11 and Matthew 6:26). Most of those mentioned are either wild, livestock, or working stock, but it surprised me to find the mention of pets. I can't help but chuckle at God's question to Job about the Leviathan (crocodile?): "Can you make a pet of it like a bird or put it on a leash for the young women in your house?" (Job 41:5).

Despite the title of a Disney movie of some years back, I've always been quite sure that all dogs *don't* go to heaven. But I can't help but wonder when I read Isaiah's grand vision of the future, when lions will lie down with lambs. . . . Fact is, we just don't know what we'll encounter in the new earth.

Prayer Prompt: Does God's concern for animals affect your treatment of these, his creatures?

odly woman,
YOU CAN'T OVERESTIMATE HIS LOVE.

$\mathcal{A}$ piece of work

Verses: "The mind governed by the flesh is hostile to God; it does not submit to God's law, nor can it do so. Those who are in the realm of the flesh cannot please God" (Romans 8:7–8).

"A sinner can no more repent and believe without the Holy Spirit's aid than he can create a world" (CHARLES SPURGEON).

Reflection: My daughter Khristina shared with me that she had just run into a "piece of work" at a gas station. A young woman, she said, had removed the oxygen tube from her infant's nose to go into the station, only to return to the car, reinstate the baby's oxygen flow—and light up a cigarette.

Much as we shake our heads at such irresponsible behavior, we have to concede, if we think about it further, that we all act at times in much the same way. The question becomes whether we're allowing ourselves to be *controlled* by the sinful nature.

Each one of us is indeed a "piece of God's work," and as such beloved by him. But it's only when we willingly submit ourselves to his law, allowing his Spirit to change us from the inside out, that we can make moment-by-moment decisions that please him.

Without the Spirit's foresight and insight, our shortsightedness will be evident to us only in hindsight.

Prayer Prompt: What sinful behavior comes closest to controlling you?

Godly woman,
CHERISH THE INSIGHT THE SPIRIT WORKS IN YOU.

*L*ittle ones at worship

Verse: "Through the praise of children and infants you have established a stronghold against your enemies, to silence the foe and the avenger" (Psalm 8:2).

"Would Christ have made a child the standard of faith if He had known that it was not capable of understanding His words?"
(D. L. MOODY).

Reflection: Two or three times now I've been caught inadvertently interrupting Adelyn's devotions. We're mutually enjoying a new children's CD of gospel songs and choruses, which we regularly play in the car. I can't get enough of listening to her just-four-year-old voice chiming in on the lyrics from the backseat.

For the first while I joined in, but she politely asked me to let the sing-along be her exclusive domain. I've also tried to talk to her, pointing out something about a song or asking a question. Her response has been long-suffering but serious: "Please be quiet, Granna. I'm singing to Jesus."

I can only imagine that the "foe and the avenger" strongly dislikes catching Addie at praise. Habits ingrained that early in life will (hopefully) be hard for him to break.

In the words of Jean Paul Richter, "The smallest children are nearest to God, as the smallest planets are nearest the sun."

Prayer Prompt: Concentrate on a child who is close to your heart and pray for his or her continued and uninterrupted faith development.

odly woman,
ENCOURAGE DEVOTION IN THE YOUNG.

$\mathcal{D}$eep and wide

Verses: "I pray that you, being rooted and established in love, may have power, together with all the Lord's holy people, to grasp how wide and long and high and deep is the love of Christ, and to know this love that surpasses knowledge—that you may be filled to the measure of all the fullness of God" (Ephesians 3:17–19).

> *"There is no surprise more magical than the surprise of being loved; it is God's finger on man's shoulder"* (CHARLES MORGAN).

Reflection: Paul describes God's love as encompassing infinity in every direction. We might say that the God who is almighty, omniscient, and omnipresent is also all-loving (or omni-loving?).

OK. My attempt at coining words may have fallen flat, but love is more than just an attribute of God—it defines him, just as he defines love (1 John 4:8). BTW, if you're looking for a shot in the arm in the area of love, 1 John is a good place to turn.

Paul's words in Romans 8:38–39 beautifully complement those in Ephesians 3, above. It's precisely because God's love is infinitely wide and long and high and deep that "neither death nor life, neither angels nor demons, neither the present nor the future, nor any powers, neither height nor depth, nor anything else in all creation, will be able to separate us from the love of God that is in Christ Jesus our Lord."

That just begs for a Paul-inspired "Praise be to God!" doesn't it?

Prayer Prompt: Before going to God in prayer, consider the implications of his infinite love in your life.

$\mathcal{G}$*odly woman,*

HIS LOVE IS MEASURELESS.

ℒoving confrontation

Verses: "Better is open rebuke than hidden love. Wounds from a friend can be trusted" (Proverbs 27:5–6).

"Only your real friends will tell you when your face is dirty"
(SICILIAN PROVERB).

Reflection: Albert Camus put both of the above proverbs in perspective by reminding us that the ideal of friendship presented in them isn't always the reality: "Don't believe your friends when they ask you to be honest with them. All they really want is to be maintained in the good opinion they have of themselves."

He's talking, of course, about the other side of the equation: our invitations for our friends to "wound" us. If we ask the questions—and truly want the answers—we'd better be prepared, and gracious enough, to accept them.

One of my daughters saw fit earlier this week to criticize my honest confrontation of her sister—ironically, on the subject of honesty. The upshot, if not the exact words: "You haven't seen her in months. Can't you just listen instead of telling her what she's doing wrong?"

I felt bad for a short time. But I keep going back to my original response: "Do you think I challenge my kids because it's easy? I do it because I love you guys." "Friendship," stated Eustace Budgell way back in 1711, "is a strong and habitual inclination in two persons to promote the good and happiness of one another." The saying fits family relationships just as well.

But in order to promote the good, we sometimes have to relegate the happiness, at least temporarily, to second place.

Prayer Prompt: How would you rate yourself on the "honesty in friendship" spectrum, in terms of both giving and taking?

odly woman,
CHOOSE TACTFUL HONESTY.

When wrong Is right?

Verse: "The city [Jericho] and all that is in it are to be devoted to the LORD. Only Rahab the prostitute and all who are with her in her house shall be spared, because she hid the spies we sent" (Joshua 6:17).

"Never let your sense of morals prevent you from doing what's right" (ISAAC ASIMOV).

Reflection: The timing was unplanned, but three-year-old Amanda moved in with me on the day of my thirtieth birthday. Her foster placement was intended to have been pre-adoptive, but being flanked in the household by rough-and-tumble two- and four-year-old boys did little to meet the needs of this fragile and needy little girl. She herself sabotaged the placement in no uncertain terms.

Amanda and I bonded immediately, and the foster mom called in frustration the morning after our first visit. Amanda had cried inconsolably for me: "For the first time in her life, this child has fallen in love."

I shouldn't have been surprised a few weeks later to encounter resistance in my attempt to return Amanda after a long weekend. It seemed surreal to me, as I made my way up the long driveway, that "Mom" was seated, unsmiling, at the picnic table at the far end. After we had established that our respective weekends had gone well, she stated her intention: "If yours was great and ours was great, why don't you just take her *right now*?" She was ready with a large cardboard box of clothing to follow through on her "suggestion."

If there are instances in which other rightness trumps correct procedure, this was one of them; I agreed immediately. My social worker's belated consent came in the form of "Do what's right for Amanda, but please don't tell me about it." Before the "illegal" weeks of Amanda's placement had passed, I asked myself repeatedly whether extenuating circumstances ever do make a wrong "right." In Rahab's case, I reminded myself, God both condoned and rewarded lying (check out Joshua 2). At the very least I'll have to concede that his ways are not simplistic.

Prayer Prompt: When have you wrestled with a moral or ethical dilemma like this? Were you comfortable with the resolution?

Godly woman,

HE WORKS IN THE GRAY AREAS TOO.

*W*atered-down wisdom

Verses: "Woe to those who are wise in their own eyes and clever in their own sight. Woe to those who are heroes at drinking wine and champions at mixing drinks, who acquit the guilty for a bribe but deny justice to the innocent" (Isaiah 5:21–23).

"Fight to escape from your own cleverness. If you do, then you will find salvation and uprightness through Jesus Christ our Lord"
(JOHN CLIMACUS).

Reflection: Sitting at my desk just now, my eye fell on a ready-to-be-discarded McDonald's soda cup. I could hardly believe what I read: "A toast to your wisdom, clever drink buyer—you have selected a classic fountain beverage, precisely mixed for maximum enjoyment." Whoa! Somebody's concept of wisdom has gotten seriously watered down (no pun intended in terms of the leftover beverage diluted with long-since-melted ice cubes).

It's interesting in the above passage that the prophet uses some similar words: "wise," "clever" (and, yes, in a totally different context, "mixing drinks"). A far-fetched comparison, yes, but the end of this verse puts it in perspective for me. The self-proclaimed wise and clever individuals of whom Isaiah is speaking accept bribes and pervert justice.

I don't know about you, but "wise" and "clever" are not in my mind synonymous. My connotations of the second word are, in fact, often negative. Criminals can be masterminds in their chosen field, but they're seldom wise. And being wise in my own eyes is a contradiction—a little like seeing myself as humble. When it comes to wisdom, the only critic who counts is God.

Prayer Prompt: Ask God for true, Spirit-imparted wisdom, applying your request to some specific situation in your life.

odly woman,

HIS ESTIMATION COUNTS.

"Dutcher"

Verse: "For there is no difference between Jew and Gentile—the same Lord is Lord of all and richly blesses all who call on him" (Romans 10:12).

"One day our descendants will think it incredible that we paid so much attention to things like the amount of melanin in our skin or the shape of our eyes or our gender instead of the unique identities of each of us as complex human beings" (FRANKLIN THOMAS).

Reflection: From the time we kids were small, we understood that we were Dutch. All four of our grandparents had emigrated from the Netherlands, and because our church affiliation had a strong ethnic component, our identity was tied as much to our racial/cultural heritage as to our American citizenship.

Dad tells the story of our family visiting the San Diego Zoo when we older kids were preschoolers. Walking behind a dark-skinned family of a different ethnicity, my sister Debbie, impressed, blurted loudly, "Look, Daddy. Those people are *Dutcher* than we are!"

I listened to an NPR newscaster this morning commenting on the surprisingly multiethnic German team that has been so successful at the World Cup soccer finals currently taking place in South Africa. Eleven of the twenty-three players, though German citizens, could have qualified to play on teams from other countries. The German gentleman interviewed commented that his country (like the United States) is to a larger and larger degree embracing its diversity. Our world is changing!

My own denomination, the Christian Reformed Church, will never lose its Dutch roots. But my particular congregation includes refugees from several different countries, as well as associate members from all over the world who have come to Grand Rapids, some with their families, for three or four years of seminary training.

All of us who together call on the Lord's name are benefitting richly from the mutual blessings we offer one another.

Prayer Prompt: Pray for a sister or brother in Christ who comes from a cultural, racial, or ethnic background unlike your own.

Godly woman,
EMBRACE DIVERSITY.

$\mathscr{B}$etween two thieves

Verse: "Can any one of you by worrying add a single hour to your life?" (Matthew 6:27).

"It is not the experience of today that drives us mad; it is remorse or bitterness for something which happened yesterday and dread of what tomorrow may bring" (AUTHOR UNKNOWN).

Reflection: "Many of us," observes Fulton Oursler, "crucify ourselves between two thieves—regret for the past and fear of the future." Not only will worry fail to add an hour to our lives, but it will most likely detract from them, both quantitatively and qualitatively. And it tells God that our trust in him is conditional.

Moving back in the opposite direction, regret may sound more godlike. But what we really need is repentance, not regret, because repentance moves us on, putting us in a position to embrace an altogether different quality of future. In the words of Anne Sophie Swetchine, "Repentance is accepted remorse." Listen also to Paul: "Godly sorrow brings repentance that leads to salvation and leaves no regret" (2 Corinthians 7:10).

It's possible with the Spirit's help to extricate ourselves from those thieves threatening to diminish us from both sides. Repentance, through which we receive forgiveness, liberates us from our past, and faith frees us from fear of our future. The prophet Isaiah put it this way: "In repentance and rest is your salvation, in quietness and trust is your strength" (Isaiah 30:15; see also my meditation for February 27).

Prayer Prompt: Which one of these thieves is the bigger issue for you?

odly woman,

AVOID REGRET AND DOUSE FEAR.

$\mathcal{U}$nconditional forgiveness

Verses: "If anyone has caused grief, he has not so much grieved me as he has grieved all of you, to some extent—not to put it too severely. The punishment inflicted on him by the majority is sufficient. Now instead, you ought to forgive and comfort him, so that he will not be overwhelmed by excessive sorrow. I urge you, therefore, to reaffirm your love for him" (2 Corinthians 2:5–8).

"Most of us can forgive and forget; we just don't want the other person to forget that we forgave" (IVERN BALL).

Reflection: When a member who has caused a rift in a congregation repents, we don't expect to talk about comforting that person and reaffirming our love. When a fellow church member has given us all grief, we're much more likely to tolerate her presence than to worry about whether she'll be overwhelmed by regret.

Our forgiveness (if it truly is that) might be tight-lipped or cool at first. We'll feed her some slack after a while, but she deserves the arm's length treatment for now, just in case she starts to forget what we forgave.

Mark Twain once referred to forgiveness as "the fragrance that the violet sheds on the heel that has crushed it." What church, or hurting church member, couldn't use a little more of that fragrance? The church owes it to our Lord Jesus Christ to tend those flickering candles and bruised reeds (see Isaiah 42:3 or Jesus' quotation of this verse in Matthew 12:20)—including and perhaps especially those who got that way by hurting us.

The principle applies just as well to families and friendships.

Prayer Prompt: To whom are you holding out grudging forgiveness? Have you considered that this kind of "holding" may not be much different from withholding?

$\mathcal{G}$odly woman,
HELP MAINTAIN UNITY.

ℒ**ittle church**

Verse: "Where two or three gather in my name, there am I with them" (Matthew 18:20).

> *"No government, no matter how well-intentioned, can take the place of the family in the scheme of things"* (GERALD R. FORD).

Reflection: Pope John Paul II had a high estimation of marriage and family, as expressed in these words: "Marriage is an act of will that signifies and involves a mutual gift, which unites the spouses and binds them to their eventual souls, with whom they make up a sole family—a domestic church."

Some time ago I spent two days attending church board meetings, during which we discussed the roles of family and church in the spiritual nurture of children. A phrase used in a proposed new vision statement for a denominational publishing venture was "little church." The reference was to the family, particularly as it relates to Christian education and the instilling of moral values in the young. The intention was to honor the institution of family as the most basic (but certainly not the lowest) common denominator in the discussion. Ironically, in the opinion of some the "little church" hook failed to do justice to the significance of the family role.

As fall approaches, church activities for a new season are in the final stages of preparation. A challenge facing many churches is how to generate parental interest and involvement in the church education program. When the "little church" abnegates this responsibility, the whole church—present and future—pays a price.

Prayer Prompt: If you're a mom, a grandma, or any woman with child-related gifts to offer your congregation, how seriously will you take the opportunity?

odly woman,

OF WHAT "LITTLE CHURCH" ARE YOU A MEMBER (HONORARY COUNTS)?

$\mathcal{T}$imes of refreshing

Verse: "Repent, then, and turn to God, so that your sins may be wiped out, that times of refreshing may come from the Lord" (Acts 3:19).

> *"Christ is not a reservoir but a spring. His life is continual, active and ever passing on with an outflow as necessary as its inflow. If we do not perpetually draw the fresh supply from the living Fountain, we shall either grow stagnant or empty. It is, therefore, not so much a perpetual fullness as a perpetual filling"*
>
> (A. B. SIMPSON).

Reflection: "This was one of those perfect New England days in late summer," writes novelist and poet Sarah Orne Jewett, "where the spirit of autumn takes a first stealing flight, like a spy, through the ripening country-side, and, with feigned sympathy for those who droop with August heat, puts her cool cloak of bracing air about leaf and flower and human shoulders."

For me nothing could be more welcome than that hint of cooler times to come. My comfort radius runs between about fifty and seventy degrees—with sunshine but without humidity, thank you very much. Otherwise I'd be cold on the lower end of that spectrum and verging on hot at the higher.

I revel especially in that occasional mid-summer cool front that seems to spring out of nowhere—in that "undeserved" refreshment I appreciate all the more for its brevity. When it comes to the extreme seasons, "unseasonable" is always for me a welcome descriptor. It's the same way with spiritual refreshment. It's never something we merit, but its presence is all the more appreciated during our seasons of discontent, of unwelcome spiritual cold or heat.

Prayer Prompt: What in your situation makes you yearn for refreshment? Have you asked for it?

$\mathcal{G}$odly woman,

SEEK AND APPRECIATE SPIRITUAL REVITALIZATION.

ℒeast likely to succeed

Verse: "When the angel of the LORD appeared to Gideon, he said, 'The LORD is with you, mighty warrior" (Judges 6:12).

*"God deliberately chooses weak, suffering and unlikely candidates
to get His work done, so that in the end, the glory goes to God and
not to the person"* (JONI EARECKSON TADA).

Reflection: Where in this passage do we make the jump from cowering farmer to mighty warrior? Ironically, the skeptical Gideon doesn't question the angel's strange form of address but only God's ability to rescue his people.

We see this thread throughout the Bible as God again and again calls unlikely and flawed characters to do his bidding. Look at Nathanael, who was to become one of the Twelve, in John 1:45–51. When Philip approaches him with the news that "We have found the one Moses wrote about," his write-off is sarcastic, even scathing: "Nazareth! Can anything good come from there?"

God often chooses and uses weaker vessels to showcase his own glory. But we also see in the Bible evidence of characters growing to fit and fill the audacious purposes God has for them. Just look at Moses and Peter.

God alone sees our true potential. Whether he's calling you to something intimidating or comfortable, he has picked the right person for the job. This isn't to say that our every undertaking for the Lord will be successful. Sometimes we attempt an avenue of service that just isn't "us." In such situations, instead of questioning God's judgment, we're wise to ask whether that particular function was truly in line with his calling for us.

Prayer Prompt: As church activities gear up this fall, what is God asking of you?

Godly woman,
SEEK HIS WILL FOR YOUR SERVICE.

$\mathcal{P}$ride prevention

Verses: "Three hundred of them drank from cupped hands, lapping like dogs. All the rest got down on their knees to drink. The LORD said to Gideon, 'With the three hundred men that lapped I will save you and give the Midianites into your hands'" (Judges 7:6–7).

"I know I owe my all to Thee. O, take this heart I cannot give.
Do Thou my Strength my Saviour be; and make me to Thy Glory
live!" (ANNE BRONTË).

Reflection: Not long ago three-year-old Adelyn opened the refrigerator door, inadvertently knocking a filled plastic tumbler to the floor. Before I could react, Annabelle was lapping up orange juice, and Addie was dropping to the floor, ready to assist, doggie-style, in the cleanup effort. I think I'm getting too old for this . . .

Seriously, though, we may wonder why God chose so unlikely a criterion for inclusion in Israel's army. Without doubt the Lord wanted to make sure that no one would later on connect any dots between Gideon and Israel's improbable victory.

Paul's words seem pertinent: "[I]n order to keep me from becoming conceited, I was given a thorn in my flesh, a messenger of Satan, to torment me" (2 Corinthians 12:7). God was evidently ensuring that the glory would remain his own by allowing Satan some leeway with regard to Paul's body—just as he had done much earlier with Job. (Do I rightly detect in these examples an element of Satan playing himself directly into God's hand?) One way or another, we can rest assured that God will never mislead us. And he'll make certain no one misunderstands the power source behind divine victory.

Prayer Prompt: What "victories" in your experience can be attributed only to God?

$\mathcal{G}$*odly woman,*
THE GLORY BELONGS TO HIM.

$\mathscr{L}$onging for the sea

Verses: "If you have any encouragement from being united with Christ, if any comfort from his love, if any common sharing in the Spirit, if any tenderness and compassion, then make my joy complete by being like-minded, having the same love, being one in spirit and of one mind" (Philippians 2:1–2).

> *"A successful team beats with one heart"* (AUTHOR UNKNOWN).

Reflection: "If you want to build a ship," counsels Antoine de Saint-Exupery, "don't herd people together to collect wood and don't assign them tasks and work, but rather teach them to long for the endless immensity of the sea."

Unity, fellowship, like-mindedness, love, commonality, equality—all noble aspirations for God's people. Notice that Paul speaks first of unity and fellowship with Christ, making this the model for interrelationships among believers.

The above quotation by Saint-Exupery reminds me, though, that much more is needed for the oneness of a congregation than assuring that all tasks and assignments are covered, based on the deliberations of pastors, staff, counsels, committees, and subcommittees. Unity of purpose must begin with unity of vision, and this isn't something we can work into our plans at the beginning of each fall season or quote as a preface to our blueprint for yet another year of doing church.

If our focus, week in and week out, remains fixed on teaching—or inviting—people "to long for the endless immensity of the sea," the common feeling, purpose, energy, and shared vision will follow naturally.

Prayer Prompt: How united is your congregation in terms of vision and purpose? What's the state of your union?

odly woman,
INVESTMENT PRECEDES ASSIGNMENT.

God's storytellers

Verses: "Joshua set up at Gilgal the twelve stones [the Israelites] had taken out of the Jordan. He said to the Israelites, 'In the future when your descendants ask their parents, "What do these stones mean?" tell them, "Israel crossed the Jordan on dry ground"'" (Joshua 4:20–22).

"'Thou shalt not' is soon forgotten, but 'Once upon a time' lasts forever" (PHILIP PULLMAN).

Reflection: I love reading—and listening. Although I can become engrossed in nonfiction, though, I'll have to classify myself first of all as a sucker for a good story. When someone starts to tell one, whether it's a sermon illustration, a long-ago and far-away nostalgic recollection, a humorous snippet or high adventure account from the *Reader's Digest*, or even a cartoon episode tickling my subconscious from the background while I'm working at my desk, I look forward to the unfolding. A story is a treat.

"If a nation loses its storytellers," notes Peter Handke, "it loses its childhood." And if the church loses its childhood, it stands to lose something in the transition to its future (an occurrence the Spirit, thankfully, is at work to prevent).

Ever wonder why the story of Paul's conversion, so pivotal to the church's infancy, is related three times in Acts (check out Acts 9:1–19; 22:2–21; and 26:4–18)? Why did Luke bother to record Paul's first and second retellings word for word when he could have said something like "Paul related to the people in Jerusalem [or to King Agrippa] the story of his conversion experience on the road to Damascas"?

In the words of Anne Watson, "Stories tell us of what we already knew and forgot, and remind us of what we haven't yet imagined." I'm not quite sure what she means by that last clause, but I do at least sense what she's getting at. It's one of those ponderables, like a good story.

Prayer Prompt: What Bible story means the most to you? Why does it move you as it does?

Godly woman,

RESPOND TO STORIES OF FAITH, ANCIENT OR PERSONAL.

TELL THEM TOO!

*R*outine

Verse: "There is a time for everything, and a season for every activity under the heavens" (Ecclesiastes 3:1).

"For pragmatic reasons, I love the routine. I love the structure of it. I love knowing that my days are free. I know where I'm going at night" (ANDREA MARTIN).

Reflection: I like Annie Dillard's perspective on the routine our work imposes on our days: "A schedule defends from chaos and whim. It is a net for catching days. It is a scaffolding on which a worker can stand and labor with both hands at sections of time." How many of us as busy women haven't encountered the irony that our productivity at home is directly proportional to our productivity outside the home?

It amazes me to think back on my days of full-time employment while raising a family. My kids and I had fun, but we always completed our work first, including a fairly thorough housecleaning every Saturday. That standard began to slip when I developed chronic fatigue syndrome more than a decade ago, but I didn't jettison routine altogether until I lost my job several years later. Sure, the work gets done, generally a little at a time—when I feel an energy surge, catch a vision for change, or start to get bugged by a particular need. The house stays orderly, but it isn't super clean.

As a freelance writer and editor, I tell myself that my professional work comes first. Seriously, though, I believe this is because I enjoy it so much. One way or another, working from home does blur the boundaries in terms of schedule.

The Bible doesn't include words like "routine" and "schedule." Routine was a given in ancient times, and schedule for the common person was largely dictated by what needed to be done, and when, in order to survive. Along that line, have you noticed that the Teacher of Ecclesiastes nowhere mentions a time for work and a time for leisure? How scheduled a life do you desire or prefer? Do you need that buffer against chaos and whim? That net for catching days?

Prayer Prompt: Have you ever thought of thanking God for agendas, routines, boundaries, and predictability? Does an uncluttered mind and environment enhance your life, including the spiritual dimension?

odly woman,
APPRECIATE THE GIFT OF ORDER.

$\mathcal{G}$ood gifts

Verse: "If you . . . though you are evil, know how to give good gifts to your children, how much more will your Father in heaven give good gifts to those who ask him!" (Matthew 7:11).

> *"Mommy talks to herself and says yes to herself. Her*
> *always does that when she wants me to have something"*
> (ADELYN HUISJEN, AGE FOUR).

Reflection: Who of us doesn't enjoy gifting a child—our own, if we're blessed with them, or others about whom we care? "Occasional" giving (Christmas, birthdays, Valentine's Day, and the like) is fun, but perhaps especially delightful for both giver and recipient are those occasional "for no special reason" surprises.

When it makes sense, we give according to a child's expressed wishes or requests; as much as possible we give what will be beneficial as well as pleasing. I enjoy offering unexpected little extras in anticipation of a new school year, like now.

God's gifts to me are anything but occasional. Like the daily manna enjoyed by his people in the wilderness, they're continual, dependable, ample, and always good. So why does Jesus want me to ask for them? To acknowledge my dependency, I suppose, as well as to express my gratitude, even in advance of those regular blessings on which I rely.

But there's another reason. In Psalm 37:4 David urges us to "Take delight in the Lord," going on "and he will give you the desires of your heart." God delights in our delight, and we express it best when we tell him about it, acknowledging the connection to him.

Prayer Prompt: Make it a point both to articulate your needs and to thank God for his ongoing provision.

$\mathcal{G}$*odly woman,*
HE DELIGHTS IN YOUR PLEASURE.

$\mathcal{T}$raveling light

Verse: "I was ashamed to ask the king for soldiers and horsemen to protect us from enemies on the road, because we had told the king, 'The gracious hand of our God is on everyone who looks to him'" (Ezra 8:22).

"Christianity is not a message which has to be believed,
but an experience of faith that becomes a message"
(EDWARD SCHILLEBEECK).

Reflection: It's easy for us as Christians to profess faith while screaming doubt. There's nothing wrong with insurance policies and prudent precautions, but we need to stop short of undue anxiety about the future. When Jesus sent out the seventy to evangelize, he instructed them not to take along any provisions.

Several years ago my aunt and uncle traveled to Central America on a missions trip to visit various church plants. They traveled light, but because my uncle's luggage failed to arrive, he traveled much lighter than anticipated. Some Christians deliberately operate this way. Many others who have found themselves in dire circumstances attest to God's seemingly miraculous provision of exactly what they've needed, exactly when they've needed it.

I'm reminded of God's supplying of manna in the wilderness, and especially of his stipulation that his people not gather more than they would need for that day. How consistent are your verbal and lifestyle messages when it comes to God's provision?

Prayer Prompt: Is there a limit to your degree of trust in God?

odly woman,

HE KNOWS WHAT YOU NEED.

ℬeyond expectation

Verses: "Now to him who is able to do immeasurably more than all we ask or imagine, according to his power that is at work within us, to him be glory" (Ephesians 3:20–21).

> *"Many live in dread of what is coming. Why should we? The unknown puts adventure into life. . . . The unexpected around the corner gives a sense of anticipation and surprise. Thank God for the unknown future"* (E. STANLEY JONES).

Reflection: When has God wowed you by doing infinitely more than you had asked, imagined, or expected? I appreciate the vignette in Acts 12:11–17, just after Peter's miraculous escape from prison. In my mind, there's something of a dreamlike quality to this slow-moving conclusion to the story. Cluelessness and bumbling predominate.

We're told that Peter "came to himself" and that when the truth of the situation "dawned on him" he proceeded to the house "where many people had gathered and were praying." This was no general prayer meeting. It had arisen spontaneously in response to the sobering news of Peter's arrest.

Peter knocks, and Rhoda, the servant girl, comes to the door. Recognizing Peter's voice on the other side, she's so overjoyed that she runs back to announce that "Peter is at the door." Instead of urging her to let him in, these prayer warriors conclude that she's out of her mind, insisting that it must be Peter's angel.

Peter's persistent knocking finally causes someone to come to enough to open the door. The believers' failure to recognize the direct answer to their prayer lends a comic aura to this improbable conclusion to a miracle.

How human is that? And how divine God's (through Peter's) continued, insistent knocking.

Prayer Prompt: When have you failed to recognize a direct answer to prayer? If you did notice it, were you so shocked that you treated God's response like an amazing coincidence?

G odly woman,

EXPECT HIS ANSWERS.

$\mathcal{N}$eedless pain

Verse: "Is any of you in trouble? He should pray" (James 5:13).

*"Trials always change our relationship with God. Either they drive
us to Him, or they drive us away from Him. The extent of our fear
of Him and our awareness of His love for us determine in which
direction we will move"* (JERRY BRIDGES).

Reflection: Even the best-intentioned adoptive parent may come to a point at which fear—for the placement and even of the child—becomes a dominant motivating factor. What many fail to recognize is that the kids may want it that way. When a child who has spent her lifetime "failing" finds herself in a hopeful situation, she may be unable to cope with waiting for the bomb to drop. Her fear that the outcome of her self-fulfilling prophecy is taking too long to unfold may prove nearly intolerable. And if she finds herself tempted to attach, the suspense may become unbearable.

The summer my middle daughter was sixteen brought me to my knees—more in fear than in prayer, I'm ashamed to admit. That was the summer when, afraid I had run out of options, I did the unthinkable: I left her for a week in a mental health facility, asking the doctor to prepare her for not returning home. But I was warned that the State of Michigan no longer allowed adoptive disruptions and that I ran the risk of losing her twelve-year-old sister if I followed through. Thankfully, I didn't. And I can't imagine today how I would feel if I had.

Have you ever found yourself so preoccupied with a difficult or desperate situation that it didn't occur to you to pray? Did you accept as a foregone conclusion that there was no way out? Did the circumstances seem too complex to "explain" to God? Or were you too angry with God at the time to trust his heart? The words of an old hymn speak to me on this issue: "Oh, what peace we often forfeit. Oh, what needless pain we bear, all because we do not carry everything to God in prayer."

Prayer Prompt: What difficult situation do you need to take to God, on your own behalf or on that of someone else?

odly woman,

ACCESS AND ACCEPT HIS PEACE.

$\mathcal{A}$ mystery

Verse: "The secret things belong to the LORD our God, but the things revealed belong to us and to our children forever, that we may follow all the words of this law" (Deuteronomy 29:29).

"I leave God's secrets to himself. It is happy for me that God makes me of his court, and not of his council" (JOSEPH HALL).

Reflection: After searching unsuccessfully last week for an item missing from my desktop, I asked little Adelyn whether she knew where it was. Addie has a habit of confessing to sins committed by the dog, so I have to make sure my questions don't come off as accusations. With a guilty expression on her face, she replied seriously, "It's a mystery." As it turns out, she wasn't responsible.

God has been selective in what he has chosen to reveal to us. And although we aren't wrong to speculate, we can go only so far in terms of delving into mysteries that haven't yet been explained. My assumption is that God has already told us what we're capable of handling—certainly, at any rate, what we need to know.

Jesus had this to say to his probing disciples: "About that day or hour [when heaven and Earth will pass away] no one knows, not even the angels in heaven, nor the Son, but only the Father" (Mark 13:32).

One day, when we see God face-to-face, all will be clear. Until that time, let's cherish the revelation he has seen fit to share.

Prayer Prompt: About what not-yet-revealed spiritual issues are you most curious? Are you willing to trust his heart for the time being?

$\mathcal{G}$odly woman,

THANK HIM FOR THE WONDERS HE HAS CHOSEN TO REVEAL.

Open borders

Verse: "If my people, who are called by my name, will humble themselves and pray and seek my face and turn from their wicked ways, then I will hear from heaven and I will forgive their sin and will heal their land" (2 Chronicles 7:14).

> *"Sir, my concern is not whether God is on our side; my greatest concern is to be on God's side, for God is always right"*
> (ABRAHAM LINCOLN).

Reflection: I spent some time thinking about what I wanted to say in my 9/11 meditation, only to recognize that none of my thoughts—patriotic, sensitive, or trusting—were all that biblical. No matter what angle I pursued, I ran smack into nationalism.

We make a mistake expecting God's automatic blessing on his people just because they happen to live in a particular land or culture. God's people and kingdom transcend national borders, as they do any other artificial "boundaries" human being are so skilled at erecting around themselves. I see this in his Old Testament concern for nations and rulers that were arch-enemies of Israel, as well as in his ready acceptance of proselytes, aliens, and other assorted hangers-on to his people Israel, not to mention the Gentile converts who so rapidly swelled the early church.

Baron Robert Alexander Kennedy Runcie (now *there's* a name!) of the United Kingdom had this to say: "Those who dare to interpret God's will must never claim Him as an asset for one nation or group rather than another. War springs from the love and loyalty that should be offered to God being applied to some God substitute—one of the most dangerous being nationalism."

We as Christians should certainly pray for God to heal our land. But if we view ourselves as a shoo-in for blessing, we're setting ourselves up for disappointment.

Prayer Prompt: Do you find yourself assuming that your nation is on God's side, or vice versa, in a confrontation?

odly woman,

HE ALONE CAN HEAL OUR LAND. BUT HE WANTS

US TO ASK.

$\mathcal{R}$ebar

Verse: "Jesus said, 'It is not the healthy who need a doctor, but the sick'" (Matthew 9:12).

"The healthy, the strong individual, is the one who asks for help when he needs it. Whether he has an abscess on his knee or in his soul" (RONA BARRETT).

Reflection: When Khristina was in her mid teens she was involved in a missions trip to Honduras to build homes for victims of Hurricane Mitch. During one work session she accidently jumped onto a rebar protruding from the cement. It penetrated her arch through her tennis shoe, requiring emergency room treatment and a pair of crutches she tolerated for all of a day or two.

Nearly two years later she developed a severe, painful, and persistent abscess in that area of her foot. Finally, stumped, her podiatrist opted for exploratory surgery—only to discover a circle of tennis shoe rubber embedded in her insole.

We were fortunate to discover the source of the infection when we did; it was rapidly advancing up the nerve sheath into her ankle. I couldn't help but shudder at the thought of how filthy that piece of shoe must have been and how much damage it could have done there in her sole.

There's plenty of dirt that can make its way into our soul too, lurking and festering there until it brings about a putrid situation. Whether an infection is physical, emotional, or spiritual in nature, we need to address it—no matter how tough we may think we are on the basis of youth, independence, success, or whatever else is making us feel invulnerable.

We won't be inclined to accept Jesus' words, above, as applying to ourselves unless and until we first acknowledge our true condition before God. The beauty is that Christ's earthly mission was all about saving us—and that he, through the Spirit, continues to be there for us throughout our earthly lives. We just need to muster the meekness to acknowledge our need.

Prayer Prompt: What contagion is multiplying in your soul? Have you asked for the help you need?

$\mathcal{G}$odly woman,
SEEK AND ACCEPT HIS HEALING.

$\mathcal{D}$ust motes rising

Verses: "As a father has compassion on his children, so the LORD has compassion on those who fear him; for he knows how we are formed, he remembers that we are dust" (Psalm 103:13–14).

"Beauty is everlasting and dust is for a time" (MARIANNE MOORE).

Reflection: Did you know that most household dust is comprised of sloughed off skin cells? And that our body replaces *all* of its cells every seven years? Our physical bodies are a part of our "package" (and we'll have them for eternity), but in their current condition they change on a moment-by-moment basis.

Not so our spirits. Within each of us is a core, untouchable "me" that remains remarkably intact throughout life. We come to understand ourselves differently, and hopefully better, as time goes by, but the continuity is never disrupted.

"It appears to me impossible," reflected Mary Wollstonecraft, an eighteenth-century British philosopher and feminist, "that I should cease to exist, or that this active, restless spirit, equally alive to joy and sorrow, should be only organized dust." She's right, of course, despite an absence of Christian faith to back her statement.

Muhammed Iqbal, an Islamic poet, made a statement that also seems to convey biblical truth: "It is true that we are made of dust. And the world is also made of dust. But the dust has motes rising."

How comforting to know that our God has compassion not only on those who fear him (quote from Psalm 103 above) but on all who bear his image—that he implants within each human psyche a core of intuition pointing in the direction of truth.

Prayer Prompt: Thanks God for his concern for your physical vulnerability. Then express your gratitude for your undying, indomitable spirit.

odly woman,
HE CREATED AN ETERNAL, UNIFIED YOU.

ℐnformation overload?

Verse: "Of making many books there is no end, and much study wearies the body" (Ecclesiastes 12:12).

"We now accept the fact that learning is a lifelong process of keeping abreast of change. And the most pressing task is to teach people how to learn" (PETER F. DRUCKER).

Reflection: Thomas Szasz reflects that "Every act of conscious learning requires the willingness to suffer an injury to one's self-esteem. That is why young children, before they are aware of their own self-importance, learn so easily." I love Adelyn's perspective on this issue. When a challenge turns out to be beyond her four-year-old capability, rather than second-guessing herself she waits for her abilities to catch up with the demands. "Practice makes perfect!" she quotes airily, assuming that whatever she desires to do (perhaps a cartwheel) will come with repeated trying. What a great approach to learning!

Yesterday I was asked by my agent to edit an author promotion manual, based on the premise that publishers increasingly expect authors to do their own promoting, requiring speaking ability and what appears to me to be a daunting amount of technical skill. I completed my editorial task with no problem but felt, as a writer, overwhelmed and deflated. The subject matter involved skills sets that are almost entirely foreign to me.

Notice that Solomon didn't end with the disheartening reflection above, instead going on, "Now all has been heard; here is the conclusion of the matter: Fear God and keep his commandments, for this is the duty of all mankind" (verse 13).

Far from expecting me to acquire ever-increasing mastery of intimidating volumes of factual material in order to legitimate myself as a person, God invites me to rest in awe of himself and to revel in the fascinating store of knowledge he has made available for my enjoyment and betterment.

Prayer Prompt: What perceived demands make lifelong learning off-putting for you?

Godly woman,
EMBRACE KNOWLEDGE AS HIS GIFT.

$\mathcal{M}$outhpiece

Verse: "Moses was educated in all the wisdom of the Egyptians and was powerful in speech and action" (Acts 7:22).

> *"If you think you are too small to be effective, you have never been in bed with a mosquito"* (BETTY REESE).

Reflection: In light of Moses' response to God recorded in Exodus 6:30, "Since I speak with faltering lips, why would Pharaoh listen to me?" I'm a little surprised by the above declaration in Acts 7. Stephen may have inferred the persuasive speech from Moses' court upbringing, and there can be little doubt that Moses underestimated his own ability. More likely, though, Moses' powerful speech was the result of obedience to God, who graciously provided what his appointed spokesman lacked—or thought he lacked.

Paul shared Moses' self-assessment when it came to oratorical skills. Referring to himself, he acknowledged that "some say, 'His letters are weighty and forceful, but in person he is unimpressive and his speaking amounts to nothing'" (2 Corinthians 10:10). The truth is that the Holy Spirit is never hampered by our inhibition, as long as we make every effort to be truthful, open, and genuine.

I experienced this on a small scale a couple of weeks ago while waiting at the Grand Rapids bus terminal for my daughter Angie to come in from Detroit. Sharing a bench seat with a rough- and defeated-looking Texan (he had made his way to West Michigan on the unsubstantiated claim that there was work to be had in the "ole fields" here), I found myself opening a conversation that soon found its way to the Lord. I didn't pray with him, but my assurance of God's presence during a bewildering time brought tears to his eyes.

Like Paul, I consider myself to be less than articulate in person. So it was reassuring to acknowledge to myself, even at the time, that my words were Spirit-prompted. When have you, like me (and like Moses and Paul, not to place myself in the same category), experienced the Spirit speaking to someone else through you?

Prayer Prompt: Pray for the courage not to let personal reserve squelch the Spirit's voice when he wants you as his mouthpiece.

odly woman,
LET HIM LEVERAGE YOUR FAITH AND EXPERIENCE.

$\mathcal{D}$epth perception

Verse: "Oh, the depth of the riches of the wisdom and knowledge of God! How unsearchable his judgments, and his paths beyond tracing out!" (Romans 11:33).

"The nature of God is a circle of which the center is everywhere and the circumference in nowhere" (EMPEDOCLES).

Reflection: Over the last couple of years I've developed an increasing distaste for nighttime driving. Too much of the time I end up behind the wheel without remembering to exchange my computer glasses for my bifocals—of which the computer glasses represent the bottom third. A lack of depth perception just might be an understandable outcome.

I just returned (in the dark) from a trip that included a stop at my ATM to extract a twenty dollar bill. As I reached toward the screen I inadvertently touched it (evidently in the $400 fast-cash box), producing a dutiful response from the machine, which shot out twenty twenties.

This particular problem can be resolved by stowing a spare pair of specs in the glove compartment. But it doesn't come close to rivaling my bigger depth-perception challenge: perceiving and beginning to appreciate the incredible depths of God's wisdom and knowledge.

This is not to suggest that I could ever—or may ever—begin to *understand* God's profound wisdom. My appropriate response is one of awe and praise. Romans 11:33, above, opens a resounding doxology that concludes like this: "Who has known the mind of the Lord? Or who has been his counselor? Who has ever given to God, that God should repay them? For from him and through him and for him are all things. To him be the glory forever! Amen." And Amen!!

Prayer Prompt: The word *awesome* has suffered some serious depreciation in the last few years. To what degree do you experience real awe—astonishment and even trepidation—in the presence of God's majesty? Approach him now with wonder and admiration.

$\mathcal{G}$odly woman,
HIS WISDOM IS INFINITELY BEYOND YOUR COMPREHENSION.

$\mathcal{P}$ushing the limit

Verses: "I will always obey your law, for ever and ever. I will walk about in freedom, for I have sought out your precepts" (Psalm 119:44–45).

"Once we accept our limits, we go beyond them" (ALBERT EINSTEIN).

Reflection: The city of Wyoming, where I live (yes, that's Wyoming, as in Michigan), was recently ordered by the state to raise several speed limits. Many of the changes apply to streets that include both residential and commercially zoned areas, and all of the affected limits have gone up ten miles per hour (from 30 to 40 or 35 to 45).

While I tended in the past to push the limits a bit when I could get away with it—like when the flow of traffic indicated a consensus among drivers to establish a new, if temporary, norm (the power of "everybody's doing it" has its allure), the surprise for me is that I'm finding it hard to keep up with the higher threshold.

I'll be "flying" along at seven or eight miles above the previously posted limit when it occurs to me that I can legitimately go faster. The exhilaration I feel at this unaccustomed license is almost laughable. Yet it seems as though I have to concentrate to push that pedal hard enough to maintain a "reasonable" five miles over the limit.

The verses above from Psalm 119 sound like a contradiction, with the author declaring both that he will obey God's law and walk about in freedom. Truth is, though, that there's no inconsistency here. I can drive about in freedom too, when I follow the rules of the road, which are as generous as they can be without compromising my own or others' safety. As I learned from this speed limit change, though, there's something to be said for the habit of abiding by the law—whether God's law or those other laws he has instituted through the state.

Prayer Prompt: In what area do you tend to push the limit? If that limit were unexpectedly raised, would you pull back on the basis of habit or take advantage of the liberty?

odly woman,
RESPECT HIS LIMITS.

$\mathcal{G}$od's people

Verse: "I will take you as my own people, and I will be your God" (Exodus 6:7).

"These are the gifts of God for the people of God"
(PART OF MY CHURCH'S COMMUNION LITURGY).

Reflection: Adelyn, who can be both painfully shy in public and lonely at home in her only-child status, has picked up what appears to be a bevy of imaginary friends. Off and on, when we make plans or designate spaces, she makes sure her "girls" are taken into consideration. I tried last Sunday to capitalize on this by suggesting she invite one of her girls to the three-year-old Sunday School class. She chose Pluto (yes, her girl's name is Pluto), and while she didn't participate in class verbally, I'm told that she did at least participate.

I don't carry the clout to have any "people," but God does—and by his grace I'm one of them. Our numbers have expanded exponentially since the birth of the Church. This wonder can't be expressed better than in the words of two of Christ's apostles:

Paul: "We wait for the blessed hope—the appearing of the glory of our great God and Savior, Jesus Christ, who gave himself for us to redeem us from all wickedness and to purify for himself a people that are his very own, eager to do what is good" (Titus 2:13–14).

And Peter: "But you are a chosen people, a royal priesthood, a holy nation, God's special possession, that you may declare the praises of him who called you out of darkness into his wonderful light. Once you were not a people, but now you are the people of God; once you had not received mercy, but now you have received mercy" (1 Peter 2:9–10). *Amen!*

Prayer Prompt: What does your status within the people of God mean to you?

$\mathcal{G}$*odly woman,*
YOU'RE HIS VERY OWN.

$\mathcal{T}$wo or three together

Verse: "Those who feared the LORD talked with each other, and the LORD listened and heard" (Malachi 3:16).

"It is impossible to enslave mentally or socially a Bible-reading people" (HORACE GREELEY).

Reflection: God hears when we talk to him. But he also listens and hears (a combination that goes beyond overhearing) when we talk *about* him. Typically in the Bible God's hearing implies his acting. The verse above suggests that he is pleased by our sincere, godly conversations with other believers.

In verses 14–15 we learn that the talk in Jerusalem had been cynical and faultfinding. The rank and file were grousing about the evident futility of serving God. But a minority risked political incorrectness to encourage each other's faith.

Acts 17:10–11 recounts the response of the citizens of Berea to the message of Paul and Silas. Luke tells us that they "received the message with great eagerness and examined the Scriptures every day to see if what Paul said was true." The Bereans engaged in regular, impromptu Bible study. Do you think God heard? Do you think he rejoiced as he listened in?

When did you last get together with an individual or group for the express purpose of talking about God and his Word? This fall, is there a Bible study group from your church or in your neighborhood with which you could affiliate? Would you feel comfortable initiating one?

If you've participated in such a discussion, were you aware of God's presence as your appreciative audience? Better yet, did you sense the Spirit's active participation? Jesus promised that "where two or three gather in my name, there am I with them" (Matthew 18:20).

Prayer Prompt: How regularly do you make God the focus of your conversation?

odly woman,

SHARE HIM.

$\mathcal{D}$ark circles

Verses: "The eye is the lamp of the body. If your eyes are healthy, your whole body will be full of light. But if your eyes are unhealthy, your whole body will be full of darkness. If then the light within you is darkness, how great is that darkness" (Matthew 6:22–23).

> *"There is a road from the eye to the heart that does not go through the intellect"* (G. K. CHESTERTON).

Reflection: A recent television commercial has been touting a cream to reduce dark under-eye circles. Little Adelyn, after asking what this was about, commented that her circles are green. Her mention that their color is changing alerted me that she was referring to the circles/orbs within, not underneath, her eyes. In this case, it was all in the preposition.

Jesus had a lot to say about eyes, and the verses above touch on two prominent New Testament themes: spiritual blindness and light versus darkness. Two issues come into play when we consider the function of our eyes: what they take in and how truthfully they reveal or interpret that image.

The first has to do with exposure, and that's where we come in. What our eyes see depends in large part on where we choose to direct our focus. Interpreting what our eyes take in, however, relies on the Holy Spirit at work within us, helping us to make sense of whatever reality confronts us.

The issue of whether we're taking in light or darkness, or correctly interpreting either one, has to do with our redemption status. "For God, who said, 'Let light shine out of darkness,' made his light shine in our hearts to give us the light of the knowledge of God's glory displayed in the face of Christ" (2 Corinthians 4:6).

BTW, what color are your circles?

Prayer Prompt: Assess what you're allowing your eyes to take in on a regular basis. Then ask the Spirit to help you interpret this input.

$\mathcal{G}$odly woman,

BE CAREFUL WHAT YOU SEE.

*E*ternity in nature

Verses: "Mortals, born of woman, are of few days and full of trouble. They spring up like flowers and wither away; like fleeting shadows, they do not endure" (Job 14:1–2).

> *"How beautifully leaves grow old. How full of light and color are their last days"* (GEORGE BURNS).

Reflection: It's officially the first day of fall. Here in Michigan the leaves are already putting on their autumn hue, and the round orange sun has been providing free spectacular seasonal shows. Except for spring, the "official" seasons always begin a little later here than I would intuit based on the signs of nature.

Having grown up in Southern California, where one season inches into another, I appreciate the onrush of nature here in the Midwest. And while I hate to see autumn leaves beginning to mute or spring tree blossoms to drop, the changes themselves are always a prelude.

On the other hand, fleeting beauty has a poignant, nostalgic quality, calling out to us to enjoy it while we can. Isaac Bashevis Singer put it this way: "What nature delivers to us is never stale. Because what nature creates has eternity in it."

Ironically, the very changes in nature, so breathtaking and yet so predictable, showcase God's enduring faithfulness as each year cycles through its phases. How comforting to remind ourselves that, despite the rush of seasons, God remains forever the same.

Prayer Prompt: How does the irony of fleeting beauty in concert with God's faithfulness play out in your life and experience?

odly woman,
RELISH THOSE REMINDERS OF HIS GRACE.

Conflict within God's family

Verses: "I plead with Euodia and I plead with Syntyche to be of the same mind in the Lord. Yes, and I ask you, my true companion, help these women since they have contended at my side in the cause of the gospel" (Philippians 4:2–3).

"I don't have to attend every argument I'm invited to"
(AUTHOR UNKNOWN).

Reflection: I don't get the feeling these two church women were disputing over a major doctrine. Paul doesn't hint that either was advocating a Gnostic heresy or claiming Jesus Christ to be a created being. Instead, I picture them quibbling about sanctuary decor or the demerits of plastic communion cups.

Both, says Paul, had contended for the gospel at his side, and he deeply appreciated each one. But their squabble was disrupting the Philippian church, with members scrambling to take sides.

How mortifying to plug in my own name, along with that of a friend from church: "I plead with Donna and I plead with Kris to agree with each other in the Lord." No wonder Euodia (despite the name's distinction of using all five regular vowels!) has yet to make it big as a baby name.

Prayer Prompt: Is there someone in your church with whom you don't see eye to eye? Remember that grudges are subject to growth spurts!

Godly woman,
DO YOUR PART TO RESOLVE DIFFERENCES WITHIN CHRIST'S BODY.

Gentle among them

Verses: "Just as a nursing mother cares for her children, so we cared for you. Because we loved you so much, we were delighted to share with you not only the gospel of God but our lives as well" (1 Thessalonians 2:7–8).

"Being an extrovert isn't essential to evangelism—obedience and love are" (REBECCA M. PIPPERT).

Reflection: Most of my evangelistic efforts, if I can call them that, have over the years involved my daughters' friends and acquaintances. My two older special-needs children in particular have attracted friends, room-mates, hangers-on—yes, and husbands—with similar challenges. I've had occasion to interact with many such people at community church suppers, health care clinics, bus depots, courtroom lobbies, and the like.

The prerequisite for sharing in this context is a Christlike view of the lost. "How you believe God perceives people," points out Jacquelyn K. Heasley, "will determine how you respond to them." I don't by any means want to convey that I'm "there." Sharing conversationally with such people often makes me feel as shallow as I think they are. If they're to find me com-panionable, though, I need to show some appreciation for the silly and the insignificant.

In many cases I do feel like a mom caring for little children—and it's amazing how many have over the years taken to calling me Mom. Requests for small favors, like rides, come repeatedly. "Great opportunities to help others seldom come," notes Sally Koch, "but small ones surround us daily."

Prayer Prompt: What opportunities do you have to interact with people you consider "peripheral"?

odly woman,

VALUE ALL HIS CHILDREN HIGHLY, AS HE DOES.

$\mathscr{L}$ifelong service?

Verses: "They are . . . always learning but never able to come to a knowledge of the truth" (2 Timothy 3:6–7).

> *"The amount of time we spend with Jesus—meditating on*
> *His Word and His majesty, seeking His face—establishes our*
> *fruitfulness in the kingdom"* (CHARLES STANLEY).

Reflection: Paul is talking in the above verses about godlessness in the last days. In verses 2–5 of this chapter he delineates through a series of negative descriptors just what these godless people will be like. Interesting as it would be to discuss the portion of the above quote replaced by the three-dot ellipsis, I'll limit myself to the "always learning . . ." clause. These words speak to me of our postmodern age, in which truth is considered to be absolutely relative (are those two words a contradiction or what?), valid only to the individual and subject to rethinking at that.

In terms of the verb phrase "always learning," I must acknowledge a difference between the lifelong learning to which we all aspire and the ambitions (or lack thereof) of those whom we have for the last several decades dubbed "professional students."

September, late in the calendar year as it is, still speaks of beginnings in terms of the traditional school year. Other learning opportunities, including some that are church related, are also getting underway. Expectations run high for students and teachers/leaders alike as the still young semester begins to pick up energy and momentum.

At this point we as adult learners do well to ask ourselves to what use we intend to put the information we're soaking up. If we as Christian women have indeed come to the point of acknowledging the Truth (hopefully long ago), what will we do with and in light of that Truth today and in the days to come? To what extent will our enhanced knowledge enhance our ability, desire, and opportunity to serve?

Prayer Prompt: Consider learning opportunities you might be able to translate into immediate, practical kingdom service.

$\mathscr{G}$*odly woman,*

HE SEEKS EQUIPPED AND WILLING SERVANTS.

$\mathscr{R}$eady to blow

Verses: "Inside I am like bottled-up wine, like new wineskins ready to burst. I must speak and find relief; I must open my lips and reply" (Job 32:19–20).

> *"I pray on the principle that wine knocks the cork out of a bottle.*
> *There is an inward fermentation, and there must be a vent"*
> (HENRY WARD BEECHER).

Reflection: We all find ourselves at that emotional bursting point, in need of a release valve. And we respond in different ways. If the issue evokes anger, this is the difference between being quick-tempered, huffing whiffs of smoke on a frequent basis, and hot-tempered, long-suffering until those around us recognize the need to take cover: *"Thar she blows!"* If it's anxiety rather than anger that's making your head feel like an inflating balloon, the relief you need may come in a different form—prayer, for example.

Job was amazingly patient, not just with God and adversity but with those exasperating friends of his. So much so that it's almost a relief for us to see him reach the boiling point. Even Jesus benefitted from an adrenaline rush when he overthrew those tables in the temple courtyard. That demonstration of "righteous anger" (do you think you experience that phenomenon?) must have been something to see.

In one way or another, unhealthy and unrelieved stress take their toll on human beings. In the words of Terri Guillemets, "If your teeth are clenched and your fists are clenched, your lifespan is probably clenched."

In times like that it helps to have a God in the relief-vent business.

Prayer Prompt: Pray back to God the words of David in Psalm 143:1: "LORD, hear my prayer, listen to my cry for mercy; in your faithfulness and righteousness come to my relief."

odly woman,
ALLOW HIM TO UNCLENCH YOUR LIFE.

Unfinished business

Verses: "As Jesus was getting into the boat, the man who had been demon-possessed begged to go with him. Jesus did not let him, but said, 'Go home to your own people and tell them how much the Lord has done for you, and how he has had mercy on you'" (Mark 5:18–19).

"Having a place to go—is a home. Having someone to love—is a family. Having both—is a blessing" (DONNA HEDGES).

Reflection: Unlike the disciples, at least some of whom may have left behind happy families and settled households (we know for certain that Peter was married), the man about whom Mark spoke had been estranged from his loved ones in the most tragic way for a very long time.

Understandable and commendable as it was for him to want to follow Jesus, the Lord understood that this man had urgent, unfinished business right there at home. Not only were his family members in dire need of healing, but his countrymen in the area were so terrified over what had happened that they begged Jesus to vacate their territory. Jesus needed this revitalized man to evangelize the neighborhood as only he could.

Jesus values our service, but he wants us to customize and prioritize it in ways that fit our unique circumstances. In some cases he calls on us to focus on home, family, and close vicinity. If that seems to be the case for you (as I believe it was for me while my daughters were growing up), know that he doesn't appreciate your kingdom involvement any less.

Prayer Prompt: Ask God for a fresh perspective on his calling for your life in its current season.

Godly woman,
ARE YOU TAKING CARE OF BUSINESS AT HOME?

$\mathcal{A}$ special favor

Verses: "When [Aksah, his daughter,] got off her donkey, Caleb asked her, 'What can I do for you?' She replied, 'Do me a special favor. Since you have given me land in the Negev, give me also springs of water.' So Caleb gave her the upper and lower springs" (Joshua 15:18–19).

> *"My faith tells me that God is always working for the coming of the kind of Kingdom in which we all are respected, all are valued, all are included"* (BISHOP V. GENE ROBINSON).

Reflection: Some background on this vignette may help. Remember Caleb—the one Israelite spy who along with Joshua brought back a glowing minority report on the land of Canaan? Of the men alive at the time of the spy mission, only Joshua and Caleb made it, more than forty years later, to the Promised Land.

In response to God's command, Joshua gave Caleb a portion of the allocation for the tribe of Judah, of which he in turn handed down a field to his daughter Aksah and her husband (see Joshua 15:13–19 for this parenthetical story squeezed into the itemized list of tribal allotments). For an earlier story similar in theme and spirit, check out the more lengthy account of the negotiations of Zelophehad's daughters from Numbers 27:1–11 (that story is finalized in Numbers 36:1–13).

No, biblical women had nowhere near the rights of men—or of those women of our day who regularly conduct business on a par with men. But the stories of exceptions in the Bible never cease to catch me off guard. Why, I ask myself, would the lowly account of Aksah's business interaction with her dad have warranted inclusion in the fast-moving book of Joshua? Such ordinary stories by their very presence speak volumes, both about God's inclusivity and about his orientation.

Prayer Prompt: Intercede for the high percentage of women in our world who still lack basic human rights. On a personal level, what request have you resisted bringing to God, considering it too minor for his attention?

odly woman,
YOU SERVE A DETAIL-ORIENTED, INCLUSIVE GOD.

$\mathcal{R}$eminders

Verse: "Taste and see that the Lord is good; blessed is the one who takes refuge in him" (Psalm 34:8).

> *"However many blessings we expect from God, His infinite*
> *liberality will always exceed all our wishes and our thoughts"*
> (JOHN CALVIN).

Reflection: "Time to sleep, Addie. Lie down now and be still."
"Hey! That beminds me—"
"Of what?"
"Be still and know that I am God."

Chuckling now, an hour or so later, I ask myself what it is during the course of a routine day that reminds me of God. The obvious answer, of course, is my writing. It would be hard to spend the better part of a day flipping through the pages of a Bible without thinking of God.

Beyond that, I would have to say my ever-present blessings, from the lake view outside my front door to the comfort of home and coffee to that very granddaughter finally still and oblivious during her afternoon "nipper nap."

As we all know too well, though, there's another side to that equation, one that Job had to explain to his cynical wife: "You are talking like a foolish woman. Shall we accept good from God, and not trouble?" (Job 2:10). What the Jobs didn't realize is that their troubles hadn't originated with God. But the point remains that even our good days are punctuated by problems.

For me as a believing woman, though, the good so far outweighs the trouble that I can't even begin to compare. I suppose perspective plays a big role. But the very acts of tasting goodness and taking refuge in God have a lot to do with my perceptions.

Prayer Prompt: What is there about today that "beminds" you of God?

$\mathcal{G}$odly woman,
HE'S SO GOOD TO YOU.

$\mathscr{B}$oxing God

Verse: "I saw all that God has done. No one can comprehend what goes on under the sun. Despite all their efforts to search it out, no one can discover its meaning" (Ecclesiastes 8:17).

Your God Is Too Small (TITLE OF BOOK BY J. B. PHILLIPS).

Reflection: In the estimation of Albert Schweitzer, "As we acquire more knowledge, things do not become more comprehensible, but more mysterious." Knowledge often works like that, serving to startle us with how little we actually comprehend. It isn't like that for God. Listen to Psalm 147:4–5: "[The Lord] determines the number of the stars and calls them each by name. Great is our Lord and mighty in power; his understanding has no limit."

How far will God allow humans to go in uncovering the mysteries of the universe? Possibly a lot further. Those most knowledgeable in the field of medicine, for example, are quick to point out how little we understand about the causes and treatments of many illnesses and mutations.

In astronomy, as in virtually every other field of scientific inquiry, the explosion of new knowledge serves more than anything else to highlight how tightly we have drawn the limits of perceived reality. The evidences of infinity are expanding at, well . . . an astronomic rate! When I consider, for example, that our Milky Way Galaxy is one of *millions* like itself, and that the illumination from some stars takes *billions* of light years to reach my purview in a cloudless night sky, how can I begin to fathom a God who counts the hairs I daily pull from my brush? The words of David reverberate in my ears: "When I consider your heavens, the work of your fingers, the moon and the stars, which you have set in place, what is mankind that you are mindful of them, human beings that you care for them?" (Psalm 8:3–4).

When we box God in, making him appear constrained and constricted, he has a way of breaking out.

Prayer Prompt: What boxes have you personally constructed around God? Do you find the ever-increasing scope of scientific knowledge a threat to your faith or a confirmation of his awesome power and love?

odly woman,
YOU SERVE A BIG GOD.

ℳansions

Verse: "My Father's house has many rooms; if that were not so, would I have told you that I am going there to prepare a place for you?" (John 14:2).

"Death . . . is no more than passing from one room into another.
But there's a difference for me, you know. Because in that other
room I shall be able to see" (HELEN KELLER).

Reflection: I'll always remember this verse as part of the passage I memorized by accident. The assigned text for my fourth-grade class had been John 10:1–5. But the younger me, a habitual daydreamer, got it almost—but not quite—right. I recall thinking at the time that what I did commit to memory (the right verse numbers but four chapters off) was pretty good too—and I still think so.

The KJV translation of "mansions" (in lieu of "rooms") left plenty of scope for the imagination, and I was struck for some reason by the logic of Jesus' remark, rendered in that version as "If it were not so, I would have told you."

It wasn't until several years ago, when I joined the Bible department of a Christian publishing house, that my managing editor pointed out to me the difference between "heaven" and the new heavens and the new earth. I guess I'd never given it a thought.

Immediately associating this new knowledge with my personal situation, I understood that the mom I haven't seen in almost fifty years is in heaven now, in a disembodied state. But after Christ's return, when he ushers in the new heavens and the new earth, she'll be reunited with her glorified body. *And me with her?!*

I like to imagine that the new earth might be right here, but there's so much we're not yet privileged or intended to understand. One thing is certain: I hope and dream that the afterlife will be complicated, interesting, and satisfying, full of arts and hobbies and avocations and learning and loving, stimulating relationships.

Prayer Prompt: What does it mean for you that Jesus has gone ahead to prepare your place?

𝒢odly woman,
YOUR FUTURE IS BEYOND WONDERFUL.

*I*mmortal you

*F*OR THE FIRST thirty days of October, I invite you to join with me in an exploration of the creative predisposition and ability to make and appreciate beauty with which God in his grace has endowed each of us as a Christian woman. If you don't view yourself as artistic, please don't take this as an opportunity for a devotional break.

Verse: "[God] has saved us and called us to a holy life . . . because of his own purpose and grace. This grace was given us in Christ Jesus before the beginning of time" (2 Timothy 1:9).

"Life is the childhood of our immortality" (GOETHE).

Reflection: Has it ever struck you that the first three words of Scripture, "In the beginning," are a concession to our finite ability to understand? During our brief stay on Earth, our minds are hardwired to think in terms of time, to organize reality as we experience it in linear terms. We have to accept on faith the mind-boggling reality that God is infinite, that his existence knew no beginning and will know no end.

In some sense our status as God's image bearers is all about infinity too. Each of us existed in God's mind from those earliest days that never began. And once created, we're around to stay.

Has it ever struck you what an investment God made when he fashioned *you*, his permanent, immortal daughter? He gave you his gift of grace, in the person of his Son, *before* the beginning of time! He endowed you with your creative bent and called you to a holy life as part of his eternal purpose and grace.

Prayer Prompt: Does the truth of your immortality ever blow you away? Nothing ever can, you know (blow you away, that is)! How does this knowledge affect your self-image? Your appreciation of those other image bearers like yourself . . .?

odly woman,
YOU'RE GOD'S TIMELESS INVESTMENT.

In-genius

Verse: "[A wife of noble character] gets up while it is still night; she provides food for her family and portions for her female servants" (Proverbs 31:15).

"Creativity often consists of merely turning up what is already there. Did you know that right and left shoes were thought up only a little more than a century ago?" (BERNICE FITZ-GIBBON).

Reflection: I don't know when that century started, but can you just imagine the blisters from wearing two identical shoes? The up side, if there is one, is that little kids would be spared the bafflement of matching the right foot to the right (or left, as the case may be) shoe. Adelyn nearly always gets it wrong, and we recognized only recently that she holds up the bottom of the shoe to the bottom of her foot to check—invariably resulting in a missed fit.

Regardless of what ingenuity means for you, of one thing you can be certain: As God's image bearer you enjoy that wonderful quality called creativity. God made you *in*-genius—able to dream, imagine, plan, and design. Maybe your creative outlet is cooking or baking. (I'll have to admit that mine is not—which makes me admire you all the more!) Do you whip up a specialty that never fails to collect *mmm*s and smiles?

Ask a young child where apples come from, and the answer is likely to be the grocery store. This line of questioning has "always" (yes, there are some infinity words in our language) been a tried-and-true means to get a little one to stretch his mind backward in the direction of creation. No, you don't truly bake your prized dessert "from scratch." But has it ever occurred to you that an animal is totally lacking in the ability to conceive, concoct, or follow something as original as a recipe?

Enjoy your creative predispositions, whatever they might be. Relish your ability to sprinkle some zest into the day. Titillate, tease, and tickle your own and others' God-given senses.

Whether or not you realize it, you're delighting your Maker at the same time.

Prayer Prompt: Don't take your creative genius for granted. Your gifts from God are also your gifts for him and others.

Godly woman,
HE FASHIONED A CREATIVE YOU.

$\mathscr{A}$ beautiful thing for Jesus

Verse: "Jesus said to [his disciples], 'Why are you bothering this woman? She has done a beautiful thing to me'" (Matthew 26:10).

"I don't try to imagine a God; it suffices to stand in awe of the structure of the world, insofar as it allows our inadequate senses to appreciate it" (ALBERT EINSTEIN).

Reflection: What sense makes your adoration? Which of your five senses, that is, most meaningfully constitutes your praise? Maybe you're an auditory person. If appreciating and/or making music is your thing, does your praise accompany the rendition? Or do you take delight in the beauty you take in visually? Does the sight of a sunset, a waterfall, or a masterful painting prompt you to hold your breath as your soul exhales its gratitude?

God created us with the ability to distinguish and appreciate fine nuances of taste. Do you respond to the bouquet of a fine wine or the variety of a well-spread table? Then again, do your creative expressions incorporate texture and patina? If so, you may be the kind of person who's touched by touch.

The woman in Matthew 26:6–13 was moved by scent. Our ability to smell calls forth all kinds of associations. Whether the aroma is of coffee, pine needles, pumpkin pie, a new vinyl doll—or even a dairy farm—scent can trigger nostalgia, even *déjà vu*. In Ephesians 5:1–2 Paul urges believers to imitate Christ, who "gave himself up for us as a fragrant offering and sacrifice to God."

If you could offer God a particular "scent" of adoration, what would it be? What quality makes your praise beautiful to God?

Prayer Prompt: Praise God for your five senses. How are you using them for his glory?

odly woman,

YOUR PRAISE IS LOVELY TO HIM.

𝒟iffering gifts

Verse: "Bless all his skills, LORD, and be pleased with the work of his hands" (Deuteronomy 33:11).

"I am as my creator made me and since He is satisfied, so am I"
(MINNIE SMITH).

Reflection: "A man who works with his hands," says Louis Nizer, "is a laborer; a man who works with his hands and his brain is a craftsman; but a man who works with his hands and his brain and his heart is an artist."

Bezalel and Oholiab were artists, artists God himself raised up, filled with his Spirit, and appointed to take charge of tabernacle construction (see Exodus 31:1–11). "Also," God added in his instructions to Moses (and his words were more than a postscript), "I have given ability to all the skilled workers to make everything I have commanded you" (verse 6).

In Romans 12:6 Paul points out that "We have different gifts, according to the grace given to each of us." The apostle goes on to list the spiritual gifts of prophesying, serving, teaching, encouraging, contributing, leading, and showing mercy. Since we know that the artisans and craftsmen referred to in Exodus were both called and Spirit-filled, we can, I believe, legitimately add to Paul's list the creative and tactile abilities.

To what area of service is Christ calling you? Don't forget that he uses and values laborers and craftsmen as well as artists. An unknown author has observed that "Every job is a self-portrait of the person who does it," going on to urge: "Autograph your work with excellence." That's a good re-minder for each of us, no matter the nature of our work.

Prayer Prompt: Thank God for your particular gifts, whether they be hands-on abilities or personality traits. God makes no mistakes in doling out temperaments and skills.

𝒢odly woman,

NEITHER UNDERESTIMATE NOR UNDERUSE YOUR GIFTS.

$\mathcal{D}$oing It better

Verse: "Speak, for your servant is listening" (1 Samuel 3:10).

> *"'Not called' did you say? 'Not heard the call,' I think you should say. Put your ear down to the Bible . . ."* (WILLIAM BOOTH).

Reflection: "Creativity," to quote John Updike, "is merely a plus name for regular activity. Any activity becomes creative when the doer cares about doing it right, or better." Without a doubt, some tasks lend themselves to innovative thinking and action, while others depend on a lack of originality. Imagine, for example, the potential chaos from a free spirit turned loose on an assembly line. (My daughter Angie is presently working a line at a recycling station two mornings a week. Her delight is adding to her burgeoning collection of wine corks, but she has to move fast to catch them.)

How do you, or could you, bring creativity to bear in your daily work? Do you consider it a waste of time to explore how a task could be handled more efficiently or with less documentation or busywork? Are you willing when the situation warrants it to respectfully buck a "We've always done it this way" mentality? Most importantly, do you view your daily work, no matter how mundane or repetitive, as a sacred calling? Have you paused to ask God why he led you to your position and what he wants from you in it?

If your vocational future is uncertain and you've been asking God for direction, consider approaching him as young Samuel did when he thought Eli was calling his name: "Here I am; you called me" (1 Samuel 3:8). Then have the courage to ask for direction (see the verse above). You might be surprised at God's highly personal revelation in response to your invitation.

Prayer Prompt: Do you view your present position as the result of happenstance or of divine direction? In what ways are you employing your creative gifts on a daily basis?

odly woman,
BE ASSURED THAT YOUR VOCATION, TEMPORARY OR PERMANENT,
ISN'T A MISTAKE.

$\mathcal{A}$rt's commentary

Verse: Cleanse me with hyssop, and I will be clean; wash me, and I will be whiter than snow (Psalm 51:7).

> *"Beauty deprived of its proper foils and adjuncts ceases to be enjoyed as beauty, just as light deprived of all shadows ceases to be enjoyed as light"* (JOHN RUSKIN).

Reflection: In Pablo Picasso's assessment, "Art washes away from the soul the dirt of everyday life." While I understand this artist's sentiment, I'll have to say as a Christian that he's missing the mark: God in his grace, through the atoning work of his Son on the cross, offers soul-washing to all who will reach out and accept it by faith.

Yet there is a sense in which art is redemptive. This has to do with the light good art has to shed on the not-always-so-beautiful realities all around us. Through so many means—whether by selection or emphasis or exaggeration or contrast or positioning or lighting or color or style—the artist makes a statement about reality, helping us to see it for what it is—or to notice it at all.

I like to think of good "secular" art in its many genres as complementary to God's general revelation of himself in nature, including within that term the realities of the human condition. No matter which of our senses is stirred, art "cleans" in the sense of extracting something from a "dirty" background and examining and clarifying it.

Prayer Prompt: What art forms point you to the Creator?

$\mathcal{G}$*odly woman,*

APPRECIATE BEAUTY IN CONTRAST.

$\mathcal{S}$ensual praise

Verse: "God created mankind in his own image, in the image of God he created them; male and female he created them" (Genesis 1:27).

> *"Listen to your life. See it for the fathomless mystery that it is.*
> *Touch, taste, smell your way to the holy and hidden heart of it*
> *because in the last analysis all moments are sacred moments and*
> *life itself is grace"* (FREDERICK BUECHNER).

Reflection: Reflect briefly on the following verses (emphasis added), each showcasing one of your five God-given senses and its unique role in your knowledge and praise of God:

"Those who *look* to [the LORD] are radiant; their faces are never covered with shame" (Psalm 34:5).

"Come, my children, *listen* to me; I will teach you the fear of the LORD" (Psalm 34:11).

"May my prayer be set before you like *incense*; may the lifting up of my hands be like the evening sacrifice" (Psalm 141:2).

"*Taste* and see that the LORD is good; blessed is the one who takes refuge in him" (Psalm 34:8).

"'Why are you troubled, and why do doubts rise in your minds? Look at my hands and my feet. It is I myself! *Touch* me and see'" (Luke 24:38–39).

In the words of Jean Houston, "Our senses are indeed our doors and windows on this world, in a very real sense the key to the unlocking of meaning and the wellspring of creativity."

Prayer Prompt: Which sensual experiences are most meaningful to you? Why?

odly woman,

BE SENSE-ITIVE TO AND FOR HIS GLORY.

$\mathcal{T}$he sound of feeling

Verses: "By the rivers of Babylon we sat and wept when we remembered Zion. There on the poplars we hung our harps, for there our captors asked us for songs. . . . How can we sing the songs of the LORD while in a foreign land? If I forget you, Jerusalem, may my right hand forget its skill" (Psalm 137:1–5).

"Where words fail, music speaks"
(HANS CHRISTIAN ANDERSEN).

Reflection: Decades ago, for a freshman speech class at the Christian college I attended, I selected this hauntingly beautiful psalm as the subject of an interpretive reading. Its words have moved me in a special way ever since. Someone has reflected that "music is what feelings sound like." It's certainly true that, especially in our highest and lowest moments, whether or not we're musically inclined, music can move us like nothing else.

I've recently been touched by a series of television commercials from the ASPCA (American Society for the Prevention of Cruelty to Animals). While the photographs of hurting dogs and cats are certainly poignant, I doubt that the songs chosen as background music could fail to move even the most stolid, non-animal-oriented viewer.

When in your life has music played a role in healing a gaping emotional wound? Or, in contrast, seemed intolerable to you in light of associations you weren't yet ready to face? Try for a moment to imagine life without music. What special memories would be lost to you? What pleasures or comforts would you have to forego?

Prayer Prompt: What music draws you closest to God? Be specific in your praise. If appropriate, sing that praise back to him (he'll hear you even if you opt to sing in silence).

$\mathcal{G}$*odly woman,*

REVEL IN THE BEAUTY YOU (OR OTHERS ON THE BASIS OF YOUR

RENDITIONS) TAKE IN AURALLY.

Quiet and dark

Verse: "I form the light and create darkness" (Isaiah 45:7).

"For sleep, one needs endless depths of blackness to sink into; daylight is too shallow, it will not cover one" (ANNE MORROW LINDBERGH).

Reflection: It's easy for us to think of darkness not as something God-made but as the absence of his created light. Yet the word "create" in the above verse, applied specifically to the darkness, doesn't connote deficiency, nonexistence, or lack.

It occurs to me that seeing and hearing are unique among our five senses in that their absence can also be a gift. Associating darkness and silence with God is a universal experience. While I intended the following poem for a younger audience, most of us have savored the experience I was recalling:

> One time when we were camping,
> something woke me in the dark—
> no, not a thud or thump or thunk,
> no screech or growl or bark.
>
> No cricket violin, no flapping tent,
> no rustling leaves.
> No crunching footstep, buzzing fly,
> no branch brushed by a breeze.
>
> I *felt* the quiet, nothing like
> I'd ever *heard* before.
> I felt like God had held his breath.
> I strained to listen more!
>
> The silence was like music,
> softer that I'd ever heard.
> Then, silently, I praised the Lord
> without one single word!

Prayer Prompt: When have you praised God in an absolutely dark and noiseless environment? Try to recall your impressions before repeating your praise.

odly woman,

SEE AND HEAR HIM WITH YOUR EYES CLOSED AND YOUR EARS STRAINING

TO EXPERIENCE THE SILENCE.

*H*olding wonder

Verse: "I have calmed and quieted myself, I am like a weaned child with its mother; like a weaned child I am content" (Psalm 131:2).

"One of the virtues of being very young is that you don't let the facts get in the way of your imagination" (SAM LEVENSON).

Reflection: Poet Sara Teasdale "teases" my sense of wonder with this exquisite little offering:

"Life has loveliness to sell,
All beautiful and splendid things,
Blue waves whitened on a cliff,
Soaring fire that sways and sings,
And children's faces looking up,
Holding wonder like a cup."

Earlier this week Adelyn, pleased with some trifle I don't even remember, observed solemnly from her car seat behind me, "This is a great day for me." I have my great days too, and typically they're fairly mundane ones. I would imagine you do too. It's the kind of day that starts out well and ends up being fulfilling and "complete"—the kind of day preceding the kind of evening when my head hits the pillow with "Thank you, God, for a good day" on my lips. The kind of day when I complete a project I enjoyed, relax on an outing with a friend, or attend a stimulating conference or book club meeting. The kind of day culminating in a night when I lie awake for at least a little while simply relishing my contentment and gratitude.

There's nothing wrong with reflecting on "things too wonderful for me" or of learning all I can about those topics, as long as I can maintain throughout my sense of the wonder of the Almighty. Imagine yourself holding your wonder up to God, wonder in the form of cupped hands you're waiting for him to fill with more of himself. Is there a vague memory somewhere in the recesses of your mind of lying contented, filled and fulfilled, in your mom's embrace? God longs for that kind of relationship with you.

Prayer prompt: Before approaching God in prayer, concentrate on stilling your soul before him.

*G*odly *woman,*

WONDER IS NEVER WASTEFUL.

*E*nlargement

Verses: "[A]ll things have been created through him and for him. He is before all things, and in him all things hold together" (Colossians 1:16–17).

"This is the truth: as from a fire aflame thousands of sparks come forth, even so from the creator an infinity of beings have life and to him return again" (MARCUS TULLIUS CICERO).

Reflection: The quotes from Paul and Cicero, above, present opposite images. In the first we see God holding together the cosmos. The picture is one of cohesion and compaction. From an emotional standpoint, Paul's words make me feel nested, safe, guarded. In the second we see thousands of individual sparks separating themselves from the flames (I'm seeing the fire here as a positive), floating or drifting upward as though irresistibly pulled back heavenward. The picture is one of expansion. I'm reminded of the rivulets of water on my rain-spattered windshield that push upward after a swish of my windshield wipers. They're resolute, those fast-flowing little tributaries that start all over again after the next swipe of the blade.

I learned recently that the universe is continuously expanding outward. Just as the Creator is impervious to boundaries, so "outer" space knows no dimensions. Yes, he holds together the creation, but that doesn't preclude its relentless expansion.

"When I look at the galaxies on a clear night," reflects Madeleine L'Engle, "—when I look at the incredible brilliance of creation, and think that this is what God is like, then instead of feeling intimidated and diminished by it, I am enlarged. . . . I rejoice that I am a part of it."

The enlargement of which this author speaks has everything to do with God and nothing to do with herself. In fact, her comment reminds me of that of John the Baptist, the forerunner of Christ: "He must become greater; I must become less" (John 3:30). God *must* become greater, not just in contrast to myself but in terms of the infinity of his greatness. It's as though expansion is inherent in his majesty. How much less, then—and at the same time enlarged—can I become than by losing my self in him?

Prayer Prompt: Take the time to reflect on these images, picturing yourself in each scenario in relationship to the Creator.

odly woman,

REJOICE IN HIM.

Created for . . .

Verse: "We are God's handiwork, created in Christ Jesus to do good works, which God prepared in advance for us to do" (Ephesians 2:10).

"People never care how much you know until they know how much you care" (JOHN C. MAXWELL).

Reflection: I'm fairly certain that my interpretation of the following quote from actor/director Larry Silverberg differs from his intention. Still, taking it as I do from a Christian perspective, I feel that these thought-provoking words stand beautifully on their own (I love it when that happens!): "You are a powerhouse of creativity; you were born magnificently expressive, available and aware. Before you had the words for it, you had an intrinsic sense of urgency because you knew down in your bones that the stakes are high."

Paul wasn't talking in Ephesians 2:10 about our creative predispositions, godlike though they may be. His words are much more revolutionary: You and I were created to glorify our Maker not first by our creativity but by our love, by the good works we perform in his name.

My oldest daughter Amanda loves to draw, crochet, design, paint, and arrange flowers, but her disabilities have limited her capacity to refine her art. From the time she was little I have emphasized to her that what truly counts in God's eyes is character. And that the stakes are indeed high.

Kindness, sensitivity, and caring for the underdog: Amanda has excelled in these vital areas. This is what God prepared in advance for her—and for you and me—to do. In her way she is expressive, available, and aware.

The following anonymous quote reminds me of what I so appreciate in my oldest daughter: "Strength of character means the ability to overcome resentment against others, to hide hurt feelings, and to forgive quickly." What, I ask myself, could be more important? And as Paul affirms in Ephesians 2:10, God looks at it, and at us, in just this way.

Prayer Prompt: On what criteria do you base your sense of self-worth?

Godly woman,

HE CREATED YOU FOR GOOD—AND FOR HIMSELF.

𝒰nbounded

Verse: "To all perfection I see a limit, but your commands are boundless" (Psalm 119:96).

"It seems a fantastic paradox, but it is nevertheless a most important truth, that no architecture can be truly noble which is not imperfect" (JOHN RUSKIN).

Reflection: "In nature," notes Alice Walker, "nothing is perfect and everything is perfect. Trees can be contorted, bent in weird ways, and they're still beautiful." Who of us hasn't been struck by the allure of life's snapshots (of nature and revealing human nature) depicting a less than perfect state: a dog with a ragged ear, a sagging barn, an old car on blocks next to an unpainted shack in a littered yard, the wrinkled hands or face of the very aged, the beseeching eyes of a dirty-faced child, the crooked black arms of a leafless tree against a yellow sky? Such snippets invite us to invent stories, don't they? Even in architecture and design we respond to asymmetry, the eclectic, the surprise anachronistic element.

This isn't to say, of course, that we don't long to right the wrongs. As stewards of creation and representatives of our Creator and Lord in society, we're called to do our best to heal nature's gashes, erase its scars, and bind up aching hearts—all the while knowing that we can only go so far.

In contrast, according to the psalmist, God's law—and by implication his love and wisdom—is inexhaustible. This isn't to say that there's no end to the number of his commands. That was the burden imposed by the Pharisees. The New Testament summary of the law includes exactly two directives, but they're all-encompassing in their scope. Because *nothing* in this world falls outside the law of love. And love's potential, for those of us guided and empowered by the Spirit, truly is boundless.

Prayer Prompt: Does imperfection in nature and life in any way draw you to God? Or does it make you feel incomplete, unfulfilled, or restless? Is it possible you've become so complacent that you no longer care?

odly woman,

HIS LAW IS LOVE.

$\mathcal{T}$rue witness

Verse: "An honest witness tells the truth" (Proverbs 12:17).

"Good art cannot be immoral. By good art I mean art that bears true witness, I mean the art that is most precise" (EZRA POUND).

Reflection: If good art represents nature, the above quote implies what you and I already know: that creation, and by extension the Creator, are not and cannot be immoral. Nature is imperfect in its present state—our world is disaster prone, and created elements can at times be vicious—but its delicate checks and balances and inescapable points of beauty still reflect a good, sovereign, gracious, and absolutely moral God.

I turned on my computer minutes ago to be met by raw video footage of that twenty-three-foot tsunami crashing into the coast of Japan in the wake of today's 8.9 quake. How surreal to view a highway in the background, its even traffic pattern looking like that from any aerial shot, juxtaposed against the encroaching onrush of seawater carrying away everything in its path.

The imminent convergence of those two flows, traffic and water, made me shudder, and I was relieved that the video cut off before that point. Perhaps, I reassured myself, the waters petered out to a trickle before brushing the shoulder of that highway. The families and business people in those cars haunt me. What must have been on their minds as they waited for the point of contact?

No, that clip wasn't exactly art, although art bearing true witness can be fully as raw. I doubt I'll forget that footage; it touched my heart in a way the relatively lengthy online report (the one relying on words) never could.

It isn't my purpose to debate God's goodness in contrast to nature's ravages. What speaks to me right now is the precise, truthful witness of that soundless "snapshot." At first glance I might say the footage is amoral, not commenting on morality in one way or another. Truth is that I need the grounding of my faith to see the Creator's goodness and morality even in, through, and beyond this picture of devastation. Because I personally know the God who is sovereign over nature and human affairs, and I know he'll make everything all right in the end.

Prayer Prompt: An honest witness tells the truth. What kind of witness are you?

$\mathcal{G}$odly woman,

DON'T ALLOW NATURE'S RAW TRUTH TO MIS-COLOR YOUR PERCEPTION OF GOD'S TRUTH.

$\mathcal{B}$eyond the gap

Verses: "'What no eye has seen, what no ear has heard, and what no human mind has conceived'— the things God has prepared for those who love him—these are the things God has revealed to us by his Spirit" (1 Corinthians 2:9–10).

> *"Nature has perfections, in order to show that she is the image of God; and defects, to show that she is only his image"*
> (BLAISE PASCAL).

Reflection: "It's not what you see that is art," reflects surrealist artist Marcel Duchamp. "Art is the gap." Duchamp is, in my opinion, headed in the right direction with this quote.

But I would argue that the gap can't be spanned by human works of art. I'm not referring to the sin-engendered rift between God and people. Praise the Lord: That's been mended through the atoning death and resurrection of Jesus Christ. No, what comes to my mind is the gap between our imagination of eternal bliss, prompted in large part by the beauty we enjoy in nature and art, and the inconceivable reality. The reason the gap is unbridgeable from our end is that we as finite human beings lack the capacity to conceive of perfection.

In nature and art we catch enticing glimpses—glimpses that thrill our souls, aware as we are that the truth will be infinitely more breathtaking.

Just as God created us with Pascal's "God-shaped void," so he endowed us with a compulsion to reach for the sublime and the divine.

Prayer Prompt: In what ways is your soul grasping for the glory that will one day be revealed in and to us?

odly woman,
DON'T STOP REACHING.

That elusive balance

Verses: "No one can look at the sun, bright as it is in the skies after the wind has swept them clean. Out of the north he comes in golden splendor; God comes in awesome majesty. The Almighty is beyond our reach and exalted in power" (Job 37:21–23).

"Holiness, not happiness, is the chief end of man"
(OSWALD CHAMBERS).

Reflection: Some of the most stunning affirmations of God in Scripture come from an unexpected source—the book of Job. It's tempting to bypass this book as dour and black, but the verses above, bathed as they are in gold, belie this impression. Spoken by Elihu, not Job, these arresting words for all their beauty still reflect the ancient Old Testament sense of a great divide between humankind and the Almighty. I'm reminded by Elihu's reference to our inability to look full into the sun of the trepidation of the ancients when it came to the Almighty. I picture in Elihu's stance an averted glance, or perhaps eyes daring to gaze upward from beneath the protection of an upraised hand.

God in the minds of these very early saints was both preeminent (by implication far removed) and glorious. Yes, Job did dare to talk to God, and God, after a prolonged silence, did respond, but we don't get the same sense of intimacy in this exchange as we do in the close communion between God and Abraham. That relationship was outside the norm.

Our situation today is so opposite. We've grown so friendly with God that we've lost the sense of his majesty. The God who's so close to us as to reside in our hearts and to occupy every square inch of space in the universe is, we assume, there for us at our beck and call.

What will it take for us to recover a balance in our perspective on God—our Creator, Lord, Lover, and Friend?

Prayer Prompt: Do you view God more as aloof, as chummy, or as somewhere in between?

Godly woman,

HE DESERVES YOUR ADORATION . . . AND YOUR LOVE.

God's blueprint

Verse: "Unless the LORD builds the house, the builders labor in vain" (Psalm 127:1).

"Do you love me because I am beautiful, or am I beautiful because you love me?" (OSCAR HAMMERSTEIN IN *CINDERELLA*).

Reflection: Charles Dickens, one of my favorite "creators," made what I think is a neat distinction: "The whole difference between construction and creation is exactly this: that a thing constructed can only be loved after it is constructed; but a thing created is loved before it exists."

It goes without saying that nobody constructs a building without a blueprint, although the quality of the plans and the amount of investment in forethought and care that go into them varies widely. How many cookie-cutter structures aren't slapped together and then abandoned within a few years as businesses open and then close their doors? And how many older homes haven't undergone multiple renovations and taken on random new appendages that reflect little or no foresight or insight? The opposite is also true. Whether it's a cathedral or an ultra-modern stadium, a painstakingly "created" architectural structure can truly be awesome.

Taken in a non-literal sense, we can extrapolate from Dickens' quote the obvious connection that the Creator loved each of us long before we existed in a tangible way. And our Maker, whose eternal investment in us is all about love, desires also to provide our security; we know him also as our Protector.

Touching on the Oscar Hammerstein quote, you and I are beautiful, in the eyes of our Creator and of others, precisely because he made us, loves us, and enables us to be loveable from the inside out. He would, of course, love us regardless; we are, each and all, his unique and cherished works of art. On the basis of our acceptance of Christ's atoning sacrifice, the intrinsic beauty in each of us has already been redeemed and is being showcased for the world to see. I can hardly wait to glimpse the loveliness of his "architecture" following our final transformation.

Prayer Prompt: Bask in the love and loveliness that are yours on the basis of his creation of and investment in you.

odly woman,

YOU'RE A LIMITED EDITION (ONE-OF-A-KIND) MASTERPIECE.

$\mathcal{T}$he potter's prerogative

Verses: "'Shall what is formed say to the one who formed it, "Why did you make me like this?"' Does not the potter have the right to make out of the same lump of clay some pottery for special purposes and some for common use?" (Romans 9:20–21).

"Common clay must go through the heat and fire of the furnace
to become porcelain. But once porcelain, it can never become clay
again" (AUTHOR UNKNOWN).

Reflection: When I was little my aunt taught my cousin and me our first song from the grown-up hymnal we used at church. I beamed with pride upon mastering the following lyrics: "Have thine own way, Lord! Have thine own way! Thou art the potter, I am the clay. Mold me and make me after thy will, while I am waiting, yielded and still." That was more than fifty years ago, but this tune still pops into my head occasionally. And when it does it brings the same secure feeling it did so long ago, when the concept was fresh to my awakening mind.

The context of the above verses from Romans 9 is heavy reading, difficult to grasp now, let alone at the age of five or six. The argument immediately preceding: If God has mercy on some and hardens others, won't somebody say, "Then why does God still blame us? For who is able to resist his will?" (verse 19).

Those questions are still being asked today—no doubt by people who think they're the first to think this through. No, we can't understand the mind of God, which is precisely why (or because) he's God and we're not.

But we can and must wait for him to reveal himself. One day it will all make sense. Of one thing we can be sure: No matter whether God needs you or me for a special purpose or for his common use, we'll each and all emerge one day from the crucible as porcelain, never again to return to the clay from which we were formed.

Prayer Prompt: Without being overly modest, try to imagine where God sees you on the "special purposes" to "common use" spectrum? (Remember that he loves you either way.)

$\mathcal{G}$*odly woman,*
YOU'RE EXACTLY WHAT HE HAD IN MIND.

$\mathcal{T}$he eyes of the beholder

Verses: "Many of the older priests and Levites and family heads, who had seen the former temple, wept aloud when they saw the foundation of this temple being laid, while many others shouted for joy. No one could distinguish the sound of the shouts of joy from the sound of weeping, because the people made so much noise. And the sound was heard far away" (Ezra 3:12–13).

"We don't see things as they are, we see them as we are"
(ANAÏS NIN).

Reflection: Perspective, perspective, perspective. In some sense it's the old "half-empty/half-full" analogy. The ambivalence of God's people at this bittersweet moment was as much for God's sake as for their own. Just as David had once bemoaned God's dwelling in a flimsy, movable tabernacle, so the returnees from exile decried a second-rate temple for his Presence.

I'm intrigued by the mingling of sounds emanating from that scene. From keening to cheers, the clamor must have been a startling punctuation of the silence of a sparsely populated area. What message was conveyed to the people "far away" who strained to make sense of the sound?

One thing is certain: That foundation, despite its truncated dimensions and bleak backdrop, was beautiful to God. Beauty involves so much more than the physical. In this case, the beauty of worship, intentionality, hope, and a new beginning, not to mention the haunting beauty of the noise erupting from God's people, added to the mystique.

In the words of Malcolm de Chazal, "The beautiful remains so in ugly surroundings." And sometimes those surroundings are intrinsic to its allure.

Prayer Prompt: What beauty in you is dear to God? Resist the temptation to be overly modest.

odly woman,

BEAUTY IS RELATIVE AND INDEPENDENT OF ITS SURROUNDINGS.

New eyes

Verses: "I pray that the eyes of your heart may be enlightened in order that you may know the hope to which he has called you, the riches of his glorious inheritance in his holy people, and his incomparably great power for us who believe" (Ephesians 1:18–19).

"The real voyage of discovery exists not in seeking new landscapes but in having new eyes" (MARCEL PROUST).

Reflection: The theme of blindness permeates the New Testament. In John 9 the Jewish leaders attempt to entrap a man who has been healed of lifelong blindness into admitting that Jesus is not from God. His simple response: "Whether he is a sinner or not, I don't know. One thing I do know. I was blind but now I see!" (verse 25). This witness turns out to be both clever and articulate (see verses 26–34), leading Jesus to address the issue of spiritual blindness head-on.

So much of what God has to show us, both in our natural and in our spiritual lives, lies smack dab within our line of vision . . . and yet we fail to see it. Unless and until, that is, our vision has been redeemed.

In the words of Evelyn Underhill, "For lack of attention a thousand forms of loveliness elude us every day." Beauty in whatever form truly does lie in the eyes of the beholder. And that beauty won't impress our eyes unless it first impinges upon our hearts. Whatever it is we see—in God, in ourselves, in others, and in creation—we view through a filter. Those of us whose hearts and minds have been enlightened by the Spirit do indeed apprehend all that we see through the filter of redemption. Praise the Lord!

Prayer Prompt: Ask the Spirit to point out to your spirit what God would have you see.

Godly woman,
THE SPIRIT WANTS TO OPEN YOUR EYES.

God-ordained praise

Verses: "LORD, our Lord, how majestic is your name in all the earth! You have set your glory in the heavens. Through the praise of children and infants you have established a stronghold against your enemies" (Psalm 8:1–2).

"It is the childlike mind that finds the kingdom"
(CHARLES FILLMORE).

Reflection: "All children are artists," points out Pablo Picasso. "The problem is how to remain an artist once he grows up." Children may, due to their short attention spans, strike us at times as flighty and erratic, but the intensity of a little one can also be mind-boggling.

Whether the activity is creative expression or worship (or some junction of the two), their involvement can often be described as no-holds-barred. Their faith, so vital and concrete, leaves no opening for doubt or logic (which is often the precursor of doubt).

Years ago my nephew, then two years old, and his family were visiting my parents in Colorado in their tri-level home. Accustomed to a California house set on a concrete slab, he was surprised during his afternoon nap in the basement to hear footsteps from the main floor above him. Rousing his dad urgently, he asked in an awed voice, "Daddy, is that *Jesus* walkin' around up there?"

The truth of the matter: It *was* Jesus, embodied in some of the rest of us, our Lord's brothers and sisters.

Prayer Prompt: What would it take to preserve and increase the childlike quality of your faith?

Godly woman,
OFFER HIM YOUR UNRESERVED PRAISE.

$\mathcal{A}$ different kind of speech

Verses: "Speak to one another with psalms, hymns, and songs from the Spirit. Sing and make music in your heart to the Lord, always giving thanks to God the Father for everything, in the name of our Lord Jesus Christ" (Ephesians 5:19–20).

"Music expresses that which cannot be said and on which it is impossible to be silent" (VICTOR HUGO).

Reflection: It's interesting that Paul uses the verb *speak* at the beginning of this quote. There can be no doubt that music communicates in a way unlike any other.

Several years ago members of my denomination found themselves discouraged as they considered the lyrics of possible selections for a contemporary hymnal. Someone made the suggestion that the committee take the time to sing through some of the songs, with the result that the impasse was broken. Many of these melodies have become favorites of my congregation . . . and me.

I'm not musical, although I do carry a tune and love to sing. So it invariably saddens me when I see a fellow worshiper standing silent or barely moving his or her lips during a song. The poet Oliver Wendell Holmes expressed this sentiment in simple and yet memorable language:

"Alas for those that never sing,
But die with all their music in them!"

One way or another, God will have his praise. In the words of Jesus, "if [my disciples] keep quiet, the stones will cry out" (Luke 19:40). Along the same lines, John Muir had this to say: "A few minutes ago every tree was excited, bowing to the roaring storm, waving, swirling, tossing their branches in glorious enthusiasm like worship. But though to the outer ear these trees are now silent, their songs never cease."

Prayer Prompt: What role does music play in your Christian life?

$\mathcal{G}$*odly woman,*
HE SPEAKS THE LANGUAGE OF MUSIC.

*C*onsistent voice

Verse: "Pleasant words are a honeycomb, sweet to the soul and healing to the bones" (Proverbs 16:24).

"Be generous with kindly words, especially about those who are absent" (JOHANN WOLFGANG VON GOETHE).

Reflection: "When I judge art," reports Paul Cézanne, "I take my painting and put it next to a God made object like a tree or flower. If it clashes, it is not art." There's something to be said for that approach when it comes to our speech patterns too. Some of us have known fellow believers so steeped in Scripture that their words come out sounding like they're straight from the Bible. I don't mean stilted or archaic or overly formal—more like right on with the "voice" of God's Word.

Our Lord's half brother James was outspoken (carefully so) on the topic of our habits and manner of speaking: "With the tongue we praise our Lord and Father, and with it we curse human beings, who have been made in God's likeness" (James 3:9). Oops! Who of us would dare to claim exemption from this pitfall? It's in our nature—the sin nature, that is, against which we as Christians still struggle daily.

Pleasant words, sweet and healing: Now there's a worthwhile goal to keep in our mind before we engage our tongue.

Prayer Prompt: In what particular area(s) are you guilty of double-speak?

odly woman,
DON'T LET YOUR VOICE CLASH WITH GOD'S.

$\mathscr{A}$ppreciation by contrast

Verse: "You, LORD, are my lamp; the LORD turns my darkness into light" (2 Samuel 22:29).

"I will love the light for it shows me the way, yet I will endure the darkness because it shows me the stars" (OG MANDINO).

Reflection: How many of our blessings don't we notice or appreciate only in contrast? That dagger of sunlight following days of downpour, the return of appetite after a stomach bug, the absence of oppressive humidity following a cleansing thunderstorm. And the list goes on.

Finding those points of light in the darkness can be both startling and life changing. It has been said that we never truly appreciate what we have until we risk losing it. Or *what else* we have until after we've lost what we had thought was indispensible.

The one loss I feared I could never endure was that of my job. Until, that is, the employment I had taken for granted for thirty-one years was yanked from under me by a mid-afternoon summons to the Human Resources department four years ago. Informed that my editorial position had been eliminated, I was escorted to the door, forced to rely on someone else to grab my purse and coat.

Knowing God as I do, I shouldn't have been surprised to recognize almost immediately that the change would be just right for me. Already that night in the darkness I spied the star.

Prayer Prompt: When have you recognized a blessing in the light of a contrast?

$\mathscr{G}$*odly woman,*

STRAIN TOWARD THE LIGHT.

$\mathscr{S}$imply satisfied

Verses: "Why do you worry about clothes? See how the flowers of the field grow. They do not labor or spin. Yet I tell you that not even Solomon in all his splendor was dressed like one of these" (Matthew 6:28–29).

> *"Contentment is natural wealth, luxury is artificial poverty"*
> (SOCRATES).

Reflection: I'm anything but a minimalist—in clothing or in decor. I like distinctive detailing on my shirts, and there's always room in my affections for one more addition from my favorite antique store. If an area gets crowded, I'm more likely to move something than to ditch it. Yet my needs are simple and my contentment factor high.

Years ago, when my daughters were young, I would periodically spend an evening with friends touring fantastic new houses in my area's late spring Parade of Homes. It was fun to dream, and I'd often return home with some small idea from a furnished house to implement. As the girls grew older I would periodically ask one or more of them to accompany me on this dream jaunt, making it a point on our return to "tour" our mobile home, commenting on its fine features.

"Making the simple complicated," notes Charles Mingus, "is commonplace—making the complicated simple, awesomely simple—that's creativity." I'm not sure where I would fall on that continuum, other than to repeat that I'm simply satisfied. Hopefully that catches the spirit.

Prayer Prompt: Ask the Lord to increase your contentment quotient and decrease your anxiety about material things.

odly woman,
FIND CONTENTMENT IN HIM.

𝒜 Mom of noble character

Verse: "[A wife of noble character] makes coverings for her bed; she is clothed in fine linen and purple" (Proverbs 31:22).

"It is not what we take up, but what we give up, that makes us rich" (HENRY WARD BEECHER).

Reflection: I grew up with a succession of two wonderful mothers. Their styles were as different as their personalities, but both embodied for me the ideal of a stay-at-home Christian mom.

For my second mom in particular, marrying a man with five children, ranging in age from thirteen down to three, entailed giving up not only her profession but also her car, business wardrobe, and active social life.

"Home," notes Martin Buxbaum, "is where we tie one end of the thread of life." When Mom tied that end, I recognize in hindsight, she was in a real way tying herself to a tether, though I'm sure she never viewed it that way. While she may not have sewn all those unfitted white sheets (verse above), she certainly did her share of mending and patching them.

Mom didn't wear fine linen or purple, either—although she had enjoyed an impressive professional wardrobe before joining our family. I'll never forget the hand-sewn cotton chemise housedresses (we called them shifts) she wore for years—the ensemble complete with white nursing shoes to combat foot and leg fatigue from our California-style concrete floors.

Times were tight for our family in the sixties (though no more difficult than those of most of our friends), but we kids have benefitted throughout the rest of our lives from the influence of this selfless mom, this mom of noble character.

Prayer Prompt: If you're a wife and/or mother, assess where you stand on the nobility scale. Refraining from being too hard on yourself, address those issues that may need a second look.

Godly woman,
WORK OUT YOUR NOBILITY.

$\mathcal{W}$ere you there?

Verses: "Where were you when I laid the earth's foundation? . . . On what were its footings set, or who laid its cornerstone—while the morning stars sang together and all the angels shouted for joy?" (Job 38:4, 6–7).

"Music was my refuge. I could crawl into the space between the notes and curl my back to loneliness" (MAYA ANGELOU).

Reflection: "My idea is that there is music in the air, music all around us; the world is full of it, and you simply take as much as you require." So says Edward Elgar. It's true that different people have different daily requirements for beauty of all kinds. Just as some individuals crave ample doses of sunshine and others need extra amounts of certain nutrients, so God built into each of us our own unique tolerance for ugliness, sameness, or lack of sensual stimulation. There's no one-amount-fits-all RDA for beauty in the human psyche.

Do you happen to be one of those individuals with a high need for musical inspiration? Do you like to make music (give it out) as well as take it in? As a child I used to wonder whether musicians would someday deplete all possible combinations of notes and rhythms. I recognize now, of course, that the music "in the air" is an inexhaustible resource, "required" as much by our Creator as by us as human beings.

Does it ever occur to you, BTW, to wonder what your dog or cat is thinking as you sing your way through some task at home? Mine are definitely interested, as evidenced by their soulful gazes (in all honesty, in the cat's case the eyes are more unblinking than expressive), but they have yet to convince me of a high level of music appreciation. Then again, I suppose my degree of musical talent isn't all that appreciable, or appreciate-able . . .

Prayer Prompt: Thank God for the gift of music.

odly woman,
TAKE THE MUSIC YOU REQUIRE—AND GIVE IT BACK TO GOD.

ℒimiting, unlimited grace

Verse: "These are the words of the Amen, the faithful and true witness, the ruler of God's creation" (Revelation 3:14).

"Glory be to God for dappled things" (GERARD MANLEY HOPKINS).

Reflection: One advantage of attending church on a beautiful campus (my alma mater, Calvin College) is the unusually long walk from the parking lot to the chapel. For Adelyn and me the trek of nearly a block more often than not turns into a nature walk.

A few weeks ago Addie spotted drops of water clinging to the bottom of every red berry on a bush—until she shook a branch and broke the spell.

The connection may seem far-fetched, but God limiting the "wetness" of water reminds me that he also, in his grace, limits the effects of sin. Tainted though it is by the fall, the created order still bears unmistakable witness to its good designer and protector. I've quoted Romans 1:20 and 8:20–21 more than once; both are eloquent. The Old Testament also attests to the goodness and limitless knowledge of the Creator: "Do you not know? Have you not heard? The LORD is the everlasting God, the Creator of the ends of the earth. He will not grow tired or weary, and his understanding no one can fathom" (Isaiah 40:28).

When I observe one of those fleeting manifestations of his glory (those droplets of water adhering uniformly to berries, tree branches encased in ice, or the artistry on pavement or water painted by the sun's impinging rays filtered through leaves), I do know. And my other senses are whetted in similar ways.

I have to be on the alert, though. In the case of the water droplets it took the acute perception of a four-year-old to prevent me from walking right past (in all fairness in that situation, her eye level was better suited to noticing). But in so many cases the beauty remaining in a fallen creation is unmistakable and unavoidable. What must it have been like before the fall? One day we'll know. What a prospect!

Prayer Prompt: At what representation of God's glory have you stood, transfixed? Thank him for limiting the effects of sin in the natural world.

Godly woman,

HIS GLORY IS EVERYWHERE EVIDENT.

$\mathcal{U}$ltimate creative act

Verses: "You created my inmost being; you knit me together in my mother's womb. I praise you because I am fearfully and wonderfully made. . . . My frame was not hidden from you when I was made in the secret place, when I was woven together in the depths of the earth. Your eyes saw my unformed body" (Psalm 139:13–16).

"It boggles my mind that someone can see life breathed into a baby, watch the grass die and then come to life again, see leaves fall and watch the rebirth of a tree, or gaze on any of the majestic splendor that is this earth and not be overpowered by the presence of an Almighty God!" (BILL MCCARTNEY).

Reflection: "God's interest in the human race is nowhere better evinced than in obstetrics," notes Martin H. Fischer. And George Vaillant muses that "Like the birth of a child, creativity compels us not to explanation but to wonder and awe." That's because the knitting together or weaving of an unborn child in its mother's womb is without a doubt the ultimate creative act.

A single adoptive mom myself, I've had the remarkable privilege of witnessing the births of three of my four grandchildren (for the one I missed I was steps away in the waiting room caring for a one-year-old).

On the evening of Adelyn's birth, just four years ago this week (I write in June), a thoughtful nurse stamped a tiny footprint on my forearm. Fearfully and wonderfully formed, that tiny, intricate foot will, I trust, carry Addie through "all the days ordained for [her]" (verse 16).

Prayer Prompt: If you're a mom, what has the experience of giving birth meant to you?

odly woman,

EACH ONE OF US IS GOD'S INDIVIDUAL MAGNUM OPUS.

$\mathcal{P}$ainting on silence

Verse: "Be still, and know that I am God" (Psalm 46:10).

"The sound of 'gentle stillness' after all the thunder and wind have passed will be the ultimate Word from God" (JIM ELLIOT).

Reflection: If there's one thing the West fears, it's silence. While I've always been moved by Simon and Garfunkel's "The Sound of Silence," I disagree with its premise. Silence like a cancer grows?! *That does seem to be the consensus*, I think as I observe the moving lips of motorist after motorist, all cradling cell phones with crimped necks. *How can anyone possibly have that much to say?*

Having worked a twenty-one-year stint in customer service, I still occasionally cringe when the phone rings, which beyond the occasional telemarketer isn't all that often at my condo. Nor am I a background music kind of person.

After keying that last sentence I paused to listen, detecting only the hum of my computer and the deep breathing of the napping puppy (it just occurred to me that the clock is also ticking). I guess I do love to talk, but more often than not I prefer forming the words with my fingertips.

Ironically, musicians seem to revel in silence more than most. "The notes I handle no better than many pianists," observes Artur Schnabel, "but the pauses between the notes—ah, that is where the art resides!" (Ever wonder about the origin of the term "pregnant silence"?)

Or this from Leopold Stokowski: "A painter paints pictures on canvas. But musicians paint their pictures on silence."

To one fact I can attest: Knowing God as God happens best for me in the stillness.

Prayer Prompt: How can you arrange this morning to meet with God in relative silence?

$\mathcal{G}$*odly woman,*
APPRECIATE QUIETNESS.

"*It's* a moster!"

Verse: "Like one from whom people hide their faces he was despised, and we held him in low esteem" (Isaiah 53:3).

"I haven't met anyone yet who isn't handicapped in some way.
So what's the big deal? Don't hide your deformity. Wear it like a
Purple Heart" (GEORGIANN BALDINO).

Reflection: The Halloween she was two, Adelyn was awed by all things scary. A friend of my oldest daughter Amanda is afflicted by neurofibromatosis, a disease that has resulted in numerous tumors, many of them visible on her face and arms.

One evening that fall, this woman was seated with me in the front seat of my car when Khristina opened the back door to place Adelyn in her car seat. Wide-eyed, Addie addressed her mom in an urgent whisper: "It's a *moster!*" We can only hope Missy didn't overhear.

As Isaiah reminds us in his past-tense prophecy of the future, God's suffering Servant knew rejection too. Earlier the prophet had described Jesus' suffering (not his looks) in terms unexpected by our ears: "There were many who were appalled at him—his appearance was so disfigured beyond that of any human being and his form marred beyond human likeness" (Isaiah 52:14). Jesus understood the suffering caused by deformities, disfigurements, and perceived deficits. Whether external or internal, they're the stuff of fallen humanity.

How do you respond to the inclusive Jesus? To his acceptance of yourself? Of others? To those often rejected others who people your world?

Prayer Prompt: Take a moment to assess what human conditions seem monstrous to you. Then acknowledge in your heart and mind God's unconditional love for those who so suffer.

odly woman,

LOOK BEYOND THE PHYSICAL.

$\mathcal{W}$rap-up

Verse: "Remember your Creator in the days of your youth, before the days of trouble come and the years approach when you will say, 'I find no pleasure in them'" (Ecclesiastes 12:1).

"In the depths of winter, I finally learned that within me lay an invincible summer" (ALBERT CAMUS).

Reflection: Until condo ownership freed me from this late-autumn ritual, I almost invariably found myself raking crispy-leaves-turned-soggy in the toe-chilling grass under November rain.

In the quote to follow, Hal Borland catches the waning of the year in a slightly earlier snapshot, one that, for me at least, carries a spiritual connotation: "Autumn is the eternal corrective. It is ripeness and color and a time of maturity; but it is also breadth, and depth, and distance. What man can stand with autumn on a hilltop and fail to see the span of his world and the meaning of the rolling hills that reach to the far horizon?"

Perhaps the bleaker landscape of winter extends the horizon still further, but I resonate with Borland's point. The imagery of declining life, despite its loveliness, catches our attention as the year enters its wrap-up phase. With a contented maturity comes that heightened sense of breadth, depth, and distance to which Borland alludes. And the corrective lenses of advancing age snap life into a focus we may have missed during our busier, younger years.

Of one thing I'm confident: I'll never have to lament, as I stand with autumn (and God) on a hilltop, that "I find no pleasure" in life.

Prayer Prompt: In which of life's seasons are you standing? What are the implications for you, both physically and spiritually?

$\mathcal{G}$odly woman,

FIND YOUR PLEASURE IN HIM.

$\mathscr{L}$ast word

Verse: "[A wife of noble character] is clothed with strength and dignity" (Proverbs 31:25).

> *"Never take a person's dignity: it is worth everything to them, and nothing to you"* (FRANK BARRON).

Reflection: We live in a day when respect has lost its place in society—with self-respect in too many cases the first to depart. Interestingly, Solomon and Jesus cite nearly identical examples of situations inviting personal humiliation:

Solomon: "Do not exalt yourself in the king's presence, and do not claim a place among his great men; it is better for him to say to you, 'Come up here,' than for him to humiliate you before his nobles" (Proverbs 25:6–7).

And Jesus: "When someone invites you to a wedding feast, do not take the place of honor, for a person more distinguished than you may have been invited. If so, the host who invited both of you will come and say to you, 'Give this person your seat.' Then, humiliated, you will have to take the least important place" (Luke 14:8–9).

It's one thing to set ourselves up for humiliation but quite another to take advantage of someone else by refusing to allow her to save face. When have you felt the urge to rub salt in someone's wound when you've gotten the upper hand in a conflict or competition? Sometimes it's that parting barb that can hurt the most.

If you and I as believing women can indeed clothe ourselves with dignity, we'll instead find ourselves following the impulse to speak a gracious last word.

Prayer Prompt: How highly do you value your own and others' dignity?

odly woman,
SEASON YOUR LAST WORD IN PARTICULAR WITH SALT.

$\mathcal{D}$estination

Verse: "Direct my footsteps according to your word; let no sin rule over me" (Psalm 119:133).

"Goodness is love in action, love with its hand to the plow, love with the burden on its back, love following his footsteps who went about continually doing good" (JAMES HAMILTON).

Reflection: "A few days ago," recalls Eric Sloane, "I walked along the edge of the lake and was treated to the crunch and rustle of leaves with each step I made. The acoustics of this season are different and all sounds, no matter how hushed, are as crisp as autumn air." This description reminds me of my favorite kind of late autumn day, brilliant with sunshine despite the now muted hues of fallen leaves.

In terms of my footsteps, I'll have to say that winter here in Michigan is the quiet season. Tentative on any outdoor surface that might hide "black ice," I plant my feet gingerly, not sliding like my adventuresome grand-daughter, who in all fairness is much closer to the ground, and certainly not kicking as I naturally do in a mantle of leaves.

As I write this in late July, I'm reminded of my footsteps this past Friday evening, squeaking as I struggled to navigate a lengthy stretch of white sand on a Lake Michigan beach—my calves were still sore this morning. In terms of my early spring footfalls, much of the time they're more deliberate and nimble, expert through long experience at avoiding puddles and mud patches.

It's fun to contrast the nature of my footfalls from season to season. But in the final analysis, it's where I'm headed that counts. "Oh, be careful little feet where you go," I sing with Adelyn. That's a good reminder for me as well. Of one thing I'm certain: I can't go wrong if I try to match my footfalls to Christ's.

Prayer Prompt: In what particular area could you benefit, right now, from God's direction?

$\mathcal{G}$*odly woman,*
INVITE HIM TO GUIDE YOUR STEPS.

November 4

STRENGTH TO STRENGTH

Her size, not mine

Verse: "Each one should test their own actions. Then they can take pride in themselves alone, without comparing themselves to someone else" (Galatians 6:4).

"Jealousy is the fear of comparison" (MAX FRISCH).

Reflection: "Did you have fun this morning, Addie?" *(at daycare).*
"Yea. I played with Haley."
"That's nice. Is Haley your size?"
"No, Granna. Haley's her size, not my size."

I'll have to admit that I didn't phrase that question too well. Makes me wonder, though: At what point of awakening maturity does comparing become more important than just being? "There are kids," notes Mike Krzyzewski, "who don't want to do something because they're afraid of looking stupid to their peers. There comes a time when they start protecting themselves, instead of extending. I want to make sure that they're always trying to extend themselves."

One of the beautiful things about the very young is their total lack of inhibition when it comes to trying new things, their lack of awareness of their bodies in space. Adelyn is self-conscious about her speech, typically choosing not to engage others in public conversation. But she moves gracefully, apparently oblivious to the possibility of an audience.

Addie at three glows when complimented about some feat or completed task. It hasn't yet occurred to her to compete or compare. Where do you stand on the competition continuum?

Prayer Prompt: Tell the Lord your frustrations in the areas of competition or your feelings of inadequacy, superiority, or jealousy.

odly woman,

FOCUS ON BEING THE YOU GOD HAD IN MIND.

$\mathscr{S}$pontaneous favor

Verses: "Although in Christ I could be bold and order you to do what you ought to do, yet I appeal to you on the basis of love" (Philemon 8–9).

"Love does not dominate; it cultivates"
(JOHANN WOLFGANG VON GOETHE).

Reflection: Paul's letter to Philemon on behalf of Philemon's runaway slave Onesimus, who has since been converted to Christ, is a study in psychological persuasion. Paul anticipates every objection, seemingly (at least on my first read) backing his friend into a corner.

I wonder: Is Paul acting as master manipulator or impartial mediator? In verses 12–14 the apostle injects some helpful information: A prisoner himself who has benefitted from Onesimus's service, he is doing the only right thing by sending him back to his master.

And he wants any favor Philemon might do on his behalf not to "seem forced" but to "be voluntary." In light of the fact that Paul has the apostolic authority to dictate Philemon's response, his request is more than generous.

There are many situations in which Christian love demands that we act in a certain way, whether or not that response is in our own best interest. Listen to Paul's words from 2 Corinthians 5:14–15: "For Christ's love compels us, because we are convinced that one died for all, . . . that those who live should no longer live for themselves."

Prayer Prompt: What situation in your Christian life demands a gracious response?

$\mathcal{G}$odly woman,

LET LOVE DICTATE YOUR BEHAVIOR CHOICES.

Summarizing the outline

Verse: "Seek first his kingdom and his righteousness" (Matthew 6:33).

> *"The key is not to prioritize what's on your schedule, but to schedule your priorities"* (STEPHEN R. COVEY).

Reflection: Khristina as a high-schooler was much bigger on random learning than on the assigned stuff, and, like many of her peers, found writing papers particularly distasteful. So I was proud of her during the fall of her senior year when she flashed before me an impressive outline. Progress after that point was painstakingly slow, and I worried about a difficult all-nighter on the evening before the paper was due. To my surprise the announcement came soon afterward that the task had been accomplished. Khris waved in my general direction two double-spaced pages. *"No worries, Mom!"* (this is still one of her favorite sayings, although it seldom puts me at ease). "I summarized the outline."

Do you find yourself wanting to fill your calendar (outline) based on high ideals—and hopeless over-commitment? You can burn yourself out . . . or you can summarize (pick and choose from) your "to do" list. I'm a list keeper, but I've learned in the last few years to keep my outline modest, based on achievable, and hopefully important, objectives. The other stuff goes on the long-term (as in no pressure) list.

There's no getting around the fact that list-maintenance requires prioritizing. Otherwise we find ourselves stumbling along, driven by the "tyranny of the urgent." In the verse above our Lord laid out for us the key principle for setting priorities. No, he didn't mean that any and all church-related activities must automatically rise to the top. We can seek Christ's kingdom and righteousness in so many ways. Which come to mind for you?

Prayer Prompt: How realistic are your commitments? How targeted, and how Christ-like, are your priorities?

odly woman,
SEEK FIRST CHRIST'S KINGDOM.

$\mathcal{K}$nowing good and evil

Verse: "Nothing impure will ever enter [the new Jerusalem], nor will any-one who does what is shameful and deceitful, but only those whose names are written in the Lamb's book of life" (Revelation 21:27).

"If the doors of perception were cleansed, everything would appear to man as it is, infinite" (WILLIAM BLAKE).

Reflection: "Now we see only a reflection as in a mirror," reflects Paul in 1 Corinthians 13:12, going on to assert that "then we shall see face to face. Now I know in part; then I shall know fully, even as I am fully known" (1 Corinthians 13:12).

What is there about the next life that puzzles or fascinates you? For me, it's how we can expect to have no tears if we still remember unsaved loved ones. Will we understand so well the relationship between God's justice and mercy that we'll no longer perceive inequality or mourn the lost? What will be the true extent of our knowledge, even—dare I suggest the question?—in comparison with God's?

Already at the dawn of human history Satan saw the ability to "be like God, knowing good and evil" (Genesis 3:5) as the ultimate drawing card with which to tempt human beings. Adam and Eve were perfect, but this kind of knowledge hadn't been given to them.

Before the fall, sinless humans (all two of them) had the free will to opt for sin. In consequence of exercising that choice, they lost the ability not to sin. We as Christians, despite our residual sinful natures, have regained the capacity to choose to do good. In the final phase of eternity, we'll at long last lose the ability to choose evil (Revelation 21:27, above). Is that the reason, I wonder, why God will only then entrust us with full disclosure?

Prayer Prompt: In what concrete ways are you exercising your ability to choose the good?

$\mathcal{G}$odly woman,

ONE DAY WE'LL KNOW AND UNDERSTAND.

Opportunity—or danger?

Verse: "I have been constantly on the move. I have been in danger from rivers, in danger from bandits, in danger from my fellow Jews, in danger from Gentiles; in danger in the city, in danger in the country, in danger at sea; and in danger from false believers" (2 Corinthians 11:26).

> *"The optimist sees opportunity in every danger; the pessimist sees danger in every opportunity"* (WINSTON CHURCHILL).

Reflection: Paul's litany, above, runs the gamut. And all due to risks deliberately incurred in the name of a cause much larger than himself. Jesus' cause was not, of course, bigger than himself, although he chose to make our dire need his priority.

What danger or perceived threat have you faced down in availing yourself of a kingdom opportunity? Perhaps you've ventured into a part of downtown known to be unsafe in order to minister to the homeless or addicted. The possibilities are myriad.

The question "What would Jesus do?" popular several years ago, was a good motivator. But Martin Luther King Jr. points out that it isn't the only one to ask ourselves in the face of another's trouble: "The first question which the priest and the Levite asked was: 'If I stop to help this man, what will happen to me?' But . . . the good Samaritan reversed the question: 'If I do not stop to help this man, what will happen to him?'"

We can take encouragement from the author to the Hebrews, who enjoins us to fix "our eyes on Jesus, the pioneer and perfecter of our faith. For the joy set before him he endured the cross, scorning its shame, and sat down at the right hand of the throne of God. Consider him who endured such opposition from sinners, so that you will not grow weary and lose heart" (Hebrews 12:2–3).

Prayer Prompt: What joy beckons you through opportunity and despite risk?

odly woman,
SEE OPPORTUNITY, NOT DANGER.

$\mathcal{R}$estricting God

Verse: "The LORD answered Moses, 'Is the LORD's arm too short? Now you will see whether or not what I say will come true for you'" (Numbers 11:23).

> *"The strength of a man consists in finding out the way God is going, and going that way"* (HENRY WARD BEECHER).

Reflection: At five feet five inches tall, I'm not exactly vertically challenged, although there are moments when I'd appreciate the ability to reach that bowl on the top shelf. But a problem arises when I try to impose restrictions on God.

In Numbers 11 Moses presented God with just such a challenge. Irked by the people's insistence on adding meat to their diet, God vowed to gorge them on the stuff. Moses pointed out logistical problems God had evidently overlooked—to which the Lord responded, presumably with some vehemence, "What? Is my arm too short?"

If you're like me, you prefer to work out your own problems, turning to prayer as a last resort. You may doubt God's interest, ability, or availability. You may want to avoid interrupting him for some detail you can just as well handle on your own. You may even be angry at him. One way or another, your attitude and actions fling a vertical challenge toward heaven.

Psalm 44:3 addresses God on the subject of Israel's conquest of Canaan: "It was not by their sword that they won the land, nor did their arm bring them victory; it was your right hand, your arm . . . for you loved them." Ah! Those four short words say it all, don't they?

Don't doubt or disdain God's desire and ability to help you. He has your best interests at heart—*because he loves you.*

Prayer Prompt: In what areas are you trying to preempt or work around God?

$\mathcal{G}$*odly woman,*

HE ORIENTS HIMSELF TOWARD YOUR DETAILS.

*H*aven

Verses: "My people will live in peaceful dwelling places, in secure homes, in undisturbed places of rest. Though hail flattens the forest and the city is leveled completely, how blessed you will be, sowing your seed by every stream, and letting your cattle and donkeys range free" (Isaiah 32:18–20).

> *"The ache for home lives in all of us, the safe place where we can go as we are and not be questioned"* (MAYA ANGELOU).

Reflection:
> "Out of the dreariness,
> Into its cheeriness,
> Come we in weariness,
> Home."
> —*Stephen Chalmers*

I'm irresistibly drawn to Isaiah's word pictures, above. The passage speaks of undisturbed rest in the midst of a decidedly disturbed situation. The allusions to devastation most likely refer to Assyria's destruction of nearby Israel (Judah is basking in prosperity, oblivious to the more distant threat of Babylonia). Yet my study Bible clues me in to the fact that verse 20, beginning with "how blessed . . .," despite falling in the middle of a sentence, leaps ahead to the "day of the Lord" so prominent in the prophetic writings—a day or reckoning or of rejoicing, depending on one's perspective. Yet despite the characteristic jumping of Isaiah's images in terms of chronology, these verses still form a cohesive thought. It's as though the prophet is stretching a "before and after" statement across a time barrier from one phase of human history into another.

What comfort we can derive from this picture of home (in the here and now) as the safe haven in a turbulent world! In the words of Jesus of all who love and obey him, "My Father will love them, and we will come to them and make our home with them" (John 14:23). Now there's a picture of peace! A picture that, though changing in its particulars, applies both to the now and to the later.

Prayer Prompt: What qualities make your home a place of refuge? To what degree is his presence a factor?

odly woman,
HE'S AT HOME WITH YOU.

$\mathcal{F}$oretaste

Verse: "Look, I am coming soon!" (Revelation 22:12).

"The Indian summer of life should be a little sunny and a little sad, like the season, and infinite in wealth and depth of tone—but never hustled" (HENRY BROOKS ADAMS).

Reflection: No matter how often I've relished an Indian summer, I'm amazed at the exuberance it brings out in me. Henry Wadsworth Longfellow focuses on the sadness factor, but I sense in his words, as in Adams's, an element of longing nostalgia: The "gorgeous tints are gone, as if the autumnal rains had washed them out. Orange, yellow, and scarlet, all are changed to one melancholy russet hue. The birds, too, have taken wing . . . . Only the dismal cawing of a crow, as he sits and curses that the harvest is over; or the chit-chat of an idle squirrel, the noisy denizen of a holly tree . . . the absolute monarch of a dozen acorns."

In sharp contrast another American poet, Walt Whitman, hones in on the beauty of this seasonal phenomenon: "It is only here in large portions of Canada that wondrous second wind, the Indian summer, attains its amplitude and heavenly perfection, and the temperatures; the sunny haze; the mellow, rich, delicate, almost flavoured air: Enough to live—enough to merely be." (I would contest that Michigan's Indian summer days can be fully as invigorating.)

So much of what life—what God—brings our way pivots on perspective, doesn't it? If later fall symbolically coincides with life's waning, Indian summer reminds me of the second wind that often accompanies its middle years—a mellow, mature time many describe as its most vibrant. That's how it is for me. Despite physical constraints I didn't experience a decade ago, I'm savoring life as never before.

I wonder, is Indian summer a foretaste or an afterglow? With all the splendor in our world—and of the world to come—I think I could make a case for both. As travelers en route from one garden to another, trudging from Genesis 2 to Revelation 22, we experience both nostalgia and anticipation as we make our way from one oasis of strength and beauty to another.

Prayer Prompt: What glimpses of eternity have you savored today?

$\mathcal{G}$odly woman,

FOLLOW HIS LEAD FROM GARDEN TO GARDEN.

$\mathscr{S}$ignposts

Verse: "Set up road signs; put up signposts. Take note of the highway, the road that you take. Return, Virgin Israel, return to your towns" (Jeremiah 31:21).

> *"Of all the bewildering things about a new country, the absence of human landmarks is one of the most depressing and disheartening"*
> (WILLA CATHER).

Reflection: The above verse took me by surprise when I read it recently. If I've encountered it before, which must be the case, I didn't engage with it. The prophet Jeremiah was advising the Judahites to set up sign markers during their forced march to Babylon to facilitate their return when the time came. My immediate association was with the breadcrumbs futilely dropped by Hansel as he and Gretel, banished by their father and stepmother, wandered deeper and deeper into the fairy-tale woods.

Whether it's breadcrumbs or some other form of trail markers, the gesture is all about hope. Hope against hope, to be specific. When reversals or tragedies or bad decisions send us into forced "exile," what signposts are there to guide us back home, to security and to God?

Some examples may help. How about good habits or traditions? Like Bible reading, prayer, or regular church attendance. Like commemorating the holidays with God in the picture. Like an ingrained value system on which we can fall back. Like controlling or eradicating vices before they can control us. Or like cherished memories of happy family times we've had and made. The more "set" we are in the ways of God, the easier it will be to find our way back to him.

Prayer Prompt: Take an inventory of the signposts you're building into your life to keep you from wandering from God and home.

odly woman,

MAKE SURE YOU'RE "SET" IN HIS WAYS.

$\mathscr{C}$ompassion

Verse: "The LORD longs to be gracious to you; therefore he will rise up to show you compassion" (Isaiah 30:18).

"So many dolls, so little room" (SUE ANN THOMASON).

Reflection: Khristina and Adelyn were wandering through Walmart when they noticed a commotion in the wine aisle. A jiggling, giggling baby doll with an infectious (soon verging on obnoxious) laugh had been placed atop some bottles partway down the aisle, and bottles up and down the line were vibrating and clinking merrily.

"Her needs me!" Addie exclaimed, alarmed, becoming all the more insistent as Khris continued past the aisle. Moments later they returned, Khris sheepishly snatching up the abandoned waif, to the amusement of the more discriminating wine shoppers.

This plastic "adoptee" has joined the many others residing in our home. Both Khris and I are suckers when it comes to needy dolls, and Addie is an equal-opportunity playmate. I have to think my influence has a lot to do with that.

I vaguely remember a favorite dollie when I was two. This outdoor doll was particularly needy; at some point her head had become detached from her body and had gone missing. I've been "accused" as an adult of being drawn to headless dolls, and perhaps there's truth to that statement for me as the adoptive mom of special-needs girls. There can be no denying that I'm a softie for the overlooked and the underdog. (It was me who steered Khris toward a "runt" last year at the animal shelter; Annabelle is anything but that now!)

Going back further, I'll have to note that we get our empathetic streak from our dad—our heavenly Father, that is. Has it rubbed off on you?

Prayer Prompt: Intercede for that person about whom you're concerned.

$\mathscr{G}$*odly woman,*

IMITATE HIS COMPASSION.

Where charity begins?

Verses: "Get rid of all bitterness, rage and anger, brawling and slander, along with every form of malice. Be kind and compassionate to one another, forgiving each other, just as in Christ God forgave you" (Ephesians 4:31–32).

"Stubbornness does have its helpful features. You always know what you are going to be thinking tomorrow" (GLEN BEAMAN).

Reflection: "Faced with the choice between changing one's mind and proving that there is no need to do so," observes John Kenneth Galbraith, "almost everyone gets busy on the proof." Do you find yourself in one of those relationships in which it seems necessary for the two of you to take opposing views, no matter what the issue? To lock horns continually, on the basis of habit, competition, underlying personality, or role clash—perhaps even boredom or the need for an outlet for irritability or frustration? I know I do. My problem is at home, at least partially the result of having two stubborn adult women under one roof.

This kind of sparring is all too common between closely connected individuals, and we as Christian women are hardly immune. The very fact that we can be continuously aware in public of our image as Christ's representatives may leave us more susceptible to conflict behind closed doors, where we feel we can finally relax our guard.

We're all familiar with the saying that charity begins at home, but have we acknowledged that home can be the hardest place to behave charitably? Paul had this to say to the young preacher Timothy: "If I am delayed, you will know how people ought to conduct themselves in God's household, which is the church of the living God" (1 Timothy 3:15). Wow! Talk about high stakes!

Prayer Prompt: How are you doing with tolerance at home?

Godly woman,
FOLLOW HIS EXAMPLE—IN PRIVATE TOO.

The door

Verses: "Very truly I tell you, I am the gate for the sheep. . . . I am the gate; whoever enters through me will be saved. They will come in and go out, and find pasture" (John 10:7, 9).

"As the fly bangs against the window attempting freedom while the door stands open, so we bang against death ignoring heaven" (DOUGLAS HORTON).

Reflection: Last night Khristina dropped a dog treat through the rear bars of her pup's unoccupied but open crate. She and I watched for a minute or two, chuckling, as Annabelle, from the outside, tried to access this enticing morsel, slipping each paw, one at a time, through the rear bars and then attempting to maneuver the goodie closer by shifting the portable crate floor. It never did occur to her to run to the other side and enter through the door.

The analogy to Jesus' words, above, is a bit flawed, but the truth is that sheep—a common biblical symbol for you and me—aren't the sharpest tools in the shed either. Without a shepherd to lead us to pasture, we'd be goners. Matthew tells us that when Jesus saw the crowds, "he had compassion on them, because they were harassed and helpless, like sheep without a shepherd" (Matthew 9:36).

How often don't we forego something good because we refuse to make use of the door by which we can access it? Each of us knows exactly how this applies to us individually. If we think there's an easy work-around, a too-good-to-be-true backdoor solution by which we can attain the body or income or whatever else we may be after, we're apt to savor the temptation.

It just won't work that way on a spiritual level. Jesus is the gate—the only door, the only means by which we can enter the fold and find nourishment. True, his gate may be narrow, but he doesn't make it hard to find.

Prayer Prompt: To whom will you point out the door?

Godly woman,
FIND IN HIM YOUR WAY, YOUR TRUTH, YOUR LIFE.

$\mathscr{B}$uffer

Verse: "The Lord is my helper; I will not be afraid. What can mere mortals do to me?" (Hebrews 13:6).

"Worry is a complete cycle of inefficient thought revolving about a pivot of fear" (AUTHOR UNKNOWN).

Reflection: I was ill prepared for Khristina's measles vaccine, administered when she was seven, shortly after moving in with me. Unaware of her fear of needles, I was taken aback by her bloodcurdling screams. As we rose shortly afterward to leave the office, though, she was gloating over her grit. "Mom," she informed me with exaggerated confidence, "I almost didn't cry!"

Of what are you afraid? My only irrational fear is of snakes, although I love nothing better than lingering behind the shatterproof glass in the snake house waiting for the big ones to move. This gives me the same kind of vicarious chill as watching a thriller in the safety of my TV room—in the company of Khristina (blanket over her face, asking for a play-by-play of what's happening).

We all indulge, if not in outright fear, at least in worry equity. Yet I can't begin to imagine facing the uncertainties of life without my ever-present awareness of God's protective care. It's there at all times, that awareness, whether or not I'm conscious of the reason for my typically optimistic calm.

Tragically, so many do face the future not only without this buffer against calamity but without the knowledge that there is any ultimate sense to our existence, any overarching plan making hope a rational approach to living. "What can [other people] do to me?" must be a terrifying prospect for those surviving in a world they perceive as random.

Prayer Prompt: What difference does God's protection make for you? With whom can you share the news this week?

odly woman,
CLING TO YOUR CERTAINTY IN HIM.

*L*everaging our strengths

Verse: "And now, my daughter, don't be afraid. I will do for you all you ask. All the people of my town know that you are a woman of noble character" (Ruth 3:11).

"We did not change as we grew older; we just became more clearly ourselves" (LYNN HALL).

Reflection: There are different kinds of transformation a person can undergo, and I don't want to discount the renewal and sanctification that characterize our lives as Christian women. They're a given—given to us by God as one of the most precious gifts we'll ever receive.

But there resides in each of us a constant, underlying personality. I still love the blurb a classmate chose for my fourteen-year-old, ninth-grade yearbook photo: "She's gentle and she's shy, yet there's humor in her eye." I like to think that still captures me pretty well.

I remember the fourth- or fifth-grade me asking my Sunday School teacher about the difference between personality and character. I don't recall what she said, but I do know it worked for me. Our character can definitely change—this has already happened for you as God's daughters; it's the part of us that's affected by renewal and sanctification, the part that can legitimately be labeled with adjectives like good or bad, noble (like Ruth) or corrupt.

When it comes to our personalities, though, we're wise to accept them (as they are) as another of God's good gifts and to make life decisions that are a good fit. Accepting our personality entails dropping any value judgments we may have developed about it. It isn't good or bad to be extroverted or introverted or whatever other distinction we might want to make—just different. And it's those very differences that make people so delightful and attractive.

Prayer Prompt: What is there about your personality you've always labeled negatively? Ask God to help you leverage the strength of that trait.

*G*odly woman,
YOUR PERSON-ALITY DEFINES YOUR PERSON.

*B*alancing act

Verse: "Please pay no attention, my lord, to that wicked man Nabal. He is just like his name—his name means Fool, and folly goes with him. And as for me, your servant, I did not see the men my lord sent" (1 Samuel 25:25).

"If you want to get across an idea, wrap it up in person"
(RALPH BUNCHE).

Reflection: The story of Abigail, as recounted in 1 Samuel 25, seems for whatever reason to be a little known gem. If you have the time, I would suggest reading through it now. It's relatively lengthy at thirty-five verses but well worth the read. Alternatively, you can pick up the story at verse 14 without losing too much.

The point could be made, I suppose, that this remarkable woman was the ultimate diplomat. But I prefer to see her in a more positive light, as peacemaker extraordinaire. It would seem to me that her story wouldn't have been included in the Bible in so much detail if this were not the case.

Abigail's quick and decisive action averted what could have lived on in history as a serious blight on David's character. For all his positive traits, David had an impetuous streak that tended to get him into trouble. What he needed was the calming influence of someone (OK, let's get it out—of a woman) talking sense.

In terms of David's wives, we certainly hear more about Michal and Bathsheba, both of whose stories include scandal (in all fairness to Bathsheba, probably not her fault). I prefer to think of Abigail, though, as the behind-the-scenes encourager David needed in order to maintain balance.

Prayer Prompt: Pinpoint a situation in your life in which you could play a role similar to Abigail's.

odly woman,
BE FOR ANOTHER THE VOICE OF RESTRAINT.

The full life

Verse: "I have come that they may have life, and have it to the full" (John 10:10).

> *"Laugh as much as you breathe and love as long as you live"*
> (ANONYMOUS).

Reflection: There's quite a difference between existing as a warm body and truly living—between breathing in and out and being fully alert, aware, alive—overflowing with life! Jesus and Paul made good use of the word translated into English as *full*. We as Christians ought to know something about the full life, because we alone are filled with the Spirit who gives life, with "the fullness of him who fills everything in every way" (Ephesians 1:23).

The full life has nothing to do with a full calendar, as we may tend to think. Being busy with and engaged with life are not the same. And unfortunately, the one doesn't necessarily lend itself to the other. It's so easy to immerse ourselves in "church life," for example, at the expense of spiritual and family life.

"I don't want to get to the end of my life and find that I have just lived the length of it," reflects Diane Ackerman, "I want to have lived the width of it as well." The picture for me is one of fullness, a matter of quality. An anonymous quote on the subject also speaks to me: "Life is not measured by the number of breaths we take, but by the moments that take our breath away."

If we as Christian women can gain perspective on this vital distinction, we'll come a long way toward living lives of effective service to God, ourselves, and others. Yes, I was deliberate about the order at the end of that last sentence. It's like the mother on the plane using the oxygen mask first so she can be fully present to resuscitate her infant.

Prayer Prompt: What's holding you back from living to the full?

Godly woman,

BASK IN HIS FULLNESS.

Try again!

Verse: "Let us therefore make every effort to do what leads to peace and to mutual edification" (Romans 14:19).

"Experience is that marvelous thing that enables you to recognize a mistake when you make it again" (FRANKLIN P. JONES).

Reflection: The Bible doesn't talk much about goofs and gaffes and gaining experience, concentrating on the more serious matters of errors, remorse, and repentance. But it does include several references to "trying" (not as in trying times or trying patience but in trying to excel or get something right—the "try, try again" mentality).

Some such endeavors will be met with minimal success. I think of Paul's parenthetical comment in 1 Corinthians 10:33, "even as I try to please everyone in every way." Not likely. Moving beyond that scenario, I still chuckle at a ditty my dad recited at the dinner table when I was quite young:

"They told the young man it couldn't be done.
With a smile on his face he went right to it.
He tackled that job that 'couldn't be done.'
And do you know what? He couldn't do it."

My guess, though, is that this enterprising young man, perhaps once he had made it past his youthful arrogance, did experience some successes.

How willing are you to resist throwing in the towel when a first attempt doesn't work out? "While one person hesitates because he feels inferior," observes Henry C. Link, "the other is busy making mistakes and becoming superior."

Take a moment to think of the mistakes (OK, errors) of men like David, Peter, and Paul, all of whom became superior witnesses for God partly as a result of having resolved their issues.

Prayer Prompt: From what worthwhile venture are you shying away for fear of blowing it? Focus especially on behaviors that will lead to peace and to mutual edification.

odly woman,

RISK THE ATTEMPT.

$\mathcal{T}$he eyes of faith

Verse: "So we fix our eyes not on what is seen, but on what is unseen, since what is seen is temporary, but what is unseen is eternal" (2 Corinthians 4:18).

"The paradox of reality is that no image is as compelling as the one which exists only in the mind's eye" (SHANA ALEXANDER).

Reflection: I remember conversing years ago with Angie's young, literary friend Anne, then probably in the fifth or sixth grade, whom I was bringing home following an overnight stay. Anne was enthusiastic about her dad reading aloud *The Hobbit* by J. R. R. Tolkien to herself and her younger siblings. She shared that she preferred hearing the book read to viewing the movie version, which did all the imagining for her. The pictures in her own mind were much more interesting.

Artist Andrew Wyeth muses along the same lines with regard to nature's promises: "I prefer winter and fall, when you feel the bone structure of the landscape—the loneliness of it, the dead feeling of winter. Something waits beneath it, the whole story doesn't show."

It's the same way for us as Christians when it comes to our faith. Listen again to Paul: "For since the creation of the world God's invisible qualities—his eternal power and divine nature—have been clearly seen, being understood from what has been made" (Romans 1:20). Paul uses seemingly contradictory terminology in both of the verses quoted above, positing that we fix our eyes on the unseen and that God's invisible qualities can be clearly seen. Isn't that precisely what seeing through the eyes of faith is all about?

Prayer Prompt: What is there about God or heaven that you visualize in a fairly concrete way? Praise him that the actual will be so much more breathtaking.

$\mathcal{G}$odly woman,

WHAT HE HAS IN STORE FOR YOU DEFIES IMAGINATION.

$\mathcal{G}$iving birth to death?

Verse: "After desire has conceived, it gives birth to sin; and sin, when it is full-grown, gives birth to death" (James 1:15).

> *"MIND, n. A mysterious form of matter secreted by the brain. Its chief activity consists in the endeavor to ascertain its own nature, the futility of the attempt being due to the fact that it has nothing but itself to know itself with"* (AMBROSE GWINETT BIERCE).

Reflection: Sin . . . gives *birth* to *death*?! I had to read that twice. What a poignant and tragic image. And yet this triad of conception, birth, and death describes precisely the "life" cycle of the unrepentant sinner. Talk about a study in futility! Is it any wonder that so many nonbelievers approach life with cynicism or that "Is That All There Is?" sung by Peggy Lee, climbed the charts so quickly way back in 1969?

As described in Wikipedia, "The lyrics of this existentialist song are written from the point of view of a person who is disillusioned with events in life. . . . The singer tells the story of when she saw her family's house on fire when she was a little girl, when she saw the circus and when she fell in love for the first time. After each story, she expresses her disappointment," inviting the listener, "'Let's break out the booze and have a ball—if that's all—there is.'"

Pretty sobering stuff. Almost sounds worthy of the Teacher of Ecclesiastes—with one all-important distinction: King Solomon (if he is the author of that unique book) concludes not that life is meaningless, period, but that life is meaningless *without God* (check out Ecclesiastes 12:13–14). The Teacher knew, getting back to the Bierce quote, that the human mind does indeed have something beyond itself by which to know itself!

But you already knew that (that life finds its meaning only in God), didn't you? Because God in his love has seen to it that you have access to the mind of the Spirit by which to apprehend life and wisdom. What incredible news you have to share with a disheartened world!

Prayer Prompt: What disillusioned individual will you seek to reach with the message of life?

odly woman,

FIND YOUR MEANING AND PURPOSE IN HIM.

In spite of . . .

Verse: "I had the leaders of Judah go up on top of the wall. I also assigned two large choirs to give thanks" (Nehemiah 12:31).

> *"When we remember how difficult life used to be and how*
> *far we have come, we set up an explicit contrast in our*
> *mind, and this contrast is fertile ground for gratefulness"*
> (THE REVEREND PETER GOMES).

Reflection: H. U. Westermayer has observed that "The Pilgrims made seven times more graves than huts. No Americans have been more impoverished than these who, nevertheless, set aside a day of thanksgiving." The situation for the returnees from exile in Nehemiah's day wasn't much more promising. Yet they centered their dedication of the completed wall of Jerusalem, crude though it was in comparison to the wall of a brighter day, around praise and thanksgiving.

How do we approach Thanksgiving Day following a year of reversal or even of personal, national, or world tragedy? Some of my own Thanksgivings have been crisis ridden, including my first as a mom. On the Wednesday afternoon just prior to that Thanksgiving, a frantic call from the babysitter informed me that three-year-old Amanda had "gone limp" and that paramedics were on the way. (Had I realized she had suffered a seizure, from which she was resting comfortably, I would have been much less terrified.) Following a SMAK test at the hospital, we were sent home.

An incident first thing Thanksgiving morning sent us back to the ER, where Amanda suffered a grand mal seizure in my arms almost immediately after the doctor's arrival. Ironically, the situation improved quickly, and my daughter has long ago been weaned from seizure medication.

Space prohibits me from listing the circumstances surrounding that Thanksgiving that called for profound gratitude. When have you found occasion for thanks against a contrasting background of real or averted tragedy?

Prayer Prompt: What hard times in your life have resulted in reasons for praise—either in spite of or in contrast to . . . ?

Godly woman,
YOU'RE NEVER BEYOND A REASON FOR THANKSGIVING.

$\mathcal{B}$onding agent

Verses: "If two lie down together, they will keep warm. But how can one keep warm alone? Though one may be overpowered, two can defend themselves. A cord of three strands is not quickly broken" (Ecclesiastes 4:11–12).

"Friends are angels who lift our feet when our own wings have trouble remembering how to fly" (AUTHOR UNKNOWN).

Reflection: Brenda Ueland, coming at this issue from a different angle, spoke beautifully about the potential for bonding with others that God has engineered into our psyches: "Listening is a magnetic and strange thing, a creative force. When we really listen to people there is an alternating current, and this recharges us so that we never get tired of each other." The marital bond, of course, most clearly expresses these truths. Already in Genesis 2:24 God proclaimed an unfathomable mystery: "[A] man leaves his father and mother and is united to his wife, and they become one flesh."

The unity among Christians is fully as mysterious. When Jesus addressed his Father in Gethsemane, he included the following petition on behalf of all believers: "I have given them the glory that you gave me, that they may be one as we are one—I in them and you in me—so that they may be brought to complete unity. Then the world will know that you sent me and have loved them even as you have loved me" (John 17:22–23). Aha! "I in them . . ." What a beautiful picture of the Teacher's "cord of three strands"!

BTW, if you happen to be unmarried, you might enjoy the following observation, also from an unknown author: "A girl's heart should be so close to the Lord's that a man would have to seek after Him to find her." No there's a recipe for an unshakable union!

Prayer Prompt: What message is your unity (with God, your husband or fiance, your children, and/or fellow Christians) giving to a fractured and alienated world?

odly woman,

FOSTER UNITY IN CHRIST.

"*P*lease pick me up"

Verse: "The LORD your God carried you, as a father carries his son, all the way you went until you reached this place" (Deuteronomy 1:31).

"I am so weak that I can hardly write, I cannot read my Bible,
I cannot even pray, I can only lie still in God's arms like a little
child, and trust" (HUDSON TAYLOR).

Reflection: A few years ago an advertisement appeared on one side of a double billboard near my home. It pictured a young girl wrinkling her nose in protest against the "pink stuff" on her family's Thanksgiving table. I don't recall what was being promoted, but she was cute and worth a chuckle.

Around Christmas, though, I was taken aback by a new ad, also featuring a little girl, on the adjoining billboard. This waif trudged along a windswept sidewalk, hand clasped in that of an otherwise unseen guardian. I remember precisely what was being endorsed—a homeless shelter in downtown Grand Rapids.

This hapless youngster was in every way the foil of her unintended counterpart. The satiny dress gave way to a grimy coverall. Both faces were unhappy, but hers was dirty and pinched rather than peeved. She too was making an appeal: *"Please pick me up."*

Considerations of the importance of contentment in our Christian lives aside, know that God will gladly comply with our request to pick us up. In fact, we're already there in his arms. If you've never noticed the verse above, take a moment to let the words sink in. Wow! For me, they go straight to the heart of Thanksgiving.

Prayer Prompt: "Remember" or imagine the rhythm of being carried, step-by-step, in a parent's embrace. Feel the warmth and listen to the measured breathing. Then envision yourself in God's everlasting arms.

*G**odly woman*,
HE LOVES TO CARRY YOU.

$\mathscr{F}$orgotten wisdom

Verse: "The unfolding of your words gives light; it gives understanding to the simple" (Psalm 119:130).

> *"A child's world is fresh and new and beautiful, full of wonder and excitement. It is our misfortune that for most of us that clear-eyed vision, that true instinct for what is beautiful and awe-inspiring, is dimmed and even lost when we reach adulthood"* (RACHEL CARSON).

Reflection: Maybe you, like me, have learned something about security and contentment—or, for that matter, about any other basic life issue—from a child's perspective. I'm reminded by yesterday's meditation of another kid-related incident that served for me as a "pick me up." Several years ago my then-three-year-old grandson Walter, straining to see our pastor in his vestments, requested in a loud whisper from the back row of the sanctuary, *"Please pick me up, Gramma. I can't see God."*

Lifting up our little ones to introduce them to God—what higher priority could there be for us as Christian parents, grandparents, and other adult members of a congregation? But let's be open as well to the possibility of God buoying us up through the precious and precocious insights of the very young. How closely attuned are we to their observations? If we're willing to listen, they can touch our hardening hearts with long-forgotten wisdom.

Prayer Prompt: Grasp a truth about God you've known for as long as you can remember. Then thank him in simple, candid language.

odly woman,

HOLD CLOSELY THOSE EARLY INSIGHTS—YOUR OWN AND THOSE

OF THE LITTLE ONES IN YOUR LIFE.

$\mathcal{T}$he mirror

Verses: "Anyone who listens to the word but does not do what it says is like someone who looks at his face in a mirror and, after looking at himself, goes away and immediately forgets what he looks like" (James 1:23–24).

> *"There must be shedding of blood for sin. You have a mirror in your bathroom, which is a picture of the law, and there is a basin underneath the mirror. You do not wash yourself in the mirror; it only reveals the dirt. Just so, the law is the mirror that reveals our sin. And beneath that mirror there is a wash basin"* (J. VERNON MCGEE).

Reflection: "Men look *at* themselves in mirrors," observes Elissa Melamed, going on, "Women look *for* themselves." I'm not sure how well this quote reflects gender reality, but it makes a point when considered in conjunction with James's reflection above. Because each of us is present there in God's Word, not for the preoccupied glance that is so soon forgotten but for the penetrating gaze of the soul seeking to find and understand itself.

God's Word acts as a mirror for those who are willing to acknowledge their presence within its pages. It's only when we read it introspectively, allowing it to convict us, that we find it to be "alive and active. Sharper than any double-edged sword, it penetrates even to dividing soul and spirit, joints and marrow; it judges the thoughts and attitudes of the heart" (Hebrews 4:12).

There's no magical blessing to be attained through even an RDA of Bible reading (which too many of us don't come close to getting). If our approach is perfunctory and dutiful, we won't benefit, either by osmosis or by God's acknowledgment of a good effort. In fact, we're more likely under those circumstances to suffer from indifference due to a familiarity that has long since ceased to entice.

In the words of Chip Brogden, "Knowing the Word of God does not necessarily mean that we know the God of the Word." That distinction means everything.

Prayer Prompt: What is holding you back from engagement with God through his Word?

$\mathcal{G}$odly woman,

SEARCH THE WRITTEN WORD TILL YOU ENGAGE THERE WITH CHRIST,

THE LIVING WORD.

"What is it?"

Verses: "When the dew was gone, thin flakes like frost on the ground appeared on the desert floor. When the Israelites saw it, they said to each other, 'What is it?' . . . Moses said to them, 'It is the bread the LORD has given you to eat'" (Exodus 16:14–15).

> *"Seek to cultivate a buoyant, joyous sense of the crowded*
> *kindnesses of God in your daily life"* (ALEXANDER MACLAREN).

Reflection: Maybe I'm reading too much into the Israelites' knee-jerk reaction to the appearance of manna. Their question with regard to this new something under the sun was natural, as was Moses' straightforward answer. But a part of me would have preferred a different answer from Moses, implied, I think, in the question itself, which I view as sadly ironic. I'd like to have encountered a response more like "Don't you see? It's a *blessing!*"

This case of spiritual denseness reminds me of John 13:12, in which Jesus finds it necessary to ask his disciples after washing their feet, "Do you understand what I have done for you?" There are some things we just can't take for granted.

Autumn is the traditional time of year for counting our blessings—how sad if we have to be reminded. But we can't count what we don't recognize or acknowledge. Sometimes God's best blessings come to us in strange wrappings or are only recognizable long after the fact.

Manna falls in our day too. We may be tempted to discount it, complain about it, grouse about its monotony, or ask our own version of "What is it?"—often something along the lines of "What is *this* now?" (through gritted teeth). It may take some time to understand what God has done for us.

Prayer Prompt: What blessings in your life have you recognized only in hindsight? What others might you be missing altogether?

odly woman,

LOOK FOR AND ACKNOWLEDGE THE MANNA.

*R*ecognition

Verses: "After the earthquake came a fire, but the LORD was not in the fire. And after the fire came a gentle whisper. When Elijah heard it, he pulled his cloak over his face and went out and stood at the mouth of the cave" (1 Kings 19:12–13).

"The self-appointed spokesmen for God incline to shout; He, Himself, speaks only in whispers" (MARTIN H. FISCHER).

Reflection: Twentieth-century expressionist artist Louise Nevelson mused, "A whisper can be stronger, as an atom is stronger, than a whole mountain." When has a whispered message sent shivers of pleasure or prickles of apprehension up and down your spine?

What impresses me about the Elijah narrative in 1 Kings 19 isn't so much the fact of God being present in the whisper; this is so often the case, as, for example, in our prayer life. The Spirit's nudges seldom bowl us over; we need to be attuned—as in quiet, receptive, and deliberate—to catch them.

No, what surprises me here is that Elijah recognized God's modus operandi, emerging to the mouth of the cave only at the sound of that hushed voice.

An anonymous reflection speaks to this issue of recognition: "Eating lunch with a friend, hearing the rain patter against the window. There is no event so commonplace but that God is present within it, always hidden, always leaving room to recognize Him or not to recognize Him."

Prayer Prompt: How does God make himself known to you? To what degree do you look for, acknowledge, and welcome his voice?

*G*odly woman,

STAY TUNED FOR THAT VOICE; THE MORE FAMILIAR IT IS, THE MORE READILY YOU'LL CATCH IT.

$\mathscr{C}$onfidence in the revelation

Verse: "For truly I tell you, until heaven and earth disappear, not the smallest letter, not the least stroke of a pen, will by any means disappear from the Law until everything is accomplished" (Matthew 5:18).

> *"In all of knowable reality, God is unique. He is knowable not like the multiplication table or the table of elements; he alone is knowable as the one totally in control of being known"* (JOHN PIPER).

Reflection: Khristina shared with me a trivia tidbit about mapmaking. Word has it that cartographers typically include some small error to identify a map as their own. That sounded implausible to us, but we considered the inclusion of some short, nonexistent cul-de-sac no one would have reason to look for.

Speaking of details, "jots" and "tittles" (points or strokes in conjunction with letters) can make a big difference in language. The diacritical marks that differentiate one language or phonetic sound from another can indeed be critical (*e*, for example, is hardly the same as *ė*, *ę*, or *ě*).

If Jesus' words, above, are true, then what do we make of the so-called Adulterer's Bible? *Come again?* you're saying. In this 1631 edition of the Authorized Version (KJV), the word *not* was inadvertently omitted from the seventh commandment, rendering it "Thou shalt commit adultery." Oops!

Having personally spent years in Bible publishing, I know that in this technological age, before a new edition of a Bible in any translation is released, a "compare" program is run, making sure no jot or tittle (or comma or apostrophe) deviates from the database. A discrepancy caught after publication invariably results in recall.

What a comfort that, despite the possibility of correctable human error, God sees to it that his Law (his Word) never misleads us. What a blessing that we can approach his revelation of himself with absolute confidence.

Prayer Prompt: Imagine trying to live your Christian life without God's Word. Pray for those around the world who are forced to do just that.

odly woman,

TRUST HIS REVELATION.

$\mathcal{T}$he whole truth?

Verse: "Truth has stumbled in the streets, honesty cannot enter" (Isaiah 59:14).

"He that complies against his will, is of his own opinion still"
(SAMUEL BUTLER).

Reflection: We all routinely make major purchases and then fill out survey questionnaires assessing the level of service. I'm generally more than happy to do this, appreciating the expected freedom to be completely honest. Perhaps even to take the time to include a well-intentioned constructive criticism.

I've run into several situations recently, though, in which I've been cautioned ahead of time that if I mark less than the highest possible rating on any given item the sales or service person stands to lose their job. I wouldn't want to be responsible for that happening to anyone, least of all to the friendly individual who just helped me purchase a new car or who installed laminate flooring in my living room.

Such a survey popped up on my computer minutes ago. I sailed through this mildly distasteful task without reading it, filling in the "excellent" box for each question, only half believing that the ramifications of opting for just "good" might without my knowledge be devastating. The only real assessment that can result from a questionnaire based on coercion, I reflected, is the level of loyalty or kindness on the part of the customer.

When we as Christians reflect on the ethics of honesty, we typically focus on whether full disclosure is necessary, and, if not, whether it might potentially hurt someone. While outright lying may be permissible if we're hiding a fugitive from oppression, and tact may dictate leaving a truthful observation unstated, though, we recognize that God's Word is unequivocal on the subject of truth telling.

Maybe, I tell myself, I'm being overly picky here. What's your take on this kind of "iffy" scenario? Do you shake your head and assume the company just doesn't want to know or improve, or do you view this as an ethical dilemma? The lines can be pretty sketchy at times.

Prayer Prompt: Which parts of the combination "the truth, the whole truth, and nothing but the truth" tend to trip you up? Is there a situation that stands out for you right now?

$\mathcal{G}$odly woman,
HE VALUES AND EXPECTS YOUR HONESTY.

The wonder of Immanuel

Verses: "Submit yourselves, then, to God. Resist the devil, and he will flee from you. Come near to God and he will come near to you" (James 4:7–8).

"Immanuel. In this one name, everything humankind needs and the entire plan of God's salvation is subsumed. How blessed we are that Jesus Christ became Immanuel, God with us"
(RICHARD P. BUCHER).

Reflection: Demonic forces are scary. Jesus, we know, has already defeated Satan through the victory of his resurrection, but God continues for the time being to allow the enemy limited sway. The caveat: He has to be invited in order to exert any clout!

Most of us as Christians have little, if any, recognition of the extent of the power we wield over Satan. Read again and marvel at James's simple words: "Resist the devil, and he will *flee from you*" (emphasis added). All it takes is a firm but gentle *No!* in response to his advances.

The parallel sentence in these verses is fully as reassuring: "Come near to God and he will come near to you." All through Advent (the word means "coming") we celebrate the "coming near" of God, until the arrival on Christmas Day of Immanuel, "God with us." Since the descent of the Spirit on Pentecost, God is with each of us personally every step of the way—the only signal Satan needs to keep his distance.

In his discussion of life through the Spirit in Romans 8, Paul says the following: "The Spirit you received does not make you slaves, so that you live in fear again; rather, the Spirit you received brought about your adoption to sonship"—or, if you'll permit me to coin a word, "daughtership" (verse 15).

Demonic forces need not be so scary after all.

Prayer Prompt: Acknowledge to God your power over the devil, and thank him for his presence in your life and heart.

odly woman,

SEND SATAN PACKING.

ᴬnticipation

Verses: "We know that the whole creation has been groaning as in the pains of childbirth right up to the present time. Not only so, but we ourselves, who have the firstfruits of the Spirit, groan inwardly as we wait eagerly for our adoption to sonship, the redemption of our bodies. For in this hope we were saved" (Romans 8:22–24).

> *"It's so much better to desire than to have. . . . The moment of desire, when you know something is going to happen—that's the most exalting"* (ANOUK AIMEE).

Reflection: Despite the fact that a meditation on these verses could move in any of several directions, they do form a complete thought. While I can't pass by the obvious association with Advent in the first sentence, I'm going to consider instead the correlation between adoption and hope—or, more specifically, the joy of anticipation, another Advent theme.

I can personally relate to the keen expectancy that precedes adoption from both sides, that of the "adoptee" and, later on, the adopter. The Christmas of my twelfth year was charmed; Dad was going to remarry two days later, bringing a new mom into our lives. Of the five of us kids, I was the believer in magic. I can attest from experience that, for a particularly imaginative child, the flights of fancy in advance of the real thing can be beyond idyllic.

No, Paul isn't talking about hope in quite the same way. For one thing, my ecstasy was immature—the bliss of, well, a kid waiting for Christmas morning. Paul's image here is of a more patient, plodding kind of hope (let's not forget that he mentions groaning). But that doesn't mean our hope is to be joyless. In Paul's words, "For in this hope we were saved"!

As we look forward to Christmas in our more subdued adult manner, let's anticipate just as eagerly the promised redemption of our bodies.

Prayer Prompt: Focus your thoughts beyond the babe in the manger to the implications, for you personally, of his death and resurrection.

ᴳodly woman,

REJOICE IN HOPE.

$\mathcal{M}$ore than a place

Verse: "While we are in this tent, we groan and are burdened, because we do not wish to be unclothed but to be clothed instead with our heavenly dwelling, so that what is mortal may be swallowed up by life" (2 Corinthians 5:4).

"There are no ordinary people. You have never talked to a mere mortal" (C. S. LEWIS).

Reflection: Paul's vocabulary and imagery are so rich that it's often easy to read right over a particular clause or phrase and miss its implications. In my last reading of the verse above, I was struck by the concept of the mortal being "swallowed up by life."

Now that I think about it, being *swallowed up* by immortal, imperishable life is a lot like being *clothed* with my heavenly dwelling. The imagery is all about being enveloped, wrapped, securely enfolded, made invulnerable. Contrast this with the exposure of tent living.

Being swallowed up by life or clothed with my heavenly dwelling makes me a part of that life and that destination—limiting as the word *destination* may seem. Perhaps the English language needs a new word to encompass the reality of our heavenly home, which we sense to be so much more than a place.

Then again, maybe the issue isn't as much our language as it is our mindset; we can't label what we can't begin to conceive.

Prayer Prompt: Close your eyes and allow these amazing images to sink in. What role has Jesus Christ, whose coming we celebrate, played in making these concepts real for you?

odly woman,

LOOK FORWARD IN CHRIST TO LIFE'S FINAL, UNENDING PHASE.

*C*hanged and changing

Verses: "Listen, I tell you a mystery: We will not all sleep, but we will all be changed—in a flash, in the twinkling of an eye, at the last trumpet. For the trumpet will sound, the dead will be raised imperishable, and we will be changed" (1 Corinthians 15:51–52).

> *"The Advent mystery is the beginning of the end of all of us that is not yet Christ"* (THOMAS MERTON).

Reflection: ". . . and we will be changed." Perhaps it's the emphasis on these five words in Handel's *Messiah* ("and we shall be changed") that makes them so climactic in my mind.

We don't yet have our changed resurrection bodies, but in another, very real sense we have already been changed and continue to change. What a wonder and privilege during this Advent season to acknowledge that, as we spend time in Christ's presence, we're becoming more and more like him.

Paul expressed the truth of our formation into the image of Christ from a negative angle, yet his point is striking: "My dear children, for whom I am again in the pains of childbirth until Christ is formed in you, how I wish I could be with you now and change my tone, because I am perplexed about you!" (Galatians 4:19–20). At another point the same apostle rejoiced in the new creation that defines each of us as a Christian: "Therefore, if anyone is in Christ, he is a new creation; the old has gone, the new has come!" (2 Corinthians 5:17).

The wonder of Advent goes far beyond the physical birth of a Jesus Christ long since returned to heaven. Jesus' long-ago coming and its aftermath in his death and resurrection allow us to exult with Paul: The new has indeed come!

Prayer Prompt: Consider carefully the implications of this "mystery" before going to God in prayer.

*G*odly woman,
YOU'RE A NEW CREATION IN CHRIST.

Opening our present

Verse: "I will be fully satisfied as with the richest of foods; with singing lips my mouth will praise you" (Psalm 63:5).

"I only want a few presents. Too many presents make me crazy!"
(ADELYN HUISJEN, AGE FOUR).

Reflection: "We tend to forget," observes Frederick Keonig, "that happiness doesn't come as a result of getting something we don't have, but rather of recognizing and appreciating what we do have." I learned my lesson the hard way in terms of this principle. Almost from the time my first adopted daughter had been placed with me I began pining for a second. While I'm not saying that Amanda's first ten years in my home were joyless from my perspective, I'd be less than honest if I didn't admit to squelching much of that satisfaction by my yearning for a repeat adoption experience.

I learned something else during the decade of my thirties: The less satisfied I am with my life, the more bitter I become against God. And the more bitter I become against God, the less likely it is that I will find satisfaction in him, myself, my loved ones, or my circumstances. "One of the most important discoveries I have ever made," observes John Piper, "is this truth: God is most glorified in me when I am most satisfied in him." My own experience in the Christian life has taught me that I'm restless and out of my element as long as I'm not glorifying God.

The circle of failure to find satisfaction and failure to glorify God for his blessings is vicious and unending unless we make deliberate change in one or the other area. In the words of Bertolt Brecht, "Everyone chases after happiness, not noticing that happiness is right at their heels." Provided, that is, their relationship with the Lord is on track.

"Life is a gift," invites Rain Bojangles. "Open your present."

Prayer Prompt: Try praising first and then counting your blessings.

odly woman,
APPRECIATE YOUR PRESENT.

*H*eart to heart

Verse: "You show that you are a letter from Christ, the result of our ministry, written not with ink but with the Spirit of the living God, not on tablets of stone but on tablets of human hearts" (2 Corinthians 3:3).

"I am a little pencil in the hand of a writing God who is sending a love letter to the world" (MOTHER TERESA).

Reflection: We all know the formula: For a principle or behavior to be truly learned, it has to be internalized—integrated into our personal belief and value system. In order for you or me, Christian woman, to be a letter from Christ, it's necessary for this step to have taken place within us.

The issue of authenticity is huge on the twenty-first-century radar. The single most pressing demand of the younger generations: Don't bother to tout it (whatever *it* is) unless it's "real"!

If we're speaking from the heart, we can communicate only to the heart. "Heart to heart" is really the only path when the message starts there. Circumventing head knowledge eliminates a step, so no complaints there. The catch: It's so easy for others to spot phony when our heart is involved.

My "kid" sister recently talked me into signing up on Facebook, and I've been amazed at how many younger people, from my kids' friends to nephews and nieces, have invited me to join their friends lists. I still don't know what to *do* with this functionality, but that's another issue . . .

During this busy Advent season, what are others—perhaps in particular younger others—reading in your letter from Christ, either in your lifestyle or through conversation with you? Call it a heart letter or call it a face book, you might be surprised to discover who's reading. Just make sure you don't negatively surprise them by what they read.

Prayer Prompt: What content does your letter from Christ offer its readers?

*G*odly woman,
YOU REPRESENT THE LORD.

$\mathcal{T}$he wiggle road

Verses: "A voice of one calling: 'In the wilderness prepare the way for the LORD; make straight in the desert a highway for our God. Every valley shall be raised up, every mountain and hill made low; the rough ground shall become level, the rugged places a plain" (Isaiah 40:3–4).

> *"Christ, our most honored and eagerly anticipated guest desires to meet with us in a heart prepared for his arrival. So eager is he to meet with us that he offers to help us with our spiritual housecleaning, working with us; creating a resting place for Himself within our hearts"* (KATHERINE WALDEN).

Reflection: One of the streets leading to my condo community runs in a semicircle, and this has grabbed little Adelyn's attention. I may think she's asleep in the car seat behind my back, but if we're heading home after dark she'll often rouse herself to request, "Let's take the wiggle road, Granna." The designation has caught on to the point that we'll deliberately "wiggle our way home" when we have the choice, even if it means going slightly out of our way.

In contrast, the consistent request of biblical authors (and of John the Baptist in Matthew 3:3) is for the straight path. I suppose that if I had to walk everywhere I went, I wouldn't want to waste steps either—or run the risk of exposing myself to unnecessary danger or of losing my way.

Passages like Proverbs 2:12–15 alert me, though, to a correlation between *crooked* and *perverse* or *devious*—which is more to the biblical point. Still today we refer to thieves as "crooks."

The analogy in Isaiah 40:3–4 of preparing a straight (and level) path in the desert goes further, referring to the custom of making ready a processional highway for a coming king.

Prayer Prompt: What, specifically, can you do this Advent to make ready your heart for his arrival?

odly woman,
PREPARE YOUR HEART; HE'S COMING.

Our desires

Verse: "Delight in the LORD and he will give you the desires of your heart" (Psalm 37:4).

"We trifle when we assign limits to our desires, since nature hath set none" (CHRISTIAN NESTELL BOVEE).

Reflection: It's easy for us to assume that God cares more about our needs than our desires. That he's "don't-get-your-needs-and-your-wants-mixed-up," no-nonsense sensible. Somehow we've gotten the idea that desiring is akin to coveting. That desiring in and of itself is selfish. That a desire is by its nature frivolous.

Come early December, there's a whole lot of desiring going on, isn't there? Just a minute or two in a concordance was enlightening for me as I considered the word *desires*. While the Old Testament talks a lot about God granting our desires—even delighting to do so—the New Testament focuses primarily on a certain category of desires, repeating adjectives like *evil*, *sinful*, *deceitful*, and *harmful*. The word *pleasures* is treated, Testament for Testament, in much the same way.

We do well at this time of year to remind ourselves that our desires are indeed wrong when they're wrongfully motivated, misguided, or self-serving. Certainly, too, it's more blessed to give than to receive. But we aren't wrong in accepting and appreciating gifts, in allowing the givers—or the Giver—to take pleasure in our gratitude and delight.

Prayer Prompt: What are your deepest desires? Not just at Christmastime but in the longer term.

Godly woman,

HE DELIGHTS IN DELIGHTING YOU.

$\mathcal{T}$he call

Verses: "Israel has experienced a hardening in part until the full number of the Gentiles has come in. . . . As far as the gospel is concerned, they are enemies for your sake; but as far as election is concerned, they are loved on account of the patriarchs. For God's gifts and his call are irrevocable" (Romans 11:25, 28–29).

> *"When you say cross, Christian, it creates images of a gentile faith.*
> *We're trying to open up the understanding in a Jewish person's*
> *mind that this is all part of our Jewish faith that was prophesied"*
> (MARLENE ROSENBERG).

Reflection: According to Paul in the verses above, the message of salvation encompasses God's original chosen people, the Jews. In the words of Pope Benedict XVI, "Our Christian conviction is that Christ is also the messiah of Israel. Certainly it is in the hands of God how and when the unification of Jews and Christians into the people of God will take place."

The temporary hardening but eventual inclusion of the Jewish people in salvation is indeed a mystery for us as Christians—as well as a powerful reminder of the force of God's call, the extent of his love and faithfulness, and the scope and reach of his plan. We're wise to approach this issue with humility and overflowing gratitude: God's willingness to include us as Gentile Christians in his marvelous redemption is fully as mysterious as his long-suffering faithfulness with his people Israel.

From very early in salvation history God's covenant promises included clauses about his chosen people blessing the rest of the world. And the Old Testament refers repeatedly to God's concern for non-Israelites. Rahab and Ruth stand as shining examples for us as Christian women of God's willingness to embrace diversity even within and among his own people.

Prayer Prompt: What comfort does it give you, a Gentile recipient of God's grace, to know that his gifts and call are irreversible? What is your attitude toward the original recipients of God's grace?

odly woman,
YOU'RE NOT ALONE IN BEING CHOSEN, CALLED, AND GIFTED.

$\mathcal{N}$ot to bear sin

Verse: "Christ was sacrificed once to take away the sins of many; and he will appear a second time, not to bear sin, but to bring salvation to those who are waiting for him" (Hebrews 9:28).

"For Christians, Christ's [first] coming only makes sense in light of
his promise to come again" (JURGEN MOLTMANN).

Reflection: It's easy to pass right over four words in this Verse: "not to bear sin." If we pause there for a moment, we realize what a heavy image they present. The contrast in this verse between Christ's first and second comings is arresting.

Has it ever struck you that we're living in a new advent—not in retrospect, in anticipation of the commemoration of Jesus' past-tense birth, but in real time?

As we live out our lives in the Church age, we're still in some sense awaiting, in the words of a well-loved carol, our "long-expected Jesus, born to set [his] people free." Still yearning and praying: "From our fears and sins release us; let us find our rest in thee." The same writer to the Hebrews reminds us in chapter 4 of the coming Sabbath rest for the people of God.

This year, as you reflect on Christ's coming, keep in mind that we're privileged to be living in the second advent, prior to the fourth and final phase of salvation history. That after creation, fall, and redemption comes *consummation*.

Unlike the situation prior to Christ's first advent (coming), Satan and death have already been defeated. How much closer we are to home than were God's Old Testament people, anxiously scanning the horizon for redemption!

Prayer Prompt: Reflect on the reality of Jesus' birth as the fulcrum point of human history. Consider the privilege—and responsibility—of living as a new covenant believer.

$\mathcal{G}$odly woman,
LONG FOR CONSUMMATION.

"Martha, Martha"

Verses: "'Martha, Martha,' the Lord answered, 'you are worried and upset about many things, but few things are needed—or indeed only one. Mary has chosen what is better, and it will not be taken from her'" (Luke 10:41–42).

"Thanks be to God for his unspeakable Gift—indescribable,
inestimable, incomparable, inexpressible—precious beyond words"
(LOIS LEBAR).

Reflection: What do you think of Jesus' response to Martha's demand? The answer depends on who you are. On whether you're spontaneous or structured, inclined toward improvising or impressing. If you're by nature driven, Jesus' reply to Martha might get your hackles up.

But was Jesus playing favorites? That question has everything to do with how the Creator views intrinsic differences among the beings he created to crown his work.

Could it be that we Martha types can find our "aha" in this story without trying to fill a void beyond verse 42? Let's listen together to Jesus' opening words to this sister, using our best interpretive ability to infuse them with his love and pathos: *"Martha, Martha."*

Notice that Jesus didn't say Mary was better. In fact, Jesus wasn't commenting on Mary at all, except parenthetically. Jesus appreciated the younger sister, but she wasn't the object of his immediate concern. Martha was. That frazzled, disheveled, perspiring, *wonderful* woman standing before him blurting out her pain. That sister with all the commendable qualities—who was hurting so profoundly at that moment when time stopped and two pairs of eyes locked.

Jesus had something to give, something Martha needed, and he wasn't willing to pass up the opportunity to state his offer.

Prayer Prompt: Why do you think God arranged to include this home-spun account in his Word? Where do you stand this Christmas season on the Martha/Mary spectrum?

odly woman,

DON'T LET WORK NEGATE YOUR WONDER.

$\mathcal{U}$pturned eyes

Verse: "Since, then, you have been raised with Christ, set your hearts on things above, where Christ is, seated at the right hand of God" (Colossians 3:1).

"Well, what was [the star], an astronomical event or the Shekinah Glory, manifesting God's presence among men? In my mind the mystery remains. Perhaps that is how God intends it to be"
(RAY BOHLIN).

Reflection: Nativity scenes to the contrary, most of us are well aware that the wise men didn't mingle with the shepherds, greeting the King in a crowded stable. But we do, in retrospect, greet and adore him there.

For me, the gripping element of the story of the Magi is their single focus on the star. Have you ever paused to wonder why, or for whom, God went to the trouble of planting that clue in the heavens? Has it occurred to you that no one else evidently noticed?

Those other "wise men," the ones in Jerusalem, had their noses in the books (see Matthew 2:3–6). They knew all about the prophecy concerning Bethlehem, but it evidently never occurred to them to pinpoint that sleepy village and watch for the action. Even the strange inquiry from these foreigners failed to pique their interest enough for them to raise an eyebrow or breathe a tremulous *"Could it be?"*

We might conjecture that the star was intended specifically for these distant astrologers. Throughout the Old Testament and continuing into the New we find hints of God's intention to include the world in the salvation story. Did the Magi return home and plant seeds of hope? Matthew doesn't say. But while we're in a wondering mode . . .

Prayer Prompt: Engage in some wondering of your own before approaching God in praise.

$\mathcal{G}$*odly woman,*
LIFT YOUR GAZE.

$\mathcal{F}$aithful Joseph

Verse: "When Joseph and Mary had done everything required by the Law of the Lord, they returned to Galilee to their own town of Nazareth" (Luke 2:39).

> *"God found the perfect couple to raise His Son—as perfect as He could find among the Jews who had the right lineage at the time. They are wonderful examples of submission to God. Even though His intervention in their lives threw a huge monkey wrench into their personal plans, they selflessly said, 'So be it, Lord. What would You like us to do next?'"* (RICHARD T. RITENBAUGH).

Reflection: Throughout Matthew's and Luke's accounts of Jesus' early life, we see his stepfather, Joseph, as a one-dimensional figure. Nearly every reference to this understated individual highlights one characteristic—steadfast, unquestioning obedience.

Joseph obeyed God without suspicion when the reports seemed preposterous, when the instructions involved embarrassment, inconvenience, danger, and displacement. No less than four times, directed by an angel in a dream, he immediately complied.

We see in Joseph a reliable and righteous middle-aged man. Luke refers to him as Jesus' father; for all practical purposes this obscure descendant of David took on that role without question or grudge. A carpenter by trade, he trained "his" son in the intricacies of his craft.

We don't know to what extent Joseph understood the implications of the virgin birth or grasped the divine identity and mission of the Son of God under his care. Jesus wasn't a "son of man," though harking back to the prophecies of Daniel he called himself that; still he was, through Mary's genetic contribution, fully human.

By the time of Jesus' public ministry Joseph had faded from sight, presumably having lived out his expected life span and died in humble dignity. Still, this faithful Jewish tradesman was God's agent in one of the most important roles any human being has ever undertaken.

Prayer Prompt: Reflect on the implications for salvation history of Joseph's unhesitating obedience.

odly woman,
OFFER HIM YOUR FULL SUBMISSION.

*I*nnocent?

Verse: "When Pilate saw that he was getting nowhere, but that instead an uproar was starting, he took water and washed his hands in front of the crowd. 'I am innocent of this man's blood,' he said. 'It is your responsibility!'" (Matthew 27:24).

"Pilate's response crucified Christ. Our sins do that as well. Pilate lived in the deception of artificial innocence. He rejected the gift of God's visit to him" (WESLEY J. GABEL).

Reflection: There's something so innocent about Christmas, isn't there? Other than Herod, there aren't a lot of bad guys in the story. How easily we picture a sweet pastoral scene, domestic barn animals hovering in the flickering firelight around the latest newborn, their lipid eyes doleful but curious within the sanctuary of the barn.

A low level of sound, like the regular bleeping of a fetal monitor—shufflings, sighs, murmurings, an infant's squalling bleats—lends credibility to our mental picture, while the punctuation of an occasional *moo* prevents us from nodding off. Peace, goodwill, and joy are the prevailing sentiments. Innocent.

Fast-forward some thirty-three years (make that about three months on the church calendar) to Good Friday. How easy it is for us, like Pilate, to absolve ourselves of responsibility for Jesus' death. Innocent. Or at least we'd like to so pronounce ourselves.

Oh, we thrill to the sentiment of vicarious guilt; the minor chords of "Were You There?" or of "Ah, Dearest Jesus" may send shivers up and down our spines. But deep down we cherish the dream that we, unlike the fickle eleven, would have hung in there for our Lord.

Prayer Prompt: Imaginatively transport yourself to the night preceding Jesus' death. Who are you, and what—realistically—would your reaction have been?

*G**odly woman,***

CHRIST'S INNOCENCE PURCHASED YOUR SALVATION.

$\mathcal{A}$ call to stand

Verse: "Stand up in the presence of the aged, show respect for the elderly and revere your God. I am the LORD" (Leviticus 19:32).

"Christmas is a holiday that persecutes the lonely, the frayed, and the rejected" (JIMMY CANNON).

Reflection: People watching has always been one of my favorite pastimes. A couple of weeks before Christmas this year I was driving Addie home from preschool when I noticed a gaunt elderly gentleman hurrying down the sidewalk carrying a flower-shaped bundle wrapped in florist's paper. Talk about a story in the making. I'd love to know where he was headed, not to mention the detail behind his errand.

One of the fringe benefits for me of providing transportation to others comes during those idle moments spent in a parking lot, observing whatever cross-section of humanity happens to be in view. A random "sampling" of people can tell us a lot about a community, a culture, an economy—hinting even at such issues as health, eating habits, ethnic particularities, and the like. Yet it's often the elderly poor, typically alone and often physically challenged, who catch my attention.

Last night I sat for five minutes outside a pet store waiting for Angie and Bowen (Bo), her boyfriend. From a rusted car in a handicapped spot emerged an elderly lady, bent almost double. Angie emerged from the store minutes later, followed somewhat later by the old lady and Bo, toting her fifty-pound sack of pet food. Had no one in the store volunteered to help, how could she possibly have managed her load?

Are the elderly and disabled really so invisible in our culture, or is ignoring them a learned behavior? In the verse above God in one sentence commanded his people to respect the elderly and to revere himself. How does he look upon societal apathy to the needs of the old, the infirm, the lonely? What can you do this Christmas, in Christ's name, to benefit one of these?

Prayer Prompt: Ask God to show you an opportunity to share your festivities—and your hope—with someone who is overlooked and alone.

odly woman,

HE CALLS YOU TO LOVE AS HE DOES.

At home with God

Verse: "Jesus [said], 'Anyone who loves me will obey my teaching. My Father will love them, and we will come to them and make our home with them'" (John 14:23).

"Winter is the time for comfort, for good food and warmth, for the touch of a friendly hand and for a talk beside the fire: It is the time for home" (EDITH SITWELL).

Reflection: "Where thou art—that—is Home," wrote Emily Dickinson. We all know the saying "Home is where the heart is." More importantly, if our heart is with God, and God is in our heart, then home is where God is.

Feeling at home and being at home don't necessarily evoke the same associations. Many people who have no place to call home, whether physically or emotionally, nevertheless manage to find somewhere they can feel secure and relaxed. Throughout my years of raising my daughters, our mobile home became that place for a long string of unattached neighborhood kids. Even after Amanda was married, she and Doug introduced me to numerous displaced adults (primarily but not exclusively men), many of whom lived with them for periods of time. Some were ex-cons and others mentally disabled. Yet nearly all took almost immediately to calling me Mom and treated me with respect throughout our period of acquaintance.

I've always been drawn to strays, primarily of the people variety. And I've never kept my faith a secret from any of them. I'd like to think that these lonely individuals I've known have been attracted as much to God's presence in my home as to my own.

Prayer Prompt: To what degree do acquaintances identify your home as a place to meet God?

Godly woman,

HE'S AT HOME WITH YOU. IS THE ASSOCIATION MUTUAL?

$\mathcal{N}$o, never alone

Verse: "After he has suffered, he will see the light of life and be satisfied; by his knowledge my righteous servant will justify many, and he will bear their iniquities" (Isaiah 53:11).

> *"The greatest negative in the universe is the Cross, for with it God wiped out everything that was not of Himself: the greatest positive in the universe is the resurrection, for through it God brought into being all"* (WATCHMEN NEE).

Reflection: Jesus' physical suffering leading up to his death wasn't his ultimate source of pain. If that had been true, how easy it would be to discount that agony based on an argument that someone's else's pain trumped it. Jesus' real angst lay in the areas of sin bearing and God forsakenness.

Who of us can't recall a sleepless night based on nagging guilt over unconfessed sin? David expressed this powerfully in Psalm 32:3–4: "When I kept silent, my bones wasted away through my groaning all day long. For day and night your hand was heavy on me." And that's the sin, or a sin, of one person. Imagine bearing the iniquity—all of it—for all of us!

We've all experienced guilt, but none of us has ever been God forsaken. God doesn't forsake his children—except for One, for a brief time, so the rest of us could escape that consequence.

In the same way that Easter culminates in our deepest joy, so Christmas is merry and blessed on the basis of two events, one seemingly tragic and the other triumphant, some thirty-three years later.

Prayer Prompt: Consider the ramifications of Christmas, thinking beyond the infant Jesus to the suffering, dying, and risen Savior.

odly woman,

TO TRULY APPRECIATE CHRISTMAS, FAST-FORWARD TO EASTER.

$\mathcal{S}$neaky pride

Verses: "In your relationships with one another, have the same mindset as Christ Jesus: Who, being in very nature God, did not consider equality with God something to be used to his own advantage; rather, he made himself nothing by taking the very nature of a servant, being made in human likeness" (Philippians 2:5–7).

> "Humility does not mean you think less of yourself. It means you think of yourself less" (KEN BLANCHARD).

Reflection: In all fairness, many of us Christian women find it easy to practice humility, if by that we mean a self-deprecating attitude. If this sounds like you, watch out for that ugly pride factor! The temptation for pride in humility is one of Satan's best tools.

The truth is that humility has nothing to do with downgrading ourselves. In the words of the nineteenth-century American theologian Tryon Edwards, "True humility is not an abject, groveling, self-despising spirit; it is but a right estimate of ourselves as God sees us."

"Many people," notes Rabino Nilton Bonder, "believe that humility is the opposite of pride, when, in fact, it is a point of equilibrium. The opposite of pride is actually a lack of self esteem. A humble person is totally different from a person who cannot recognize and appreciate himself as part of this world's marvels."

Jesus understood himself to be coequal with the Father but chose not to grasp that prerogative. Let's not be afraid this year to approach his birthday with a spirit of humble pride—rightly acknowledging our cherished status in the eyes of the Father while following Jesus' model of self-denial unhampered by self-disdain.

Prayer Prompt: Pray for the humility of authentic self-pride, coupled with a servant attitude.

$\mathcal{G}$*odly woman,*

ASSESS YOUR STATUS FROM HIS PERSPECTIVE.

$\mathcal{J}$oy in their presence?

Verse: "You make known to me the path of life; you will fill me with joy in your presence, with eternal pleasures at your right hand" (Psalm 16:11).

"Your children need your presence more than your presents"
(JESSE JACKSON).

Reflection: An anonymous quote has it that "The best Christmas of all is the presence of a happy family all wrapped up with one another." Wow! That sounds ideal, doesn't it? And daunting. As I've found in my own family life, my physical presence doesn't guarantee that I'm present, or that I necessarily want to be. It's easy for me to function in the company of my kids in a preoccupied manner.

When it comes to Christmas, I enjoy the worship, the preparations, the shopping, the decorating, and the gift exchanges (I'm not much for food prep, generally preferring the cleanup phase). But after that point, particularly if the atmosphere has become raucous and adolescent, with family members arguing and baiting one another, I find myself ready to retreat into myself. Or, better yet, to take a long nap.

The fact is that my kids are grown, and, well, I'm finished raising them, despite some growing deficits I can't help but notice in terms of their functionality. Frankly, I'm tired. And discouraged. I'd much sooner indulge my desire to write or read or even watch a worthwhile TV program than engage in disappointing interactions.

My kids, though, continue to crave my love and are quick to point out my increasingly standoffish tendencies. The question I must ask myself: If God fills me with joy in his presence, isn't it still my responsibility as a mom to shore up my daughters, perhaps especially during those traditional family times?

Prayer Prompt: To what degree does disappointment with one or more family members or with the dynamics of family interaction in general undermine your Christmas spirit?

odly woman,
HE LOVES WITHOUT RESERVATION OR CONDITION.

$\mathcal{I}$nviting the light

Verse: "Pray that this will not take place in winter . . ." (Mark 13:18).

*"How did it get so late so soon? It's night before it's afternoon.
December is here before it's June. My goodness how the time has
flewn. How did it get so late so soon?"* (DR. SEUSS).

Reflection: The first day of winter is much more likely to pass unnoticed than the first day of spring. We're immersed in planning for or are already enjoying Christmas festivities. We may consider the beginning of winter to be palatable because of nostalgic holiday associations. The snow of December is less likely to be yellowed or dirt-tinged, more apt (so we think) to be fluffy and picturesque and conducive to celebration.

Has it ever occurred to you that we in the northern hemisphere celebrate the coming of God's Son only days after the year's deepest darkness has settled in? Easter morning, on the other hand, arrives on the heels of spring, during that time when dawn arrives earlier each day and the natural world is beginning to respond to the nudges of warmth and light.

Darkness is hard on people. For many in cold, bleak climates depression settles in during those long months with their dearth of light. The proximity of Grand Rapids to Lake Michigan produces dank air and gloomy skies. It isn't uncommon to move through weeks seeing the barest fraction of "possible sunlight." Our spirits are noticeably lifted on those rare crisp and cloudless days.

Jesus' coming occurred in the dark—of night and of sin. In early traces of coming grace, God punctuated that darkness by an angel choir and an unusually bright star. But Easter Sunday will dawn in the effulgent glory of sunrise—the full light of salvation.

Prayer Prompt: Invite the Light to penetrate and permeate your January, February, and March.

$\mathcal{G}$odly woman,

HIS PRESENCE IS MOST EVIDENT IN THE DARK.

$\mathcal{H}$ang tight!

Verse: "I am coming soon. Hold on to what you have, so that no one will take your crown" (Revelation 3:11).

"The child of God should not be overanxious to make new gains; what he essentially requires is to keep what he already has, for not losing is itself a gain. The way to retain what he possesses is to engage it" (WATCHMAN NEE).

Reflection: It's easy for us to become acquisitive this time of year. In contrast, John as he meets us here is in a holding pattern—a pattern of holding on and holding fast. The author of Hebrews makes one of the most sobering statements in the Bible when he states that it "is impossible for those who have once been enlightened . . . , who have fallen away, to be brought back to repentance. To their loss they are crucifying the Son of God all over again and subjecting him to public disgrace" (Hebrews 6:4–6).

We might argue based on other Scriptural evidence that the person so described was never truly enlightened in the first place. In the words of John Calvin, "Those who fall away have never been thoroughly imbued with the knowledge of Christ but only had a slight and passing taste of it." Without taking a deep dive into theology, though, we do well to heed Paul's challenge to Timothy to "take hold of the eternal life to which you were called" (1 Timothy 6:12).

No, I'm not attempting to dampen our celebration of Jesus' birthday. This pivotal point of history precedes, defines, and paves the way for our own rebirth—the most amazing gift ever given.

Prayer Prompt: Take the time to assess the meaning, for you personally, of that greatest gift ever given—or received.

odly woman,

HOLD FAST TO WHAT HE HAS GIVEN.

$\mathcal{S}$heepish?

Verses: "For I am not ashamed of the gospel, because it is the power of God that brings salvation to everyone who believes . . . . For in the gospel the righteousness of God is revealed—a righteousness that is by faith from first to last" (Romans 1:16–17)

> *"God is a philosophical black hole—the point where reason breaks down"* (KEDAR JOSHI).

Reflection: I felt a little sorry for Adelyn's preschool teacher a few days ago—a Christian "forced" on the basis of public-school employment to inform eighteen three- and four-year-olds that Santa's travels encompass the globe.

I had attended in Khristina's place the class party on the last day before vacation. Before beginning to read an illustrated holiday story, the teacher interjected a bit of humor from earlier in the week for the benefit of the adults present. She had been reading a story in which Santa stopped to talk to a duck when she was interrupted by one of her young learners: "That's just silly. Everybody knows ducks can't talk." Whatever mental leap it took to believe in Santa evidently posed no problem.

Speaking of leaps, what about us and the story of the virgin birth? Or of Jonah and the big fish, or of creation, or whatever other biblical "tale" might raise the eyebrows of the uninitiated—not to mention many of the initiated? We've become so accustomed to these accounts that we accept them with unquestioning faith. Which is a good thing, right?

But what, you may ask, if my lack of skepticism is based more on apathy or tradition than on . . . well, reason? Does it make you feel a little sheepish to admit to an incredulous, "enlightened" acquaintance that you actually "buy this stuff"? Faith by its nature counters reason. That's why it's called faith. Nor is God's Word an inherently "reasonable" book, if by reason we mean human wisdom. "Has not God made foolish the wisdom of the world?" Paul asks rhetorically. "For since in the wisdom of God the world through its wisdom did not know him, God was pleased through the foolishness of what was preached to save those who believe" (1 Corinthians 1:20–21). Hallelujah!

Prayer Prompt: Thank God for the gift of faith, for enabling you through his Spirit to overcome the natural objections that might otherwise stand in your way.

$\mathcal{G}$*odly woman,*

TRUST HIS WISDOM—AND HIS HEART.

$\mathcal{T}$ime to wonder

Verse: "But Mary treasured up all these things and pondered them in her heart" (Luke 2:19).

> *"Philosophy begins in wonder. And, at the end, when*
> *philosophic thought has done its best, the wonder remains"*
> (ALFRED NORTH WHITEHEAD).

Reflection: "Christmas renews our youth by stirring our wonder. The capacity for wonder has been called our most pregnant human faculty, for in it are born our art, our science, our religion." So states Ralph Sockman. I don't know his stance on faith. And although I resonate to some degree with his statement, I question his cause-and-effect thinking. Could be it's one of those chicken/egg scenarios. I'd be more inclined to say something like *The capacity for faith is our most pregnant human faculty; in it is born our wonder.*

I love that one short verse in Luke 2, above. Why, I wonder, does Luke pause for breath during a fast-moving narrative (we've just read that the shepherds "hurried off") to tell us about the "but" of Mary sitting still, wondering? Makes us want to exhale slowly before moving on, doesn't it?

About that business of wondering: It takes time. Time you have to give in order to take.

Prayer Prompt: Carve out a block of time this busy Christmas Eve to thrill anew to the wonder of God's incredible gift.

odly woman,

MAKE AND TAKE THE TIME TO WONDER.

$\mathcal{R}$emember

Verse: "I will remember the deeds of the LORD; yes, I will remember your miracles of long ago" (Psalm 77:11).

"God gave us memories that we might have roses in December"
(J. M. BARRIE).

Reflection: I was still a young child when my mom related to me her memory of a Depression-era childhood Christmas. Grandpa was employed in a department store, but the position wasn't "gainful" enough to cover holiday gifts for the couple's five children. He and Grandma resolved this dilemma in a unique way: by borrowing toys from the store—to be enjoyed on Christmas Eve and Christmas day, before being boxed back up and returned on December 26.

When I first heard this story, the gesture seemed to me more heartless than heartwarming. Reflecting back on it now, though, it occurs to me that my grandparents were giving their children something precious—the gift of memory. And what could have been more appropriate to commemorate Christ's coming?

The Bible is all about remembering. God's Word is a story, a cherished saga that begins with creation and weaves its threads through sixty-six books, through the fall and redemption of humanity all the way to the consummation of human history. Its memories are truly incomparable.

Prayer Prompt: What verses, passages, and stories from Scripture mean the most to you? Thank God for his Word—including the gift of the Living Word, the Lord Jesus Christ (John 1:1–5).

$\mathcal{G}$odly woman,
USE WELL THE GIFT OF MEMORY.

$\mathscr{B}$usted!

Verses: "You have searched me, LORD, and you know me. . . . You discern my going out and my lying down; you are familiar with all my ways" (Psalm 139:1, 3).

"Most of our faults are more pardonable than the means we use to conceal them" (FRANCOIS DE LA ROUCHEFOUCAULD).

Reflection: When I was little, my mom had a choice saying she would pull out at opportune moments: "Be sure sin will find you out" (I wasn't aware until recently that this comes straight from Numbers 32:23). I was duly impressed from an early age by this truth, and it has stood me in good stead. Another such coded "word," along the same lines and also associated with my early childhood: "You cannot hide from God." There's a cautionary tone to that sentence, but what I remember most is the comfort: God wouldn't let me wander far.

Temptation of one kind or another assails all of us. The Christmas Adelyn was two, Khristina and I were tickled to locate a partially unwrapped Christmas package pushed far back under the tree, the ripped portion secured with a child's sticker. *Busted!*

When I was five our family camped with my grandparents in a rustic campground somewhere in the Sierra Nevadas. I remember several things about that vacation: The steep slope back to the road the old cars could barely navigate, my imaginary friend in the woods (Mom would give me a snack for two prior to my "disappearance" several feet away into the trees), but most of all the result of my tiff with Debbie and Ricky (siblings flanking me in age)—the reason for which has long ago escaped me. What I do recall is that in retaliation I took their squirt guns and released them into the lake. And sure enough, my sin did find me out (actually, unable to bear the suspense, I incriminated myself). I simply found it unbearable trying to hide from God.

When have you tried to conceal a sin? You can rest assured (better make that "experience unrest, convicted") of one thing: It won't work! Because "Everything is uncovered and laid bare before the eyes of him to whom we must give account" (Hebrews 4:13).

Prayer Prompt: Identify one sin you've tried to cover up, maybe even from yourself. Then confess it and experience the sweet release of forgiveness.

odly woman,
HE KNOWS YOU MUCH BETTER THAN YOU DO.

*T*he triumph

Verse: "You yourselves have seen what I did to Egypt, and how I carried you on eagles' wings and brought you to myself" (Exodus 19:4).

"Your worst days are never so bad that you are beyond the reach of God's grace. And your best days are never so good that you are beyond the need of God's grace" (JERRY BRIDGES).

Reflection: I've seen an eagle once in the wild, traveling by Amtrak shortly after Christmas with Khristina over the Rockies, en route to Grand Junction, Colorado, to visit my parents. It was perched high in a pine directly adjacent to the track on our side of the car—evidently its habitual roost, since the engineer stopped the train as though on cue to point it out. What a magnificent, lordly bird! That second adjective came to my mind unbidden as I recalled that sighting just now.

The comfort of the Exodus verse above is echoed in Deuteronomy 30:10–12: "He guarded him . . . like an eagle that stirs up its nest and hovers over its young, that spreads its wings to catch them and carries them aloft. The LORD alone led [his people]."

But God also used the eagle image in a very different way to refer to his dealings with his Old Testament people: "The LORD will bring a nation against you from far away, from the ends of the earth, like an eagle swooping down" (Deuteronomy 28:49). We can be thankful that, based on the atoning death of Jesus Christ, God doesn't punish his new covenant people in this way.

We do well at Christmastide to reflect on the reason for Christ's incarnation. God's justice demanded punishment for sin—the only way to mend the jagged rift between himself and humankind reported in Genesis 3. But the other side of his nature, his infinite mercy, triumphed through the advent, death, and resurrection of his only Son.

"The eagle has landed!" I suppose we could proclaim of Christ's birth. A little far-fetched, perhaps, but I believe the metaphor works in this context. And our Savior and Lord will follow through, carrying us on wings of love to the Father's waiting arms. Hallelujah!

Prayer Prompt: How does this eagle imagery affect your perception of God?

*G*odly woman,
PRAISE HIM FOR THE TRIUMPH OF GRACE.

𝒯his little light of mine

Verse: "If we walk in the light, as he is in the light, we have fellowship with one another, and the blood of Jesus, his Son, purifies us from all sin" (1 John 1:7).

*"Christmas is most truly Christmas when we celebrate
it by giving the light of love to those who need it most"*
(RUTH CARTER STAPLETON).

Reflection: At our house we have a tangible "this little light of mine"— two of them, in fact, a matched pair. They started out as dollar-store-variety, battery-operated Christmas window candles. But their glow is narrow-spread and ineffective.

Still, it didn't take long a year ago at Christmas time before three-year-old Adelyn saw possibilities as a night-light. I loved to watch her during that phase, padding along, barefooted and red-plaid-flannel-nightgown clad, "this little light of mine" clutched in both hands.

Addie's candle afforded her comfort, associated, I hope, in her mind with the God who watches over her when "it's darking." Hopefully, this comfort will morph into an inkling of what it means for us to carry God's light as we thread our way through the dark hallways of our world.

Prayer Prompt: What does it mean for you to carry with you the message of God's light?

odly woman,

HE DELEGATED YOU AS HIS LIGHT BEARER.

God within us

Verse: "He who raised Christ from the dead will also give life to your mortal bodies because of his Spirit who lives in you" (Romans 8:11).

"It is imperative that believers recognize a spirit exists within them, something extra to thought, knowledge and imagination of the mind, something beyond affection, sensation and pleasure of the emotion, something additional to desire, decision and action of the will" (WATCHMAN NEE).

Reflection: The New Year's festivities are still around the corner. But after that, winter settles in for a long stay (at least here in West Michigan), unpunctuated by holiday cheer. It's easy to give in to post-Christmas doldrums, isn't it?

How long does it make sense for us to leave some of those unwrapped surprises under the tree? At what point do you muster the motivation to retrieve the outdoor ornaments and truck the boxes of holiday paraphernalia back down to the basement?

We as Christian women sometimes find it hard after Christmas to let go of the fresh wonder of Immanuel, "God with us" (not that we have to). But has it ever struck you that Pentecost (coming up fifty days after "Resurrection Sunday" on the spring church calendar) is vitally important as well? If Jesus Christ is "God with us," remind your heart that his Spirit is God with*in* us!

Prayer Prompt: You've thanked God for Jesus Christ during Advent and Christmas. How about focusing now on the Holy Spirit dwelling within you?

Godly woman,

MAKE THE MOST OF YOUR RELATIONSHIP WITH THE SPIRIT.

ꞈttend to the light

Verse: "We also have the prophetic message as something completely reliable, and you will do well to pay attention to it, as to a light shining in a dark place, until the day dawns and the morning star rises in your hearts" (2 Peter 1:19).

*"I have found the paradox that if I love until it hurts, then there is
no hurt, but only more love"* (MOTHER TERESA).

Reflection: What more appropriate image so soon after the winter solstice than the promise of morning light shining in a dark place? Peter is referring to the light of revelation we carry within us, a light foreshadowed by prophecy and "completely reliable" based on the birth, death, resurrection, and ascension of Jesus Christ.

If it's early morning, the insubstantial light of day may not yet have dawned. You may be nested comfortably in the warmth and artificial light of home, possibly looking ahead to yet another low-key day before a return to busyness as usual.

Norman B. Rice, Seattle's first African American mayor, offered this challenge: "Dare to reach out your hand into the darkness, to pull another hand into the light." As you gaze ahead into the yet-to-be-revealed possibilities of the year to come, consider ways in which you can do just that. We do well to remember that an eternal light of day lies around the corner—a light that waits to brighten the face behind that hand in the dark.

Prayer Prompt: How will you answer the call to make a difference in the coming year?

odly woman,

YOU BEAR HIS REVELATION LIGHT.

𝒫assages

Verses: "I trust in you, Lᴏʀᴅ; I say, 'You are my God.' My times are in your hands" (Psalm 31:14–15).

> *"Her grandmother, as she gets older, is not fading but rather becoming more concentrated"* (PAULETTE BATES ALDEN).

Reflection: We like to use the word *passages* with reference to the times or seasons of our lives. In a certain sense our life passages are predictable. They include or may include, not necessarily in this order or without overlap, infancy, childhood, an "awkward age," adolescence, the teen years, young adulthood, spiritual awakening, youthful idealism, higher education, career, marriage, parenthood, middle age, empty nest, retirement, grand-parenting, elder care, diminishing strength, and that last finite (but hardly final) phase of our eternal lives—old age.

In addition, we go through other periods not directly related to our linear lives: seasons of doubt; periods of illness, cynicism, disillusionment or depression; winters of discontent. On the opposite end of the spectrum, we may at various times experience the euphoria of infatuation, the thrill of adventure or of newly realized independence, the mellow contentment of mature love . . . and the list goes on.

You may find yourself at the end of this year planted solidly in some particular phase while tentatively exploring or breaking from another. Wherever you are, you can take comfort in the knowledge that God both knows and cares.

The end of another year offers both a vantage point for reflection and assessment and a springboard for change. How will you and God together negotiate the passages—the times—of the fresh new year riding in on the next dawn?

Prayer Prompt: Reflect on these meaningful verses before praying them back to God.

Godly woman,
YOUR TIMES ARE SECURE WITH HIM.

"*B*lessed are those whose strength is in you,

whose hearts are set on pilgrimage. . . .

They go from strength to strength,

till each appears before God in Zion"

(Psalm 84:5, 7).

"You have no strength but what God gives

and you can have all the strength that God can give"

(ANDREW MURRAY).

$\mathscr{A}$fterword

We humans live according to a built-in cycle of work (or weariness) and re-freshment. At those times when we're really depleted, like after an especially concentrated effort or trying experience, we may experience what we know as a crash. During other periods, when we're wise enough to refresh our-selves periodically, we can benefit from a briefer dip into relaxation—like a coffee break or even a shared laugh. One way or another, we as Christian women understand the reality of moving along on life's journey from one oasis—or steppingstone—of strength to the next. And we understand and appreciate from where that strength derives. I particularly relate to the image of steppingstones. I picture them as regularly spaced and envision a rhythm of step (or hop) and pause. What better steppingstone can we incorporate into our everyday routine than a devotional pause for rejuvenation?

My approach in this set of 366 daily devotions (wouldn't want to miss a February 29!) has been personal. Even though the conversation has of necessity been one-sided, I've approached my subject matter (that sounds so cold, but I don't intend it to be) and you . . . as me. Although not every reflection includes a personal backdrop or touch, many do. I wrote these devotions over the course of a year, during which time there has obviously been some flux in my situation. You've probably noticed that the medita-tions weren't written in any particular order (my granddaughter's age, for example, jumps around between three and four and back again; kids don't take steppingstones in quite the same way we do!).

To make sure this hasn't caused confusion, please allow me to introduce myself. I'm the single adoptive mom of three grown daughters, Amanda, Angela, and Khristina, and the proud grandmother of Adelyn, Khristina's little girl. Oh yes, you've heard a little about three other precious grand-kids—Walter, Becky, and Tavis. They're Angie's, but I haven't seen them in more than four years, during which time they've been in foster care in Kentucky. Although I have no grandparental rights, their social worker was willing to share with me the recent good news of their incorporation into a Christian forever family. I look forward one day to reuniting with these three, now ages ten, nine, and eight.

These days I'm pretty much a fulltime freelance editor and writer (a lifestyle I love!), having lost a job of thirty-one years at a Christian publishing house four years ago on account of an eliminated editorial position in the Bible department. I say "pretty much" because the bulk of my income arrives each month in the form of a Social Security disability check based on my chronic fatigue syndrome / fibromyalgia.

I think that's enough about me to clear up any major confusion as you read. I'm not the focus, of course, but I have "run" my perceptions of at least some of the Scripture passages through the prism of my own experience.

You've already seen from my copious use of quotes that I appreciate perspectives beyond my own. Each devotion opens with a Scripture verse or verses, followed by a quote from some other source, ancient or modern, well-known or even anonymous. You'll notice that I didn't say Christian, simply because not all of the speakers are. Please don't get hung up on the names, if you know them. I prefer to allow the quotes to speak for themselves, to expand on the point of my chosen Scripture.

It may be that from time to time you prefer a thematic approach to your devotions. Perhaps you're struggling with a contentment issue, for instance, or are experiencing grief . . . or the stimulation of anticipating an exciting experience. For that reason I've included an index in the back of the book.

By the way, I want to reiterate my awareness that a one-sided conversation is less than ideal. The conversation that counts, of course—and the one I've tried throughout to encourage—is between you, God's cherished daughter, and your doting Abba.

Blessings, believing sister!

*I*ndex

$\mathcal{A}$cknowledgments

TITLE PAGE

http://www.suffering.net/godpurp.htm

JANUARY 1

David Parsons: http://thinkexist.com/quotation/today-s-process-is-god-s-faithfulness-to-his/765711.html

JANUARY 2

Jacob Bronowski: http://www.finestquotes.com/author_quotes-author-Jacob%20Bronowski-page-0.htm

Dan Millman: http://www.brainyquote.com/quotes/keywords/uncertainty.html#ixzz17ja5hK65

JANUARY 4

Jean Paul: http://www.quoteland.com/topic/God-Quotes/404/

JANUARY 5

Edith Wharton: www.quotegarden.com/light.html

Arlo Guthrie: www.quotegarden.com/light.html

Terry Pratchett: www.quotegarden.com/light.html

JANUARY 6

Mother Teresa: http://thinkexist.com/quotes/with/keyword/faithfulness/

JANUARY 8

Maynard James Keenan: http://www.brainyquote.com/quotes/keywords/reflection.html

JANUARY 9

D. A. Carson: http://www.suffering.net/godpurp.htm

JANUARY 11

Martin Luther: http://exploringthepathhome.blogspot.com/2006/10/100-quotes.html

Charles L. Allen: http://thinkexist.com/quotations/god/3.html

JANUARY 12

Oscar Wilde: http://quotes.maxabout.com/paradox-quotes/991/page-1

Søren Kierkegaard: http://www.goodreads.com/author/quotes/6172.S_ren_Kierkegaard?page=2

"You, Lord, are both Lamb and Shepherd": Sylvia Dunstan (1955–93). From . Grand Rapids, Mich.: The Calvin Institute of Christian Worship, Faith Alive Christian Resources, and Reformed Church in America, 2001)

JANUARY 13

Martin Luther: http://www.suffering.net/suffinev.htm

JANUARY 14

Aiden Wilson Tozer: http://thinkexist.com/quotes/with/keyword/obey/2.html

JANUARY 16

John Updike: http://thinkexist.com/quotes/with/keyword/reverence/4.html

JANUARY 17

Samuel Taylor Coleridge: http://www.quotelucy.com/quotations/7399/201499-samuel-taylor-coleridge-quote.html

JANUARY 19

Ralph Waldo Emmerson: http://pslinstitute.com/inspirationalquotes.html

John Kenneth Galbraith: http://www.brainyquote.com/quotes/keywords/devil.html

Watchman Nee: http://christian-quotes.ochristian.com/Watchman-Nee-Quotes/page-8.shtml

JANUARY 20

Erica Jong: http://thinkexist.com/quotations/advice/

Woodrow Wilson: http://www.brainyquote.com/quotes/quotes/w/woodrowwil110374.html

JANUARY 21

Oscar Wilde: http://thinkexist.com/quotations/hope/

Friedrich Nietzsche: http://thinkexist.com/quotation/he_who_has_a_why_to_live_can_bear_almost_any_how/205853.html

JANUARY 22

Steven Estes: http://www.suffering.net/godpurp.htm

JANUARY 23

Alfred, Lord Tennyson: http://thinkexist.com/quotation/music_that_gentler_on_the_spirit_lies-than_tired/161097.html

JANUARY 24

Alfred North Whitehead: http://quotes.maxabout.com/god-quotes/280/page-3

Jules Renard: http://www.quotegarden.com/laziness.html

JANUARY 25

Alicia Britt Chole: http://www.quoteland.com/topic/God-Quotes/404/

JANUARY 26

Abraham Lincoln: http://exploringthepathhome.blogspot.com/2006/10/100-quotes.html

John Piper: , p. 255; http://www.pietyhilldesign.com/gcq/quotepages/sanctification.html

Leighton Ford: http://thinkexist.com/quotations/god/3.html

JANUARY 27

Florence Nightingale: http://www.finestquotes.com/quote-id-15130.htm

JANUARY 28

William Ellery Channing: http://www.dumb.com/quotes/vigilance-quotes/

Jerry Seinfeld: http://exploringthepathhome.blogspot.com/2006/10/100-quotes.html

JANUARY 30

Woody Allen: http://www.quotegarden.com/singing.html

JANUARY 31

Henri-Frédéric Amiel: http://www.quotationspage.com/subjects/talent/

FEBRUARY 1

Miguel de Cervantes: http://www.quoteland.com/topic/God-Quotes/404/

FEBRUARY 2

Bertrand Russell: http://www.quotegarden.com/kindness.html

FEBRUARY 3

Herodotus: http://www.brainyquote.com/quotes/keywords/presumption.html

FEBRUARY 4

Joni Eareckson Tada: http://www.suffering.net/godpurp.htm

Viktor Frankl: http://thinkexist.com/quotation/what_is_to_give_light_must_endure_burning/203844.html

FEBRUARY 5

Stephen Colbert: http://www.woopidoo.com/business_quotes/internet-quotes.htm

FEBRUARY 6

Cliff Richard: http://www.thoughts-about-god.com/quotes/quotes-god.htm

FEBRUARY 7

Henry David Thoreau: http://www.quotesea.com/quotes/with/aroma

Henry Ward Beecher: http://en.thinkexist.com/quotation/a_man_ought_to_carry_himself_in_the_world_as_an/192356.html

FEBRUARY 8

Oswald Chambers: http://christian-quotes.ochristian.com/Stewardship-Quotes/

FEBRUARY 9

Sarah Ban Breathnach: http://quotations.about.com/cs/inspirationquotes/a/Reflection1.htm

Victor Hugo: http://quotes.dictionary.com/One_is_not_idle_because_one_is_absorbed

FEBRUARY 10

Elizabeth Barrett Browning: http://www.thoughts-about-god.com/quotes/quotes-god.htm

FEBRUARY 11

Socrates: http://www.suffering.net/godpurp.htm

FEBRUARY 12

Garth Henrichs: http://www.quoteworld.org/quotes/6468

FEBRUARY 13

Augustine: http://christian-quotes.ochristian.com/Salvation-Quotes/

FEBRUARY 14

Henry David Thoreau: http://quotes.possumstew.com/quotes/rationalizing

FEBRUARY 15

Bernadette Roberts: http://blog.gaiam.com/quotes/topics/knowing-god

FEBRUARY 16

William Lloyd Garrison: http://www.quotegarden.com/integrity.html

FEBRUARY 17

Martin Luther: http://christian-quotes.ochristian.com/Contentment-Quotes/page-5.shtml

FEBRUARY 18

Bishop Gore: http://thoughts.forbes.com/thoughts/god-bishop-gore-god-does-not

Kathryn Hulme: http://en.thinkexist.com/quotation/never_forget_that_god-tests_his_real_friends_more/213048.html

FEBRUARY 19

C. S. Lewis: http://www.quoteland.com/topic/God-Quotes/404/

FEBRUARY 20

William Mathews: http://www.quotelucy.com/keywords/proverbs-quotes.html

FEBRUARY 21

Marche Blumenberg: http://www.quotegarden.com/winter.html

FEBRUARY 22

A. W. Tozer: http://www.quoteland.com/topic/God-Quotes/404/

Albert Einstein: http://thinkexist.com/quotations/time/

FEBRUARY 23

Erica Jong: http://www.finestquotes.com/select_quote-category-betrayal-page-0.htm

Benjamin Franklin: http://www.quotationsbook.com/quote/18788/

FEBRUARY 24

"Jesus Bids Us Shine with a Clear, Pure Light": http://library.timelesstruths.org/music/Jesus_Bids_Us_Shine/

James Keller: http://www.brainyquote.com/quotes/quotes/j/jameskelle192856.html

FEBRUARY 25

Paul Little: http://www.quotesea.com/quotes/with/holy-spirit/3

FEBRUARY 26

Abraham Lincoln: http://www.brainyquote.com/quotes/keywords/god.html

FEBRUARY 27

Vance Havner: http://www.quoteland.com/topic.asp?CATEGORY_ID=783

Etty Hillesum: http://www.quotationsbook.com/quote/31943/

FEBRUARY 29

Albert Einstein: http://thinkexist.com/quotation/the_most_incomprehensible_thing_about_the_world/15590.html

MARCH 1

Ann Landers: http://thinkexist.com/quotation/hanging_onto_resentment_is_letting_someone_you/193233.html

MARCH 2

Henry Miller: http://thinkexist.com/quotation/true_strength_lies_in_submission_which_permits/208927.html

MARCH 3

William Barclay: http://thinkexist.com/quotes/with/keyword/arms/4.html

MARCH 4

Oswald C. Hoffman: http://www.quoteland.com/topic/God-Quotes/404/

MARCH 5

Frank A. Clark: http://www.quotegarden.com/helping.html

Dr. Seuss: http://exploringthepathhome.blogspot.com/2006/10/100-quotes.html

MARCH 6

Henry David Thoreau: http://thinkexist.com/quotes/with/keyword/shadow/

Maori proverb: http://quote-book.tumblr.com/post/1729302196/turn-your-face-to-the-sun-and-the-shadows-fall

MARCH 7

Nelle Morton: http://exploringthepathhome.blogspot.com/2006/10/100-quotes.html

MARCH 8

Lewis B. Smedes: http://www.iloveulove.com/wisdom/50quotes.htm

MARCH 9

Laurie Anderson: http://thinkexist.com/quotations/paradise/

Charles Dickens: http://thinkexist.com/quotation/it_was_one_of_those_march_days_when_the_sun/343114.html

Lilja Rogers: http://www.famousquotes.com/show/1040051/

Nathaniel Hawthorne: http://en.thinkexist.com/quotation/our_creator_would_never_have_made_such_lovely/262145.html

MARCH 10

Mae West: http://thinkexist.com/quotations/sin/

MARCH 11

Chester Brown: http://www.brainyquote.com/quotes/keywords/accepting_4.html

MARCH 12

Douglas Engelbart: http://www.brainyquote.com/quotes/keywords/embarrassment_2.html

MARCH 13

Thomas Jane: http://www.brainyquote.com/quotes/keywords/loss_8.html

MARCH 15

Leonard Ravenhill: http://christian-quotes.ochristian.com/Holy-Spirit-Quotes/page-3.shtml

Friedrich Nietzsche: http://www.quotationsbook.com/quote/18893/

MARCH 16

John Vance: http://thinkexist.com/quotes/with/keyword/rainbow/

MARCH 17

C. S. Lewis: http://christian-quotes.ochristian.com/Eternity-Quotes/

MARCH 19

Max DuPree: http://www.leadership-tools.com/customer-service-quotes.html

MARCH 20

Mark Twain: http://www.quotegarden.com/spring.html

MARCH 21

Lewis Grizzard: http://www.quotegarden.com/spring.html

Virgil A. Kraft: http://www.quotegarden.com/spring.html

Ellis Peters: http://www.flickr.com/photos/tuanh/3379341769/

MARCH 22

Polly Berrien Berends: http://www.christian-parenting-source.com/family-quotes.html

MARCH 23

Wilfred Peterson: http://www.joy4u.org/Quotes/JoyQuotes.htm

MARCH 25

Henry Morris: http://whygodreallyexists.com/archives/quotes-about-the-resurrection-of-jesus-christ

MARCH 26

William Blake: http://thinkexist.com/quotations/eternity/3.html

Vladimir Nabokov: http://www.brainyquote.com/quotes/quotes/v/vladimirna159120.html

Rabindranath Tagore: http://thinkexist.com/quotation/death_is_not_extinguishing_the_light-it_is_only/144007.html

MARCH 27

William Ralph Inge: http://www.quotegarden.com/god.html

John Rohn: http://exploringthepathhome.blogspot.com/2006/10/100-quotes.html

MARCH 28

Karl Barth: http://www.happylifeu.com/Gratitude-Quotes.html

MARCH 29

Robert Grosseteste: http://www.brainyquote.com/quotes/keywords/household.html

MARCH 30

Emily Dickinson: http://www.americanpoems.com/poets/emilydickinson/10060

MARCH 31

John Calvin: http://www.suffering.net/godpurp.htm

Aristotle: http://exploringthepathhome.blogspot.com/2006/10/100-quotes.html

APRIL 1

Mark Twain: http://www.brainyquote.com/quotes/keywords/household.html

APRIL 2

Charles Stanley: http://www.dumb.com/quotes/christ-quotes/2/

Robert Service: http://www.quotationcollection.com/tag/priorities/quotes

APRIL 3

Herman Bavinck: http://www.desirespiritualgrowth.com/tag/quotes/

APRIL 4

Augustine: http://www.quotegarden.com/god.html

APRIL 5

Jonathan Edwards: http://www.brainyquote.com/quotes/keywords/glory_3.html

APRIL 6

C. S. Lewis http://christian-quotes.ochristian.com/Joy-Quotes/

APRIL 7

Martin Luther: http://www.brainyquote.com/quotes/keywords/resurrection.html

APRIL 8

Sinclair Ferguson: http://www.thegracetabernacle.org/quotes/Christlikeness.htm

Trevor Huddleston: http://www.finestquotes.com/select_quote-category-Responsibility-page-0.htm

APRIL 9

Henry Benjamin Whipple: http://bibleinsong.com/Promises/Spiritual_blessings/Grace/Grace.htm

APRIL 10

Blaise Pascal: http://www.brainyquote.com/quotes/keywords/justice.html

APRIL 11

Lyn Lomasi: http://www.associatedcontent.com/article/2366448/why_parents_shouldnt_have_a_favorite.html

APRIL 12

Peter Larson: http://www.tentmaker.org/Quotes/jesus-christ.htm

APRIL 13

Helen Rowland: www.famousquotes.com/show/1040512

APRIL 14

Henry David Thoreau: http://www.buzzle.com/articles/wisdom-quotes-and-bible-verses-about-it.html

Josh Billings: http://exploringthepathhome.blogspot.com/2006/10/100-quotes.html

APRIL 15

Charles Bent: http://www.brainyquote.com/quotes/keywords/righteousness.html

APRIL 16

Ann Landers: http://www.forgivenessweb.com/RdgRm/Quotationpage.html

William Blake: http://thinkexist.com/quotation/it_is_easier_to_forgive_an_enemy_than_to_forgive/12382.html

Lewis B. Smedes: http://thinkexist.com/quotation/you_will_know_that_forgiveness_has_begun_when_you/214404.html

APRIL 17

Voltaire: http://www.famous-quotes.net/Quote.aspx?The_perfect_is_the_enemy_of_the_good

Henry Van Dyke: http://quoteworld.org/quotes/10487

APRIL 18

Kela Price (two quotes): http://www.todaysmodernfamily.com/index.php/tag/blended-family-quotes

APRIL 20

Neil Anderson: http://www.suite101.com/content/great-quotes-for-christians-on-trusting-god-a153323

APRIL 21

Alexander MacLaren: http://dailychristianquote.com/dcqprovision.html

APRIL 22

Paul Little: http://www.quoteland.com/topic/God-Quotes/404/

Robert McCloskey: http://www.quotationspage.com/quote/26806.html

Stephen Crotts: http://thinkexist.com/quotations/god/3.html

APRIL 23

Abraham Kuyper: http://thinkexist.com/quotations/security/

APRIL 24

Pearl Bailey: http://www.selfhelpdaily.com/quotes-about-god/

APRIL 25

T. D. Jakes: http://sites.google.com/site/worshipbasic101/about-praise--worship/praise--worship-quotes

APRIL 26

Robert C. Edwards: http://www.randomterrain.com/favorite-quotes-human-and-nature.html

Ben Okri: http://www.atozquotes.com/authors/author_10833/quote_122400

APRIL 27

George Whitefield: http://christian-quotes.ochristian.com/Death-Quotes/page-3.shtml

APRIL 28

Helen Keller: http://blog.gaiam.com/quotes/topics/blindness

APRIL 29

Edward V. Lucas: http://www.karlonia.com/2008/09/13/quotes-about-fake/

APRIL 30

James Baldwin: Love takes off masks that we fear we cannot live without and know we cannot live within. --James Baldwin

"The B-I-B-L-E": childbiblesongs.com/song-23-b-i-b-l-e.shtml

MAY 1

Stephen Grellet: http://www.desktop-quotes.com/caring-quotes.html

MAY 2

Francis Bacon: http://www.famous-sayings.net/francis-bacon-quote-prosperity-is-the-blessing-of-the-old-testament/

MAY 3

Charlie Chaplin: http://www.sayingsnquotes.com/quotations-by-subject/help-quotes-proverbs-sayings-6/

MAY 4

Nadine Hawthorne: http://www.examiner.com/christian-living-in-new-york/vulnerability

MAY 5

Albert Einstein: http://thinkexist.com/quotations/god/2.html

MAY 6

Eric Bentley: http://thinkexist.com/quotes/with/keyword/jargon/

MAY 7

Rollo May: http://thinkexist.com/quotations/depression/

MAY 9

Roger Babson: http://www.quotegarden.com/worry.html

MAY 10

Mary Webb: http://www.someworthwhilequotes.com/TRADITIONTRANSIENCE.html

MAY 11

Leighton Ford: http://en.thinkexist.com/reference/love_of_god_quotes/

MAY 12

Madame de Stael: http://www.finestquotes.com/select_quote-category-Speech-page-1.htm

MAY 14

Ivy Baker Priest: http://www.quotegarden.com/perspective.html

MAY 15

Audrey Hepburn: http://www.boloji.com/quotes/cis.htm

MAY 16

William Gaddis: http://www.brainyquote.com/quotes/quotes/w/williamgad388096.html

MAY 18

Epicurus: http://quotationsbook.com/quote/17793/

MAY 19

Henry Ward Beecher: http://www.quoteland.com/topic.asp?CATEGORY_ID=40

MAY 20

James Thurber: http://www.abundance-and-happiness.com/purpose-quotes.html

MAY 22

Billy Sunday: http://christian-quotes.ochristian.com/Joy-Quotes/page-4.shtml

MAY 23

Martina Navratilova: http://www.quoteland.com/topic.asp?CATEGORY_ID=548

MAY 24

George Washington Carver: ttp://parenting.families.com/blog/more-great-quotes-about-kids

MAY 25

Christopher Logue: http://www.conures.net/stories/edge.shtml

MAY 26

L. J. Suenens: http://thinkexist.com/quotes/with/keyword/holy_spirit/

MAY 27

Peter Drucker: http://thinkexist.com/quotation/efficiency_is_doing_things_right-effectiveness_is/218648.html

MAY 28

Leonard Ravenhill: http://christian-quotes.ochristian.com/christian-quotes_ochristian.cgi?query=children&action=search

MAY 29

George Bulwer-Lytton: http://www.quotegarden.com/stress.html

MAY 30

Steven Estes: http://www.suffering.net/godpurp.htm

John Updike: http://thinkexist.com/quotation/you_cannot_help_but_learn_more_as_you_take_the/254827.html

MAY 31

Fran Lebowitz: http://thinkexist.com/quotes/with/keyword/offended/2.html

JUNE 1

Karl Barth: http://www.quoteland.com/topic.asp?CATEGORY_ID=90

JUNE 3

Angela at Refresh My Soul Blog: http://www.chrysaliscafe.com/2007/11/marriage-memorable-quotes-on-submission.html

JUNE 4

C. S. Lewis: http://christian-quotes.ochristian.com/Lust-Quotes/

JUNE 5

Jane Sellman: http://www.allgreatquotes.com/mother_quotes.shtml

Mother Teresa: http://www.dictionary-quotes.com/love-begins-at-home-and-it-is-not-how-much-we-do-but-how-much-love-we-put-in-that-action-mother-teresa-of-calcutta/

JUNE 6

J. B. Priestly: http://www.quotegarden.com/generations.html

JUNE 7

Bern Williams: http://www.quotesdaddy.com/quote/75107/bern-williams/if-a-june-night-could-talk-it-would-probably-boast

JUNE 8

Benjamin Whichcote: http://www.quoteland.com/topic.asp?CATEGORY_ID=382

JUNE 9

Guillermo Mordillo: http://thinkexist.com/quotations/god/3.html

JUNE 10

Robert Quillen: http://www.tentmaker.org/Quotes/lovequotes.htm

JUNE 11

Letty Cottin Pogrebin: http://www.famousquotesandauthors.com/keywords/plowing_quotes.html

JUNE 12

Matthew Henry: http://www.quotesdaddy.com/author/Matthew+Henry

JUNE 13

Ann Landers: http://www.sayingsnquotes.com/quotations-by-subject/help-quotes-proverbs-sayings-9/

Jean Houston: http://www.quotegarden.com/laughter.html

Bill Cosby: http://thinkexist.com/quotations/hope/

JUNE 15

May Sarton: http://www.sayingsnquotes.com/quotations-by-subject/help-quotes-proverbs-sayings-9/

JUNE 16

Granni Nazzano: http://www.famousquotearchive.com/Granni_Nazzano/Quote_15998.aspx

Richard Whately: http://www.worldofquotes.com/topic/loss/index.html

JUNE 17

Gertrude Stein: http://www.brainyquote.com/quotes/keywords/vegetables.html

Will Rogers: http://www.quotationspage.com/quote/34158.html

Doug Larson: http://en.thinkexist.com/quotation/life_expectancy_would_grow_by_leaps_and_bounds_if/202850.html

JUNE 18

Richard Whately: http://thinkexist.com/quotes/with/keyword/dinner_table/

F. Scott Fitzgerald: http://thinkexist.com/quotation/family_quarrels_are_bitter_things-they_don-t_go/206099.html

Margaret Laurence: http://www.friendship-quotes.org.uk/friendship-and-family-quotes/08-friendship-and-family-quote.htm

JUNE 19

Thomas Dekker: http://www.notable-quotes.com/w/work_quotes.html

Alexander Graham Bell: http://thinkexist.com/quotation/concentrate_all_your_thoughts_upon_the_work_at/12669.html

JUNE 20

G. K. Chesterton: http://www.quoteland.com/topic.asp?CATEGORY_ID=41

Bertrand Russell: http://thinkexist.com/quotation/the_world_is_full_of_magical_things_patiently/200400.html

JUNE 21

H. Jackson Brown: http://thinkexist.com/quotation/in_the_confrontation_between_the_stream_and_the/339965.html

JUNE 22

George Herbert: http://christian-quotes.ochristian.com/The-Heart-Quotes/page-4.shtml

JUNE 23

Golda Meir: http://www.brainyquote.com/quotes/keywords/blessing_3.html

JUNE 24

Francis E. Willard: http://www.quoteland.com/topic.asp?CATEGORY_ID=467

Thomas Fuller: http://www.brainyquote.com/quotes/keywords/blessing_3.html

JUNE 26

Edward Everett Hale: http://www.quotegarden.com/helping.html and http://www.stresslesscountry.com/helpingothersquotes/index.html

JUNE 27

Elisabeth Kübler-Ross: http://thinkexist.com/quotation/people_are_like_stained-glass_windows-they/8840.html

JUNE 28

Macrina Wiederkehr: http://www.notable-quotes.com/p/prayer_quotes.html

Mother Teresa: http://www.quoteworld.org/quotes/11159

JUNE 29

George Whitefield: http://christian-quotes.ochristian.com/Scripture-Quotes/page-10.shtml

JUNE 30

Martin Buxbaum: http://www.quoteland.com/topic.asp?CATEGORY_ID=157

Marie Stopes: http://www.quotegarden.com/beauty.html

JULY 1

C. S. Lewis: http://blog.gaiam.com/quotes/authors/cs-lewis/47867

JULY 2

George Washington Carver: http://www.kevinstilley.com/general-revelation-quotes/

JULY 3

Augustine: http://christian-quotes.ochristian.com/Truth-Quotes/

Ralph W. Sockman: http://www.brainyquote.com/quotes/quotes/r/ralphwsoc403011.html

JULY 4

Marilyn vos Savant: http://quotes.liberty-tree.ca/quote_blog/Marilyn.vos.Savant.Quote.70CA

George Bernard Shaw: http://www.quotationspage.com/quote/32958.html

Bernard Baruch: http://www.quotes-museum.com/quote/6172

JULY 5

Ray Bradbury: http://exploringthepathhome.blogspot.com/2006/10/100-quotes.html

JULY 6

George MacDonald: http://en.thinkexist.com/quotation/god-s_finger_can_touch_nothing_but_to_mold_it/345881.html

JULY 7

John Balguy: http://www.achieving-life-abundance.com/contentment-quotes.html

John Balguy: http://www.achieving-life-abundance.com/contentment-quotes.html

JULY 8

Billy Graham: http://www.heartlight.org/cgi-shl/quotemeal.cgi?day=20100704&s=christian

JULY 9

Charles Swindoll: http://thequotes.wordpress.com/2006/11/13/god-will-give-us-rest/

JULY 10

C. S. Lewis: http://christian-quotes.ochristian.com/Truth-Quotes/page-2.shtml

JULY 11

Theodore Ledyard Cuyler: http://quoteworld.org/quotes/3340

Robert Brault: http://www.robertbrault.com/2009/10/thoughts-mostly-on-art-and-artists.html

JULY 12

Robert Updegraff: http://quotations.about.com/cs/inspirationquotes/a/Time1.htm

Robert Green Ingersoll: http://www.quotes-museum.com/author/Robert%20Green%20Ingersoll/3128

JULY 13

Warren Wiersbe: http://www.hurtingchristian.org/PastorsSite/otherscripture/isaiahstudies/isaiah40-25-31.htm

JULY 14

Alexander MacLaren: http://thegracetabernacle.org/quotes/Eschatology-Second_Coming.htm

JULY 15

John Calvin: http://thinkexist.com/quotations/blessings/2.html

JULY 16

Gilbert Chesterton: http://quoteworld.org/quotes/2695

JULY 17

Anne Lewis: http://www.famousquotesandauthors.com/topics/prayer_quotes.html

JULY 18

Paul Chappell: http://christian-quotes.ochristian.com/Paul-Chappell-Quotes/page-2.shtml

JULY 19

Arnold H. Glawgow: http://thinkexist.com/quotations/patience/

JULY 20

Charles Baudelaire: http://quotes.dictionary.com/
The_insatiable_thirst_for_everything_which_lies_beyond

JULY 22

St. Jerome: http://thinkexist.com/quotation/good-better-best-never_let_it_rest--til_your_good/151162.html

JULY 23

A. W. Tozer: http://preceptaustin.org/holiness_quotes.htm

Oswald Chambers: http://preceptaustin.org/holiness_quotes.htm

JULY 24

Martin Luther King Jr.: http://thinkexist.com/quotation/we_must_accept_finite_disappointment-but_never/8113.html

Samuel Johnson: http://www.famousquotes.com/show/1030280/

JULY 25

John Leonard: http://thinkexist.com/quotation/it_takes_a_long_time_to_grow_an_old_friend/210119.html

JULY 26

R. W. Raymond: http://www.self-help-healing-arts-journal.com/quotes-afterlife.html

JULY 27

Arthur Somers Roche: http://thinkexist.com/quotation/anxiety_is_a_thin_stream_of_fear_trickling/221176.html

JULY 28

Georges Bernanos: http://www.famousquotesandauthors.com/topics/prayer_quotes.html

JULY 29

Charles Haddon Spurgeon: http://www.tentmaker.org/Quotes/biblequotes.htm

Kurt Vonnegut: http://www.brainyquote.com/quotes/quotes/k/kurtvonneg112524.html

Albert Camus: http://quotationsbook.com/quote/3818/

JULY 30

William Barclay: http://www.famousquotesandauthors.com/keywords/drowning_quotes.html

JULY 31

Rich Vincent: http://www.suffering.net/godpurp.htm

Ramona C. Carroll: http://thinkexist.com/quotation/faith_is_putting_all_your_eggs_in_god-s_basket/224515.html

AUGUST 1

Cyril Connolly: http://thinkexist.com/quotations/vulgarity/

AUGUST 2

Jesse Jackson: http://thinkexist.com/quotation/never_look_down_on_anybody_unless_you-re_helping/9447.html

Eric Hoffer: http://thinkexist.com/quotation/kindness_can_become_its_own_motive-we_are_made/205101.html

AUGUST 3

Marianne Goldweber: http://blog.gaiam.com/quotes/topics/accountability

AUGUST 4

Blaise Pascal: http://christian-quotes.ochristian.com/The-Heart-Quotes/

AUGUST 5

Ralph Waldo Emerson: http://www.inspirational-quotations.com/faith-quotes.html

C. S. Lewis: http://thinkexist.com/quotation/if_the_whole_universe_has_no_meaning-we_should/201245.html

Mother Teresa: http://thinkexist.com/quotes/like/words_which_do_not_give_the_light_of_christ/215932/

AUGUST 6

Billy Graham: http://math.fullerton.edu/sannin/Hobbies/quotes/quote-challenges/quote-challenges.html

James Montgomery: http://www.cptryon.org/prayer/special/index.html

AUGUST 7

Eubie Blake: http://www.quoteland.com/topic.asp?CATEGORY_ID=287

AUGUST 8

Mason Cooley: http://www.famouspoetsandpoems.com/thematic_quotes/compassion_quotes.html

AUGUST 9

Dwight Eisenhower: http://quotations.about.com/cs/inspirationquotes/a/Victory1.htm

Dietrich Bonhoeffer: http://www.quotecosmos.com/quotes/37396/view

AUGUST 10

Hudson Taylor: http://www.selfhelpdaily.com/quotes-about-god/

AUGUST 12

Rick Warren: http://www.beliefnet.com/Faiths/Christianity/2009/01/Christian-Quotes-About-God-and-Love.aspx?p=4#ixzz1Ccs1PfF9

AUGUST 13

Paul Chappell: http://twitter.com/ChristianQuote

AUGUST 14

Madame Guyon: http://christian-quotes.ochristian.com/Contentment-Quotes/page-4.shtml

AUGUST 15

Henry Wadsworth Longfellow: http://www.answers.com/topic/song-stay-stay-at-home-my-heart-and-rest

Vernon Joseph Baker: http://heartquotes.net/Heart-quotes.html

AUGUST 16

Warren Christopher: http://www.brainyquote.com/quotes/keywords/temper.html

"Jesus, Tender Shepherd, Hear Me": http://www.prayer-and-prayers.info/prayers-for-children/jesus-tender-shepherd-hear-me.htm

AUGUST 17

Levende Waters: http://www.quotesinternet.com/tag/life/

George Elliot: http://quoteworld.org/quotes/4288

AUGUST 18

Anthony J. D'Angelo: http://thinkexist.com/quotation/smile-it_is_the_key_that_fits_the_lock_of/10294.html

Denis Waitley: http://thinkexist.com/quotation/a_smile_is_the_light_in_your_window_that_tells/327588.html

AUGUST 19

Mother Teresa: http://thinkexist.com/quotes/with/keyword/god%27s_will/

AUGUST 20

Martin Luther: http://www.brainyquote.com/quotes/keywords/resurrection.html

AUGUST 21

Charles Spurgeon: http://christian-quotes.ochristian.com/Holy-Spirit-Quotes/

AUGUST 22

D. L. Moody: http://christian-quotes.ochristian.com/Children-Quotes/

Jean Paul Richter: http://thinkexist.com/Children_Quotes_for_Scrapbooking/

AUGUST 23

Charles Morgan: http://thinkexist.com/quotation/there_is_no_surprise_more_magical_than_the/201486.html

AUGUST 24

Albert Camus: http://thinkexist.com/quotation/don-t_believe_your_friends_when_they_ask_you_to/222881.html

Eustace Budgell: http://en.thinkexist.com/quotes/like/friendship_is_a_strong_and_habitual_inclination/205336/

AUGUST 25

Isaac Asimov: http://www.quotegarden.com/integrity.html

AUGUST 26

John Climacus: http://www.tentmaker.org/Quotes/faithquotes.htm

AUGUST 27

Franklin Thompson: http://www.inspirationalquotes4u.com/diversity/index.html

AUGUST 28

Fulton Oursler: http://thinkexist.com/quotation/many_of_us_crucify_ourselves_between_two_thieves/174882.html

AUGUST 29

Ivern Ball: http://thinkexist.com/quotation/most_of_us_can_forgive_and_forget-we_just_don-t/172269.html

Mark Twain: http://thinkexist.com/quotation/forgiveness_is_the_fragrance_that_the_violet/215234.html

AUGUST 30

Gerald R. Ford: http://equotes.wetpaint.com/page/Gerald+Ford+Quotes

Pope John Paul II: www.brainyquote.com/quotes/quotes/p/popejohnpa158582.html

AUGUST 31

A.B. Simpson: http://christian-quotes.ochristian.com/christian-quotes_ochristian.cgi?query=living%20water&action=search

Sarah Orne Jewett: www.gardendigest.com/summer.htm

SEPTEMBER 1

Joni Eareckson Tada: http://www.suffering.net/godpurp.htm

SEPTEMBER 2

Anne Brontë: http://www.iwise.com/tag/Glory/page/4

SEPTEMBER 3

Antoine de Saint-Exupery: http://thinkexist.com/quotation/if_you_want_to_build_a_ship-don-t_drum_up_people/170927.html

SEPTEMBER 4

Philip Pullman: www.brainyquote.com/quotes/keywords/shalt.html

Peter Handke: http://thinkexist.com/quotation/if-a-nation-loses-its-storytellers-it-loses-its/410057.html

Anne Watson: http://www.kampman.nl/quotes/page/2/

SEPTEMBER 5

Andrea Martin: http://brainyquote.com/quotes/keywords/routine.html

Annie Dillard: http://thinkexist.com/quotation/a_schedule_defends_from_chaos_and_whim-it_is_a/221210.html

SEPTEMBER 7

Edward Schillebeeck: ttp://www.tentmaker.org/Quotes/faithquotes.htm

SEPTEMBER 8

E. Stanley Jones: http://www.famousquotesandauthors.com/keywords/surprise_quotes.html

SEPTEMBER 9

Jerry Bridges: http://christian-quotes.ochristian.com/Trials-Quotes/

SEPTEMBER 10

Joseph Hall: http://christian-quotes.ochristian.com/Contentment-Quotes/page-5.shtml

SEPTEMBER 11

Abraham Lincoln: http://www.brainyquote.com/quotes/keywords/god.html

Baron Robert Alexander Kennedy Runcie: quotationsbook.com/quote/41091

SEPTEMBER 12

Rona Barrett: http://www.quoteland.com/topic.asp?CATEGORY_ID=287

SEPTEMBER 13

Marianne Moore: http://www.brainyquote.com/quotes/keywords/dust.html

Mary Wollstonecraft: www.brainyquote.com/quotes/quotes/m/marywollstonecraft

Muhammed Iqbal: www.brainyquote.com/quotes/quotes/m/muhammediq232451.html

SEPTEMBER 14

Peter F. Drucker: http://thinkexist.com/quotes/with/keyword/lifelong_learning/

Thomas Szasz: http://quotes.dictionary.com/Every_act_of_conscious_learning_requires_the_willingness

SEPTEMBER 15

Betty Reese: http://quotes.possumstew.com/quotes/determination

SEPTEMBER 16

Empedocles: http://www.sapphyr.net/smallgems/quotes-religion-god.htm

SEPTEMBER 17

Albert Einstein: http://thinkexist.com/quotations/limits/

SEPTEMBER 19

Horace Greeley: http://www.keyway.ca/htm2002/biblquot.htm

SEPTEMBER 20

G. K. Chesterton: http://thinkexist.com/quotations/eyes/

SEPTEMBER 21

George Burns: www.brainyquote.com/quotes/quotes/g/georgeburn119565.html

Isaac Bashevis Singer: www.quotes.net/quote/10537

SEPTEMBER 23

Rebecca M. Pippert: www.quotationsbook.com/quote/12795

Jacquelyn K. Heasley: www.tentmaker.org/Quotes/evangelismquotes.htm

Sally Koch: http://thinkexist.com/quotation/great_opportunities_to_help_others_seldom_come/254238.html

SEPTEMBER 24

Charles Stanley: http://christian-quotes.ochristian.com/Service-Quotes/page-2.shtml

SEPTEMBER 25

Henry Ward Beecher: http://quoteworld.org/quotes/11575

Terri Guillemets: www.brainyquote.com/quotes/keywords/brushing.html

SEPTEMBER 26

Donna Hedges: www.quoteworld.org/quotes/6374

Bishop V. Gene Robinson: http://www.everyoneisincluded.us/inclusionquotes09.html

SEPTEMBER 28

John Calvin: http://thinkexist.com/quotations/blessings/2.html

SEPTEMBER 29

Bill McCartney: http://thinkexist.com/quotes/with/keyword/rebirth/

Albert Schweitzer: www.quotationsbook.com/quote/23091

SEPTEMBER 30

Helen Keller: http://www.allgreatquotes.com/heaven_quotes.shtml

OCTOBER 1

Goethe: http://www.finestquotes.com/select_quote-category-Immortality-page-0.htm

OCTOBER 2

Bernice Fitz-Gibbon: http://www.famouspoetsandpoems.com/thematic_quotes/creativity_quotes.html

OCTOBER 3

Albert Einstein: http://thinkexist.com/quotations/god/4.html

OCTOBER 4

Minnie Smith: http://thinkexist.com/quotes/with/keyword/creator/

Louis Nizer: www.quotelucy.com/quotes/louis-nizer-quotes.html

OCTOBER 5

William Booth: http://www.pietyhilldesign.com/gcq/quotepages/calling.html

John Updike: www.brainyquote.com/quotes/quotes/j/johnupdike393205.html

OCTOBER 6

John Ruskin: www.brainyquote.com/quotes/quotes/j/johnruskin161591.html

Pablo Picasso: www.allgreatquotes.com/art_quotes56.shtml

OCTOBER 7

Frederick Buechner: http://thinkexist.com/quotation/listen-to-your-life-see-it-for-the-fathomless/1211006.html

Jean Houston: quotationsbook.com/quote/9027

OCTOBER 8

Hans Christian Andersen: http://quotations.about.com/cs/inspirationquotes/a/Music2.htm

OCTOBER 9

Anne Morrow Lindbergh: http://www.brainyquote.com/quotes/keywords/depths.html

OCTOBER 10

Sam Levenson: quotations.about.com/cs/inspirationquotes/a/Imagination2.htm

Sara Teasdale: www.americanpoems.com/poets/Sara-Teasdale/4426

OCTOBER 11

Marcus Tullius Cicero: http://www.brainyquote.com/quotes/keywords/creator_3.html

Madeleine L'Engle: www.inspirational-quotations.com/faith-quotes.html

OCTOBER 12

John C. Maxwell: http://www.sayingsnquotes.com/quotations-by-subject/help-quotes-proverbs-sayings-7/

OCTOBER 13

John Ruskin: www.brainyquote.com/quotes/keywords/paradox_2.html

Alice Walker: www.brainyquote.com/quotes/quotes/a/alicewalke132291.html

OCTOBER 14

Ezra Pound: www.wisdomquotes.com/topics/art/index3.html

OCTOBER 15

Blaise Pascal: http://thinkexist.com/quotes/with/keyword/image/

Marcel Duchamp: http://en.thinkexist.com/quotation/i_am_interested_in_ideas-not_merely_in_visual/156421.html

OCTOBER 16

Oswald Chambers: www.quotationsbook.com/quote/18291

OCTOBER 17

Oscar Hammerstein in : http://www.tentmaker.org/Quotes/lovequotes.htm

Charles Dickens: www.famousquotes.com/show/1020816

OCTOBER 19

Anaïs Nin: http://www.quotegarden.com/perspective.html

Malcolm De Chazal: http://www.brainyquote.com/quotes/keywords/surroundings_2.html

OCTOBER 20

Marcel Proust: www.quotationspage.com/quote/31288.html

Evelyn Underhill: www.wisdomquotes.com/quote/evelyn-underhill.html

OCTOBER 21

Charles Fillmore: http://www.brainyquote.com/quotes/keywords/childlike.html

Pablo Picasso: www.quotedb.com/quotes/3197

OCTOBER 22

Victor Hugo: www.quotationspage.com/quote/39942.html

Oliver Wendell Holmes: www.quoteworld.org/quotes/12281

John Muir: http://www.quotegarden.com/singing.html

OCTOBER 23

Johann Wolfgang von Goethe: www.brainyquote.com/quotes/keywords/kindly.html

OCTOBER 24

Og Mandino: www.brainyquote.com/quotes/quotes/o/ogmandino140597.html

OCTOBER 25

Socrates: http://www.quotedb.com/quotes/1573

Charles Mingus: www.brainyquote.com/quotes/quotes/c/charlesmin130345.html

OCTOBER 26

Henry Ward Beecher: http://quotations.about.com/cs/inspirationquotes/a/Sacrifice1.htm

Martin Buxbaum: www.yesterdayontuesday.com/2010/10/home.html

OCTOBER 27

Maya Angelou: http://www.quotegarden.com/music.html

Edward Elgar: www.famous-quotes-and-quotations.com/music-quote.html

OCTOBER 28

Gerard Manley Hopkins: http://quotes.yourdictionary.com/glory/3

OCTOBER 29

George Vaillant: www.inspirationfalls.com/birth-quotes

OCTOBER 30

Jim Elliot: http://www.famousquotesabout.com/on/Stillness#ixzz1DZiKpsVt

Artur Schnabel: www.quotationspage.com/quote/30238.html

Leopold Stokowski: www.brainyquote.com/quotes/keywords/paints.html

OCTOBER 31

Georgiann Baldino: http://blog.gaiam.com/quotes/topics/handicap

NOVEMBER 1

Albert Camus: http://pslinstitute.com/inspirationalquotes.html

Hal Borland: www.great-inspirational-quotes.com/autumn-quotes.html

NOVEMBER 2

Frank Barron: www.quotelucy.com/keywords/dignity-quotes.html

NOVEMBER 3

James Hamilton: http://thinkexist.com/quotes/with/keyword/footsteps/

Eric Sloane: www.quotationspage.com/quote/37704.html

NOVEMBER 4

Max Frisch: www.brainyquote.com/quotes/keywords/jealousy_2.html

Mike Krzyzewski: www.quotelucy.com/quotes/mike-krzyzewski-quotes.html

NOVEMBER 5

Johann Wolfgang von Goethe: http://www.lovingabundance.com/loving-quotes/

NOVEMBER 6

Stephen R. Covey: http://thinkexist.com/quotes/with/keyword/priorities/

NOVEMBER 7

William Blake: http://thinkexist.com/quotation/if_the_doors_of_perception_were_cleansed/179709.html

NOVEMBER 8

Winston Churchill: www.quotationsbook.com/quote/28661

Martin Luther King Jr.: http://www.sayingsnquotes.com/quotations-by-subject/help-quotes-proverbs-sayings-4/

NOVEMBER 9

Henry Ward Beecher: http://www.worldofquotes.com/topic/strength/index.html

NOVEMBER 10

Maya Angelou: http://www.brainyquote.com/quotes/keywords/home.html

Stephen Chalmers: chattahoocheehillshistoricalsociety.org/homeplaces.htm

NOVEMBER 11

Henry Brooks Adams: http://thinkexist.com/quotes/with/keyword/indian_summer/

Henry Wadsworth Longfellow: http://www.giga-usa.com/quotes/topics/indian_summer_t001.htm

Walt Whitman: www.brainyquote.com/quotes/authors/w/walt_whitman.html

NOVEMBER 12

Willa Cather: http://www.brainyquote.com/quotes/keywords/landmarks.html

NOVEMBER 13

Sue Ann Thomason: http://www.quotesquotations.com/famous/dolls-quotes.htm

NOVEMBER 14

Glen Beaman: www.worldofquotes.com/author/Glen-Beaman/1/index.html

John Kenneth Galbraith: quoteworld.org/quotes/5179

NOVEMBER 15

Douglas Horton: http://brainyquote.com/quotes/keywords/door_3.html

NOVEMBER 17

Lynn Hall: www.quotationspage.com/quote/1818.html

NOVEMBER 18

Ralph Bunche: http://www.great-quotes.com/quotes/category/American_Diplomat_Quotes.htm

NOVEMBER 19

Diane Ackerman: quotationsbook.com/quote/23459

NOVEMBER 20

Franklin P. Jones: www.quotationspage.com/quote/827.html

Henry C. Link: www.quotationspage.com/quote/3139.html

NOVEMBER 21

Shana Alexander: http://thinkexist.com/quotes/with/keyword/image/3.html

Andrew Wyeth: www.quotegarden.com/winter.html

NOVEMBER 22

Ambrose Gwinett Bierce: http://www.famousquotes.com/category/futility/

NOVEMBER 23

The Reverend Peter Gomes: http://www.suffering.net/godpurp.htm

H. U. Westermayer: www.wisdomquotes.com/quote/h-u-westermayer.html

NOVEMBER 24

Brenda Ueland: www.quotationspage.com/quote/26408.html

NOVEMBER 25

Hudson Taylor: http://www.selfhelpdaily.com/quotes-about-god/

NOVEMBER 26

Rachel Carson: www.quotationsbook.com/quote/20397

NOVEMBER 27

J Vernon McGee: http://www.sermoncentral.com/illustrations/quotes-about-immanuel.asp

Elissa Melamed: thinkexist.com/quotes/with/keyword/mirrors/4.html

Chip Brogden: www.tentmaker.org/Quotes/biblequotes.htm

NOVEMBER 28

Alexander Maclaren: http://www.quoteland.com/topic/God-Quotes/404/

NOVEMBER 29

Martin H. Fischer: http://www.quotegarden.com/god.html

Louise Nevelson: www.worldofquotes.com/topic/whisper/index.html

NOVEMBER 30

John Piper: http://www.goodreads.com/quotes/show_tag?name=revelation

DECEMBER 1

Samuel Butler: http://quotes.liberty-tree.ca/quotes_about/coercion

DECEMBER 2

Richard P. Bucher: http://www.orlutheran.com/html/immanuel.html

DECEMBER 3

Anouk Aimee: www.quotes.ubr.com/subject-quotes/d/desire-quotes.aspx

DECEMBER 4

C. S. Lewis: http://www.cslewisinstitute.org/files/webfm/aboutcslewis/DeathImmortality.pdf

DECEMBER 6

Rain Bojangles: http://www.quotesdaddy.com/quote/1390513/rain-bojangles/life-is-a-gift-open-your-present

Frederick Keonig: thechatpage.com/open/Quotes,Happiness.htm

John Piper: http://www.quotesea.com/quotes/on/satisfaction

Bertolt Brecht: freequotesomg.com/famous_quotes_topics/Happiness_Quotes

DECEMBER 7

Mother Teresa: http://www.quotegarden.com/helping.html

DECEMBER 8

Katherine Walden: http://www.christmascarnivals.com/quotes/christian-christmas-quotes.html

DECEMBER 9

Christian Nestell Bovee: www.quoteland.com/rate.asp?QUOTE_ID=11005

DECEMBER 10

Marlene Rosenberg: www.quotesea.com/quotes/with/gentile

Pope Benedict XVI: www.nutquote.com/search?topic=unification

DECEMBER 11

Jurgen Moltmann: www.new-life.org/answers.php?id=15

"Come, Thou Long Expected Jesus": www.cyberhymnal.org/htm/c/o/m/comtlong.htm

DECEMBER 12

Lois Lebar: http://dailychristianquote.com/dcqchristmas2.html

DECEMBER 13

Ray Bohlin: http://bible.org/article/star-bethlehem

DECEMBER 14

Richard T. Ritenbaugh: http://www.bibletools.org/index.cfm/fuseaction/Topical.show/RTD/cgg/ID/4200/Mary-Josephs-Humility.htm

DECEMBER 15

Wesley J. Gabel: http://www.bethanyum.com/sermons2007/sermon030407.pdf

DECEMBER 17

Edith Sitwell: magazine (December–January 2011).

Emily Dickinson: www.desiquotes.com/subject/home_quotes

DECEMBER 18

Watchman Nee: http://christian-quotes.ochristian.com/Atonement-Quotes/

DECEMBER 19

Ken Blanchard: http://pslinstitute.com/inspirationalquotes.html

Tryon Edwards: www.leadershipnow.com/humilityquotes.html

Rabino Nilton Bonder: www.leadershipnow.com/humilityquotes.html

DECEMBER 20

Jesse Jackson: www.sfpcn.org/Quotes%20Give.htm

DECEMBER 21

Dr. Seuss: www.goodreads.com/quotes/show_tag?name=late

DECEMBER 22

Watchman Nee: http://christian-quotes.ochristian.com/Anxiety-Quotes/

John Calvin: http://www.christian-resources-today.com/christian-quotes-2.html

DECEMBER 23

Kedar Joshi: http://www.quoteland.com/topic/God-Quotes/404/

DECEMBER 24

Alfred North Whitehead: www.quotegarden.com/philosophy.html

Ralph Sockman: quotations.about.com/od/specialdays/a/christmas1.htm

DECEMBER 26

Francois de La Rouchefoucauld: http://www.brainyquote.com/quotes/keywords/conceal_2.html#ixzz17iGvzzFh

DECEMBER 27

Jerry Bridges: http://thequotes.wordpress.com/category/grace-of-god/

DECEMBER 28

Ruth Carter Stapleton: www.myangelcardreadings.com/christmasquote23.html

DECEMBER 29

Watchman Nee: http://christian-quotes.ochristian.com/Holy-Spirit-Quotes/page-5.shtml

DECEMBER 30

Mother Teresa: http://www.quotegarden.com/helping.html

Norman B. Rice: www.joyofquotes.com/light_quotes.html

DECEMBER 31

Paulette Bates Alden: http://www.finestquotes.com/select_quote-category-Grand%20Parents-page-0.htm

My steppingstones

_____

_____

_____

_____

_____

_____

_____

_____

_____

_____

_____

_____

_____

_____

_____

_____

_____

_____

_____

_____

_____

_____

_____

$\mathcal{M}$y steppingstones

My steppingstones

$\mathcal{M}y$ *steppingstones*

www.ingramcontent.com/pod-product-compliance
Lightning Source LLC
Chambersburg PA
CBHW060958280326
41935CB00009B/756